R.
OXUS R.
Aq Chah
Mazar-i-Sharif
Andkhui
Tushkurgan
KUNDUZ R.
Shibargan
Balkh
Robatak
Pul-i-Khumri
Qaisar
Maimana
Doshi
Shakh
Bala Murghab
Doabi
Chardeh Ghorband
Charikar
Bamian
Qal'eh Nau
SHIBAR PASS
Kabul
Jelalabad
Sarobi
Dakka
ROPAMISUS MTS.
HARI RUD
RMAST PASS
KHYBER PASS
Peshawar
HINDU KUSH
GILGIT
Kalam
Saidu
Sharif
Malakand
Attock
Nathiagali
Murree
Rawalpindi
JAMMU AND KASHMIR
Jhelum
Torkham
INDUS R.
JHELUM R.
CHENAB R.
Lahore
AFGHANISTAN
HELMAND R.
RAVI R.
SUTLEJ R.
WEST
PAKISTAN
INDUS R.
Sukkur
Mohenjodaro
INDIA
Hyderabad
Karachi
Thatta
SEA

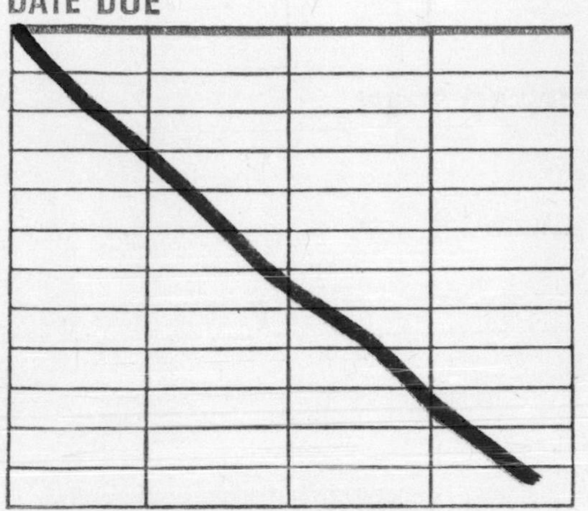

US

BOOKS BY WILLIAM O. DOUGLAS

WEST OF THE INDUS

THE RIGHT OF THE PEOPLE

RUSSIAN JOURNEY

WE THE JUDGES

AN ALMANAC OF LIBERTY

NORTH FROM MALAYA

BEYOND THE HIGH HIMALAYAS

STRANGE LANDS AND FRIENDLY PEOPLE

OF MEN AND MOUNTAINS

West of the Indus

BY

WILLIAM O. DOUGLAS

1958

DOUBLEDAY & COMPANY, INC., GARDEN CITY, N.Y.

Four lines from "Gunga Din" and 2 stanzas from "Arithmetic on the Frontier," both from DEPARTMENTAL DITTIES AND BALLADS AND BARRACK-ROOM BALLADS by Rudyard Kipling. Reprinted by permission of Mrs. George Bambridge, The Macmillan Company of Canada Ltd., and Doubleday & Co., Inc.

Library of Congress Catalog Card Number 58–13276

Designed by Alma Reese Cardi
First Edition

TO ALI,

the Persian peasant of Hamadan, who offered me his jug of cold water on a blistering hot day.

PREFACE

This is an account of a seven-thousand-mile automobile trip which Mrs. Douglas, Mary Watkins, and I took from Karachi, West Pakistan, to Istanbul, Turkey, in the summer of 1957. On that trip we crossed five countries, one of which was Iran.

On August 15, 1957, after we had left Iran and arrived at Baghdad, Iraq, the Moscow radio beamed the following Persian-language broadcast to Iran:

"Dear listeners, every day you turn a new page in your calendar, and it can be said with confidence that it is not often that you remember the days gone by. But many of the events of the past are extremely edifying.

"Seven years ago, in August, 1950, a senior American justice, William Douglas, visited Iran. In those days he came to Iran as a mountaineer, but no one ever saw him in climbing gear or carrying a rucksack. That lover of tourism who is a member of the U. S. Supreme Court visited Iranian Azerbaijan, Kurdistan, and Luristan. Later on, early in September, he visted Isfahan, Shiraz, and the areas inhabited by the Bakhtiari and Qashqai tribes. It should be said that Douglas did not go to the Iranian provinces to enjoy the natural sights. In any case, he would not have had time for that.

"That 'mountaineer' was engaged in provocations among the tribes, and he incited them to rebellion. As the paper *Dad* reported, in the tribal areas of Iran, Douglas met certain tribal leaders. It is difficult to say that during those meetings they discussed various ways of climbing up to the mountain peaks.

"In connection with those meetings more interesting details were also published at that time. Douglas called on one of the tribal leaders to form 40 groups, each 150 strong, train them in the methods of guerrilla warfare, arm them with American weapons, and keep them supplied with U.S. funds.

"In those days the Iranian press closely followed the trip of such a well-known 'mountaineer' as Douglas. None of his athletic feats escaped the notice of Iranian journalists. For instance, the paper *Kasra* said that when Douglas was wandering in the south of Iran he concluded some agreements with certain tribal leaders. The paper said that the agreement did not concern ways and means of climbing the peak of the Kallar mountain. In the agreement which they signed, the tribal leaders undertook to rise against the government if any efforts were made to disarm them.

"No one ever saw Douglas with an alpenstock. He was equipped with other things which bore no resemblance to sports equipment and which could not be hidden in a rucksack.

"In any case, Douglas kept way from sports equipment. He left that to others. At the same time Douglas was pedaling about the south of Iran, a ship was anchored off Bushire. A warm and gentle breeze waved the U.S. flag which was fixed to its high mast. The hold of the ship was full of war equipment.

"At that time the paper *Atesh* reported that in the course of several days 250 jeeps, 2000 rifles of the latest design, and a number of heavy machine guns were distributed among the tribes. The paper then added that 5000 fully armed partisans were organized in Fars.

"As a result of Douglas' 'mountaineering' new graves appeared in Iran. That is to say, early in September, 1950, the Javenroud tribes in northern Kermanshah staged a rebellion against the government. The members of the Javenroud tribe carried weapons marked 'Made in USA.' Government forces, accompanied with aircraft, were sent to suppress the tribes and fighting lasted more than a week. Thus, as a result of the secret promises of Douglas, the blood of a great number of Iranians was shed.

"Now it will probably occur to the Iranian listeners to ask what is the object this time of mountaineer Douglas' trip to Iran. And what plans does that mountaineer have this time for his 'mountaineering'?"

I let pass without comment the innuendo that I am a decrepit mountaineer, though that accusation hurts most of all. The broadcast is interesting for its composition. It puts isolated facts together and manufactures a relationship between them. The Russian mind, being bent on intrigue in foreign affairs, attributes like intrigue to everyone else. Travel for travel's sake without an ulterior political aim is beyond the Kremlin's understanding. When one travels the Russian border, he is endowed by the Russians with the same designs which they themselves harbor.

If Russia had real freedom of the press, her people and leaders could learn from these pages that the people south of the Soviet border want freedom with their bread, not dictatorship. The modern Russian has a high degree of literacy, a high level of health, and a standard of living surpassing anything in Asia. Yet more than these are necessary to make one ready for a viable world community. The Russian communist, reared and trained in an atmosphere of scheming and plotting, has not come to be a world citizen, interested in ideas and people as such.

The Russian is not the only one who needs to know the world. We all tend to become provincial in our interests; we measure the common good by our own parochial standards. We see the world we live in by our own image. Yet it is vastly different. It must be known if we are to understand the impulses that motivate it. The only way to know it is to travel. Yet just as a visit to Washington, D.C., does not acquaint one with America, so one must avoid the capitals of Asia to feel her pulse.

This automobile trip across the Middle or Near East shows one way to explore Asia. It also proves that any man can travel hot and dusty Asia by car with safety and comfort—provided he has an urge for adventure and a wife who is a good mechanic.

WILLIAM O. DOUGLAS

CONTENTS

PART V—PERSIAN KURDISTAN AND AZERBAIJAN

PART VI—TURKEY

PART 1

WEST PAKISTAN

CHAPTER 1

THE CAR AND THE MECHANIC

The car that took us seven thousand miles across the hot and wind-blown Middle East performed herculean feats. So did Mercedes, my wife and mechanic. The pictures I took, mostly in color, of Mercedes under the hood, under the car, or fixing a flat tire in some valley of fierce heat; pictures of the car stuck in deep ruts or caught on a peaked culvert; and the battered underside of the car tell the story. On my return I showed some of these pictures to a small group. A rather pompous lady, who was an old friend, spoke up:

"Do you mean to say that you stood by while Mercedes changed tires?"

"Yes, ma'am."

"Do you mean to say you sat in the shade while your wife crawled under the car to fix the muffler?"

"Taking pictures of her at work."

"You mean to say you let a woman do all that work and you never lifted a finger?"

"I was busy taking pictures."

"Why, I never heard of such a thing—and Mercedes coming from the South, too."

"But you forget she's the mechanic. I, myself, can't tell one end of a screwdriver from another."

"Never heard of such a thing," she snorted.

"Neither had the people of the Middle East, where traditionally the men do everything mechanical, except churn butter."

"I would think," said our friend, "that it would have been much more proper if Mercedes had taken the pictures, while you fixed the car."

"But you see, pictures of a man fixing a car are a dime a dozen. Pictures of a woman fixing a car—especially pictures taken by her husband—tell a better story."

"Well," our friend snorted, "I think that under the car is no place for a woman."

Mercedes is a good mechanic. She developed her talents early while helping on her Dad's cotton plantation in Louisiana. And there is nothing she can't do with an automobile. When news of our proposed seven-thousand-mile auto trip from Karachi in West Pakistan to Istanbul in Turkey got around, the Washington, D.C. reporters got interested and asked for a conference. I met them in my chambers and told them about the forthcoming trip. One commented that the roads of the Middle East were notoriously bad, and asked what I would do about repairs for the car. I said I would take my mechanic with me.

"And who is your mechanic?" he asked.

"My wife," I replied. And then I added, facetiously but with a straight face, "I'm sending her to a General Motors school for a refresher course."

She actually went to no mechanics' school. But she did brush up on Chevrolets with some of the local mechanics. And we bought the Chevrolet mechanic's repair manual and a nice set of tools for the trip.

The car that took us across the hot Middle East was an ordinary Chevrolet station wagon, vintage of 1956. It was two tones of green, with a standard gearshift, and ordinary springs and shock absorbers. It was owned by Mrs. Mary Watkins of Rockville, Maryland, who had had it in India for a year and who drove it to Karachi to meet us.

When we ended the long, dusty trip at Istanbul, over two months later, Robert G. Miner, of the American Consulate, and his wife asked if we had had much trouble. We all replied in the negative. For the unpleasant parts of a journey—punctured gas tanks as well as dysentery—fade away in time. Only the pleasant experiences remain. Yet when I tabulated the disasters our car encountered, I realized we had seen much trouble.

We lost five tires. The muffler came off six times; and in Afghanistan the roads were so poor we had to keep it off. We had to replace the carburetor once and the generator once. We lost one fan belt. We wore out a battery, three sets of points, and a dozen spark plugs. We broke two shock absorbers and six leaves in the springs. The carburetor flooded or got clogged several hundred times. The automatic choke ceased to be automatic. We lost the side-view mirror on the left front door and broke one of the small ventilator windows, when we were attacked by an Afghan sheep dog. We lost all but one bolt in the steering mechanism and as a result almost went off a cliff near Kabul. We scored our brake drums so often, they had to be ground down several times. The constant jostling from the rough terrain kept Mercedes tightening the nuts and screws every day. Once near Meshed the gearshift rod came loose and we drove for miles in second gear before we could repair the trouble. Once near the Caspian Sea we punctured the gas tank. The rocks had played such a severe tattoo on the bottom of the car that finally one single rock had done the damage. Apart from that we had no trouble except getting stuck in sand and in ditches. But more of that anon.

If I were to go again on such a trip, I would have heavy-duty equipment underneath. Moreover, I would arrange for more clearance than our modern cars give. But our journey proved that poor roads are no impediment to adventure by automobile if a man brings along his own mechanic and keeps her reasonably happy and satisfied by constant praise.

CHAPTER 2

BY AIR TO KARACHI

The Pan American plane came in for a landing at Karachi midmorning on a hot June day, 1957. The outside heat was so great that the interior of the air-conditioned plane got oppressive as we came down. The flat land that stretched to the horizon was brown and seared. A moving white line showed the surf of the Arabian Sea breaking on the coast below us. Nothing else moved except shimmering waves of intense heat that rose from the scorched plain.

Any approach to Karachi in summer is an oppressive view. And to one who knows history it is doubly so. This was the plain across which Alexander the Great led his army in 325 B.C. on his return from the Indus. This is the home of poisonous insects and poisonous herbs. Hot sand hills stretch as far as the eye can see. When one leaves the blistering sand, he comes to laminated clay cliffs and ridges that are barren of water and life. Here Alexander lost thousands of his troops and practically all of the women and children who made up the camp followers. This is Sind, a province of West Pakistan, which was conquered for the British by Sir Charles Napier in the 1840s.

Soon the city of Karachi itself came into view. It is sprawled along the coast—nondescript, and parched, marked by flat mud roofs with only a few domes, spires, or trees to break the monotony. And, unknown to us, it had at this time 400,000 cases of

Asian flu. Farther to the east I saw streaks of brown where the many mouths of the Indus join the sea. Then the plane turned to the runway for our landing.

It was 110°F. at the airport. Arthur Gardiner, of the American Embassy, and his wife were there to greet us. So was the Chief of Protocol of the Pakistan government, Brigadier Mirza Hamid Hussain, and Mary Watkins with her station wagon.

The asphalt was oozing under the intense heat. The air conditioning in the limousine that took us to Government House, where we stayed, broke down. Now the windows were open and we were traveling in the same furnace heat as everyone else. In many ways Karachi had not changed from my first view of it in 1950.

The white-collared crows—among the best scavengers of the East—were still there by the thousands. They seemed to be on every lamppost, on every telephone wire. They seemed to say to me now as on previous trips, "You're ill. You're ill." I remembered that on earlier trips I had been, and hoped that this time I would have better fortune.

While the crows were the same, the tramcars, run by diesels without overhead wires, were new. But the rubber-wheeled drays, piled high with cotton and pulled by single camels, had not changed. Neither had the two-wheeled carts drawn by burros and loaded with crates, creaky wagons pulled by bullocks, three-wheeled motorcycle taxis, bicycle rickshaws, ordinary rickshaws drawn by barefooted men in dirty shorts and sweaty turbans (*lungis*) and tongas drawn by pitiful horses which were pounding out their last few days on blistering pavements.

In 1950, when I first saw Karachi, the city was piled high with refugees. Like Calcutta, its counterpart in India, Karachi had been a magnet for the discontents who found themselves on the wrong side of the religious line when Partition came in 1947. Karachi grew almost overnight from a few hundred thousand to 1,500,000. The people lived in crates, in shelters fashioned from pieces of tin, or under canopies made from rags. They were wrapped in blankets of poverty and misery. They had little shelter from the weather, no water supply, no toilets except the gutter, no privacy.

I saw on my entrance to Karachi in 1957 tens of thousands of these emigrants still living in filth and misery. The stench had not changed. On Victoria Road, where the refugees piled up, a great clutter of slums and ramshackle markets grew mushroomlike. One shack among the slums, adorned with makeshift minarets, was used as a mosque. Though it was little more than a prayer platform, it became almost overnight a holy place. The government wanted to tear down the whole collection of packing-case structures to build quarters for the refugee businessmen who had their little shops on this site. But the *mullahs* put up a great protest against demolition of the little mosque—a protest so great that by the time of our visit the government had not dared to move.

These refugees still eke out a precarious existence. Some drive tongas and taxis; some are porters; others work on the docks; but it seems that most are miserable merchants of small stocks of goods—cigarettes and candies, pottery, cloth, sea shells. They squat all day in their baggy trousers (*shalwars*) beside their racks or carts of meager produce, calling out their wares. Their income is a pittance—a few rupees, barely sufficient for food. At day's end they go back to the hovel made from a packing box, unite their family, and share a bowl of food. I wondered as we passed these breeding grounds of disease and misery how many of us could live this way even for a week. I had come to have profound respect for the fortitude of these creatures of misfortune. Thousands of them had had only a gutter for a home for over a decade.

On the way from the airport I saw one refugee's home that was different. This man lived on a higher scale. Years back he had taken up his residence on the low ledge or window sill of a large office building. I went back several times to get his picture; but he was always absent. His blanket, however, was neatly rolled up in one corner and his brightly polished pots and kettles in the other. Later I was to see the Drigh Road Resettlement Project for the refugees. It lies to the north of Karachi off the road to Lahore. There are one- or two-room houses of concrete—flat-roofed and closely packed. Some the government built and rented to the refugees. Others were built by the refugees on land and with materials contributed by the government. The completed plans in blueprint form call for a model community—homes with water and sewerage, schools through high school, dispensaries and maternity wards. Nazimabad, a city of one thousand acres on the outskirts of Karachi, is another modern refugee center. But public housing drags in Pakistan for lack of capital.

The refugees and the packing cases apart, the drive into town from the airport showed remarkable changes from my first visit seven years earlier. Suburbs have grown up, mushroom fashion. Some are built around factories, newly established. Many new homes belong to commuters who ride the busses each morning and night. Though Pakistan is heavily committed to the welfare state, both housing and transportation by bus are largely in private hands. The busses, which we met and passed coming in from the airport, were a nondescript lot owned by many different operators. Up until recently each had run on such schedules as it chose and charged such fares as it liked. Interurban bus transportation was, indeed, in a condition of anarchy, until the government imposed a system of close supervision and regulation similar to our own.

The new houses we passed were of stucco, brightly colored, and in the $20,000 to $50,000 class. They had the Spanish touch, reminding me of the new housing developments in our own Southwest. While the yards were fairly spacious, all the lawns were brown. Karachi is short of water—so short there is water rationing. There is a waterkeeper for each district of the city, who makes his rounds, turning the water on for a few hours each day, and then off. One who wants to keep his garden green must buy water by the tank. It's expensive but the only way to have a lawn and flowers in the blistering heat of summer.

The water mains are not pressurized. Each house has its own pump to bring the water into tanks that are roof-high. The lack of pressure in the mains means that they are subject to leakage from sewage drains. So the water supply of Karachi is unsafe for drinking, though a new pressurized system is on its way down from the Indus.

These are the matters we discussed on our drive from the airport. The slums meant that the problems of Partition lay as heavily on Karachi as they still do on Calcutta. The presence of the bright new houses for merchants, government executives, business and professional people meant, however, that Pakistan is fast developing a middle class—the hated *bourgeois* the Communist rail against. The absence of a real middle class has been a great weakness in the societies left behind by the Western colonial powers. In colonial days there were economic and financial rewards for the powers that be and for a few favored few of the native population. But there was no real opportunity for peasants on the farm or residents of the slums to aspire to membership in that class—to reach it and indeed pass through it to higher positions in industry, finance, and government. No avenues of education were open to the masses. The opportunities for self-help were few. The colonial system created a vast gulf between the top and the bottom. It was that gulf that the Communists seek to fill. The *bourgeois* were always the chief opponents of the Communists. For the *bourgeois* were literate and articulate and eager to defend a way of life that keeps society fluid. Moreover, the *bourgeois* proved by their existence that the Communist class conflict is not inevitable.

This was our discussion as the car wheeled into the spacious yard of Government House. A smartly dressed soldier in khaki presented arms. We climbed long, carpeted stairs to a balcony off which our rooms were located. When I opened the door, I knew at once that we would be captives of the heat inside as well as out. For the air-conditioning machine, located in the balcony window, wheezed and puffed in the losing battle it waged against the intense heat.

CHAPTER 3

HAWK'S BAY

We arrived in Karachi on a Sunday and planned to spend the entire day getting acquainted with the station wagon that was to take us on our seven-thousand-mile journey to Istanbul. It now stood in the sun at Government House, filled with packages and supplies, and hot enough inside to melt the steering wheel. The intense heat helped us decide to put off the preparation of the car until Monday, and accept the invitation of the Gardiners to spend the day at their summer place on Hawk's Bay.

Hawk's Bay is a half-hour drive northwest from Karachi, located on the Arabian Sea. After we left the city proper, the asphalt road was mostly empty. We passed one refugee settlement that was still in tatters but had been "cleaned up," and was neat and orderly. On the highway there were a few drays piled high with bales of cotton and pulled by single camels. One tonga, pulled by a horse of skin and bones, was filled with three men dressed in white muslin, headed for the beach. A few motorcycles streaked by. But the traffic was sparse. We passed some huge cotton gins and came to the estuary of the Hab River, where there was great activity. It seemed that this was washday. Some taxi owners had their cars on the bank giving them a wash. Water buffalo soaked in the muddy waters. Dozens of men had their camels in the stream, scrubbing them with zeal and shaving their hair with long razors.

The owners of these camels are getting organized these days. Camels still take the place of trucks in Karachi. Camel drivers specialize in hauling freight from the railroads to warehouses. The government moved in with regulations, fixing the rates these camel drivers may charge. When the drivers sought to charge more, the police moved in. The rebels sought to bribe the police into silence. Then they moved *en masse* against the government to get the rates increased. These were some of the rumblings among the men who washed and shaved their camels this blistering day in June, 1957.

Shortly before the beach was a toll station, where one rupee is exacted for every car entering the beach. The custom prevails in the East to contract out to private persons certain functions of government and to grant monopolies over certain activities. In Pakistan we found numerous small towns and district boards auctioning out the right to collect taxes, because the cost of maintaining a tax-collection agency of government did not seem commensurate with the income from the taxes. The toll tax at Hawk's Bay is, therefore, in a great tradition.

Hawk's Bay is lined with modest summer houses well spaced for privacy and equipped with well water and septic tanks. Apart from the houses, the beach is a barren expanse. There is no shrubbery, like Scotch broom, that adorns our beaches in the Pacific Northwest. There is sand and gravel, low desert scrub, and the ever present white-collared crow.

A southwest wind was blowing. It carried some of the coolness of the water with it, so that the shade was quite comfortable. The wind brought with it a heavy surf that pounded the beach without mercy and stirred up mud. The pretty blue coast line I had seen from the air was now murky. The sea was too dangerous for swimming because of a tremendous undertow. So we settled for some dips in the surf, and for napping in wet bathing suits in the shade after a lunch of baked potatoes and delicious fried chicken.

A man with a camel came down the beach. For a rupee the camel came to his knees, took Mercedes aboard, and went for a canter. Other men with camels came up the beach, looking for customers. Several men with monkeys appeared. One man's monkey was trained as an acrobat. Another man with two monkeys put on an act of the Drunk and the Policeman. This parade was something like our own TV. At Hawk's Bay on a weekend, one could sit by his cottage and, for one rupee a performance, be entertained the whole day long by traveling vaudeville.

Instead, I went for a hike down the beach. The sand is coarse, not choice. But the beach is wide, sloping, and inviting. This day numerous sailboats were tacking in the bay; and farther out huge freighters were headed for the Persian Gulf. A few fishing boats made for the Karachi harbor—a port the British started to develop about a hundred years ago. Sir Charles Napier, the British General who conquered Sind, saw the need to avoid the long overland transshipment from Bombay by developing the potential harbor at Karachi. He built a lighthouse and a mole (that still bears his name); and today Karachi has twenty-one deep-sea berths and eighteen moorings.

The Arabian Sea is a great fishing area. But the absence of refrigeration long kept its potential from being fully exploited. Since independence, Pakistan has gone in heavily for refrigeration of fish as well as meat. As a result, the fishing industry in the Arabian Sea has experienced a resurgence. That sea now produces a great abundance, especially of shrimp, small oysters, and mackerel. I saw for the first time in Karachi stores where frozen fish can be bought. I learned that Karachi shrimp now reach the New York fish market.

My particular interest this summer day was the turtles for which Hawk's Bay is famous. These are green turtles over three feet long (*Chelonia mydas*) that weigh in the neighborhood of four hundred pounds. They come in from the sea in the full of the moon, dig holes in the sand, and lay their eggs. Each female lays about a hundred eggs, covers them, and returns to the sea. In a month or so the young turtles hatch and return to the sea.

Few turtles are molested by the Pakistanis, as Moslems do not eat shellfish; and the market for turtle meat has not yet been exploited. The eggs are largely unmolested because the local people do not like them. So at Hawk's Bay the turtles flourish and complete in peace their unending cycle.

I found a few of the mounds where eggs had once been laid; but no turtles or eggs were there. I could not wait for the full moon that would bring these resolute animals up from the depths.

It was oppressively hot when we returned to the city before sunset. The nights in Karachi during the summer months are usually stifling. But this night on the lawn of the Gardiners was comfortable. The conversation ran from turtles to freedom of the press to water. Once the subject of water was raised there was no stopping. Water in hot, parched, wind-blown Sind is gold. Adequate water for Sind means a liberal apportionment of the waters of the Indus that rises in India and runs the length of West Pakistan. The main tributaries of the Indus—the Jhelum, Chenab, Ravi, Beas, and Sutlej—also rise in India and are in fact implicated in the bitter dispute over Kashmir. The future needs of both India and Pakistan probably exceed the potential of the whole river system. The argument over its apportionment is an argument involving life and death. A new crisis looms, for India has started a 400-mile canal, which will divert waters now flowing into Pakistan, to reclaim over three million acres of India's Rajasthan Desert.

India got its Constitution adopted and a stable government formed nearly ten years before Pakistan. That gave India a head start on all internal improvements, including irrigation and flood control. Pakistan is beginning to feel the pinch of India's appropriation of water. Pakistan is beginning to feel frustrated at India's advance and Pakistan's delay. Pakistan is hurrying to catch up. Yet in 1957 most of her irrigation and drainage projects were still in blueprint.

The Pakistani voices this night were tense and troubled. They followed me back to Government House. They had a familiar ring. They reminded me of the passionate pleas of Wyoming and Nebraska for the waters of the North Platte River, which, like the waters of the Indus, are inadequate for the total needs of all the states that the river drains.

CHAPTER 4

THE CAR AND ALI

The first business Monday morning was getting the station wagon in condition for its long, dusty journey.

We had some extra parts that we had brought from the States—a carburetor, fuel pump, fan belts, radiator hose and clamps. In Karachi we added an extra ignition coil, condenser, carburetor repair kit, headlight beams, fuses, fuel-pump diaphragm, oil filter, extra caps for the radiator and gas tank, battery leads, radiator cement, valve caps, hot patches, three sets of points, a dozen spark plugs, an oilcan, and brake fluid. We also added what eventually turned out to be our most valued ally—odds and ends of ordinary baling wire.

The acquisition of these parts required some shopping around. We then took the station wagon to a highly recommended garage. The manager was a very pleasant man who bowed at every request and answered, "Yes, Sahib." He hurried around in his white duck pants and white shirt, giving orders in Urdu to a busy staff. His mechanics wore grimy *shalwars*. They changed the oil and lubricated the car. They tuned the engine and adjusted the brakes. We had only one extra wheel but three extra tires and several extra tubes. Two of the tires were taken off the car when it arrived and examined. They had slight breaks in the casings which we decided to vulcanize. It was an unwise decision because a vulcanized tire turned out to be a poor risk in heat of 140° which we were to experience. But we had a fine new tire for the spare and a new tube for it. This spare was carried in the well under the floor of the car. The manager with a pleasant "Yes, Sahib," assured me he had put the new tube in the spare.

"Twenty-eight pounds pressure?"

"Yes, Sahib. Yes, Sahib."

I was to remember that smile early one morning in a remote village near the Russian border in northern Afghanistan. I went out to load the car, only to discover that the left rear tire was flat. When I pulled out the spare, I discovered that it had no tube in it! Perhaps the garageman in Karachi with the ready "Yes, Sahib," had not filched the tube. But I was morally certain that he or one of his underlings was guilty.

Before then I had learned that there was something wrong at the Karachi garage. For when we looked for the new spark plugs in Lahore, a whole dozen had disappeared.

Though we traveled light, we ended up with four suitcases of clothes, one of medicines, three overnight bags, one box of film, two bags of cameras and light meters, a basket of food, a kerosene stove, a box of tools and spare parts, two jerry cans of gasoline, two cases of kerosene and oil, one brief case, a movie camera on a tripod, three sleeping bags, and the two extra tires. The jack was the last article placed in the car before the rear doors were closed. Five canvas water bags were kept filled and hung on the rear handle.

Manipulate as we would, we could never squeeze all the baggage into the station wagon. So we put a rack on top; and it too was filled. Up there went the extra tires, the sleeping bags, and two suitcases. A large tarp was lashed over them and carefully tucked underneath as a protection against dust.

At the beginning of the trip we took a long time to pack, for we were experimenting with various methods of loading. But after a week or so, each bag, box, can, and package had its place and we could pack and be off in a quarter hour.

At the beginning, the car was a stranger. But as the days passed it became an intimate friend. Its squeaks and noises were soon messages of comfort or alarm. The hum of the motor indicated whether trouble was ahead. It had a mood about it that was specially noticeable in the morning. If delicately handled, it would start right off. If roughly treated, it would cough once or twice and stop. Then Mercedes would have to raise the hood and tinker with the carburetor. The load was heavy and our clearance slight. American cars have been getting lower and lower as our roads have got better and better. But Middle East roads are like American roads at the turn of the century—mostly dirt and filled with washboard ridges and deep ruts. Open irrigation ditches often run across them. And culverts are sometimes built up so high and are so steep that it is very difficult to take a loaded American car over the top without either hitting or getting impaled.

So we soon learned how to angle the approach to a culvert to get the greatest clearance. We discovered the arc the springs would follow on a series of dips. We discovered how to weave back and forth across a washboard so as to break the up-and-down movement of the car. We learned the maximum speed in which we could stop at fifty feet without having all the baggage land in the front seat. We learned the shoulders to avoid, the dangers of ruts in deep dust, the dreadful hazards of being attacked by Afghan sheep dogs, the maximum speed on rock-strewn roads.

I had traveled the Middle East before, much of it by jeep. But I had never been so heavily loaded; my car had never had such low clearance; my wheels had never been so close to the fenders. I knew something of the ruts in the loess dust of Afghanistan. I knew we had five huge mountain ranges to cross—the Hindu Kush and the Paropamisus in Afghanistan, the Elburz in Iran, the Zagros between Iran and Iraq, and the Pontic Border Range in Turkey. I also knew that the roads were not good and that several of the passes were in the 10,000-foot zone. As I thought of the ordeal ahead and looked at the overloaded station wagon in Karachi, I knew it had a real job cut out for it. It needed, I thought, a good name, an inspirational one.

I picked Ali as the name.

Ali was the cousin and son-in-law of the Prophet and the fourth of the Caliphs or successors of Mohammed. To the Shiite Moslems or Shi'as (those who dominate the religious thought of Persia and Iraq) he is the most important Imam since Mohammed. Shrines commemorate him. Men often invoke the help of Ali in their arduous tasks.

I remembered a visit to Kermanshah in west central Iran in 1950. I went out from the city one bright warm summer day to visit Taq-e Bostan, the remnants of a hunting lodge built in the fifth century A.D. by the Persian King, Firuz of the Sassanid dynasty—the dynasty that ruled when the Arabs conquered Persia. What is left today is a sheer rock wall and small caves under the cliff. The lower rock surfaces are covered with delicate carvings.

There is a neat, tidy park lined by shade trees facing the cliffs, where I sat admiring the artistry of the carvings. A man, who turned out to be the gardener, appeared and talked with my interpreter. He had the oval head, the lean build, the graceful gait of the Persian. His fingers were long and delicate. His brown eyes were earnest and deep-set. Though barefoot and dressed in the dirty pantaloons of a workman, he had the air of an aristocrat. It appeared that he was making a proposition to me. For one toman (thirteen cents) he would scale the cliff barefoot. The cliff, which rises perhaps a hundred feet, is not perpendicular; but it inclines at about an eighty-degree angle. I assented by paying the man in advance. He trotted to the base of the cliff, went like a goat up the skirt, and then angled his way along the face of it looking for toe and finger holds. All the time he kept invoking the aid of Ali. "Alee, Alee," he would shout as he reached a seeming cul-de-sac or a difficult ledge. Once out of one danger point, he would reach another. "Alee, Alee," he would cry; and so on to the top.

Ali became the name of the station wagon as we loaded it for the first stage of the journey to Lahore. Ali it was the whole way to Istanbul. And, strangely, I was to hear on this seven-thousand-mile journey dozens of natives invoke the aid of that Caliph as they sweated and toiled to lift Ali, the car, or get it out of a rut. "Ali, Ali," was with us the whole way to Istanbul.

CHAPTER 5

MOHENJODARO

Mohenjodaro—"The Hill of the Dead"—was a flourishing city in 2500 B.C. It is on the west bank of the Indus about two hundred and fifty miles north of Karachi and about a hundred miles below the point where the Jhelum, Chenab, Ravi, and Sutlej join the Indus. We decided to visit it; and to save time we went by plane.

The plane was a one-engined De Havilland carrying four people. The pilot was a capable young Pakistani who spoke both English and Urdu. I sat up front with him, Mercedes and Mary in back. We took off at 6 A.M. and put down at Mohenjodaro at eight o'clock.

We flew north by east, roughly parallel to the winding Indus. Below us for most of the way was the hot road which the station wagon was to follow to Lahore. It's a good road for the most part and largely black-surfaced. But there are stretches where it is no more than two narrow strips of brick and rock—one for each set of wheels—running through sandy gullies.

For a hundred miles or so the road and river wind through broken, hilly country. The scene is one of utter desolation. The land has marks of severe erosion. Deep gullies gouge every slope. The *average* summer temperature in this part of Sind is 120°F., which means that 130° and 140° are quite common. And the winter extremes are below freezing. There is no vegetation except desert scrub and now and then a tamarisk or babul tree. There are many outcroppings of salt in this area. There are, indeed, stretches where acres and acres are so deeply encrusted with salt that from a distance one gets the cruel illusion of snow.

This is a land of howling hot winds, as well as blistering heat. In the summer the wind through a car window is practically unbearable. When I opened the window of the De Havilland plane at 9000 feet, I discovered that the air was only moderately cool.

For all of this, the land is not lifeless. There are scorpions and vipers in the wasteland; and I have seen pythons twenty feet long by the Indus. After mid-November there is excellent partridge hunting on these plains. In the winter great flocks of duck and geese come down from the communist north.

It was up and down and across this country that Sir Charles Napier marched his British troops in the 1840s. When Sind fell, Napier made a pun. *"Peccavi"* (meaning "I have sinned") was the message he sent the British War Office. The British troops under Napier marched by night, and by day lay in double tents with wet towels on their heads. Even so, the casualties from heat prostration were staggering. The water, too, was a curse, for it was mostly foul. Malaria, dysentery, cholera, boils also plagued Napier. Far more Britishers met their end in this fiery desert from disease than from the Baluchis. Though today malaria is largely under control in Pakistan and though cholera is curbed, the ravages of heat and foul water still take their toll.

Sind is cursed not only with hot winds and blistering heat but with oppressive landlordism as well. In Sind 90 per cent of the agricultural land is owned by absentee landlords whose tenants have little security and few statutory rights. The political union of reactionary landlords and conservative *mullahs* is closer in Sind than in any other part of the continent.

Below Hyderabad, the ancient capital of Sind, the land close to the estuary of the Indus is watered only in flood season. Inundation canals then come into service. Above Hyderabad the area receiving year-round irrigation increases, particularly on the east side of the Indus. By the time Manchhar Lob is reached a few villages appear and green acres with occasional patches of woods roll on and on to the eastern horizon. By 1960, when the new irrigation dam at Kotri, above Hyderabad, is in free operation, some of the barren wastes which we traveled will be cultivated.

The hundreds of miles of irrigation canals, nourished by the irrigation projects at Sukkur, water the plains around Mohenjodaro. They are as intensively cultivated today as they were in 2500 B.C., when the ancient city flourished. The cotton and barley they grew then still grow there; and today the melons and mangoes of Sind are as sweet as one can find anywhere.

The dirt, weed-covered runway at Mohenjodaro is short and dusty. There is not even a wind sock to show the direction of the wind. Our arrival was a signal to the few dozen villagers who live there. They all came running. Shamsul Haque Chishty, the young curator of the museum at Mohenjodaro, was there dressed in a white tunic and white trousers. He is a man of thirty with a slight build and a thin line of dark mustache. With him were two gendarmes dressed in khaki. The latter had two jeeps to take us to the site of the ruins, about a mile distant. Before we left, the pilot whispered that since there were thieves in modern Mohenjodaro, he would lock up in the plane any articles of value we wanted to leave behind. I believe the pilot maligned these good people. For never were we more graciously received.

It was now eight o'clock and by eleven the sun would be unbearable. One cannot see the ancient ruins in less than two hours. So we went at once to the site.

As one approaches the ruins from the present village along a walk where scatterings of tamarisk and olive trees grow, he sees only a nondescript mound or hill with thin mud bricks strewn everywhere. This mound—at least the visible part—is not from the ancient city. It is probably the remains of a Buddhist temple built hundreds of years after Mohenjodaro perished. The bricks that lie like rubble all around were the product of the excavation of the city. As long as they were buried they were in perfect condition. But now that they are exposed, Mr. Chishty told me, they may be completely disintegrated by sun and rain in a couple of decades.

The hill, which is almost 40 feet high, commands an arresting view. The remains of this derelict city are outlined by a series of mounds about 4000 yards long and 200 yards wide. Not all of the space has been excavated. But enough has been done to show an upper and a lower city. The upper city is to the west and includes structures which apparently had relation to the administrative functions of the ancient town. There is a pillared hall, a magnificent residence, a huge bath, a granary, and watchtowers.

The pillared hall, which apparently was a place of assembly, is 90 feet square and had a roof supported by 20 brick columns.

The residence is 230 by 78 feet, probably the home of a very high official.

The bath is 39 by 23 feet and 8 feet deep. The floor and the sides were of bricks set on edge in gypsum mortar. At one corner was a huge drain. There are remains of a series of small bathrooms, all designed for privacy and probably serving members of some priesthood.

The granary is 150 by 75 feet and was designed to have circulation of air from below. It had loading facilities on the outside.

The watchtowers are remnants of an ancient defense system.

To the east of these large buildings lay the lower city. The main streets ran north and south and east and west, leaving blocks 1200 by 800 feet. The lower city was probably a mile across. The main streets are 30 feet wide; and narrow lanes (from 5 to 10 feet wide) run off these avenues. The lanes are often dog-legged; and the curator suggested they were so designed to break the force of the wind.

The houses, which were two-storied, were built around courts just as they are in most of Asia today. Each house had a bathroom—some with a seat-latrine and all with an outside drain in the form of an eathenware pipe, discharging waste and sewage into some kind of a soil tank, probably of brick. Earthenware pipes carried drainage from the roof. Each house had a small room where water was stored. A larger residence suggests a hotel for travelers and another a restaurant.

There are neat drains in the streets; and manhole covers for the main drains.

I felt as I saw these ruins that the city had been conceived by master planners who built from blueprints and who had close supervision over every detail. An intelligent civic authority was obviously behind these neat and orderly projects.

We spent three hours walking the hot streets of this ancient ghost town, climbing stairs in the glaring sun, exploring alleys and basements under a searing sky. By eleven o'clock the heat of the bricks was burning through the soles of my shoes; and the temperature was so high we all felt faint. So we withdrew to the shade by a small one-story museum recently erected near the ruins.

From the works of art both in the museum at Mohenjodaro and in the one at Karachi, it seemed plain that Mohenjodaro was an ancient center of a great civilization that covered a large area. The gold, silver, alabaster, tin, and lead plainly came from scattered sources. So did all the precious jewels.

Bullock carts, similar to those that groan along the roads of Sind today with their solid wood wheels, are among the toys dug up at Mohenjodaro. Exquisite seals, both flat and cylindrical, were found in large numbers. Many interesting sculptured articles have been unearthed. A bronze dancing girl, with hair coiled at the nape of the neck and pinned over the left ear, caught my fancy. There are pieces of jewelry galore, many delicately designed. There are vases by the dozens, some small and others five feet high, some ceramic with geometric or abstract forms. Many tools of stone, of copper, and of bronze have been dug up. One that caught my eye was a 16½-inch bronze saw with three rivet holes for a handle. And then there were the toys—a cow with an adjustable head that wags with a string, a monkey that slides down a rope so designed that he can be stopped by tightening the rope, a whistle of pottery that makes a noise like a hen, numerous clay dolls or figurines, and finally dice. These dice are like our own, except that each is ten times as large. They never could be palmed. But they are precision-made and, so far as I could detect, they were not "loaded."

The minutiae can be gleaned from Sir Mortimer Wheeler's masterful description in *The Indus Civilization* (1953). As he points out, Mohenjodaro was only one of over sixty known sites extending from the Himalaya to the Arabian Sea. The archaeologists have learned enough from their recent diggings to tell us that about 2500 B.C. there existed a great civilization in the Indus Valley—one that ranks with the one in Mesopotamia and the one in Egypt.

Who were the people of Mohenjodaro? Skeletal remains, as analyzed by Wheeler and others, suggest that they were predominantly of the Mediterranean type—slight, medium height, olive complexion, dark hair, fine features. But the community was apparently mixed or cosmopolitan. Some were doubtless "aboriginals" with thick lips; others were Mongols.

They were literate, for they had a language and an alphabet. Their script, however, has never been deciphered. They were seemingly far advanced in many respects, not only as shown by their elaborate social organization but also as indicated by their system of weights and measures and their use of the decimal system.

What happened to this great non-Aryan civilization?

This is the question we discussed as we sat with the young curator under a banyan tree at Mohenjodaro. A servant poured water from a pitcher over our hands into a basin. Then we had a lunch of sweet mangoes and cold fried chicken.

Perhaps change in weather played a part. There is evidence that the area is more arid now than it was in 2500 B.C. or even later when Alexander the Great came through.

Increased salinity of the soil doubtless played a part.

But the experts are more and more inclined to the belief that it was the Aryans, arriving from the northwest about 2000 B.C., who destroyed the great civilization of the Indus. These days the finger points more and more to the Rigveda for some clues. This collection of ancient Hindu hymns or poems recites an invasion and many assaults upon the walls of aboriginals or barbarians. The Rigveda has lines that suggest over and again that this invasion was not imaginary, as often supposed, but actually a conquest of the Indus Valley and an assault against Mohenjodaro and its companion cities.

The leader of the Aryans was Indra, the war god. He headed the invasion of the lands of the barbarians who lived in walled cities. The Sanskrit word is *"pur,"* which means "fort," "stronghold," or "walled city." The Rigveda describes these cities as made of stone or of bricks. There are passages that relate how Indra destroyed ninety of these cities or forts; others where he destroyed ninety-nine; and Wilson's translation of the Third Ashtaka recites, "Indra has overturned a hundred stone-built cities for Divodas, the donor of oblations."

Wheeler gives circumstantial evidence that the people of Mohenjodaro were massacred *en masse* and that Indra, the Aryan warrior god, the famous "fort destroyer" of the Rigveda, is guilty.

All the way back to Karachi in the De Havilland plane I had dark thoughts about us Aryans and our aggressions. I was brought back to reality by a glance at the gauge of the gas tank. It showed "empty" and we still had fifty miles to go. When I turned to Mercedes and showed concern, she put on a front of nonchalance: "When the Oldsmobile's gauge at home shows empty, I pay no attention."

I tried to pay no attention to the gas gauge of the plane. But all I could remember were the blocks I had walked to get gas for Mercedes. And all I could see below me were gullies and crags where nothing larger than a buzzard could land in safety. As it turned out, my worry was needless, for we landed at Karachi without a sputter or a cough. The Pakistani pilot, who apparently had noticed my concern, grinned as he wheeled the plane up to the airport gate and said, "I always figure we're good for fifty miles once the gauge shows we are out of gas."

CHAPTER 6

THE PUNJAB

It is over eight hundred miles by road from Karachi, capital of Sind, to Lahore, capital of Punjab. One could spend weeks in that area rummaging among ruins and catching up with some of the tides of history that swept the Indus basin.

Thatta, located on the Indus not far from Karachi, is a town chock-full of history. The Arabs conquered Sind in A.D. 711. In 1555 the Portuguese, who sailed far up the Indus, sacked Thatta. In 1592 the Mogul, Akbar, seized the town. When the British conquered Sind in the 1840s, Thatta was a city with one thousand looms. Its last decline began when the East India Company flooded Sind with cheap goods from Manchester. In Thatta, as in other parts of Pakistan and India, the British destroyed local industry, capturing the markets for their own factories.

Thatta today is not the busy city it once was. It has mostly relics of towers, tombs, and mosques that span about five hundred years of time. And outside Thatta is a graveyard of six square miles containing a million bodies.

Upstream is Hyderabad, the city famous for the wind catchers on the roofs of the homes. Though Hyderabad is a hundred miles or more from the sea, the breeze from the salt water, blown through a house, is somewhat cooling. Hyderabad, a city of 250,000, is in the semidesert region of Sind where the rainfall is about eight inches a year and the main crops are rice, wheat, and cotton. Hyderabad is the home of the University of Sind. Hyderabad, too, is filled with tombs and shrines.

Sukkur, farther upstream, also has tombs and shrines of historic interest. These days, however, Sukkur is most famous, first, for a biscuit factory that is the largest in the subcontinent, and second, for an irrigation dam that is nearly 5000 feet long. A great network of canals takes off from this project, their total length being about a quarter of the circumference of the earth. Sukkur, which produces wheat, cotton, and rice, is largely dependent on irrigation, as its rainfall is less than five inches a year.

Since I had seen many of these historic places between Karachi and Lahore on earlier trips, we decided to skip them this journey and concentrate on the antiquities of Lahore. So we flew there, sending the station wagon ahead.

Lahore is one of the most beautiful cities of all Asia. It sits on the banks of the Ravi River, to the east of the Indus. It has ample water from the river and uses it well. The city is, indeed, a lush garden.

There are streets, such as the Mall, with wide green center strips.

Near the School of Arts on the Mall stands Bhangian-di-Top, the famous brass gun dating back to 1757 that is mentioned in the opening pages of Kipling's *Kim*.

A huge park—containing fields for cricket and baseball and carefully manicured—is named after the late Liaqat Ali Khan, one of Pakistan's first great leaders.

Lahore, captured by the Afghans in the twelfth century and burned by Babur (whose name means Tiger) in 1524, has long been a center of learning and trade and the capital of the Punjab. It is still a great seat of learning, the home of Punjab University, one of the finest on the subcontinent, and numerous other colleges. The Moguls came to Lahore in the sixteenth century, headed by Babur. Babur was followed by a long line of Mogul rulers including Akbar. It was Akbar, his son Jehangir, and grandson Shah Jahan who made Lahore the city of stately buildings. Aurangzeb, whose death marked the beginning of the disintegration of the Mogul Empire, built here one of the world's most famous mosques.

We saw the old fort which dates back to the Afghan invasions of the twelfth century. It was rebuilt by the Moguls, and finally was turned into an archaeological exhibit by the British. I sat in the shade of some peepul trees opposite one of its walls, scanning the ancient ramparts. Though it would be an easy target for modern artillery, it would frown ominously on men with spears and swords. Bullocks, unhitched from their two-wheeled carts, were resting in the shade from the hot sun. I talked with one of their masters—a barefoot man in a dirty loincloth and a soiled turban. His stomach was concave and his ribs protruded through a half-starved body. He knew nothing of the history of the fort. It was there and had been for years. But who built it and whence the builder came, he had no idea. Another turbaned man sat in the shade puffing on a water pipe. Down the street came four barefoot women carrying hay on their heads in great bundles of cloth. A grassy slope beyond the peepul trees led down to a small creek. Men and women were busy under the hot sun beating laundry with clubs, rinsing it, and laying it out on the grass to dry. I talked with one of those characters; and he, too, knew nothing of the fort.

The same day we visited the fort we took pictures at Jehangir's tomb, located on the opposite bank of the Ravi and four miles northwest of Lahore. The tomb is a one-story building, about 266 feet square, built of red sandstone inlaid with marble. Four graceful minarets rise about 100 feet at the corners. Each has four successive platforms protruding at regular intervals; and at the top is a white marble cupola. The building sits in the spacious Dilkusha Garden, which has small canals dividing it into sixteen separate units. A graybeard with white turban and white flowing robe sat at the entrance to the tomb. We left our shoes with him and, putting on rented slippers, went inside to the tomb itself. We were to see many tombs on our seven-thousand-mile journey. But apart from those in Iran, none contained such delicate, colorful mosaics of tile as this one.

On a blistering hot day when the temperature soared to 114°F. we spent several hours in the famous Shalimar Gardens at Lahore. This beauty spot, built by Shah Jahan, has three terraces and occupies forty acres of land. It is planted with a wide variety of fruit trees—from apples to mangoes. A canal, one hundred miles long, was built to water it. The garden was not only a residence of the Emperor when he was in Lahore but also a place where guests were entertained. It is filled with pavilions and summer-houses. It has pools and promenades. One huge pool, nearly 200 feet square and adorned by stately cypress, has 152 fountains. Overlooking the pool is a stately throne—a white open marble platform slightly raised and contained by a low railing.

These days people flock to the garden in great numbers; and in the spring it is the site of a famous fair. It takes over one hundred gardeners to keep these forty acres green and manicured.

The fourth historic site that we visited at Lahore was Badshahi Masjed, the famous mosque built by Aurangzeb in A.D. 1673. One reaches the main entrance after a steep climb of dozens of steps. The courtyard of the mosque measures roughly 528 feet square. Four corner minarets rise about 175 feet. The building is red sandstone inlaid with white marble. The roof has three huge domes of white marble with golden spires. The interior is divided by immense arches into seven rooms. The walls are plaster relief delicately decorated and trimmed with black marble.

As we entered the main gate, workers were painting a tile mosaic that had faded. Following the noise of hammers working on stone, I turned a corner into a small alcove and found a dozen or more artisans, dressed in turbans and loose trousers, making material for needed repairs. Some were chiseling out blocks of stone; others were marking the design of a mosaic on tile; others were cutting the tile; still others were putting the pieces together to make the finished jigsaw pattern. This mosque, severely damaged by an earthquake last century, today is as carefully maintained as a clockmaker's watch.

What interested me most on this tour of historic sites in Lahore was Iqbal's tomb. It lies to the left of the Badshahi Masjied as one enters. It is a plain rectangular edifice of marble raised five low steps from the ground and capped by a rather heavy roof. Above it flies the Pakistan flag. The flag and the tomb brought back a flood of memories.

Mohammed Iqbal, who died in Lahore in 1938, was a poet, a philosopher, a politician. I had known Iqbal as a philosopher:

"Physically as well as spiritually man is a self-contained centre, but he is not yet a complete individual. The greater his distance from God the less his individuality. He who comes nearest to God is the complete person."

Iqbal recognized that the great contribution of the West to the East was the scientific attitude. He recognized what science, introduced into ancient and underdeveloped Asia, might do. He saw its potential for good, its potential for evil.

> Love fled, Mind stung him like a snake; he could not
> Force it to vision's will.
> He tracked the orbits of the stars, yet could not
> Travel his own thoughts' world;
> Entangled in the labyrinth of his science
> Lost count of good and ill;
> Took captive the sun's rays, and yet no sunrise
> On life's thick night unfurled.

Iqbal recognized that if science were to treat kindly with Asia—not make it a sweatshop of capitalism on the one hand or the victim of Communist regimentation on the other—it must be controlled in the public good:

> The object of science and art is not
> knowledge,
> The object of the garden is not the bud
> and the flower.
> Science is an instrument for the preservation of
> Life,
> Science is a means of establishing the
> Self.
> Science and art are servants of Life,
> Slaves born and bred in its house.

The most remarkable phenomenon of modern history to Iqbal was the need for a new spiritual understanding between the East and the West. He put this thought into verse:

> In the West, Intellect is the source of life.
> In the East, Love is the basis of life.
> Through Love, Intellect grows acquainted with Reality,
> And Intellect gives stability to the work of Love.

Arise and lay the foundations of a new world,
By wedding Intellect to Love.

Before this trip, I had read most of Iqbal's poetry and philosophical writings. It was in Lahore that I first realized how critically important Iqbal was in the movement to establish Pakistan as a separate nation.

An anagrammatist coined the word "Pakistan"—P for Punjab, A for the Afghan province, K for Kashmir, S for Sind, and Tan for Baluchistan (in Urdu, the national language of Pakistan, the *i* is not written as a separate letter). Iqbal gave wings to the idea of a separate Moslem state for Northwest India. He was President of the All-India Moslem League in 1930 when he declared that the creation of Pakistan was "the final destiny of the Muslims at least of North-West India." It was this idea that Qaid-i-Azam Mohammed Ali Jinnah enlarged to include East Pakistan. It was this idea that led to an independent nation on August 14, 1947. Liaqat Ali Khan, the man whose marble tomb we visited in Karachi, was the inspired leader of this political program until his death in 1951.

To many Moslems, the idea of an Islamic state was the only solvent of the ills of the area. That apparently was Iqbal's point of view. How he would solve it if he had lived, no one knows. It's a difficult problem, as difficult as it would have been in this country at the time of the Constitution to make one of our states Catholic, another Presbyterian, etc. There are minorities in every land whose conscience, tastes, predilections, politics, religion must be given the same respect as those of the majority. To make religion the *sole* unifying force and to build a state around it is to sacrifice minority rights.

These were some of the problems I discussed with Pakistanis, particularly in Karachi and Lahore.

In Karachi the Minister of Law, F. A. Karim, gave us a luncheon at the Metropole Hotel. In Karachi I met many lawyers at a dinner tendered by the Bar Association in the beautiful garden of the Beach Luxury Hotel. A. K. Brohi of the Karachi Bar also gave us a small tea in his new home. In Lahore Justice and Begum Shahabuddin of the Supreme Court of Pakistan tendered us a dinner in their lovely air-cooled home. In Lahore

Sri Chaudri Nazir Ahmad Khan, President of the Lahore Bar Association, and Begum Ahmad Khan gave us a buffet luncheon in their cool home. And in Lahore the Bar Association tendered us a tea in the garden of the graceful High Court building where palm trees line the walks.

At these social engagements we met many lawyers and judges; and when members of the profession congregate the talk usually turns to law. Much of the talk on these occasions was about the difficulty of constructing a sectarian state. India had avoided the problem by completely separating church and state, as we do in the United States. Pakistan, after nearly a decade of debate, finally adopted a compromise Constitution on March 2, 1956.

The preamble proclaims the Islamic principles of justice. Article 198 provides that "No law shall be enacted which is repugnant to the Injunctions of Islam as laid down in the Holy Quran . . . and existing law shall be brought into conformity with such Injunctions." Article 25 provides that the state shall endeavor "as respects the Muslims of Pakistan" to make the teaching of the Koran "compulsory." Other sections set the Islamic ideal as the ideal of government. But there is only one fixed religious requirement in the Constitution and that is Article 32, which requires that the President be a Moslem. In all other instances accommodation of the rights of minorities is guaranteed. While Article 28 pledges the state to outlawry of alcoholic liquor, there is added the phrase "otherwise than for medicinal and, in the case of non-Muslims, religious purposes." Religious freedom is guaranteed. The office of the President aside, there is no religious test for the public service. No person attending school need receive religious instruction or take part in a religious ceremony, if it relates to a religion not his own.

Freedom of speech and of press, freedom of movement, freedom of assembly, freedom to form trade unions—these are all guaranteed.

The levy of a tax to support a religion other than one's own is prohibited.

Universal suffrage is guaranteed; and discrimination on the basis of sex is outlawed.

Though the Islamic tradition that relegates women to *purdah* still persists in Pakistan, the Constitution does not sanction it; and the rising generation repudiates it.

Pakistan is now revising all laws to bring them into conformity with the Koran. A commission of eleven, headed by Justice Mohammed Sharif of the Supreme Court, is hard at work on it. There are the fanatics who want the literalness of the Koran adopted. There are the liberals who want strict principles ameliorated in the broader interests of a democratic society. The struggle between the two groups has not yet been resolved; and it promises to be a bitter controversy.

Religion aside, Pakistan's Constitution goes far beyond anything we have toward committing the nation to the welfare state. It pledges the state to prevention of "the concentration of wealth and means of production and distribution in the hands of a few to the detriment of the interest of the common man." It pledges all citizens "facilities for work and adequate livelihood with reasonable rest and leisure," all the "basic necessities of life," and "social security."

Although there is no guarantee of jury trial, there are numerous procedural safeguards comparable to our own.

I found on our journey that the Pakistanis are proud of their Constitution. While they are mostly Moslems, they have in their midst Christians, Hindus, Buddhists, and Sikhs who make up about 15 per cent of the population. *There are nearly 7,000,000 Christians alone in West Pakistan and they live in over 230 villages.* Likewise, India is not solidly Hindu. *There are many minorities in India, including more than 40,000,000 Moslems.* The Pakistanis I met had no idea of holding their Hindus as hostages for India's Moslems. The Pakistani Bar was unanimous in its pledge to accommodate all minorities and defend their rights.

Yet I detected an ominous overtone in these discussions about religion and politics; and it related to the electorate register system. The British introduced this system into the subcontinent to distribute seats in the legislature among the various religious groups. One district could return only a Moslem, another only a Hindu, a third only a Sikh, and so on. This was a vicious system that perpetuated the problems of religious minorities and prevented the communities from developing a unity over and above race and religion. Most students of the subject have agreed that the electorate register system tore communities apart, accentuated religious differences, kept the democratic principle of equal opportunity with the best man winning from taking hold. For the best man, if he were a Moslem, could never win in a Hindu section, or vice versa. India rid herself of that system.

My friend Huseyn Shaheed Suhrawady of the Awami Party, when he was Prime Minister, sponsored a bill, passed by the National Assembly, abolishing the electorate register system and approving a joint electorate. But Suhrawady resigned in the fall of 1957 in opposition to mounting demands for a return of the electorate register system. Thus the religious problem remains a vital, burning one in the politics of Pakistan.

In Lahore especially, we had many hours of relaxation. We stayed at Government House—a luxurious, imposing residence constructed by the British and now used by the Governor of West Pakistan for his residence. It is set well back on a vast estate that is taken care of tenderly. The lawns are sunken so as to permit flooding. The winding driveways are lined with banyan trees. There must be miles of garden strips for flowers and shrubs. The lawns are mowed with a huge machine pulled by five barefoot men. Flowers are sprinkled from goatskins of water, filled from a central tap.

We stayed in a wing of the residence that was built for the Prince of Wales when he visited Lahore in the 1920s. The British also built for him a large swimming pool. It is four feet deep at one end and eleven at the other. It is covered by a roof, thus keeping the water from heating up in the intense sun. And it, like all other swimming pools in Lahore, is entirely enclosed with screens to prevent frogs and toads from filling it. The water in the pool, which comes from a deep well, was 78°. The temperature outside stayed right close to 114°, night and day during our visit there. I spent at least three hours a day in the cool depths of this wonderful pool.

One evening after a swim, I found the Governor—M. A. Gurmani, a middle-aged man, short and stocky—on the lawn by a lone pine tree. He had a huge electric fan that stood six feet high set up on the grass, for the summer nights in Lahore are about as hot as the days. We sat for an hour or more in the breeze of the fan, sipping delicious mango sodas and talking about the problems of Pakistan.

Punjab, which produces chiefly mutton, wheat, rice, sugar cane, and cotton, is the granary of Pakistan—its most fertile, productive area. As such, it has immense strategic importance to the country, for this young nation is suffering a food shortage. The shortage has been so acute that it has been necessary to import about 1,000,000 tons annually during recent years. Of the $170,000,000 American *economic* aid extended in 1956–1957, nearly half went to provide food imports.

The crisis is not an easy one to resolve. The water supply for West Pakistan is limited; there is much wasteland in the region; there is other land—vast stretches of it—that has become salty and that can be reclaimed only through extensive drainage projects. Worse still, West Pakistan is losing 100,000 acres of *irrigated* land and 12,000 acres of non-irrigated land a year to salinity.

Fifty per cent of the irrigated lands of West Pakistan are affected by increasing deposits of salt. Of the 14,000,000 acres of land under irrigation in the Punjab, over 3,000,000 acres are now badly affected by salinity. Of these 3,000,000 acres, almost half have been withdrawn from cultivation and the rest have been so seriously affected that their yield has been reduced by an average of 50 to 60 per cent. Our agricultural expert in West Pakistan, John O. Bell, has predicted that, if this rate of salinization continues, the great valley of the Indus will become a desert in less than half a century.

The growth of increased salinity is not modern. It is the product of years of irrigation without proper drainage. Subsurface waterlogging (which keeps the salts close to the earth's crest) has apparently been under way for centuries.

Where is Pakistan to get the capital funds to reclaim her land and to prevent further depletion? Iraq and Iran have oil. Pakistan has none. During the period 1948–1956 roughly 40 per cent of all Pakistan's expenditures from capital funds and from annual revenues was spent on defense. If annual revenue receipts alone are taken, the amount spent on defense is 58 per cent per year. These figures are exclusive of American aid. Where are the rupees for internal development coming from?

Pakistan has an ambitious educational program. The segregation of boys from girls in the schools—a pattern set by Islamic tradition—has been abandoned. In most primary schools the classes are now mixed, though the old pattern persists in secondary schools. But today Pakistan has schools for only 15 per cent of her children. Vast funds for education are needed.

Pakistan under the British was only 9 per cent literate. Today it is 18 per cent literate. Much has been achieved. But Pakistan has barely started on her basic problems.

The Governor expressed great urgency to get ahead fast on all Pakistan's social and economic problems. It was an urgency I felt throughout the length of the nation. Pakistan, like India, Burma, and other Asian countries, is hurrying to catch up. The capital, as well as the technical skills, are not there to do the job quickly. Military preparedness is deemed essential. But the allocation of resources to social and economic problems must be increased, lest the people become frustrated. Frustration is the quick road to Communism. This was the concern of gray-haired Governor Gurmani, who sat with me under the lone pine tree that hot night in Lahore; and I found as I traveled the country that it was also the concern of most of the thoughtful people of this young Republic.

CHAPTER 7

RAWALPINDI AND THE HILL STATIONS

It's a little over a hundred and fifty miles from Lahore to Rawalpindi (known as Pindi), which is located in the northern corner of the Punjab. The road has an excellent black surface and climbs about a thousand feet, twisting and turning through rough ravines and jagged outcroppings of rock. At the top of the climb is a large plateau where cotton, corn, melons, and rice are grown.

En route to Pindi, we stopped at Jhelum for lunch. We parked the station wagon under some peepul trees at the railroad station. Here several men were squatted in the shade making shirts on rather old-fashioned hand-operated sewing machines. A vendor wearing a bright-colored skullcap sat on his haunches beside the road selling cigarettes. He also had cardamon seeds and betel nuts, which the people of the subcontinent especially enjoy after meals. All of his wares were in a folding wooden box, making him a true itinerant. Across the street were a dozen or more tongas lined up waiting for the next passenger train. We got cold drinks inside the station and sat under the far-spreading peepul tree to eat the sandwiches we had brought from Lahore. The other people there were reserved and polite, probably more so than the three of us. They left us completely alone. But we prowled around them taking their pictures until they must have thought that no Westerners had manners.

We were in and out of Pindi for several days, making the Circuit House our headquarters. Its portico was heavy with bougainvillea in bloom and guarded night and day by soldiers nattily dressed in khaki with highly polished brown boots, Sam Browne belts, and cartridge clips over their shoulders.

Pindi is the headquarters of the Pakistan Army, and its cantonment is one of the largest military stations in the country. Here also are the Liaqat Gardens, marked by a bandstand facing a large lawn lined with trees, where Liaqat Ali Khan was assassinated in 1951 as he addressed a crowd.

During the day the heat was as oppressive as at Lahore. But the summer nights in Pindi are cool. We spent one evening with the Rotary Club of that city—an energetic group of young business and professional men, headed by M. T. Faizi, dedicated to a better understanding of world conditions. We spent another at a dinner tendered by Lieutenant General Mohammed Musa, on the spacious lawn of the Officers' Club, where some of the cream of Pakistan's young officers were present. Present were Brigadier and Mrs. H. M. el Effendi, who had shared with me a wonderful fishing expedition in the remote province of Gilgit some years earlier. I learned from them about the mahsir fishing in the Indus and its tributary, the Pindi Gheb. The mahsir, which resembles somewhat our salmon, runs over sixty pounds in these waters and is so strong it straightens out the ordinary hook. Fresh-water trout are found in the streams running off the western slopes of the Himalayas. I learned that more people in Pindi have fishing as a hobby than golf. The glass casting rod I chose for the Effendis in New York City some years back still lands the fighting mahsir in Pakistan and the glass fly rod I selected works beautifully on the trout streams near Murree and Abbottabad.

One afternoon we drove to Murree, where I was to address the American-Pakistan Society. It's about thirty-seven miles to Murree and the roads are paved. But they are so winding and the ascent is so sharp that it takes an hour and a half or more to make the climb.

The heat of Pindi was so great when we started the drive that we had to close the car windows against the fiery blast of the wind. We left about two o'clock, right after a luncheon tendered by Amanullah Khan, Assistant Commissioner of Rawalpindi, when, according to Noel Coward, only "mad dogs and Englishmen" go abroad. The people of Pakistan are more sensible. In the summer, activities come to a halt or slow down to a walk from about noon to four o'clock. This is the period of the leisurely luncheon and the long siesta.

The shops were mostly closed as we left Pindi; and when we reached the outskirts, the fields were empty of workers; bullocks were unhitched from their two-wheeled carts and tied under trees, while long-legged birds hopped from back to back looking for lice. Some women were washing clothes in an irrigation ditch, while children played. Most men, using their turbans as pillows, lay curled up in the shade, sound asleep.

Murree is one of the most historic hill stations in the Himalayas. It was an important military post and summer resort under the British. It is one of the few hill stations left to Pakistan as a result of the partition. Murree is about 7500 feet above sea level and a great refuge for all who flee the heat of Sind and Punjab.

There are rice paddies in the lower stretches of the climb from Pindi. Then come terrace upon terrace of potatoes and maize. Every available piece of ground on the lower slopes of the Himalayas is tilled. The homes in the valley are mostly of mud. Above Pindi they are mostly thatched. On its climb to Murree the road passes through numerous small villages. We stopped at one, called Charapani, where a cascade of cold water pours from the hillside. The spring has been carefully cemented and is one of the most popular watering places in all West Pakistan.

We first saw the pines at about 5000 feet. These are the long-leaf Chiel pine, slightly reminiscent of the yellow pine of our West. Below Murree they grow in thick stands that are carefully protected. Never have I been so happy to reach the pines. We had been in the suffocating heat of Sind and Punjab for a week, perspiring night and day. I had suffered so much that I was developing the painful rash of prickly heat. The pines below Murree, therefore, were to me a refuge and a haven. We stopped the car so that I could climb among them and inhale their fragrance. Then I lay on a bed of needles looking up through ragged branches to a sky that was no longer oppressive.

This was July 4 and Murree was crowded. This hill station has many summer homes and a dozen or more rather old-fashioned, but very neat, hotels. Almost every porch, every window, every yard has a wonderful view, for Murree sits on a high perch. All available homes and hotel rooms had been reserved weeks in advance. No space was available except and unless a friend would put an extra cot in his room for a traveler. The town was so crowded that automobile traffic had been banned from most streets. They are narrow ones, designed on an earlier day when the cart was supreme; and they are incapable of handling the heavy traffic which moves up the mountains these days. So we parked our car on the outskirts and walked to Sam's Restaurant where the American-Pakistan Society was having its meeting—a meeting arranged by Chester Neudling of the American Consulate in Lahore, who had a small but enterprising USIA reading room in Murree.

Sam's Restaurant is on a winding paved road crowded with small shops and so narrow that two cars cannot pass. The restaurant is reached by climbing thirty-odd steps. From below, the building seems ramshackle. But beyond the wooden porch is a large attractive room, filled with small tables. At one end is a platform, where this afternoon a horn, a fiddle, and a drum produced loud music in a patriotic vein.

We sat at the opposite end with Chief Justice M. Munir of the Supreme Court of Pakistan, General Mohammed Ayub Khan, Commander-in-Chief of the Pakistan Army, and others. In Asia, unlike America, tea is not a euphemism for cocktails. Real tea was served and after tea came the speeches. The Chief Justice, introducing me, spoke in eloquent terms of the new Constitution of Pakistan. I spoke of it and of our own Constitution. I said that the greatness of a nation was not in the number of factories it had or its wealth or the size of its army. Its true greatness was its tolerance for religious, social, racial, and political diversities. The American Bill of Rights, I commented, was the symbol of the real greatness of America. We are not perfect; we have our problems and our difficulties; discrimination exists in America as elsewhere. But we have political remedies for it; and we apply those remedies vigorously.

In Pindi I had met Pakistan's first woman judge—the attractive Miss Parvez Yusafzai, who is in her early thirties. She presides with dignity and authority over an important trial court handling civil matters. She is a symbol of the emancipation of women in modern Islam. There are other symbols of that emancipation both in the professions and in business. Though on the streets one sees more women veiled than unveiled, Pakistan repudiates the Islamic tradition that relegates women to an inferior position. I congratulated the Pakistanis on their emancipation of women and on their declaration of the fundamental rights of man in their Constitution and added a word about Communism. I said I was happy to find the leaders of Pakistan agreed that to wage war on Communism one must have more than an army, navy, and air corps; that he must have a social program which will make sure that people do not end up in despair. I was sure, I added, that the Pakistanis knew of George Washington, Thomas Jefferson, Abraham Lincoln, and Franklin D. Roosevelt. But did they know about Benjamin Franklin? A chorus of ayes went up from the crowd; and I was happy that the fame of the one who was perhaps more responsible than any single man for the final draft of our Constitution had reached Asia. So I ended my talk by quoting Franklin at the time our Declaration of Independence was being signed and applying his wisdom to the fate of the free world today.

"We must all hang together," said Hancock.

"Yes," answered Franklin. "We must all hang together, or most assuredly we shall all hang separately."

The three-man band played the two national anthems; but the horn never quite made the high notes of the "Star-Spangled Banner."

On another hot day we retraced our steps to Murree and then went beyond to the village of Nathiagali, which rests on a ridge 8200 feet high. The road is tortuous and winding. The viewpoints show scenes of startling beauty. The temptation is to go slow so as not to miss any of the glimpses of the Kashmir Snows in the distance. There are several military check posts we had to clear, manned by men in khaki shirts and short khaki pants. At one point woodcutters were weighing wood. They had brought it to the roadside and were using huge old-fashioned scales suspended from a tripod to determine the kilos in each log. All at once we negotiated the last tortuous turn and reached the top of the ridge. Here the British years ago built a high rambling wooden building that served as the summer residence and administrative headquarters of the Governor. It is a mountain garden with a cricket field and tennis courts, all beautifully maintained. It is now the summer headquarters for the amiable President, Iskander Mirza.

Village names that end with "gali" are very common in West Pakistan. In Urdu "gali" means a narrow road and "nathia" means the little nose rope by which a bullock is controlled. So by one version, the summer home of the President has to do with a narrow lane and a bullock's nose rope. There is still another version. In the old days several settlements were built on these high ridges to accommodate the army in summer months and later the civilian branches of government. Nathiagali, according to this story, got its name from the ranking officer in charge of the military camp—a Sikh by the name of Natha Singh. By that version, Nathiagali is this officer's narrow lane.

President Mirza and his wife entertained Mercedes, Mary, and me at a buffet luncheon. It was a perfect summer day with only a few fleecy clouds in the sky. The view from the front porch is one of grandeur. To the east are the Snows of Kashmir, not over thirty-five miles as the crow flies. To the northeast are some of the peaks of the Karakoram. We went down the ridge a mile or so to see Nanga Parbat (26,660 feet). I had flown the western wall of Nanga Parbat a few years previously and had scouted its eastern approaches. It seemed to me then to be a mountain that men would not climb. Yet in 1953 the late Herman Buhl of Austria climbed it.

Today at a distance it seemed even more imposing than it had close at hand. It is a cold, rough spire of snow and ice, reaching into heights where mountains are not supposed to be. I felt as if I were looking into another world. This peak, like Everest, Kanchenjunga, Godwin Austen, and Annapurna, reaches far above the abode of man into the supernal land. One who sits and watches it becomes lost in thoughts of the supernatural. It is no wonder that among the hill people Nanga Parbat is the home of spirits and gods and mysterious force of life. This day at Nathiagali my musings about Nanga Parbat were cut short by a bustling Swiss who climbed over the fence, where Mercedes and I were sitting in a field of asters and cinquefoil, to take movies of Nanga Parbat through the pines. He worked diligently, getting down on his stomach for choice shots, yet wholly oblivious of the fact that he had a cover over his lens.

All along this ridge are terraces of maize and potatoes and strawberries. They run 9000 feet high, some higher. The strawberries are the sweetest in Asia. There are grass huts on the ridges as well as in the valleys. The ones high up are the summer homes of those who work the terraces.

From the high ridge of Nathiagali the canyon walls seem well terraced and safe from ugly erosion. But farther down—along the skirts of these hills—great erosion is in fact taking place. The Rawalpindi hill area is notorious for floods. Recently 143 villages were heavily washed with floodwaters when a downpour struck. Mud huts turned to mud heaps and most of the crops were ruined. The reports are alarming. The disastrous runoffs are due partly to overcutting of trees and partly to improper terracing or contouring of steep fields. The forests are not regenerating as they should, for animals eat the saplings as the trees retreat. In this region I noticed that the birch zone had completely disappeared. In the Pindi area alone, lands which yesterday produced good crops and fine pasture are being regularly and incessantly washed away. The damage is estimated in terms of millions of tons of soil a year.

In the winter there are eight feet of snow at Nathiagali. Then the peasants gather in the valleys and huddle together to keep warm. There are as yet few schools for them; no hospitals; no theaters. Medical care is expanding in Karachi; but the country people are the last to get its benefits.

This afternoon Mirza, the tall, heavy-set President of Pakistan, paced with me the ridge of Nathiagali that faces Kashmir. He has a military background and is often impatient with democratic processes. He feels the central government does not have enough power under the Constitution. He favors a strong executive. The President of Pakistan does not have the power of our President, for Pakistan is organized under the parliamentary system. The President of Pakistan is more analogous to the King or Queen of England. He does, however, have a great reserve of authority under the Constitution. When the National Assembly is not in session, he can promulgate laws of his own until the next National

Assembly meets. And the President has authority to declare an emergency in any province and transfer the lawmaking powers of that province to the National Assembly. But the President's real authority is in the force of his personality and in his power to summon and dissolve the National Assembly.

In terms of American orientation we would classify Mirza as a Hamiltonian, not a Jeffersonian. But he knows that the real enemies of modern Pakistan are hunger, disease, illiteracy, ignorance, and superstition. He knows that continuous victories must be achieved over these enemies, if Pakistan is to progress as a democracy.

These were the concerns of this restless man the July afternoon we walked the ridge of Nathiagali together.

CHAPTER 8

THE ROAD OF THE INVADERS

Peshawar—about seventy-five miles northwest of Pindi on a good macadam road—lies on one of the most popular invasion routes of history. The Himalayas protect the city on the north and east; and the hot sands of Sind have prevented most invasions from the south. But to the west of Peshawar is the low-lying Safed Koh Range of mountains that has numerous passes in it, the most famous being the Khyber. Peshawar sits on the plain near the mouth of the Khyber; and as a result it has been stomped on more than any other city in Asia. Peshawar and the other cities of the plain (once called Gandhara) have been invaded by at least ten peoples in addition to the Greeks, White Huns, Moguls, and British.

About twenty miles out of Pindi on the road to Peshawar we turned right on a dirt road leading north a few miles to the ancient city of Taxila. We stopped first at the archaeological museum, a long one-story stone building, marked by stately cypress, to meet and pick up the curator, Riaz Hussain Shah, a brilliant dark-complexioned young man in the thirties. He showed us some of the ancient ruins.

Taxila was a prosperous city and a great educational center from about 500 B.C. to A.D. 500. It was a part of the empire claimed by Darius I; and it was taken by Alexander the Great in 326 B.C. Ambhi, the King of Taxila, did not resist Alexander.

He had other enemies against whom he needed the Macedonian's help; so he submitted. Alexander stayed in Taxila for some time; and he left it intact, since he, unlike most invaders of the Middle East, destroyed only armies, not civilizations. We know from the annals of the Greeks that Taxila at this time was a well-governed community, heavily populated, a wealthy town on a Central Asian trade route, and a city proud of a great university. Polygamy was practiced; young girls were bought and sold on the market; the dead were not buried but fed to the vultures.

Shortly after Alexander—probably about 300 B.C.—the Buddhists came to the Punjab. They converted King Asoka, who proceeded with zeal to spread Buddhism far and wide—to Ceylon in the east and to the Hellenistic world in the west. Asoka made Taxila the greatest seat of Buddhist learning on the subcontinent. When Fah Hian, the Chinese Buddhist pilgrim, came through Taxila about A.D. 400, it was a thriving Buddhist center.

Over the years, many Buddhist monasteries had been built. They were all destroyed about A.D 500 by the White Huns who swept down from Northwest China. The White Huns, headed by Toramana, had broad shoulders, flat noses, and small, deeply set black eyes. They were practically beardless and made up for their apparent lack of manliness by awful cruelty. Though they fastened a tight hold on Peshawar and Taxila, it did not last long. The Turks, united with the Persians, liquidated the White Huns about A.D. 567.

It was to these ruins, which Toramana's hordes created by burning, that Hussain took us. Taxila, which means "the city of cut stone," lies in a valley, dotted with villages, that reminded me somewhat of our own San Fernando Valley in California. It's a wide valley, generously watered by the Haro River and several creeks that flow into it. Spires of the Himalayas are on the north and east and lower ridges on the south and west. The valley, which has an intense dry heat in summer, is fertile to this day and grows diversified crops including wonderfully sweet mangoes and melons. The tracts are neatly laid out, most of them marked by rows of trees planted as windbreaks.

We went first to the Buddhist ruins at Jaulian. We parked the car in a skimpy grove of wild olives and locust and climbed a winding dirt path three hundred feet to the crest of a low hill.

Here once stood a beautiful monastery, built about A.D. 200. Three hundred feet is not high; but three hundred feet at Jaulian gives a dominating view of the entire valley. There was no water here; but the monks had wells near the base of the hill. On top they had dustless air, a view of snow-capped mountains, quiet and calm, and complete command over a green and peaceful valley.

The dirt path reaches stone steps that lead to a courtyard. It is a rather large open quadrangle with five small shrines or *stupas,* now roofed over for protection from weather. Their square bases are decorated with stucco reliefs—the Buddha and his attendants, with elephants and lions that support the superstructure.

A few steps more lead to an upper court where the main *stupa* is located. Here sits a Buddha figure with a circular hole in the navel where a suppliant could rub his finger when praying for relief against intestinal pain. Many small and highly decorated *stupas* surround the main *stupa.*

To the east of these two courts and connected with them is the monastery. At its entrance on the left is a chapel, with one seated and two standing Buddhas which still have traces of the red and black paint and the gold leaf that once adorned them.

The monastery is a two-story affair in the form of an open quadrangle with cells on the four sides. There are broad verandahs above, a bathroom, assembly hall, kitchen, refectory, and storeroom. In alcoves and in niches are many images of the Buddha in various postures. Clay was used for plaster in the monastery and in the *stupas;* and the fierce heat that destroyed these buildings turned the clay to terra cotta.

The fire that destroyed these Buddhist monasteries and the cities of Taxila was started, as I have said, by the fair-skinned Huns who brought only destruction, not ideas, to the Indus Valley. Before the White Huns, seven invaders or conquerors, starting with the Persians and the Greeks, had rolled over Taxila, leaving imprints in art and culture. But the White Huns brought only havoc and destruction. By the seventh century A.D. when Hsüan Tsang, a famous Chinese Buddhist pilgrim, visited Taxila, the monks were few, the monasteries desolate, and only a few hardy people remained in the Buddhist flock. Any existing Buddhist monasteries that he saw were all destroyed about A.D. 1000 by the invading Moslems.

We visited one of the three destroyed cities—Sirkap. This town shows the remains of six successive periods of building. Over the seven or eight hundred years of its existence, buildings fell and new buildings were built on the debris (a century of debris furnishes approximately three feet of dirt). The last of the six cities was a huge metropolis surrounded by a thick wall of rubble masonry. It had a large palace—400 by 350 feet. There were temples and shrines, some of them Buddhist. One shrine features the double-headed eagle, which, according to Sir John Marshall, who made the excavation at Taxila, was probably introduced by the Scythians, one of the seven invaders of Taxila who preceded the White Huns.

The shops and houses were made of brick and stone; and the houses had no access to the outside streets. One entered them from courtyards; and the ground floor was a cellar, access to the living rooms being had by stairways or ladders.

The streets are almost as neatly laid out as those at Mohenjodaro. They are wide and spacious. Today only grass grows there. Today this is grazing land for livestock, whose herdsmen walk among the ruins, unmindful both of the glorious and of the sad history of the place. There are a few chenar trees among the ruins. I sat for perhaps a half hour under one, trying to take in the enormity of the destruction rendered this ancient civilization by men whose minds were insensate to art, religion, and culture. A great loneliness swept over me, a loneliness increased by the repeated sad call of a mourning dove.

I was awakened from my soliloquy by the curator, who had taken Mercedes and Mary for a longer tour. We went to a bungalow next to the museum, where we had tea and mangoes under a huge *punkah* pulled back and forth by a turbaned Moslem who sat on his haunches outside on the porch. Then we went for a visit to the museum to see the glories of ancient Taxila that had been unearthed.

The details are too great to give here. I saw gold jewelry that reminded me of Scythian ornaments on display at the Hermitage in Leningrad. There were silver vessels of fine lines, lamps and drinking goblets of many shapes, tiny pots and huge ones, bridles, swords, arrowheads, daggers, thousands of coins and rings, ink-pots, and perfume bottles, bronze cups and copper cups. Taxila had entered the Iron Age. So its people used iron vessels and utensils of a wide range. The two that caught my fancy were, first, folding iron chairs, and second, iron grills for cooking, standing on three legs.

I was to see in the bazaars at Peshawar and in other bazaars across Asia many folding iron chairs and iron grills on tripods of the same design as those at Taxila. Both are intensely practical even in these modern days; and the grill would be one of the handiest items for a pack trip, if the legs were only collapsible.

Beyond Taxila on the winding road to Peshawar, we reached Attock. It is located at the confluence of the swift and muddy Indus and Kabul rivers. Here Alexander is supposed to have crossed on a pontoon bridge. We crossed on a massive bridge heavily guarded by troops. Commanding the point is a huge fort of stone and brick built by Akbar to protect the route leading down from the north whence all invaders came. This Indus basin, now hot, dusty, and wind-blown, was the home of the rhinoceros and tiger as late as the sixteenth century.

Today, as in older times, Peshawar has on its western edges a dozen tribes of Pathans whose history has been filled with intrigue and battle. Peshawar, now as always, is the terminus of a principal caravan route leading west across Afghanistan and Iran. Peshawar today is still the Paris of the Pathans where drugs, love, and murder are for sale.

We stayed at Government House, formerly the residence of the British Commissioner and after independence the residence of the Governor of the Northwest Province. It's a huge, spacious place beautifully proportioned and gracefully set in a lovely garden and decorated with palm and banyan trees. Here in an oak-paneled dining room are shields bearing the names and dates of all the Commissioners and Governors of the Northwest Frontier Province from the Britisher Sir Harold Deane to the Pakistani Qurban Ali Khan, the last in the long line that served until the Northwest Frontier Province was placed directly under the Governor of West Pakistan. Now Government House is almost a relic —a guesthouse for traveling dignitaries.

In Babur's day the gardens of Peshawar were beautiful, the

mangoes sweet, and the bazaars colorful. The same is true today.

On this and earlier trips I had often walked through the bazaars of Peshawar; and always the scene seemed unending and the same: swaggering Sikhs with heavy beards and tightly wound turbans; *mullahs* with green turbans; Arabs with white *kafeyahs;* dancing boys with bobbed hair, walking hand in hand; blind beggars; dwarf beggars; one-legged beggars; toothless beggars; fakirs traveling as holy men; great giants of Pathans—Afridis, Mohmads, and Shinwaris with knives in their belts and rifles in their hands; aesthete-looking Hindus; men with trousers filled with so many tucks that if they were stretched out they would measure twelve feet at the waistline.

These bazaars are on winding streets. The merchants often live on the second floor where balconies command a view of the street. The word is that *hashish, bhang,* and opium—all fierce drugs—can be bought upstairs. The prostitutes are dressed in black with veils sufficiently low to show rouge. The streets are winding, lined with small shops. In the heat of summer many shops have ragged awnings to protect the merchandise, especially fruit. The bazaars of Peshawar are not as splendid as those in Isfahan, which we later visited; but they show many fine wares. Coppersmiths hammer away at their trade. Potters apply their skills. There are shops filled with bandoliers and bullet belts. Tobacco, snuff, and spices are on display. There are blocks of stalls filled with luscious fruit. There are many teahouses where Afghans, Pathans, Turkmen, Sikhs, and Hindus foregather, and where the proprietor keeps a large brass Russian samovar constantly boiling. There are shops full of sweets; there are shops where live birds are sold. There are small dens where the palmists and fortunetellers work. And above the roar of the bazaar are the cries of the hucksters who peddle their trinkets or sell cold drinks along the walks. One hawker sold a cold lemon drink. He carried on his back a huge copper jug with long curving beak that bent over his shoulder. He carried cups in his pockets; and all that he needed to do to pour a drink was to lean forward and hold the cup under the spout—and out would come the lemonade.

The bazaar that always interests me most is Qissa Khani, the famous Street of the Storytellers. Here one finds storytellers galore. The Street of the Storytellers is famous in Central Asian history. One can find a storyteller in almost any teahouse; and often they can be found in the center of the street with a crowd gathered round. For a rupee, a wizened old man in flowing gown, a turban, and a skimpy white beard, whom I found in a teahouse, told me a tale of Alexander that has currency in the Middle East.

Alexander, who conquered Afghanistan and swept around the plains of Peshawar in a great circling movement, hardly ever looked at a woman. A woman to him was a danger far greater than an armed man. But in Afghanistan Alexander met the beautiful Roxana, daughter of the great Oxyartes. Roxana, a virgin, was a beautiful dancer and she danced for Alexander, who was overpowered by her beauty. They married and Roxana bore him a son. But Roxana, though faithful as a wife, harbored resentment against the Greeks who had conquered her country. She got her revenge. One day she and Alexander gave a great feast by a deep pool in their garden. There was much to eat and drink and Alexander ate more and drank more than any other man. When he had finished, Roxana, pointing to the pool, said, "You would not dare to swim now." Alexander, moved by the wine that surged in his veins, jumped to his feet and plunged into the cold water. From that he got a fever, and died. "That is how," the old storyteller cackled, "an Afghan woman outsmarted the man who conquered Asia."

For another rupee he told another tale of Alexander, who was tired out by the time he reached the Hindu Kush mountains. After that crossing, Alexander gave orders to his soothsayers to find him the fountain of youth. They went forward and found by the Jhelum a cold spring where they made a sacrifice and studied the entrails. The signs were propitious. So they hurried with a skin of the precious water to the camp of Alexander on the plains of Peshawar. Alexander raised the skin to his mouth and was about to drink when a toothless man with gnarled thin hands and sunken face came forward shouting. The ancient one prostrated himself before Alexander and then cried out: "O King, if you drink that water you'll be like me—too old to live, too old to die. I drank some five hundred years ago and look at me now."

On Eid-ul-Adha, which in 1957 fell on the ninth of July, I

went to mass. This is an important Moslem religious holiday which starts with services at eight o'clock in the morning. I took my cameras to a mosque of white marble that glared even in the early sun. It was roofed over and closed on the street side. But the other three sides were open. Canopies of canvas had been extended beyond the edge of the roof on the side opposite the altar, so that three times the number inside could sit outside. There must have been five thousand Moslems there that morning—all male, for women do not celebrate Eid publicly.

I took off my shoes at the entrance, carrying them inside. Then I put them on the floor and went to work with my Leica. No sooner had I dropped my shoes than a turbaned Pathan picked them up, placed them sole to sole, and replaced them on the ground. Thus did I learn one lesson in religious protocol.

The men first sat on their haunches, listening to the *mullah* recite the Koran. Then at a command they started their prayers. There are seven movements in these prayers, though their sequence this day was slightly different than the normal. These several thousand men sitting on their haunches touched their foreheads to the ground and then sat back on their haunches. This they did five times. Then they stood and, after reciting in unison passages from the Koran, bowed from the hips and straightened up. This they did twice. After another prayer from the *mullah,* the meeting broke up and we all left the canopy for the blistering sun.

Immediately after Eid mass, it is the bounden duty of a good Moslem to go home at once and sacrifice a sheep and give a portion of it to a poor family that lives in the neighborhood. This is in commemoration of the episode which we of the West know from Genesis 22 and the Moslems from the Koran, Chapter 37—how Abraham at the call of the Lord did not sacrifice Isaac but sacrificed a ram instead.

Throughout our Pakistan trip we had seen many sheep gaily painted in yellow, blues, and reds. These were marked for the Eid sacrifice. Mercedes and I attended one sacrifice ceremony at the home of Dr. Abdul Samad Khan, a physician and surgeon who was once Minister of Health in Peshawar. Pakistan has a modified form of socialized medicine, made necessary by the dearth of doctors and hospitals. Medical graduates work for the state as civil servants. A new law makes it compulsory for all graduates of medical schools to serve the government for five years, either in the civil medical departments or in the army. They are assigned to hospitals or other posts, pretty much as members of the medical branch of our army and navy. After retirement as civil servants, whether at the end of the five years or later, they can practice medicine privately. Dr. Samad, middle-aged, tall, and heavy-set, is retired and now practices privately in Peshawar.

He greeted us warmly at the gate of his one-story yellow stucco home and escorted us to the shade of the front porch where we met his wife and children. I do not know how warm it was in the sun but the porch recorded 110°F. Dr. Samad put two electric fans to work and served us cold and refreshing lemon sherbet, while we waited for the sheep to be prepared.

The slaughter took place in a shady corner of the courtyard. A black-fleeced ewe was hog-tied. As the family gathered round, Dr. Samad sharpened a large knife and cut the throat of the sheep. When the last reflex kicking of the ewe had ended, a professional butcher took over. The carcass was hung in a doorway and the skinning and butchering took place.

While this was going on, professional entertainers appeared in the neighborhood, going from door to door seeking a retainer. For one rupee two men with a horn and a drum played Pathan music for us so loudly I thought the echoes from the courtyard would burst my eardrums. They had no sooner finished than three more entertainers appeared—one man playing a drum and one an instrument something like an accordion. The third was a young girl about nine or ten years old, dressed in a white skirt, yellow bandolier, and red scarf. Her brown eyes were lighted with merriment as she whirled and stomped out a mountain dance.

Then we went back to the Street of the Storytellers. The place was so packed with people it was difficult to move, let alone take a picture. Tongas, bicycles, motorcycles, camels, burros, donkeys, trucks, and people vied with each other for passage. There was less room than at Times Square when the theaters empty at night. All of Peshawar seemed to have poured into Qissa Khani on a spree. Most shops were boarded up; but the fruit stalls and teahouses were open. Beggars were out in numbers; hucksters were selling cold drinks and food. In some squares there were small ferris wheels and miniature merry-go-rounds, all hand-propelled. Trinkets and Eid souvenirs were on display on trays carried by hucksters and on corners of the unpaved street. At one corner, a storyteller had collected a crowd. He sat on the ground with his green gown gathered around him. His sallow face, straggly beard, piercing eyes, sunken cheeks gave him a satanic appearance. He had worked himself up to a frenzy, so great that the eyes of small boys around him danced with excitement as they jumped up and down at his words. His story, according to my interpreter, had something to do with the glory of the Arabs and the machinations of the British. The British were definitely the object of his scorn. He had a dagger in his waist and he used it to emphasize a point, just as a speaker uses his fist. His voice would rise to a crescendo and then break with a roar, as he pulled his dagger from his belt and drove it into the ground. Over and again he did it; and when in one last furious curse of the British he drove the dagger into the ground, the crowd tossed coins at his feet and roared approval, shouting, *"Hokay," "Hokay,"* a word that a Pushtu-speaking friend later told me had been borrowed by us and corrupted into "Okay."

One night when a full moon rode over Peshawar, we had dinner with Commissioner Musarat Hussain Zuberi and Begum Zuberi at their home. The dinner was buffet, served on a green spacious lawn dominated by five tremendous banyan trees. The wives were all there, for though by tradition Pakistani women are in *purdah,* the intelligentsia and the younger generation are free from it. Though the women mingled with the men during the meal, before and after dinner they sat together apart from the men and did not participate in their conversation. Many political figures were present. The political parties were all represented—the Moslem League, Republicans, the Congress Party, and the Awami Party. The members of the Moslem League—strongly supported by *mullahs* and landlords—were not very talkative this night. One was teased by an Awami Party member:

"We understand the *mullahs* are upset at women in bathing suits at the Peshawar Club," he said.

There was no reply. Turning to me, he whispered:

"The club at Abbottabad was burned down; and the rumor

is that the *mullahs* were responsible. You see, they are upset when women put on bathing suits. They see red when women and men go swimming together in the same pool. They sometimes get violent when women and men in bathing suits sit together drinking whisky."

There was also discussed that evening a proposal to divide West Pakistan into four linguistic areas—Sind, Punjab, Northwest Frontier, and Baluchistan. It was that division that the British maintained. But the Pakistanis in 1955 had united all into one governmental unit and placed a Governor at the head of the whole of West Pakistan. Some landlords are uneasy over this merger. They want a division of West Pakistan into the old British pattern. When all four are merged, the political power of the landlords is diluted. If West Pakistan were broken up into smaller units, the landlords would then tighten their political hold on certain areas.

Some lawyers in Peshawar had first mentioned this subject to me at a reception and tea which the Peshawar Bar Association tendered us at Dean's Hotel. The entire American community in Peshawar, including several members of ICA, were present. The discussion over the teacups centered largely on the problems of landlordism in West Pakistan.

When the British took over India, they found a land-tenure system in which a chief or *zamindar* commonly collected agricultural rents. The *zamindar* kept some for himself and remitted the balance to the rajah or other head of government. The British found this system to be a great convenience in raising revenue. They not only adopted it; they enlarged it. They turned the *zamindar* into a proprietor or landlord, giving him, for the first time, an interest in the land. This is the core of the land-tenure system that persists to this day in West Pakistan and plagues every government.

The landlords of West Pakistan are uneasy. In East Pakistan land reform is well along: (1) limits have been placed on the number of acres which may be possessed by a family; (2) tenants have been protected in occupancy rights; and (3) a program has been worked out for the acquisition (on payment of compensation) of ownership of the land by the man who cultivates it.

These reforms have lagged in West Pakistan. Some tenancy

rights have been increased; but no basic changes have been effected. Landlords still dominate the agricultural economy. Throughout West Pakistan the landlord has been strong enough to frustrate protective legislation. For example, landlords often refuse to give receipts for produce received or fail to collect their share of the crop from the field and then lodge suits for ejectment on the ground of non-payment of rent. These evasive actions are easy in West Pakistan because the peasants are illiterate and largely unorganized and inarticulate. Land reform in Pakistan is not a matter for the federal government; it rests with the states. Hence if Sind, Baluchistan, Northwest Province, and Punjab were separate states, the landlords in those states would exercise greater leverage over their respective legislatures.

The conversation in the garden of the Zuberis turned to less serious subjects; and then the dinner, with a delicious rice curry as the main dish, was served.

After dessert, when the women had gathered in one corner of the lawn again, our host took me by the arm as we strolled the edge of the lawn where the banyan trees stood. They seemed majestic in the moonlight and I stopped to admire them. As I did so, the Commissioner told a tale.

It seems that in the seventh century A.D. the famous Chinese Buddhist, Hsüan Tsang, came through Peshawar and stopped in the shade of five banyan trees. Pointing to his banyans, the Commissioner said:

"These are the same five."

When I asked how a tree could possibly live twelve hundred years, he explained that the banyan tree constantly sends new shoots down from its branches. When they reach the ground, they take root and form a new trunk. In a hundred years or so the old trunk rots and crumbles and the new ones become blended into a main stem and take its place.

"The same tree trunks, of course, were not here when Hsüan Tsang visited Peshawar," my host added. "But we all think the same trees, as living organisms, were."

It came to me as a surprise that in this part of the world one story; and during the rest of the evening all the invaders of history could link a dozen or more centuries. Yet I believed the tory seemed in my mind's eye to parade beyond the banyan trees.

It came to me then why this part of the world—Turkey and Iran as well as India and Pakistan—has more of a socialist philosophy and approach to problems than we of the West.

During this evening we had discussed many of the industrial problems of Pakistan. When Britain conquered Pakistan a hundred years or so ago, Sind and Punjab had many home industries. British policy was designed to crush these local industries so as to widen the markets for goods from Manchester and Birmingham. That policy applied to India as well as to Pakistan. Though some large industries were built under the British, Pakistan remained almost entirely an agricultural society. Pakistan was the supplier of raw materials for British factories on the subcontinent and abroad and served British colonial policy, as Soviet Russia in the early years after World War II planned that Yugoslavia should serve hers.

When independence came, one of Pakistan's greatest problems was industrialization. Peshawar, for example, had no single factory under the British. Today it has nine flourishing plants, including a spick-and-span DDT factory. Down in Lahore we had spent several hours in the enterprising plant of the Batala Engineering Company, which makes excellent diesel engines and machine tools. This plant was privately financed.

Other new industrial plants are privately financed—and some of that private capital is Hindu. But the larger percentage is governmental. That is partly due to the absence of accumulations of private capital in these areas. That is not, however, the main reason. There are great riches in Asia; but they are mostly in land and in chattels, such as jewelry. From the days of Mohenjodaro, Asia has lived under long periods of insecurity. Invaders come and pillage and loot. Maybe they stay to oppress the people; maybe they move on. One who reads the history of these troubled areas finds not only the repeated pattern of invasions. He also sees that, when there is no invader, dynasty overthrows dynasty, tribe overthrows tribe, so that there is no breathing space for solid peaceful development.

In that kind of environment, if wealth is to be secure, it must be that which on the one hand can be secreted or moved with a camel, or, on the other, tramped on but not destroyed. That is why capital has gone into jewels on the one hand or land on the other.

Asian capital needs political security if it is to come out of hiding at home or abroad and move into factories. The aura of insecurity that has overhung Asia during the centuries is a psychological factor that works even today to retard that movement. Industrialization must, however, go forward if the standard of living is to be raised. But if the rate of progress needed is to be achieved, government must be the main contributor or the underwriter.

We in America are apt to think of people consciously choosing between socialism and capitalism. There is no such choice in Asia. The psyche of man takes time to change. There are no valleys in Asia that have known the security which has blessed this continent of ours for three hundred years. Asia needs generations to settle down in an atmosphere of peace and security. Meanwhile the socialist way of life will continue to be more and more dominant.

These were the observations of the small group of us who sat under the banyan trees that moonlight night in Peshawar.

CHAPTER 9

THE KINGDOM OF SWAT

The valley of Peshawar, known historically as Gandhara, was, from the third century B.C. to the sixth century A.D., a great Buddhist stronghold. The Gandhara art that developed was almost entirely Buddhist in its subject matter. The Greek and Roman influence can be seen in the works of art that fill the Peshawar Museum. Some Buddhas have the heads of Greek Apollos and are dressed in togas. The Greek centaurs and tritons are also there. But the Roman influence—traced to the practice of importing foreign workmen from the eastern centers of the Roman Empire—is perhaps more dominant, as shown by the use of separate panels to portray distinct climactic events, rather than the device of continuous narration used in India. The style of drapery is also Roman. The Mesopotamian motifs—the sphinx and the gryphon—are also present.

These relics were of special interest to Mary, who is interested in art. "Each chiseled piece of stone," she said, "announces that the Buddhists were here. So were the Greeks. And the Chinese and Indians left their imprint too."

Gandhara art shows borrowings from many cultures. Whatever all its sources may be, it claims one distinction—the first school to portray the Buddha in human form. Yet Mary called them "stiffly stylized." Only a few, she thought, had not been frozen "by the repetition of tradition."

According to Buddhist legends, the Buddha reached perfection only after many incarnations—some 550, so it is said. In some of these existences he was a bird or a beast. In others he was a man. The Buddha never visited Gandhara. During these previous incarnations, however, he traveled extensively there. Some of the legends concerning these early journeys into Gandhara as a man are told in stone in the museum. Many engraved episodes in the life of the Buddha in his last incarnation are also in this collection. The relics were dug up from many sites in Gandhara.

The museum is in charge of Dr. M. A. Shakur, an aesthetic-looking Moslem with a Vandyke beard who is most learned as an archaeologist. What I have related is a very brief summary of what Dr. Shakur told us on a visit to the museum. The curator was excited by the subject matter and his eyes got brighter and brighter, as he talked about the Buddha. Soon he excused himself and went to a vault to reappear with a bronze bowl or urn covered by a lid. His eyes were dancing as he handed it to me. He explained that the Buddha was cremated and his relics divided into eight parts and distributed among as many communities. Legend has it that Asoka, King of Taxila, collected them and redivided them into many more portions and distributed them throughout Gandhara.

"This covered bronze urn is a casket that contained some of those relics," he said.

And gently retrieving the casket from my hands, he returned it quickly to the vault so that he could catch the afternoon train to Lahore. When I last saw this earnest, learned scholar, he was seated in a tonga en route to the railroad station, reading a book as the horse jogged along.

We were to pick up threads of Dr. Shakur's discourse when we traveled north a few days later to visit the ancient Kingdom of Swat.

I had visited Swat before, but this was the first trip for Mercedes and Mary. We left Peshawar by car one morning around eight and arrived at Saidu Sharif, the capital, at noon. It's not much over a two-hour drive, but we traveled slowly, taking many pictures as we went.

The road out of Peshawar goes west and then north to Swat. The plains of Gandhara this morning were under a sun as hot as a burning glass. It must have been over 110°. The road across the plains is black-surfaced and for miles passes between rows of tamarisk trees whose boughs touch in the middle. The fields are mostly sugar cane, cotton, and rice, worked by water buffalo. This morning they were steaming under the intense heat as men and women, most of them turbaned, plowed paddies in preparation for the rice transplanting that was soon to take place, or cultivated fields of corn and cotton. The mud villages we passed were as deep in stench as they had been on my earlier trip. They probably have not changed much since the trip of Alexander the Great, who came through here over two thousand years ago.

In an hour we reached the 2000-foot escarpment of Malakand where the black road, following the contours of the hills, climbs gradually to the higher plain where the town of Malakand sits. The limestone rocks and cliffs along these hills were roasting hot; and though we stopped once for pictures, we quickly hastened on, as the heat was almost unbearable.

Once along this escarpment the British Army fought the Pathans, who held the higher ground. It was one of the battles in which Kipling memorialized the British Tommy who was "chokin' mad with thirst," and called out the now world-famous words:

> For Gawd's sake, git the water, Gunga Din.
> It was crawlin' and it stunk,
> But of all the drinks I've drunk,
> I'm gratefullest to one from Gunga Din.

It was this hot escarpment that Winston Churchill well knew as a young lieutenant in the British Army.

Opposite, as we climbed, were several huge conduit pipes carrying the water of the Malakand River down the steep cliff to turbines that generate electricity, some of which goes to Swat. The discharged water pours out at the bottom in a huge muddy stream to join the Kabul River near Peshawar and irrigate the sun-parched land of Gandhara, which averages only thirteen inches of rain a year and is largely dependent on irrigation for its agriculture.

We did not stop in the shade of Malakand where many pleasant teahouses line a cool road, but went on at once to Swat.

Shortly out of Malakand a large river and a dirt road come in on the left. That is the Panjkora River of Dir that rises to the west of Swat. We took instead the right-hand road—the paved one—and soon came to the village of Thana. Here all the villagers were down at a creek doing laundry—men, women, and children. We stopped the car. Some were chanting in unison as they rubbed the clothes. Others were shouting discordantly as they beat the laundry at water's edge. When we listened from a distance, it seemed the whole village, like a flock of geese, was in an uproar over their common task. Shortly we entered the Kingdom of Swat at a point marked by a tiny square sign on a high pole. The road follows the blue Swat River all the way to Saidu Sharif.

Each time I see the entrance to the Swat Valley I am reminded of our own Connecticut Valley. The river is broad and purling, the water blue and sparkling. Green fields of rice and sugar cane stretch as far as one can see. The roads that lead under green arches of trees are inviting.

The first stretch of the road into Swat runs between rows of beautiful chinaberry trees, called Persian lilac in Swat. The chinaberry tree and the chenar dominate most of the roadsides in the southern part of Swat. As we were approaching Saidu, a huge lizard, about two feet long, came up from the ditch on one side of the road and headed for the other. He did not dawdle, tortoiselike, on his journey. He darted like a streak across the asphalt to disappear in a flash in the ditch on the other side.

We stayed at the Swat Hotel in Saidu. Each room has overhead fans, a toilet, and a bath. The rooms face a courtyard; and cross-ventilation is provided by a door from the bathroom that opens on the outside. There are presently only twenty rooms in the hotel; but Saidu is becoming so popular as a resort that many new rooms are being planned. We found the hotel neat, clean, and exceedingly well managed. It was run by a Swiss lady, Mrs. Sherling, who served us for luncheon the best rice and curry we had on our seven-thousand-mile journey.

Before lunch an old friend of mine and the Wali's chief secretary—Mr. Ataullah—appeared. He was, as usual, meticulously attired and most affable. He asked us what we wanted to see and do in Swat. I told him: a visit to the Buddhist ruins, a trip to Kalam, which is eighty miles upstream from Saidu, a call on the

Wali's father, the Badshah, and a visit with the Wali himself. He disappeared to return in a quarter hour with the word that all had been arranged.

Swat, like Dir, Chitral, Gilgit, Nagir, and Hunza, is a principality in West Pakistan. While it is a part of Pakistan, it has a greater degree of autonomy than the states of Pakistan. Ultimately it will be absorbed; but today, as in yesteryear, the present Wali of Swat rules as absolute monarch—collecting his own taxes, maintaining his own army, operating his own schools and hospitals, and maintaining his own roads. Though Swat is a part of West Pakistan, the powers of the Wali have been left undisturbed, pursuant to the Establishment of West Pakistan Act, 1955.

Swat is a rich country, a nation that has a food surplus. It exports each year rice, barley, and maize. The perquisites of an absolute monarch are, therefore, not all in honor and prestige. The Wali gets a flat 10 per cent of all produce of the land. No grain, for example, can leave the thrashing floor until the Wali's 10 per cent is paid. And there is an agent there who promptly makes the collection. Out of this 10 per cent and other taxes all government expenses must be paid. The Wali receives for himself a salary of 500,000 rupees ($105,000) a year, which is more than our President gets. And the Wali's salary is tax-exempt. The Wali of Dir, the neighboring principality, also takes his 10 per cent but gives nothing in return—no schools, no hospitals. As we shall see, Miangul Jahan Zeb, the Wali of Swat, has introduced into his domain a goodly portion of the welfare state.

The valley of Swat at its southern end, where we entered, is about 3100 feet in elevation. But even so, the farmers this year were somewhat in advance of those on the plains of Peshawar and were transplanting their rice.

We traveled the length and breadth of Swat and saw no farm machinery. We saw many miles of road being paved; but apart from a roller or two, the entire work was manual even to the crushing of the small gravel that underlies the asphalt. Swat is almost entirely dependent on manual labor.

Telephones connect the Wali with all police and military stations and with all important public buildings. There is some electric power in Swat generated from the power project at Malakand. The Swat Hotel, the Wali's mansion, and other public buildings have electric lights. This power reaches few farms.

With one difference, the farms of Swat are like all of Asia's—houses made of mud and bricks, located in fields worked by water buffalo. The difference in Swat is in the smell. No fecal odor overhangs a Swat village. In the first place, the standard of living is fairly high by Asian standards; in the second place, the Wali has introduced public health measures that teach, among other things, the use of sanitary outhouses, and the virtue of neatness.

Below Saidu we first saw the relics of the Buddhist civilization that once dominated this hundred-mile-long valley. There are carvings on a thirty-foot cliff to the right of the road, not in good condition but showing the Buddha. Farther on, a rock on the left showed a twenty-foot figure of the Buddha facing the river.

We were to see up and down the valley many foundation stones that mark the location of ancient Buddhist monasteries. The story of the earlier Swat diggings in these Buddhist ruins has been told by Aurel Stein in *On Alexander's Track to the Indus*. In 1957 the Italians under Professor Ricci were excavating one large Buddhist *stupa* at Batkara. Only six feet or so of the ruins had been uncovered. But it showed friezes that, even to the untutored eye, had plain traces of the Greek influence. One stretch of sculpture reminded me of the Parthenon and our own Supreme Court Building in Washington, D.C. Mary said she was startled when she first saw this model of Greek temple form with Ionic columns.

Fah Hian, a famous Chinese Buddhist pilgrim, passed through Swat about A.D. 400 and found it to be a thriving Buddhist center. When Sung Yun, the next Chinese Buddhist pilgrim, visited Swat in A.D. 519, he found Buddhism flourishing and the sound of temple bells filling the whole valley. But when Hsüan Tsang arrived in A.D. 630 the country was in sad ruins, though Buddhism was still the predominant religion. He reported that once there had been 1400 Buddhist monasteries in the valley "but many of them are now in ruins." And he added, "Once there had been 18,000 Brethren but these had gradually decreased until only a few remained."

The liquidation took place shortly after A.D. 500. It was at the hands of Mihiragula, son of Toramana, who succeeded his father as King of the empire of the White Huns. Mihiragula in Indian tradition is the most bloodthirsty tyrant of all. The murders and destruction he visited upon quiet, peaceful, serene Swat are probably unparalleled.

The story is that the Swat River was so swollen with the bodies of Buddhist monks that it rose several feet. Those Buddhists who did not expire on this wave of destruction were liquidated by the Yuzufzais, who invaded from Afghanistan in the fifteenth century.

Though Swat has had no Buddhists for five hundred years, the Buddhist legends still persist. One can pick them up in the teahouses that stretch all the way along the Swat River from Saidu to Kalam. I picked up one at Bahrin, halfway up the narrow canyon to Kalam where the roaring white water of the Dral River empties into the Swat. Here we stopped for a visit with the villagers. Here several dozen gathered on the flat rooftops to see us. Here a Swati with his wool hat with rolled-up edges told me about Buddha, the pigeon, and the hawk. It was in Swat that, during one of his incarnations, Buddha saved a pigeon in desperate flight by tearing his own flesh and offering it to the hawk.

The road to Kalam follows the narrow winding canyon of the Swat River all the way and crosses it many times on wooden cantilever bridges that tremble like reeds under the wheels of a car. At Kalam, the northernmost point in Swat, a new hydroelectric dam on the Swat River (below the confluence of the Ushu and Utrar rivers) is being built. There the peaks, knows as Falak Sar and Monkial, rise to about 19,000 feet and the canyon is filled with blue spruce, silver fir, and walnut trees. No matter which direction one travels the valley, there is always a distant peak to lift the heart. The mountain barrier on three sides creates a feeling of seclusion and safety. The sunsets show a riot of color. The roar of white water has a soothing effect. The green of the valleys and the calls of the mourning doves mean peace. While Taxila seemed an ideal valley for a Buddhist retreat, Swat was a short step from heaven. Here in the fastness of this remote valley there is a solitude that brings one close to his Creator. Wherever I stopped in Swat, I had this illusion of remoteness from man, of isolation from the world's cares. The Buddhists in picking it for 1400 monasteries had planned well. We know from the early travels of the Chinese Buddhists in this region that Swat was indeed their "garden."

Swat is filled not only with stories of Buddha but also with tales of Alexander the Great. Alexander sent one army through Gandhara and another in a sweeping pincer movement through Swat. The fiercest opposition was in the stronghold of Swat. The man who guided Alexander wanted to be left behind as Governor of Swat. But Alexander's policy was to appoint only Greeks as governors of conquered territory. This disappointed guide therefore deserted Alexander, went over to the Indian side, and eventually helped build up a force too great for Alexander. At least, this is the current legend that one hears in Peshawar and Swat. If we took a census of Swat, we would find quite a few boys being named Alexander to this day.

Swat has a fair collection of shops where a wide variety of articles can be purchased, including bicycles and alarm clocks made in America and brightly embroidered skullcaps made in Swat. But the prize product of the Saidu bazaar is the "Swat curtain." It is woven in stripes of bright colors in almost any combination. It is ideal for either spreads or draperies. The colors are not fast; but the price is so low as to make these curtains popular with the ladies.

We left by car about four o'clock one afternoon to see the Wali's father—Miangul Abdul Wadud. The father has a town home—a rambling white house built beside a large pool filled with lily pads. Next to it is a huge fortlike building where the wives and their entourage live. Opposite this town house is a beautiful shrine where the father wants to be buried. It is a building with some of the most delicate lines and best proportions I saw on our long journey. These buildings were guarded by soldiers dressed in gray, who were taking turns shaving each other, apparently in preparation for some festive occasion. The customer sat on a cot covered by a rice mat laid over a mattress of rope strands while the barber, with an old-fashioned, murderous-looking razor, stood over him.

We stopped the car at a prominence near the new shrine. Here we were three hundred feet or more above the city of Saidu. All was quiet in the hills around us. Some rock pigeons streaked down the valley. From below came the voices of hundreds of people and children, an occasional rooster's crow, and the cackling of many hens. This was the beginning of evening; and, in

Swat, as in other parts of the earth, the voices of people, especially children, seem to rise in pitch as darkness nears. The nearness of night draws all of us closer together in response to the loneliness that travels with the lengthening shadows.

We reached Sufaid Mahal, the summer home of the Wali's father, about dusk. It lies at 4100 feet at the end of a dirt road at the head of a narrow canyon where peaks rise 9000 feet high. This dirt road, like all of Swat's unpaved highways, is as excellent as our own Vermont's. It is lined with chenar and chinaberry trees; but by the time Sufaid Mahal was reached we were in pine and fir. This residence is a rather palatial L-shaped stone structure facing a courtyard that has a white stone floor and a low wall.

The Wali's father, Wadud, met us at the foot of a dozen steps leading up to the courtyard. He is seventy-four years old, with white chin whiskers, thin and wiry, toothless, and quite active. He wears large steel-rimmed spectacles and carries a heavy cane over his arm as an ornament. Taking me by his other hand, he escorted me up the steps and seated me on a stone bench in the courtyard, the ladies following.

Wadud speaks Pushtu; but he neither speaks nor understands English. So Ataullah was my interpreter. After orange squash and cherries were served, I asked my host if I could take pictures. The sun was down and it was deep dusk; but I had my strobe flash equipment along. Wadud agreed and noticeably stiffened himself for the ordeal. I maneuvered my strobe, trying not to get a reflection in his glasses. When I had what I thought was an ideal pose, I pressed the trigger of my Leica. But there was no flash. I explained to my host that all was not in order and apologized for the delay. He spoke up at once and said most seriously, "What man makes fails. Only God is perfect."

Wadud is considered a holy man today. He spends his days in prayer and meditation. He has a room at Sufaid Mahal set aside for worship. There he faces Mecca five times a day in prayer. Like other Swatis, he is an orthodox or Sunni Moslem. He strives to lead the life proclaimed by the Koran; and that includes not only abstention from pork and alcohol, five daily prayers, the acceptance of four wives, and the like, but charity to the poor. He offers food to the poor twice a week; and he is noted for his piety the length and breadth of the kingdom.

Some in Peshawar whisper that religion came late in Wadud's life. Only forty years ago was Swat welded together into a nation. Up to 1917 it was divided into twenty-four separate and often warring tribes, including the Ajjars, the Sujjars, and the Kohistanis. Wadud effected a merger of these quarreling tribes and became their acknowledged leader. The merger was not a peaceful one; many heads were lost; and the whispered talk in the bazaar at Peshawar is that Wadud's religion came only at the end of the long list of assassinations that made the merger possible. But there is no doubt today that Wadud is a devout person, a man of piety. He has, indeed, devoted much of his life to pacifying the people and improving their social and economic conditions. In 1949 he created a precedent by abdicating in favor of his son, the present Wali.

The Wali invited us to an informal dinner which was attended only by him, one of his teen-age sons, Ataullah, and the three of us. Though I have been in the Wali's home twice, I have never met any of his wives, for they, like good Sunnis, are in *purdah*. The Wali, bald, stout, broad-shouldered, five feet eight, and in his mid-fifties, is a friendly outgoing person. He was educated at Peshawar University and speaks English fluently. So this night he and I covered a lot of ground.

He is proud of the welfare state he and his father have brought to Swat. This country of over 500,000 people now has schools in most villages. There are high schools in reach of all communities. We saw the schools all the way to Kalam in northern Swat, which is a great ski resort with a small comfortable hotel. But Kalam, though remote, and all the villages below it on the roaring white water of the Swat River have at least a primary school.

In 1952 the Wali established a college at Saidu. The primary and secondary schools are segregated Moslem style—boys in one school, girls in the other. These schools are free but not compulsory. In 1957, Swat schools had 20,000 students altogether. The college is for boys only; girls are banned. The sophisticates of Swat say, "*Purdah* must ultimately go. But the people of Swat are not yet ready for it." Women of Swat who work the fields are not in *purdah;* but those from the middle class on up practice it faithfully. The women are so far in *purdah* that practically all deliveries at birth are made by midwives, though Swat has many doctors trained in Lahore and Peshawar.

The Wali is proud of his health program. There are first-aid stations everywhere. There are six hospitals in Swat with a total of 600 beds. I visited a 100-bed hospital in Saidu run by Dr. Ghulam Mohammed and found it compared favorably with one of ours in mid-America. It had well-equipped operating rooms, X-ray equipment, and a dental clinic. All medical care in Swat is free; and all doctors are civil servants of the Wali. The Wali is more proud of this medical program than anything else he has done.

I turned the conversation to law. The law of the Koran is the law of Swat in civil cases. Church and state are one. *Mullahs* sit to hear most civil cases. A case cannot get into civil court merely by the filing of a complaint, as in this country. The person who wants to sue must first petition the Wali for permission to sue, just as he was compelled to petition the King under ancient English law. The Wali hears the plaintiff, and sometimes the defendant, on whether or not the case should be brought. If he thinks the charge is a substantial one, he remits the plaintiff to a *mullah* to resolve the controversy. In that way is a writ obtained.

Criminal courts apply the customary law, and also in general follow the principles of the Koran. Criminal cases likewise start with the Wali. If the prosecutor has a criminal charge which he would like to make, he first states it to the Wali; and if the Wali agrees, the criminal case is instituted. The Wali himself will sit in the most serious criminal cases, such as robbery and murder. Murder, rape, and adultery are all punished by death. A man caught in the act of stealing can suffer the death penalty, as can an arsonist whose fire results in the death of a person. If the Wali does not sit in a criminal case, he must nevertheless approve all the sentences which are imposed. He is, indeed, the absolute monarch.

In a recent murder case the following facts appeared: A married woman disappeared. Finally her mother asked the woman's husband where she was. He said she had gone to Karachi. The mother was suspicious and went to the police, who found the wife's body in a well. The husband had choked her in a fight, put her in the well, and filled the well with stones to keep her body from floating. While the evidence to begin with was wholly circumstantial, the facts were finally well-established.

The Wali ordered the man executed. It is customary law in Swat for the nearest female or male relative of the murdered person to do the killing. But the children were all quite young; and the Wali thought it would be unwise to wait until they had reached maturity. So he allowed the brother of the wife to be the executioner. The police produced the defendant and tied him hand and foot to a tree. Then the brother-in-law stepped off a dozen paces and, turning, shot the man with his rifle.

I asked the Wali how many lawyers there were in Swat. He told me there were none. I asked him who represents the defendant in a civil suit or the accused in a criminal case.

He said, "The defendant himself. But the judge, of course, sees that he gets a fair trial."

I asked what would happen if an accused did not feel adequate to defend himself and wanted a lawyer.

"None would be appointed," the Wali said.

I asked what would happen if the accused retained a lawyer and the lawyer appeared in court.

"He would not be allowed to speak," the Wali replied.

I spoke of the complexities of many cases and of the inability of many laymen to grasp the intricacies of the law. I emphasized how easy it was for an innocent man to get trapped by circumstantial evidence. I spoke of the guarantee of our Sixth Amendment and the need of an accused for the helping hand of a lawyer at most stages of a trial.

The Wali was most patient with my inquiries and most courteous in his answers. He brought the conversation to a dramatic close as coffee was being served. Turning to me, he said, with the voice that carries authority throughout the whole length of Swat:

"You see, Mr. Justice, up here in Swat we have concluded that a lawyer only makes a lawsuit complicated and confusing."

CHAPTER 10

THE KHYBER

Ali, the station wagon, performed nicely in West Pakistan. We had no punctures, no blowouts, no engine problems whatever. We did not, however, use our car for all the side trips around Peshawar. Two capable chauffeurs at Government House, Arbab Wazir Mohammed Mohmand and Jamshaid Khan—both husky Pathans about forty years old—took us on some side trips in government cars, while we kept our station wagon in the garage. One day we went with Jamshaid to a garage in Peshawar and arranged for a checkup of the car in preparation for our trip to Kabul.

The carburetor needed adjustment, the oil needed to be changed and the car needed greasing. We decided that we should pick up an extra battery, since articles of that kind are not easy to come by in Afghanistan. We were lucky enough to obtain a Delco dry-charge battery and the garageman furnished us with six quart bottles of sulphuric-acid mixture necessary for charging it. These bottles were no great asset to our packing problems, as anything that touched their corks got a hole eaten in it.

All the way up from Karachi the car had been very heavily loaded—too much so even for paved roads. Coming out of Pindi on the asphalt road, the rear tires hit the fenders several times and the car listed to one side badly. And when we got on the dirt roads near Taxila, we had to crawl to get through the ruts.

We had tried in every major town without success to get extra leaves for the rear springs. We tried again in Peshawar and to our delight we had success.

While the English-speaking garageman did not have the extra leaves, he thought he knew where they were. He sent to the bazaar a mechanic who came back in a short while with six leaves. We found these to be too long. So off we went with the garage owner to a blacksmith. We found him in the bazaar. It was a typical Asian blacksmith shop, not under a tree or in a separate building, but only a stall perhaps fifteen feet wide and thirty feet deep in a narrow, winding lane packed with other stalls. The owner was a Pathan, without headdress, barefooted and wearing a tattered brown shirt and the usual baggy trousers. The measurements of the leaves were taken and he went to work at once, sawing off the ends, then heating them and tapering them down to the right thickness.

Jamshaid had a worried look on his face as he drove the car up to Government House that evening. I asked what was wrong. He said that he had driven the car only a few blocks from the garage when he noticed that the red light indicating oil deficiency was on. He stopped at once and measured the oil with the dip stick. There was no oil at all in the car! When my friend at the garage had drained the oil, he had been interrupted and forgot to fill it.

The car now rode so high, it reminded me of cars I had seen in the valleys of the Smoky Mountains in Tennessee where moonshine whisky is said to be made. There the rear ends of many country cars are so high that the back seat looks down on the driver. They say it takes fifty gallons of whisky in the rear seat to bring the back end down where it should be. The six new leaves caused no such distortion in our station wagon; but the rear now rode high enough to give me greater confidence for the Afghan journey ahead of us.

The weather in Peshawar was oppressively hot during our entire stay there. The nights were too hot for sleep. The Pakistanis for the most part slept outdoors. Their beds were fourposters with ropes stretched tightly across the frame to take the place of springs. Sometimes they put a blanket on this rope;

sometimes not. At other times they used mats of woven rice straw as ground cover, substituting them for beds. In one way or another, practically the whole population of Peshawar slept outdoors—on the roofs, porches, lawns, or in the parks. If one drove his car at night and pulled off to the side of the road, turning off the engine, he could always hear a chorus of snores. All of Peshawar left the heat of the houses for slumber.

We, however, did not have the courage to follow suit. We could have slept outside, for Mercedes, very wisely, had bought three woven rice mats in the Peshawar bazaar. We had found plastic seat covers uncomfortably hot on our Pakistan journey. They not only retained the heat; they also would not absorb any moisture from our clothing. The woven rice mats, when draped over the seats, were cool to the back and good absorbents of perspiration. Moreover, we were to find that they made an excellent ground cloth whenever it was necessary to get under the car for repairs. Some of my best pictures show them protecting Mercedes from the dirt of the highway as she labored to repair the muffler or the gearshift rods. But we did not use these mats to sleep on the lawn of Government House. Bound by convention, we stayed indoors and suffered greatly as a consequence.

I found only one remedy for sleeplessness on those hot nights. It was a remedy I used first in Baghdad years earlier when the night temperatures were over 100° F. I stood under the cold shower in my pajamas and went to bed dripping wet. The idea is to get to sleep before one dries off. I found in Peshawar that I had to do this once at bedtime and twice during the night in order to get eight hours' sleep. But it invariably worked. I used the dripping-pajama technique the last night in Peshawar; and to my surprise I slept nearly eight hours without waking up. The reason was that Peshawar had an unseasonable storm during the night that dropped the temperature forty points. At four-thirty o'clock, when I wakened, the air was as cool and refreshing as Seattle's; and a light drizzle was falling.

We had packed the car, Ali, the night before; so by six o'clock we were on our way to the Khyber, Abdul Qadir, the charming and efficient head boy at Government House, seeing us off. Mohammed and Jamshaid led the way in another car. Mohsin

Ali Khan, the political officer in charge of Khyber Pass matters, was to meet us at the eastern edge of the Khyber and see us through.

The sky was overcast and the drizzle continued as we rolled past the formidable old fort of Peshawar that rose on our left like a huge mountain. Peshawar had slept late this cool morning, for only a few creaking bullock carts were on the streets. As we left the city and came to the broad plains of Gandhara west of the city, I was sorry we had picked this day to leave. In the first place, I had not rummaged enough in the ancient bazaars of Peshawar, places that hold a strange fascination. Secondly, the rain continued, and the low notch that lay ahead and marked the beginning of the defile known as the Khyber was heavily overcast. My hopes for good color pictures of the Khyber were now low and in view of the long journey ahead of us there was no prospect of retracing our steps to photograph the Khyber on a day of blue skies and white clouds.

The beginning of the Khyber, which Babur called "the hill of Kheiber," is about ten miles from Peshawar. There stands Fort Jamrud (known centuries earlier as Jam), made of mud and stone and shaped like a battleship. This morning it had no sign of life; its flag was not yet flying; the earth around it had the sharp fragrance of dust freshly sprinkled by rain. We had no sooner entered the long winding defile that runs about thirty miles to the Afghan border than the clouds began to break up. In ten minutes the sky was blue; and when we stopped at the first big elbow on the road to take a picture of a fortress commanding this bend in the gorge, the photographic conditions were perfect. It was to be this way for over six weeks. With one exception, the next rain to drop on us was in eastern Turkey in late August.

There are three routes through the Khyber. The first and main one is the black-surfaced two-lane road constructed on an easy grade by the British and now well maintained by the Pakistanis. Above the highway is a railroad to Landi Kotal, also built by the British and still used. Below the highway is a caravan route that dates long before the British and long before Alexander. The Khyber was the easy funnel through which Central Asian trade has passed from time out of mind. The Khyber is, indeed, the lowest pass in the Safed Koh Range, being about 3500 feet in elevation. It was the easy route for caravans as well as invaders.

Today the caravan route, a winding trail, is marked at places, where it reaches the highway, with a sign that could not be misunderstood by anyone, no matter whether he is illiterate, no matter his language. The sign carries pictures of a camel fully loaded and a donkey carrying a pack. The auto road is marked by a sign showing an automobile. There were no camel trains in the Khyber the day we passed through. But we saw quite a few pack trains of donkeys and burros, headed for Peshawar.

Much history—mostly bloody—has been written here. The Khyber is a name better known in Asia than any other. Through it poured the main invasions of India—the Aryans about 2000 B.C. on their march to Mohenjodaro; one arm of Alexander the Great's army in 327 B.C. as he swept to the Indus in a great pincer movement; Mahmoud of Ghazni, the Afghan who, beginning in A.D. 1000, sent his soldiers of Islam onto the plains of Peshawar in twelve major invasions; Genghis Khan and his cruel Mongols in A.D. 1220; Timur of Samarkand in A.D. 1398; Babur Khan, who invaded India through the Khyber five times, the first in A.D. 1505, and who established the Mogul dynasty that ruled India until the British came; the Afghans in A.D. 1756 on their conquest of Kashmir. The British were rather newcomers to the Khyber. They first occupied the Khyber on July 26, 1838, when they fought the First Afghan War. As Russia moved south, England moved north and west. The annexations bit by bit of Soviet Central Asia by Russia were chess moves that England countered in the Sind, the Punjab, the Khyber, and Afghanistan. There was much British blood spilled in the Khyber. Slate and limestone cliffs dominate almost every foot of the passageway through the Khyber, making it an ideal place for ambush. British deeds of glory made the Khyber famous. And Kipling memorialized them in *Arithmetic on the Frontier:*

A great and glorious thing it is
To learn, for seven years or so,
The Lord knows what of that and this,
Ere reckoned fit to face the foe—

The flying bullet down the Pass,
That whistles clear: "All flesh is grass."

With home-bred hordes the hillsides teem.
The troopships bring us one by one,
At vast expense of time and steam,
To slay Afridis where they run.
The "captives of our bow and spear"
Are cheap, alas! as we are dear.

The men who ambushed the British were men of some dozen tribes headed by the Afridis, Mohmands, Shinwaris, Shilmanis, and Mullagoris. One who goes to the library to see what is written about these tribes will find ugly reports. These people are described as ruffians and murderers; they are rated as an untrustworthy, thieving lot. And so they were to the British; and it was through the eyes of the British that we who read English have come to know them.

These Pathans are Afghans, and Afghans are mixtures of Aryans, Dinarics, and Mongols. These Pathans who sat, and still sit, across the Khyber are proud hillmen—as proud, as fierce, as independent as the Scot Highlanders were in the seventeenth and eighteenth centuries. Both fought the British in the cause of independence. Both were dogged and independent. And to this day the Pathans are proud of their ancient code: (1) asylum to every fugitive; (2) hospitality to every visitor, even an enemy; (3) insult wiped out by insult; (4) do unto others what they do to you. Kipling in *The Ballad of East and West* has shown how the stuff of which the Pathan is made can be a strong bond uniting them and us.

These Pathans love a rifle above all else; and one who travels the Khyber these peaceful days will seldom see a Pathan without one. During the dark days of the British rule they made rifles by hand. A captured British rifle could be duplicated so meticulously that only an expert could tell the difference. That skill is perpetuated to this day. Under the British, traffic in those guns was illicit; but it flourished. Many villages had gun factories. There were some guns manufactured in the Khyber itself. But the main factories were in five villages in Kohat Pass, which lies forty miles south of Peshawar. I had seen these handmade guns in Peshawar and could not tell the difference from the factory-made rifles which they copied. As we passed through the Khyber by car, I saw Pathans on almost every turn of the winding road, carrying rifles under their arms.

There have been fortifications and breastworks in the Khyber from time immemorial. The forts or blockhouses that the British built here are now mostly relics. But they have a potential value to Pakistan. The Khyber today does not seethe in discontent and trouble. But all is not quiet. The area is under the Khyber Agency, a political branch of the Pakistan government that is responsible to the Commissioner in Peshawar. The agency is manned by competent, farseeing men who have the situation under control. But the seeds of trouble are still present. It is not the presence of the foreigner, the invader. It is the political idea of Pushtunistan.

The Pathans want a nation of their own. Ancient Gandhara, which took in eastern Afghanistan and the valley of the Indus, is roughly the claim which the Pathans make for Pushtunistan.

Ahmad Shah Durani, who ruled Afghanistan in the mid-eighteenth century, gave the idea historic concreteness by extending the boundaries of the nation beyond the Punjab to Delhi. Such a claim, if ever realized, would in practical effect result in West Pakistan disappearing from the map. Though visionary and impractical, the idea smolders. It is a major divisive force at work along the northwest border of West Pakistan today.

The modern Pathans are spilled across the border on both sides of the Khyber. Most of them still run sheep and goats. On a previous trip I had seen many of them with their herds high in the Hindu Kush mountains of Afghanistan. They go up in the spring and down in the fall. In recent years many Pathans have become sedentary farmers. And I learned from Mohsin Ali Khan, the political officer of the Khyber Agency, that today the Shinwaris have become mostly truck drivers. In the past they ran mule trains between Kabul and Peshawar. Now they run trucks instead. Some Afridis do the same. And many tribal members now have shops in Peshawar.

This bright cool morning in the Khyber we saw many Shinwaris with yellow, red, or blue turbans, behind the wheels of trucks. When I signaled them they invariably stopped, stepping down from the cab with wide grins that showed their excellent white teeth. These are friendly people, always ready for a visit, always eager for a story. An Afridi or Mohmand always seemed to me more reserved than the Shinwari. But under the surface I always found a friendly, warmhearted person.

We stopped at Ali Musjid to take pictures. This is the narrowest point in the pass; the cliffs are sheer and the canyon is only a few rods wide. Here the Pathans have a mosque in memory of Ali. Legend has it that Ali took off on horseback on his heavenly ascension from the Khyber; and if one has the time, he can get a Pathan to show him the hoofprints on the rocks made by the half-flying, half-running horse. I had seen them on my earlier trip and did not take the time to look them up again. Our interest this time was in the faces of the crowd that gathered from nowhere when we stopped. Most of them were Afridis dressed in white trousers, blue tunics, and blue turbans. They were eager to be photographed, full of questions about America, intensely interested in our journey, and to the last man eager to have us in their homes for lunch. They did not know who we were, except that we came from America. They were fascinated with the baggage inside and on top of the station wagon. Many faces pushed through the car windows to get a glimpse of our belongings. Yet the crowd was quiet, orderly, and extremely polite.

We made many stops this morning. We stopped briefly at Fort Meade, Shagai Ridge, and at Landi Kotal, the high point from which one sees the plains of Afghanistan. We did not tarry at any stop. The trip to Kabul was a long one and I wanted to arrive before dark. So after Landi Kotal we hurried down to the mouth of the funnel that empties onto the Afghan plain. Near the western end of the Khyber are concrete blocks that fill the whole canyon, with spare ones to roll across the road. This is a road block that the British put there against tanks. If the Russians ever burst across the Oxus and pour down toward India, they will be used again.

The Pakistan border point is Torkham, a small place set in locust trees where customs and immigration employees and a small unit of the Pakistan Army live. Here was a sign that read:

Dakka	6 Km
Jelalabad	57 Km
Kabul	165 Km

The Pakistan flag fluttered briskly in a cool breeze this bright morning, as we sat on the verandah of the administrative building having tea.

Soon it came time to say goodbye. We were anxious to be on our way across rugged Afghanistan. Yet we hated to say goodbye. Pakistan had been hospitable and friendly; we had made many new friends there; we had left undone many things we had wanted to do. We were especially sorry to leave Mohammed and Jamshaid, the two Pathan chauffeurs attached to Government House in Peshawar. They had done us many favors far beyond the line of duty. I had become especially fond of Mohammed. He had an Anthony Eden mustache and a turban with a fancy twirl to it. He was a Mohmand of the Khyber and intensely proud of his race. He knew from his tribe that I had visited it in 1951. One who is once a guest of the Mohmands becomes an honorary member. Mohammed, therefore, was my friend and protector from the beginning. He was a wholesome, outgoing person with a keen sense of humor. One day as we rode in a government car, Mercedes and Mary kept speaking up from the rear seat saying they were sure we were on the wrong road. They thought Mohammed could not speak English and kept urging me to try to convey to him in Urdu, Persian, or sign language that he was going the wrong way. Soon Mohammed leaned over to me and said in broken English, "I no lost." In many ways he had endeared himself to us. Jamshaid, too, had been most helpful. The last thing he did was to check over the motor to see if it was running well and show Mercedes again the proper carburetor adjustments to make.

At Torkham we shook hands with heavy hearts. For such occasions I had taken along brightly colored ballpoint pens. We used these inexpensive gifts as tokens of appreciation for services rendered and new friendships made. Mohammed and Jamshaid had no use for them, as they were illiterate. Yet they loved these pens. The last I saw of Mohammed Mohmand, he had the blue one in his hands and his brown eyes were moist with tears.

PART 2

AFGHANISTAN

CHAPTER 1

AN AMERICAN KAZE

Our journey across Afghanistan might well be called "Adventures in Friendship." Never has adversity worked so strongly against a traveler; never has one been so warmly and generously received along the highways and byways. Trouble seemed to follow us all the way across the Hindu Kush and for hundreds of miles along the Russian border; and at the same time good Samaritans without number always were at hand to ease the way. History books tell us that Afghans are brigands. But our journey taught us that they are the friendliest people we ever knew.

When we passed through the Pakistan gate at Torkham and entered Afghanistan, we left a black-surfaced road for gravel. Apart from a few cities, we were not to travel another paved highway until we left Ankara for Istanbul. The beginning of this two-lane gravel road across Afghanistan was propitious. It had good drainage and a surface that seemed to have been recently scraped and rolled. We were to learn later that this road was one built in Afghanistan under Russian supervision. But it is a vast improvement over the rut-ridden road I had traveled from Kabul in 1951.

On my earlier visit I had cleared customs and immigration at Dakka, a small outpost on the Kabul River about three and a half miles from Torkham. Being at the wheel of the station wagon, I naturally headed straight for Dakka, hardly noticing a big warehouse type of building on our left near the Afghan border. That was my first mistake, for it was there that we were supposed to clear customs. My second mistake was in not having an interpreter to enter Afghanistan with us. I had tried to get one. My choice was Faqir M. Mohmand, who had been with me on my earlier Afghan journey. I had written ahead, requesting that Faqir meet us in Peshawar; and I received word in Lahore that it had been arranged. Faqir, however, did not show up in Peshawar nor was he at the Afghan border to meet us.

The languages of Afghanistan are Pushtu and Persian. I know no Pushtu and my Persian is limited. We had to clear Dakka and travel the hundred miles to Kabul, all without an interpreter. This was my anxiety as I pulled into the shade of the nondescript Afghan administration building at Dakka. That building is all there is at Dakka. There's not even a tree or a shrub. There are mountains to the north and the east. A slightly alkaline meadow runs a half mile or so to the blue Kabul River which turns north at Dakka to cross the Safed Koh Range above Khyber Pass. As I pulled up at Dakka, the only sign of life was a dozen ravens wheeling in search for carrion.

There were three men at this lone outpost. One in baggy *shalwars* and tattered shirt was a servant. A thick, heavy-set, unshaven man about fifty-five who had lost half his upper teeth was dressed in Western clothes. Also dressed Western style was the man in charge. He was tall and thin with a three-day black beard. It was to him that I handed our passports and the "triptyque" for the car. I followed him inside to his barren office and sat opposite him as he fingered through the passports. In a minute he extended his hand and in Persian asked me for other papers. What those papers were I did not know. He finally called the older man and they talked simultaneously in Persian to me. I could only shrug my shoulders to indicate my ignorance. Finally there was a light in the older man's eyes and he said, "Customs." I replied that customs was *"inja"* (here). *"Na, na,"* was the reply and, pointing toward the Pakistan-Afghan border, he indicated that I must clear customs there. I was about to return for that purpose, when the thin man with the three-day stubble raised another problem, one that concerned our passports. It took nearly thirty minutes for me to understand his new difficulty. But after he had counted fifteen on his fingers and pointed to the visa, it finally dawned on me that he was saying either that our visa had expired fifteen days ago or was good only for fifteen days after issuance. I could not read the Persian script on the visa. But it had been issued by an old friend, Najib Ullah, Afghan Ambassador to the United States, who knew I would not reach his country until mid-July.

There was no way to communicate this to either of these officials at Dakka. All I could say to their discussion of our visa was *"Na, na."*

Thus was an impasse reached. We could not go on, for our way was blocked. The alternative was to return to Peshawar and get a new Afghan visa. That meant a delay of a couple of days; and Ambassador and Mrs. Sheldon T. Mills expected us for dinner in Kabul this very night. I stood perplexed, trying to think of a way out. An idea came to me. Pointing to the telephone, I said, "Please call Kabul"; and remembering another old Afghan friend, the Foreign Minister, I added, "Mohammed Naim."

The two men had a conference and shortly the younger one picked up the telephone. The older one and I went out to the porch and joined Mercedes and Mary. He and I conversed in Persian about matters as simple as the weather. Even so, his tongue was too fast for my ear and he would have to repeat his sentences very slowly for me to understand. I changed the pace, trying to teach him a few English words like "auto," "road," "watch," etc.

About this time there was great activity on the telephone. The Kabul call had come through and the tall, thin man was shouting at the top of his lungs. Soon he called for the official who was with me. When the older man returned to the porch, his face was fairly lighted up. Pointing to me, he asked in a voice expectant with hope, *"Kaze?"* And when I replied, *"Bali, bali,"* he fairly hugged me. Then he ran back to his associate shouting, *"Americani kaze, Americani kaze."*

I was, indeed, the American judge whom Kabul expected. At once, Dakka went into action. Loud shouts brought the servant running. A big room—obviously for VIPs—was opened up. We were ushered in with much bowing. Soon the servant appeared with ice-cold fruit juice. Mercedes and Mary wisely refused. But someone had to drink a toast; and I was so jubilant at having broken through the customs and immigration barriers that I accepted and drained the glass. A day later I was terribly ill. But this day protocol was satisfied and the border officials at Dakka were beaming. After the cold drink came tea, cakes, and melon; and after them the farewell.

But there was one item of business left; and the tall, thin man tried to explain it. I understood he was talking about Jelalabad, the next town; and I could tell that I was to do something there. He must mean, I thought, that I should report to some official. I could not remember the Persian words for police or mayor. Finally I remembered a Turkish word sometimes used in Persian countries. *"Vali?"* I asked.

"Bali, bali," was the happy reply. *"Niabohukma." "Vali"* and *"Niabohukma"* mean governor; and it was he I was to see in Jelalabad. So after we had written *"Niabohukma"* on a piece of paper, we said goodbye to our three newly found Afghan friends and headed for Jelalabad about thirty miles distant with four Afghan melons that had been given us by our friends at Dakka.

The dirt road to Jelalabad was excellent, except for one culvert that had washed out. It traverses what many writers call the Afghan Desert. It is a dry semi-desert belt with no touch of green except along the Kabul River. A jackal slinked off to the south with a guilty look on his face. A small herd of antelope crossed the road ahead of us, a species smaller than those we have in Oregon and Utah. There was no other sign of life and no vegetation except camel's-thorn and scrub until we reached Jelalabad and its shade of willow and locust trees.

At the time of Christ, there were many Buddhist monasteries in and around Jelalabad. They are all in ruins. Recent diggings have brought many relics to light. We were to see many Buddhist heads—all with fine Grecian noses—in Kabul. And I was to hear all across Afghanistan many tales of the travels of Buddha in this area. Legend has it that during his early incarnations he made many trips here; and near Jelalabad he once left his shadow in a cave—a shadow that reveals itself in iridescent light to the faithful.

We were far too busy to sift out Buddhist legends, let alone stop for lunch in Jelalabad, even though it was now high noon. Kabul was still many miles distant; and we had a tortuous road to travel before dark. I was tempted to stop at a large grove on the eastern edge of town. For here a large number of country people had assembled for a market. Horses, mules, burros, and camels were up for sale; the bidding seemed spirited; and the photographic possibilities looked great. But time was so short we hastened on to find the Governor of Jelalabad and obtain the necessary papers for transit to Kabul.

Jelalabad, a town of about 10,000, is the center of a fertile valley watered by the Kabul River. Near here many Mohmands have farms. The city has dirt streets with irrigation ditches on each side. The homes are all behind mud walls. The bazaars are stalls on open (not covered) streets; and this day the merchants were sprinkling them—using tin scoops at the end of long poles to lift the water from the ditches and throw it onto the streets.

We did not stop until we came to a traffic policeman standing under an umbrella affixed to a stand at a street intersection. I stopped next to him and asked, "*Niabohukma, kojast?*" The accent on my Persian must have been awful, for the officer gave me only a blank look. I tried twice more but without success. By this time a crowd of curious men had assembled. When I asked the fourth time where the Governor lived, a young man about nineteen stepped forward saying, "*Bali, bali.*" So we opened the door of the car and took him along as a guide.

In about six blocks we came to a rather imposing entrance to a large, lush garden adorning a massive residence. This once had been a winter residence for the King of Afghanistan. It was now the home of the Governor of Jelalabad. But it appeared that this official had left for Kabul. I considered my duty to Dakka fulfilled and, having no desire to lose precious hours with a minor officer's red tape, I thanked our volunteer guide and said we would go to Kabul. As he was about to leave, I noticed that we were dangerously low on gasoline. In the excitement of Torkham we had forgotten to have the tank filled. So I called our guide back, asking, "*Benzine kojast?*"

He took us at once to a filling station where I learned that our problems were still far from solved. In Afghanistan one cannot drive up to a filling station, have the tank filled up, pay for the gas, and be on his way. Coupons are necessary. The coupons must be purchased from the King and presented in lieu of cash to the filling station operator. Gasoline is a monopoly of the monarch in Afghanistan. All of it comes from Russia. The Russians agree the King may have it all, while the King agrees to import no gasoline except Russia's.

Without the coupons one can get no gas in Afghanistan. They come in units of ten gallons each; and though one needs only five gallons, he must surrender units for ten gallons, for the coupons are indivisible.

The volunteer guide, the filling station attendant, and I faced each other with blank looks. It would take all afternoon to clear the red tape in Jelalabad to get coupons. Moreover, I did not want to tangle with any more officials, since our visas apparently had some defect in them. So I pulled out my passport from one pocket and all my money from another and handed them all to the attendant. My money was all rupees; I had no afghanis. Mercedes suddenly thought of our supply of fifty one-dollar U.S. bills which we always carry and which, I have discovered, everyone, everywhere, is anxious to get. She got one of these out and laid it on top of the rupees. The Afghan attendant hesitated a minute, then took the passport and all of the money, and stepped back in the shade to talk with my volunteer guide. In a few minutes they returned with a piece of blank paper they wanted me to sign, together with the number of my passport—a document which would be a receipt for ten gallons of gasoline. When I signed the paper, the attendant picked from my currency the dollar bill and enough Pakistani rupees to make three dollars, which is the approximate cost of ten gallons of gasoline in Afghanistan. I did not mind the cost even though I needed less than eight gallons. For gasoline in Jelalabad was to me more precious than gold.

Then came another act of friendship. Both the filling station attendant and the volunteer guide asked us for lunch. They had no idea who we were because neither spoke English. They knew only that we were Americans on a long, dusty journey. I thanked them kindly, wondering if we would be as thoughtful to a traveling Afghan who came our way in America. Then we headed the car toward Ahmadzar, Sarobi, and Kabul.

Abdul Qadir at Government House had packed us a nice lunch—chicken sandwiches, fresh tomatoes, and hard-boiled eggs. We had cold water in two thermos jugs. To save time we ate as we traveled.

Apart from the oasis at Jelalabad this part of Afghanistan is semi-desert. They say it is a joy to behold in springtime when the wild flowers are out. But in July it is brown and desolate. This day the sun was fierce. The storm had passed east of here; and by noon the temperature out of Jelalabad was above 110°.

This is an ancient road, traveled by caravans. Pathans take their flocks across this valley to the high hills in the spring and bring them back in the fall. It's a road notorious for the nails that fall out of the shoes of the herders. I had puncture after puncture when I traveled here before; and I expected several this day. But we had none. The Russian road construction program had brought in earth-moving machines that apparently had covered the old shoe nails under several meters of dirt.

The road, well engineered, is a good dirt one. After Ahmadzar it follows the Kabul River through a narrow winding canyon that this day was as hot as a furnace. The canyon road had not yet been completely finished. There were tributaries to the Kabul that had to be forded; and the first one was so treacherous that I unloaded the ladies and took the car across in low. The radiator by this time was boiling. So I left the car in the shade of the canyon wall, filled the radiator from our water bags, and filled them again from the bright cool stream. Mercedes and Mary had to ford the creek—a blessing in disguise, I told them, for they got wet and refreshingly cool.

Beyond this point are bridges, built earlier by German engineers, and a big hydroelectric power plant also constructed by the Germans. Then comes Sarobi, a pleasant village on a side hill overlooking the Kabul River. At Sarobi we drove into a filling station to get road information. We had been told in Peshawar that the new Russian road followed the canyon of the Kabul River all the way to Kabul. So it does. But in July, 1957, much work yet remained to be done on it. So the Sarobi filling station man, after taking a look at the meager clearance of our car, grinned and shook his head, and waved me toward the old mountain road that I had used once before.

Knowing the steep climb ahead, I filled the radiator. Then we stretched our legs and cut some of the Dakka melons on the car's fenders and shared the sweet fruit with a group of dirty urchins who gathered around.

In another two weeks the car, Ali, would never have made the grade over Lataband Pass, which is 5900 feet in elevation. Russian gasoline is notoriously low in octane and has a foul influence on American motors. Even this day the Russian gasoline caused much knocking in the engine. But the points and spark plugs were clean and the carburetor (which was so badly gummed up by the time we crossed Afghanistan that we had to throw it away) was functioning nicely. The old mountain road out of Sarobi climbs and climbs through barren canyons, reaches many false tops, winds down for a spell, then climbs and climbs some more to reach a new summit. There are thirty miles or more of sharp curves and narrow passages. No guardrail lines the road. Apart from a truck or two ours was the only car on this dangerous, swinging road. I knew of people who had traveled it in dead of winter when the snow was thick. Then it was that trucks often went hurtling into the canyon hundreds of feet below as they mistook a snowdrift for a shoulder of the road.

This was the route taken by the defeated British at the end of the disastrous First Afghan War. On January 6, 1842, the British Army left Kabul for Peshawar with 4500 fighting men and 12,000 camp followers. It was bitter cold, the snow was deep, and the Afghans lay in wait for them on the crags that overlook this twisting canyon road. Only one man got through to Jelalabad, the rest being killed or captured.

The road was as dry as powder the day we crossed; and the weather was clear. So we had no hazards from the sky. I noticed, however, that when I applied the brakes I got a violent pull to the left. I warned Mercedes and Mary, when it came their time to drive, to be careful of the brakes. Had I known what the mechanic in Kabul told us the next day, I would have been too frightened to take those zooming canyon curves even at ten miles an hour. Our brakes were all right. We had, however, lost the nuts that hold the front inner pivot of the left lower control arm of our steering mechanism. In fact, our control of the left front wheel was nil. We were skating around the mountain curves in daredevil fashion and did not know it. Our only worry was the radiator. While climbing Lataband Pass we stopped three times to cool off the engine and fill the radiator. We reached the top about four o'clock. The dirt road down is as long, as swinging, and as treacherous as the dirt road up the Sarobi side. But when it debouches on the plains of Kabul, one is less than fifteen miles from the city.

Way out from the city—perhaps ten miles—is an old caravanserai with accommodations for many travelers and their animals. The highway, as a convenience to customs, goes right through this caravanserai. When we arrived, it took several honks to get the big wooden gate opened up. But the official, who was looking for produce, on which Kabul places a tax, saw at once we were in an exempt class and waved us on. Nearer the city were hundreds of families camped on the plains and building their evening fires. Most of them had black wool tents, typical of the Middle East. Camels were still grazing. Donkeys and burros were staked out. The cries of children at play on the edge of dark were shrill. This was an ideal setting for pictures with my strobe flash, I thought. But picture taking would consume an hour or more; and we wanted to reach Kabul before dark.

Farther on we came to the brick kilns for which Kabul is famous. They fill the sky line as one approaches from the east. I came back a few days later to get pictures of them. In the day of Babur the Kabul Valley had plenty of wood. Today the wood is mostly gone. The men who work the brick kilns use tumbleweeds as kindling; but the wood for the fires must be brought from Jelalabad.

Once the brick kilns were behind us we were in Kabul. The night wind from the north, for which Kabul is famous, was up and the dust was swirling. The sun was low and the air chill, for Kabul sits at 6000 feet.

When I was here in 1951 the streets were dirt. Now, as a result of Russian aid, the main streets are paved. I pulled up alongside a traffic policeman to inquire the way to the American Embassy. But he did not understand my Persian. I drove on until I came to the famous white column statue the Afghans erected to commemorate a victory over the British. Two Afghan soldiers in stone flank the monument. On the side facing me was the British lion in stone, chained to a rock. I stopped the car, for here I saw two men and a woman who looked like Americans to me. I hailed them and they came over.

"Where is the American Embassy?" I asked.

The man in the middle—about thirty years old with red hair—replied, pointing:

"Go straight ahead; cross three side streets; turn left at the fourth; you will see it on the right."

"Thanks a lot," I replied. "You folks here on Point IV?"

"Point IV?" the speaker said in perfect English, with a gasp. "We are Russians."

CHAPTER 2

THE RUSSIANS

Russia has kept a close watch on Afghanistan for several centuries. Russia's concern was twofold. First, her moves in the direction of Afghanistan were moves of empire against the British when they held India. Second, Russia's southern border has never been a natural barrier such as a mountain range or large body of water. It has rather been the relatively smooth plains of Central Asia. The one great barrier to serve as her southern border has been the mighty Hindu Kush that run east and west across Afghanistan north of Kabul. Russia has been drawn to the Hindu Kush as to a magnet. The substitution of Pakistan and India for the British on Asia's subcontinent has merely changed some of the characters in the play; but the drama remains the same today as it was last century.

Today Russia is in Afghanistan in force. Her embassy staff in Kabul is probably larger than that of any other, including our own. Her Ambassador at Kabul is Mikhail Vassiliyevitch Degtyar, a middle-aged, rotund, pleasant-faced man who reminded me a bit of Santa Claus without the beard. I met Degtyar in Kabul at a dinner that Foreign Minister Naim gave for the new Indian Ambassador and his wife—Sri and Mrs. Sundar Narain Haksar. Degtyar was beaming as he moved through this rather large gathering, emphasizing with every word and gesture the friendly intentions of Russia and the willingness of his nation to show Afghanistan the way to modernity.

Afghanistan has not turned wholly to Russia for technical help. The United States has numerous projects there—some twenty-four in number. In dollar volume about half of the assistance goes to projects in the Helmand Valley in southeast Afghanistan where vast hydroelectric and agricultural developments are under way. There are also projects of quite a different nature: the rendering of architectural services, educational programs for graduate and technical schools, teacher training, police, fiscal and public administration, industrial development. But from Kabul on north one sees mostly Russians.

From what I saw, I would say that the Russians in Afghanistan outnumber us. I met Russians in jeeps and trucks all across Afghanistan; and I saw them most everywhere we stopped for the night, huddled around a radio to get the six o'clock news from Moscow.

The Russians of whom I speak were technicians assigned by Russia to some engineering or industrial mission in Afghanistan. What Russia is doing in espionage, I do not know; but it would be a surprise if she did not know the height of every bridge in the entire Middle East. What Russia is doing ideologically is difficult to say. Certainly in Afghanistan her opportunities are limited. There is no press to exploit; the people are largely illiterate; radios are few and far between; the intelligentsia are few and not easy targets to reach in this ancient land. Yet for every twelve technicians Russia always sends six political agents. What the Russians are doing technologically is plain: they are helping supply the engineers and other technicians to transform Afghanistan from an ancient to a modern state.

In the old days it was always disconcerting to the British to hear of a Russian mission in Kabul. They started the First Afghan War in 1838 to put an anti-Russian King on the throne. They started the Second Afghan War in 1878 because Kabul had received a Russian mission and rejected a British envoy at the Khyber. How unnerving to the Foreign Office it would have been to find Afghanistan under the guidance of Russian engineers!

I believe it was Lowell Thomas who once said that it is longer from Peshawar to Kabul than from Peshawar to New York.

Peshawar, under the British influence for nearly two centuries, does not lag behind as far as Afghanistan. One who enters Afghanistan steps back by Western standards nearly a thousand years. There is a Parliament; but it is a legislature in form only. The King rules as absolute monarch. Pakistan has struggled hard to get a Constitution that respects the rights of minorities and avoids complete merger of church and state. But Afghanistan unites the two, making the *mullahs* supreme.

The streets of Kabul were not paved until a year or so ago, when Russia provided asphalt, rollers, and a supervisory staff. There are no paved roads outside Kabul. There is no sewage system in Afghan towns. Some have power plants; but apart from Kabul none has a telephone exchange. Even Kabul's exchange is limited to government agencies and embassies and legations. The intercity telephone lines are for military and other governmental use. There is no garbage collection and disposal system. In Kabul the householder empties his garbage can in the street and trusts to the semi-wild dogs (and in winter to the wolves) to clean it up. Afghanistan has no water system, no streetcar system, and no railroad. There are a few airports; and Kabul now has fair air service with three flights a week to Tashkent in Russia, and several to New Delhi, Karachi and Tehran. There are a few industries in Afghanistan, such as brick kilns and textile mills. But industry is still at the cottage level; and industrial development, as we of the West know it, still lies ahead.

In previous years one man tried to do something about it. He was Amanullah, who ascended the throne in 1919 at the age of twenty-six. Some say he was a rake; others maintain he was headstrong and unreliable. I never knew the man. But from my visits to his nation, I believe he was not only a great patriot but a courageous and enlightened leader.

He took his own wife out of *purdah;* he proclaimed against polygamy; he abolished slavery; he built schools for girls; he introduced Western dress; he wore a gray top hat to the mosque; he asked for tolerance of the Hindus; he introduced a Parliament; he started motor roads and built airports and textile mills; he built new political quarters for the government six miles outside of Kabul and connected them to the city with a streetcar system; he proclaimed Afghanistan independent of all foreign intervention, declared war on England in 1919, and got rid of British control over Afghan foreign affairs.

In all of these things he stepped on the toes of important people. But he had been inspired by Ataturk (Mustafa Kemal) of Turkey and Reza Shah of Iran; and, like them, he was resolved to catch up with the West and to rid his country of the religious and other shackles that held it back.

The opposition was too strong for the rate of change Amanullah demanded. The Shinwaris of Khyber Pass, inspired and instigated by the *mullahs,* led the way by marching on Kabul, calling the Queen a "shameless prostitute" for wearing an evening gown, threatening to stone to death every girl without a veil, and promising to dethrone the King. The opposition grew until by the winter of 1928 Amanullah was besieged in Kabul. In the shifting balance of power among the various groups who moved against the King, fate turned to Bacha-i-Saqao, the son of a water boy who had long been a brigand in the Afghan hills. Bacha-i-Saqao took Kabul, Amanullah fled, Bacha-i-Saqao seized the throne, taking the title Habibullah. Bacha-i-Saqao ruled for nine months until he was assassinated by Nadir Shah, his successor. During those nine months Bacha-i-Saqao concentrated on two things: looting and increasing the size of his harem.

Amanullah's reign was the closest Afghanistan came to the emulation of Turkey and Iran. Since then progress toward Westernization has been made; but it has been slow, one reform barely edging along and then discreetly halting until opinion can catch up. The most dramatic changes have been made by the Russians, who today are there in force on technical missions.

Russian jeeps and Russian diesel trucks are everywhere. There are more of them than other makes, though German and American machines follow in that order.

Russian engineers are surveying roads and designing bridges. Russian road equipment, from pneumatic drills to scrapers to bulldozers, was the only road equipment we saw.

Russian gasoline and steel products are brought down by railway to three ports on the Oxus River. Russian engineers are building facilities on the Afghan side of the Oxus to handle the imports and to receive the skins, raisins, and cotton which Afghanistan ships to Russia.

Russian engineers are designing airports and factories. Three of the Russian-built factories we saw were a combination granary, flour mill, and bakery.

The Russians have advantages over us in dealing with the Afghans. They are neighbors with a long, common frontier that presents no barrier to easy access. Trade along this frontier is no problem, as compared with the long expensive shipments we must make. Moreover, Russia has given the Afghan King a monopoly on all gasoline sold in Afghanistan. That agreement ties the King in personally to the great rewards from Russian trade.

I learned at a luncheon, which Ambassador and Mrs. Mohammed Shayesteh of Iran tendered us in Kabul, of another even greater advantage which Russia has over us in competing for Afghan business. When we (or an American company) undertake a mission abroad, we export the American standard of living with the mission. We put up air-conditioned houses and we fly out frozen steaks and all the other customary items that we consider good and healthy. They are essential if we are to induce our workers (and families) to leave the comforts of home and go out to a place where it is unbearably hot in the summer, miserably cold in the winter, unhealthy and wind-blown the year around. The Russians have no such problem. For they order their men (and families) to go and they must go. When they arrive they live like the natives and suffer with them the rigors of climate, food, water, and sanitation. This makes the Russians low-cost producers. We, on the other hand, are high-cost producers.

These matters were explained to me at the Shayestehs' luncheon by an economic adviser to the Afghan government. He explained also that Afghanistan in order to finance her development program merely increases the currency. It has found, however, that a currency increase can result in inflation.

"That's why we favor Russia, the low-cost producer," he said. "American engineering is excellent; you Americans get the job done faster; but Russian costs are lower."

Afghanistan, like Syria, seems destined to become a Russian technological state. For though we are building airports and are very active in irrigation and power projects on the Helmand River, the Russian engineering and financial influence is in the ascendancy. But all is not rosy with these Russian undertakings. They are learning that a people geared to one economy and conditioned to set patterns of conduct cannot be quickly changed. A Kabuli illustrated the point with great amusement as he told me of the combination granary, flour mill, and bakery that the Russians put up on the outskirts of Kabul.

This plant, which is most attractive, turns out a loaf bread such as we and the Russians use. But the Afghans do not like loaf bread. They prefer *nan,* the flat unleavened bread that is made in the bazaar. I usually saw five men making it: one weighed the dough on crude scales; one rolled it out in a thin sheet about fifteen inches in diameter; one used his fingernails to puncture the dough with rows of holes; one put it on a mat and pressed it against the inside wall of an earthen furnace; and another took the bread out when it was done.

One sees this *nan* the length and breadth of Afghanistan. People prefer both its taste and its shape; and before I had left this ancient land I began to share their prejudice. It is chewy but not tough. It is not only the staff of life; it takes the place of spoons and forks. A piece of this flat bread between the thumb and index finger is an instrument for picking up pieces of meat and vegetables. It is a scoop for rice. One uses it the whole meal in place of a fork and at the end it takes the place of a spoon in in getting the plate clean. Loaf bread is new and strange and less versatile. So, when the new bread from the new Russian-built bakery was put on the Kabul market, it went begging; no one would buy it; people preferred their familiar *nan.*

"So what did you do with the output of this new Russian-built bakery?" I asked my Kabuli friend.

He chuckled as he answered, "The people won't eat it. So we feed it to the army. The soldiers have to eat it, for it's the only bread they get."

CHAPTER 3

"HOW LONG IS HIS BEARD?"

Afghanistan, a country of around 12,000,000 people, is a nation of eight major groups: Pathans, Ghilzais, Tadjiks, Turks, Mongols, Kafirs, Arabs, and Qizilbashis. It was the stomping ground of many invaders. It was the highway for the great migrations of people who for centuries came down from the north in successive waves.

Ibn Battuta, the Moroccan who visited it about A.D. 1325, said that Kabul was a village "inhabited by a tribe of Persians called Afghans" who were "mostly highwaymen." Afghanistan was not united until 1737 when Nadir Shah of Persia conquered it north and south. By then the great migration of people had ended. Ahmad Shah Durani, who followed Nadir Shah, was the first Afghan King. Though Ahmad Shah gave the country its first real unity, it still was largely tribal. The tribal complexion of the country persists to this day. The Parliament, which has an Upper House appointed by the King for life, has a Lower House made up largely of tribal chiefs and heads of important families. The tribes, which have been rallying points for patriots who wanted to get rid of the foreigner who occupied Kabul, have also been dissident elements working against the central government.

Another element that kept Afghanistan underdeveloped was its role as a buffer state between Russia and England. It never had the security needed for voluntary development as an industrial state or the authoritarian direction over sustained periods of time that could force a modern economy on these ancient tribal regions.

A third element working against the modernization of the nation was the church. The *mullahs* tended to be conservatives who kept their hold on the people through ignorance and superstition. *Purdah* was an institution of the church. Education was controlled by the church. New ideas were dangerous ones. The violent reaction of the *mullahs* to Amanullah's rather modest reforms is a measure of their great power.

The priesthood is still strong in Afghanistan. All judges must be *mullahs*. The Supreme Court is composed of one *mullah,* who has the sole power of decision, and eight associate *mullahs,* who are his advisers. The Constitution makes the faith of Afghanistan "the sacred faith of Islam"; and it makes that religion the "official religion." All rights recognized by the Koran and by Islamic jurisprudence are recognized by the government. No one can be imprisoned or punished without an order in accordance with the Koran. A provision of the Koran may always be pleaded in defense of rights at issue in the court. All lawsuits must be decided in accordance with Islamic principles. The freedom of the press is conditioned by the constitutional requirement that it not be "against religion." Education of minorities in their faith is guaranteed. But in public schools no instruction can infringe the articles of the Islamic faith.

Judges in Afghanistan are very powerful. The saying is that their power extends "from frowning to death." Two men came before a *mullah* seeking settlement of a dispute. Each claimed to be the owner of several handfuls of coins. There were no witnesses. Whom should the *mullah* believe? He called for a glass of hot water and placed some of the coins in it. After a few minutes, oil from the coins came to the surface. The *mullah* made an instant decision: the coins belonged to the man who had greasy hands. Which one? He inquired their occupations. One was a cloth merchant, the other a sheepherder. Clearly, the coins belonged to the sheepherder, the *mullah* concluded, because the handling of sheep is bound to get lanolin on the hands. And so he ordered the coins delivered to the sheepherder.

That was not all. He ordered that the eyes of the merchant be removed. And that blind man lives in Kabul to this day.

The law is severe, reflecting the unruly nature of the people and their turbulent history. Abdur Rahman, who became King in 1880 and died of gout in 1901, adopted cruel procedures to deal with crime. Anyone convicted of highway robbery was placed in an iron cage which was suspended from a tree near the scene of his crime and left there to die from exposure, hunger, and thirst. People I met along the highways in 1957 remembered these cages but could not produce the remnants of one for my Leica camera. In those days, criminals were not only hanged; they were stoned to death. A merchant caught cheating had nails driven through his ears into the door of his shop.

Today robbery can be punished by cutting off a hand. But that sentence is not often imposed, imprisonment being the usual punishment.

There are various degrees of murder, turning largely on the nature of the weapon used. Killing by knife is first degree. Killing by automobile is third degree murder. A woman who rolls in bed and kills her baby must either fast two months or feed sixty poor people a meal.

Rape requires four witnesses who can speak "with the clarity of sunlight" to the offense.

Insanity is a defense. A man found insane is not tried until he is "awake." We of the West usually make sanity or insanity turn on whether the defendant knows right from wrong. In Afghanistan it turns on his answer to the following question, "Where is the sky and where is the earth?"

Sacrilege is a criminal offense. It includes blasphemy, the denunciation of Allah, the Koran, Mohammed, or his sayings. It also includes denunciation of the practice of praying. One who even proclaims against appropriation of public funds to build mosques may be charged with sacrilege.

The state does not feed people in jail; they must be fed by their relatives. A material witness or a suspect is detained in jail, bail not being a part of Afghan law. He too must be fed by his family. If the family cannot or does not feed him, recourse is had to the accuser. When I was in Kabul a Hindu merchant had been robbed in the bazaar. He gave the police the names of five men he suspected. The five were arrested and jailed. No one fed them. They sent word of their plight to the Hindu. He fed them for a while. But when he learned that the police would not complete their investigation for months and that the trial might not be held for a year, he withdrew the complaint, figuring the feeding of the suspects would be more costly than the robbery itself.

In civil cases the plaintiff must have two witnesses. If the defendant takes an oath, he absolves himself and goes free. If he lied, it's a matter for his conscience and his settlement with God.

In a criminal case the oath of the defendant absolves him of all damages but not of the public injury. Though he is acquitted of private injury, he can be convicted on the public phase of the case. But in that event he can only be imprisoned, not executed.

The status of minorities is a peculiar one in orthodox Moslem nations like Afghanistan. The Koran extended the protection of Moslems to Christians and Jews, since their religions were considered to be revealed. These minorities were called People of the Book or *dhimmi*. But there was a price for that protection. The Koran says: "Fight against such as have been given the Scripture and believe not in Allah nor the Last Day, and forbid not that which Allah hath forbidden by His Messenger, and follow not the religion of truth, until they pay the tribute readily being brought low."

The tribute was in the form of a tax known as the *bauj* or *jisya*. Payment of the tax gave this minority the right to stay in Islamic territory, security for their persons and property, freedom to practice their religion, and protection against the common enemy. But on his part a member of the minority also promised loyalty to the Moslem government. Moreover, he could not marry a Moslem woman, though a Moslem man might marry a Christian or Jew. No member of a minority could help a non-Moslem against Moslems or give him refuge. Nor were these minorities allowed to build new churches or to pray loudly, to ring their church bells noisily, or show their crosses, drink their wine, or eat pork in public. Their homes could not be built higher than those of Moslems. They had to distinguish themselves in dress by wearing a belt and colored turban. They were forbidden to ride horses or carry weapons, though they might ride donkeys or burros. This was the law; but sometimes it was not strictly enforced. In practice the People of the Book got a degree of self-rule. Their religious head settled disputes among themselves, according to their own canon law.

There were two ways to avoid payment of the *jisya*. One way was to become a Moslem; another was to take up arms for the defense of Islam.

The *jisya* still exists in Afghanistan in nominal form. In Kabul it amounts to four, six, or eight afghanis (eight to sixteen cents) a year, payable by the head of the family, the amount depending on his income. The People of the Book in Afghanistan are Hindus, Sikhs, and Jews. Recently military service has been opened to the Hindus and Sikhs. Those who serve in the army are exempt from the tax. But to this day Jews are not admitted to the Afghan Army. So they must pay the head tax.

These days when an Afghan is asked for a tip or a bribe he often replies, "Why should I pay *jisya* to you? I'm not a Jew."

Marriages are performed by the parties themselves. Two witnesses and publicity are all that are required. Polygamy is lawful; and it is extensively practiced.

In practice, a man divorces his wife as he chooses. But in law (if the wife wants to pursue the matter) he must have "just cause." Although Islamic law permits a man to divorce his wife merely by dismissing her, even the lower-class Afghan desires some documentary evidence of the event. Accordingly, a written document witnessed by a *mullah* is usually provided. Moreover, when the man divorces the woman, all gifts exchanged at the time of the wedding are returned. If the gifts cannot be returned, the value is substituted. Often the husband "buys" his bride in the sense that he gives her family fifty dollars or more for permission to marry her. The husband tries to get that purchase price back as a part of the divorce. When we were in Kabul a chauffeur working for an American was being hounded by his wife for a divorce. At the time of the wedding, five years earlier, he promised to provide his wife with 9000 afghanis ($180) if he ever divorced her. The chauffeur finally decided to rid himself of the woman and was making the rounds of friends to borrow the money. Yet only the man can get a divorce. A woman has equal rights in the law with men when it comes to the ownership and control of property.

It is not in the Islamic tradition to allow lawyers to appear in court or to have any bar association. There are, of course, lawyers in Afghanistan. A fine law school in Kabul turns out many *mullahs* well trained in Islamic law. But these lawyers work either for the executive branch of government or for the courts. If a party to a lawsuit needs representation, he either gets a relative to speak for him or leans on the judge. I found, however, that this tradition is breaking up in Kabul. Two lawyers now practice privately there; and a law has been approved making a bar association lawful. I asked a *mullah* about these developments. "Well," he said, "the country is developing so fast, so many commercial projects are being formulated, so many foreigners need advice on Afghan law, that we have decided to let the lawyers practice privately."

But in Afghanistan today it is not considered good taste or graceful for a person to be paid for legal services in the courts.

The English-American writ of *habeas corpus* is unknown in Afghanistan. Islamic law produced no such remedy for unlawful detention. Afghan law grants only a remedy in damages against one who brings an unjust charge, a remedy similar to our suit for false arrest.

Women practice *purdah* in Afghanistan. They wear the *chadhri,* a tentlike garment that slips over the head and completely covers the body. There are slits for the eyes; but these are woven over, so that a passer-by cannot see beyond them. These *chadhris* vary in color; many are pleated. One sees them everywhere in the cities. They obviously are unsuited for work in the fields. So in the country the women wear only scarves.

There are no women being educated in the law school. There are, however, women now in attendance at Kabul University in medicine and in the social sciences. A cabinet officer told me at the dinner given by Foreign Minister Naim that "there is a great upsurge among women throughout the country to be educated." The existence of the university with its nine colleges is part of the pull. The admittance of Afghanistan to the family of nations, the increased travel of its nationals, the radio and other impacts of the West on the country—all these are slowly working as a ferment in Afghan society.

But the *mullahs* still reign supreme and probably will continue to do so until a new generation with larger vision follows the lead of Turkey. I met many of these *mullahs* and found them as conservative on the one hand or as liberal on the other as our own Bar and Bench. Some knew of Marshall, Holmes, and Hughes and thus had fresh ferment in their thinking. Others were narrow and pedantic, chained to the past. Some were truly great judges who knew the ingredients of justice. Others were bigoted. The younger *mullahs* I met were uniformly forward-looking. They were adapting the principles of Islam to a new age, not applying it mechanically as if it were an inflexible code. One of these younger men was M. M. Shafik Kamawi, whom I had met a few years back in this country when he was doing graduate work at Columbia. He called on me at the residence of Ambassador and Mrs. Sheldon T. Mills, with whom we stayed in Kabul. He invited me to a tea at his home. And when the appointed time came, he called for me and we went together in the station wagon.

His reason for calling for me was that in Kabul houses do not have numbers. There are only a few streets in Kabul that are named, one being Ibn Sina Avenue, after Avicenna, the famous Persian physician. The people usually call even a named street by the profession that is dominant on it or by the biggest or most famous building located there. A street divided by the Kabul River has several names; but the people like to call it Labi Darra, the Bank of the River.

Shafik's home, like all Kabuli houses, is surrounded by a mud wall. We entered the yard through a wooden door. The low house was small but attractively decorated. Two men and several ladies were present. We had green tea, pistachio nuts, and cakes. Our conversation covered a wide range and was so interesting I hated to leave. But this was the night of the Foreign Minister's dinner and I had to return early to the Embassy to dress. As Shafik escorted me from the house and reached the yard, he turned with a twinkle in his eye and said:

"The rumor spread through this neighborhood that you were coming to tea. I had told my cook and she told everyone. I described you as an American *kaze;* and as you know '*kaze*' means judge. As I left to get you, my neighbor stuck his head over this wall and asked, 'Does this American *kaze* have a long beard?' "

"Why did he say that?" I asked.

"In our country *kaze* is always a *mullah* and a *mullah* always wears a white turban and a beard. The more important the *mullah* the longer the beard," Shafik replied.

At that point the neighbor with a grin on his face stuck his head over the wall.

Rubbing my beardless chin, I said to Shafik, "Tell him that in America the shorter the beard the more important the *kaze.*"

And Shafik, who had only started a beard, rubbed it with glee, while he and the neighbor roared with laughter.

CHAPTER 4

THE KABUL BAZAAR

We know very little of the history of Kabul. The word means "sheepfold"; but the origin of the city is lost in the mists of history. Darius was there in 516 B.C. Alexander the Great visited it in 329 B.C., coming in from the southwest and heading north to march against Samarkand, now in Soviet Central Asia. Of all the invaders who came this way, Babur stayed the longest. This young Mongol was descended on his father's side from Timur and on his mother's from Genghis Khan. He started life as ruler of Ferghana (now in Soviet Central Asia) but he was deposed. His great aim in life was to regain Timur's throne in Samarkand. But the Uzbeks always defeated him. Adventure pushed him south. He subdued the disorganized tribes of Afghanistan, beginning at the start of the sixteenth century, and made Kabul his headquarters. Kabul was indeed his base for the invasions of India that eventually led to his establishment of the Mogul Empire that lasted until the British took India.

In Babur's time, Kabul was a busy emporium on a great caravan route down from China. Slaves, cotton cloth, candy, sugar, drugs, and spices were the main commodities, with profits of the Kabul merchants running between 300 per cent and 400 per cent. Babur relates in his *Memoirs* that the caravans entering Kabul were so numerous that he counted 10,000 horses alone entering the city every year. Kabul is a lush garden, growing apricots, cherries, quinces, pears, pomegranates. Its rhubarb is extra special. Its melons are sweet. Its wheat and barley make out into good heads. Kabul has a sour cherry that Babur introduced. And its grapes make a very sweet wine.

Babur had a poem he especially liked:

> Drink wine in the citadel of Kabul,
> Send round the cup without stopping.
> It is at once a mountain and a sea,
> A town and a desert.

Kabul is to this day a beautiful yet desolate place. It sits on a vast and lonely plateau that is delightful in the summer and severe in winter. The buildings are low, for this is notorious earthquake country.

Though Babur died in India, he is buried in Kabul. His grave is at Bagh-i-Babur on the edge of town. It's a large spacious garden of many acres dominated by chenar trees. In former years it was carefully and meticulously maintained. But in 1957 the garden had a desolate look. There is a shortage of water in Kabul. Most compounds have their own wells. The open *jubes* or irrigation ditches that run down the streets furnish water by flooding for the other lawns. Why Bagh-i-Babur is neglected, I do not know. There are tennis courts in the garden, above them a large swimming pool, and above it broad steps leading up to the marble tomb that rests under a high canopy guarded by fig trees. It could be a place of splendor; but when we were there it was a dry, dusty, wind-blown garden.

We visited Paghman, which is about sixteen miles west of Kabul and a thousand feet higher. Here is Tapa, the rather modest summer home of the King. Here too are beautiful formal gardens with pools and fountains where the Afghans like to gather on any holiday in spring and summer. The afternoon of our visit a thunderstorm broke over Paghman. The high peaks of the Hindu Kush that look down on these gardens fairly echoed with thunder. The lightning was thrilling to watch as it struck all along the western fringe of the valley below us where Kabul stands. Then came the rain—a hard, cold rain that chilled us. We huddled with a hundred or more Afghans under some huge plane trees on the slopes above the formal gardens. The oneness of the crowd against the storm produced a camaraderie. Soon a group of teen-age boys started to dance. They had no instruments; one furnished the music by singing and clapping his hands. The others with their arms over each other's shoulders formed a line and danced in unison—bowing up and down, swaying left to right, and stomping. And when they noticed I was photographing the dance with my Leica, they insisted on doing it all over again so that I could have perfect pictures.

We visited Dar Ul Aman, the site of the new buildings which Amanullah built six miles from Kabul. One was a palace, sitting on a hill, that is now being converted to a government guesthouse. The other, below it, was a Parliament Building now being converted to Executive Offices. The approach to them is beautiful. A dirt road, thickly lined by chenar trees, runs straight as an arrow for six miles to the new site. The old carbarn that housed Amanullah's streetcars still stands and it contains two of them as relics. Until recently the new three-story buildings had never been occupied. But now some ministries are in possession and others are expected to move in. Part of Amanullah's dream is coming true.

We spent some hours in the Kabul Museum, an exciting place for the archaeologist, but an institution poorly equipped and not very well managed. The glass in front of priceless Buddhist figures was grimy. Silk gowns embroidered with gold were dirty and stained, and not protected from the atmosphere.

We saw not only the historic sites around Kabul but industry too. We visited the spick-and-span granary, flour mill, and bakery the Russians had built. And I climbed all over many brick kilns getting pictures of the picturesque characters who operate them.

The place in Kabul we enjoyed the most was the bazaar. There are more colorful bazaars in the Middle East; but this one has a character all its own. According to legend, the one the British burned in the First Afghan War was the best in Central Asia. The one that took its place is a rambling nondescript bazaar that apparently grew like Topsy. But it has color and charm.

A section of it extends along the Kabul River, which runs through the city. This July the river was low; and men were shoveling the silt of the river into bullock carts to take to their fields for new topsoil. Above the river were stands where Hindu merchants sat under canvas roofs displaying gaily colored cotton and silk cloth. These were sidewalk stores. The main bazaar is made up of stalls on narrow, winding dirt roads a few blocks back from the river. I never got a map of this area; but I know it goes for several dozen square blocks. Some streets are barely wide enough for a car to squeeze through. Others are too narrow for anything but an animal.

We visited the bazaar one day with Leon B. Poullada, of the American Embassy, a very fine person and an excellent Foreign Service officer, who had traveled Afghanistan extensively and knew its roads well. He had recently returned from Herat—our destination—by jeep; and although he had not traveled our precise route, he had enough information to give us alarming news. The roads were so poor and the ruts so deep and our car so overloaded that precautionary measures had to be taken. He recommended that in view of our narrow escape with the steering mechanism between Khyber Pass and Kabul, all nuts should be tightened at least once a day. He also recommended a visit to the bazaar.

First, an extra rear spring should be acquired.

Second, longer U bolts, which hold the rear springs to the axle, should be put on the car.

Third, a shovel was a basic necessity.

There is in Kabul what is known as the thieves' market. It can't be described by metes and bounds. But it runs along one side of a block for a dozen or so stalls. It was to that place we went to find an extra rear spring. We had the precise measurements, and to our surprise found the spring at the very first stop. This stall was run by two tall, thin, delicate-looking Hindus. They sat amidst a pile of merchandise that looked like junk; but they sat with great dignity. There was no order or arrangement to their shop. Pieces of hardware that would fit anything from a plow to a tractor were stacked in great disorder. Bolts, wheels, springs, rear-view mirrors, hub caps—things that could be easily stolen and things that would take more time to steal—were all there.

When we asked for a spring, one of the Hindus disappeared and returned with three. One spring was too short, the other too long, but the third one fit precisely our measurements. The matter was now one of price only.

He wanted two thousand afghanis (forty dollars).

We called him unreasonable.

He answered that he had waited months to get the rear spring and could sell it for a higher price.

We said a rear spring in America would cost scarcely half of his price.

He answered that America was a long way off.

We asked him to hold it until the next day, when we would return.

He replied that he could make no promise, that if he could get his price he would sell at once to anyone.

We said a man who charged two thousand afghanis for this spring should go to jail.

He told us that the rear spring had come from Beirut, that the transportation charges alone were one thousand afghanis.

We told him that a rear spring to be worth forty dollars had to be set with jewels.

He said this would probably be worth more than jewels in our Afghan journey.

We called him a thief.

He smiled and said it was the only rear spring in Kabul that would fit our needs.

We called him a robber.

He answered that it would cost much more than two thousand afghanis to make a rear spring in Kabul, even though Kabuli blacksmiths were very expert.

We called him a highwayman.

He blandly said the price was fair, that he expected to get far more.

We did not continue our attack on his character. We wanted and needed the rear spring so badly—and this clever merchant knew it—that we ended the debate by paying his asking price. We wrapped the rear spring tenderly in burlap, lashed it tightly to the rack on the top of the car, and went our way.

The shovel was our next purchase. We had to drive over a mile through cobblestone streets packed with stalls until we came to the "hardware" unit of the bazaar. It was on the edge of town near flat plains that stretched to distant hills. Here were tinsmiths by the dozen, each with his specialty line. They worked in full view of the street, sitting on their haunches, cutting galvanized iron with shears, heating iron in small furnaces that their small sons kept red with bellows, pounding the red metal on anvils, beating sheet metal with mallets. A din filled the street so that we could hardly hear one another talk. We went from stall to stall until we found the sturdy, sharp-nosed shovel with the short handle that we needed. Once the shovel was spotted, the bargain was short. Again we paid the asking price.

Mercedes then had an inspiration. We needed a funnel to fill our gas tank. Gas stations in Afghanistan are few and far between. We had extra jerry cans of gas that we would carry. The problem was to find a goose-necked funnel into which gas from a jerry can could be poured.

The search seemed endless, for every tinsmith had his own special funnel. We finally found a small mouselike man who wore steel-rimmed glasses and hopped around his stall in a sprightly fashion. After disappearing in the rear, he returned in a few minutes with the exact article we needed. We paid his price without haggling and went in search of a blacksmith to make the U bolts for our rear springs.

We found him in a section of the bazaar where ironsmiths and garage owners are neighbors. His blacksmith shop could have been anywhere in the world, so familiar did it seem. The only difference was in the proprietor. He was a swarthy Pathan, named Shafik, with a heavy, dark beard and a tightly wound turban. He was most intelligent and efficient. He had his son Nazim take the measurements; then he cut the heavy rods, heated and bent them in the middle, turned threads at the end, and delivered them to us in a jiffy.

We had found the Kabul bazaar enterprising as well as colorful.

Another day we visited the rug section of the bazaar.

As I have said, we had expected Faqir Mohmand to meet us at Peshawar or Dakka, and to travel with us to Kabul as our interpreter. But he had been detained at the last minute in Kabul and could not leave. He was there to greet us when we arrived; and it was to him I turned for advice about the rug markets of

Kabul. He recommended his brother Mohammed Ali Lowangin. It was Faqir's brother who went with us this warm afternoon to haggle with Kabul's rug merchants.

The rug market of the bazaar is a separate unit off a crowded, narrow cobblestone road. The stalls are crowded closely together. Each has wooden doors that are placed across the front and bolted and locked, come nighttime. The stalls are flush with the street and their floors stand about two feet off the ground. The rugs for sale cover the floor, hang on the walls, and are rolled up in every corner. The proprietors sit barefooted on their inventory with turbaned heads and inscrutable faces. All of the nationalities of Central Asia occupy these stalls—Mongols, Turks, Tadjiks, Arabs, and others I did not recognize.

Most of the people moving through the bazaar were men. Occasionally a woman would come through; and invariably she would be dressed in the *chadhri*—the tentlike dress worn by every Afghan woman who walks down the street.

Mohammed Ali knew Afghan rugs well and some of these merchants personally. At the very first stall he met a heavy-set Pathan who was an old friend. But Mohammed Ali's first loyalty was to me. So he soon whispered that he thought this Pathan was too high. On we went to another stall; then another and still another. Finally we came to one owned by a tall Mongol who wore a thin mustache and was well advanced in years. He had a rug that fit Mercedes' measurements for our upstairs hall. So the haggling started. Soon the Mongol called for help and a younger man, who was Chinese in appearance, came to take over the burden. Mohammed Ali, after a half hour of intense haggling, turned to me with a puzzled look and said, "I need help."

He was gone for a few minutes, to return with the heavy-set Pathan with whom we had been haggling up the lane an hour earlier. This merchant, who only a short while ago had tried to do us in, now turned his talents on his competitor.

The Pathan apparently had scorching things to say of the Mongol.

The conversation sounded to me like sheer invective. At one point I whispered to Mohammed Ali, "What are they talking about?"

"The Mongol's father," he replied.

The voices rose in intensity. I whispered again, "Now what do they talk about?"

"The Mongol's grandfather."

The argument continued unabated.

"Now what do they say?"

"They're discussing the Mongol's great-grandfather."

"Are his father, grandfather, and great-grandfather honorable men?"

"No," whispered Mohammed Ali, "they were all thieves."

The clenched teeth of the Mongol showed that my new Pathan ally was making telling blows.

My Pathan advocate apparently had also made a penetrating analysis of the structure of the price which the Mongol sought to extract from me. It fairly sizzled in Pushtu as he presented it point by point. He called for the meter-long metal measuring rod and reduced the rug to square meters. Then we had to reduce this to square yards, and square yards to afghanis and afghanis to dollars. The argument went back and forth as each man tussled to gain a point. Voices rose and fell. The tones were now demanding, now deprecatory. Humor seemed to enter the deal; then scoffing; then satire. Now it appeared that this affair over one lovely red and white Afghan rug was as serious as the First Afghan War. Just when I expected the worst, our Pathan ally had a few whispered words with Mohammed Ali, who turned to me and said:

"We have a good price for you."

"You mean there's going to be no physical violence?"

Mohammed Ali passed the message along to the Pathan and they both laughed.

"No," he answered. "Our friend and the Mongol are not enemies. It's only the arguments over prices that get them a bit on edge."

We thanked the Pathan, who returned to his stall. We paid for this rug and gave it to a porter to carry on his back. This miserable-looking creature, barefooted, dressed in trousers and coat that had more patches than suit, and wearing a black, brimless hat, was to follow us an hour as we continued our shopping.

At one shop we had seen another rug—this one from Herat—that interested us. Back we went for it; but the price was too high. After several more stops, we bought one at a small stall and finally ended where we started—at the first stall owned by the heavy-set Pathan. He had two rugs that I wanted badly—one from Bukhara in Soviet Central Asia, and one from Herat. So the man who an hour ago had been my protector against the Mongol was now my antagonist. He straightened his spine almost imperceptibly for the struggle. The eyes that once had been warm with friendship now were like steel. There was not a flicker of expression on his face.

"He's a tougher guy than the Mongol," I said to Mohammed Ali.

"Yes, but he's also my friend," was the reply.

So the two of them settled down for the bargain. The battle of words went back and forth; the rugs were held up both with pride and with scorn. Fists were pounded on palms; fingers were used as exclamation points. The metal measuring rod was brought out and once more square meters were reduced to square yards and the number of afghanis per each was computed.

Mohammed Ali whispered to me, "The price per square meter is almost as good as the Mongol's but the Bukhara rug is much better than the Afghan rug you bought at the Mongol's shop."

"Put the Bukhara rug and the Herat rug together in a package and if he comes down five hundred afghanis (ten dollars) I'll take both."

Mohammed Ali went back to the battle with renewed energy. The struggle ebbed and flowed. Every time it seemed that Mohammed Ali had won, the Pathan stiffened and shook his head. It seemed we had lost. I had left several times, to create the impression I was not too interested in the merchandise. But the Pathan knew better. He held it teasingly before my eyes. There was nothing I wanted more than the lovely red Bukhara rug. I could practically see it in the front hall at home to greet me every night. Finally Mohammed Ali said:

"The best he will do is to come down two hundred and fifty afghanis."

At that I made the bargain; and we returned to the station wagon, followed by the porter dressed in tatters, but proudly carrying our four new Afghan rugs on his shoulders.

CHAPTER 5

THE ROAD TO BAMIAN

We had difficulty finding in Kabul an interpreter who was knowledgeable in English, Persian, and Pushtu, and who was available to travel with us to Herat. My old friend, Faqir Mohmand, the short, wiry Pathan who had been with me on my earlier Afghan journey, was detained in Kabul and could not go. We interviewed other candidates but they either did not like the prospects of the rough journey or had limitations in personality that argued against them. No one we interviewed had the depth of knowledge of Afghan history, the range of language, and the zest for adventure which were needed. I put my problem to Ambassador Mills the morning before we were to leave for Bamian, and at lunch he had a suggestion to make.

There was an Afghan chauffeur on the Embassy staff by the name of Mohammed Aslam who was due for annual leave and who would be willing to go with us to earn additional money. According to the Ambassador, he was personable, energetic, and versatile in languages, in chauffeuring, and in mechanics. I saw the man and liked him instantly. He was dark, short, and wiry, with a spring in his walk and a broad smile on his face. He was a devout Moslem, married, with two children, and anxious to supplement his annual income by working vacation time. We made our bargain in a few minutes; and it turned out to be one of the best of our long journey. Aslam agreed to be on hand at the Embassy residence at five o'clock the next morning to help us pack. We wanted to be off by five-thirty so that we could reach the ancient Buddhist center of Bamian in time for late afternoon pictures. It was only 156 miles. But the dirt roads were only fair and we had the 9800-foot Shibar Pass of the lofty Hindu Kush to cross.

The Mills, who had entertained us generously during our four-day sojourn in Kabul, wisely decided to have a family dinner our last night there. We had met many Afghan officials and dignitaries and many members of the American community. This last night was to be spent leisurely, writing up notebooks and packing bags.

The wind was howling and the dust flying as I went to bed. I lay there for a moment thinking of Babur, who made Kabul his headquarters as he raided India over and again and finally conquered it. He and his men were hard-riding, heavy-drinking soldiers bent on plunder and pillage. He always started his battles with prayer; and he was convinced that every victory was God's will: "What God wills comes to pass." He operated under this policy: "Whoever does not submit his head must be subjected to punishment and humbled by pillage."

He was proud of the heads cut off by his soldiers. After a battle he would have whole regiments of prisoners beheaded. Then with the skulls he would build minarets, symbolic of the mastery of Islam over the infidels.

I thought of these things as the wind blew and the dust whirled, dust made up in part of the ashes of those whom Babur had slaughtered.

Aslam arrived at five o'clock sharp the next morning, with one small battered suitcase that I later learned contained only a razor, one shirt, and one suit of underwear. Mercedes supervised the packing of the car. The two jerry cans of gasoline, the new battery from Peshawar, the six bottles of sulphuric acid for the new battery, the huge galvanized funnel from Kabul's bazaar were squeezing more bags out of the rear of the car onto the top. The rather large, clumsy kerosene stove took up a lot of room, and someone suggested we leave it behind. A large wicker basket containing canned fruit, a tin or two of English biscuits, a can of cheese, powdered milk and dried soups, one each of tomatoes, sardines, and asparagus were also eyed by Mercedes and Mary and marked for the discard. But I intervened against that move. For I had seen northern Afghanistan and knew how desolate it was. In case of illness one's own portable kitchen would be especially welcome. The result was that we had so much luggage on top, the roof actually buckled when the rope holding it down was tightly lashed.

We got off at eight o'clock instead of five-thirty. Access to the King's winter home in Kabul comes with a special permit only. We had applied earlier but had given up hope. At dinnertime the night before, the Protocol Officer had called, giving permission. So at five-thirty we went across Kabul to the palace and in the low early sun photographed the main buildings in all their summer splendor. There is a small mosque on the palace grounds and offices for the King as well as quarters for the royal family. At one end a clock tower rises about four stories. The gardens are filled with geraniums. The walks are lined with tall trees of the nastrum rose. This rose, with its single white petals, is most fragrant in the early morning. Architects would call the buildings drab and nondescript. But set against twenty-foot hedges of roses, solitary pines, and huge, arching plane trees, they seem magnificent.

Bamian is west of Kabul and slightly north. But in between is the Hindu Kush, which runs across the country in a southwesterly direction to cut it in half. One road goes south and west from Kabul, passing through Ghazni, Kandahar, and Farah to skirt the western flank of the Hindu Kush. That is the way Alexander the Great reached Kabul. But we wanted to see the northern country along the Soviet border. That meant crossing the Hindu Kush. There are ten passes over this mighty range and any one of them can be used six months of the year. But with one exception, they are only trails or jeep roads. The one highway over the Hindu Kush that connects the north with the south crosses the Shibar Pass. This road is a recent one, having been completed by the Afghan King Mohammed Nadir Shah shortly before his assassination in 1933. The fact that this vital link is so new underlines the slow growth in the unity of Afghanistan.

The lighthearted Aslam did the driving. Having alerted the ladies to look out for good pictures, I settled down to a study of the map—the contours of the Hindu Kush, the drainage of slopes, the river systems. I spotted at once Charikar, a town I had visited on my earlier journey; and as I perused the map my mind turned to limericks. I had made one for each of the prominent towns of West Pakistan; now it was Afghanistan's turn and Charikar was the first. I had hardly got any further than

> There was a knife maker from Charikar
> Who took out his girl in his Buick car

when we arrived at this place of 10,000 people.

Most Afghans are Sunni or orthodox Moslems. But about a quarter of the people of Charikar are Ismailis, the followers of Aga Khan. They are farmers, shopkeepers, and artisans. This town of mud huts and wide dirt streets lined with willows has no industry except handicrafts. While Aslam looked for gasoline, I looked up the knife makers who have made the city famous in Central Asia. They make knives for trimming fingernails, knives for the kitchen and field, knives for killing bullocks and men. There are knives for the pocket, the belt, and shoulder straps—daggers, huge hunting knives, switchblade knives. These are all handmade without even a lathe. The workmanship is excellent, the steel superb.

After the knives, I strolled through a small bazaar following the odor of fresh lamb being cooked over charcoal. I soon found these stalls run by graybeards who, sitting on their haunches before small braziers, turned the skewers that held the meat. The smell made me hungry, and I was about to order a skewer wrapped in *nan* when Aslam wheeled around the corner with the car. I mentioned my hunger and he said:

"There's a wonderful teahouse at Chardeh Ghorband."

So off we went.

Shortly after we left Charikar we reached Jabal-us-Siraj, where we turned left up the Ghorband Valley. The river which comes down this valley is famous in history. The natives sometimes call it the Matuk but it's the Ghorband. Somewhere along here Alexander the Great built his capital city Kapisa. Kapisa at the time of Hsüan Tsang was a great Buddhist center with 100 monasteries and 6000 monks. But today Kapisa has disappeared, leaving no traces.

Out of Jabal-us-Siraj, we went by many vineyards. Most of the crop goes into the raisins that Afghanistan exports to Russia in great quantities. Every other farm seemed to have a tall mud tower about the height of a three-story building. These towers had many slits in their sides. The slits were for ventilation. Inside on trays the raisins are dried and made ready for the market.

People here not only dry their grapes; they preserve them in a curious way. They use soft mud to make a mold that holds a whole cluster of grapes. The mud dries, forming a hard casing around the grapes that preserves them for the winter months.

People here preserve grain in like fashion. In case of excess crops they bury it. This day Aslam pointed out a Pathan friend who once buried some grain and the next spring went to look for it. He looked and looked and could not find it. At last, he had a bright idea. He picked out the burro that had carried the grain to its burial place on its back, reloaded the animal, and turned him loose. The farmer followed the burro, which eventually retraced his steps to the unmarked vault. All of which proves, according to Aslam, that burros are smarter than we think.

In this stretch of the road we also met a traveling theatrical group. Men and women—about eight in number—traveled with donkeys and burros from village to village looking for work. In one group there were two monkeys who for a few afghanis would do their tricks. The women were unveiled and rouged. They were the musicians and dancers. The men were the singers. Each group had a variety of talent, willing to put on a roadside show or for a larger fee provide the entertainment for a wedding, taking their compensation in food, drink, and afghanis. These are the traditional entertainers of Afghan villages. They are not Afghans but Parsees—the Christians and Zoroastrians who left Persia after the Arab invasion in the seventh century and moved east to save their religion, many eventually settling in Bombay.

On my earlier journey the Ghorband River was clear and blue; this time it was dirty and brown from heavy rains that preceded us. Every square foot of the river bottom is cultivated. Rice, corn, and wheat are the main crops; and they are irrigated from the river by quaint yet apparently efficient dirt canals that sometimes travel miles to reach a few acres.

Magpies seemed to be everywhere, filling the canyon with their cries. From Charikar to Chardeh Ghorband there were no cars except our own, and only a couple of huge Russian diesel trucks filled with Russian gasoline and rumbling down toward Kabul. There were, however, small family groups with all their possessions loaded on donkeys, going our way. Men and women walked; babies rode. Chickens were tied onto the packs. Occasionally a goat led the way. These were Hazarahs who were following the harvest up the southern slopes of the Hindu Kush. They were left behind when he swept through this country. Like our seasonal workers who move north from the Mexican border in the springtime, the Hazarahs were looking for work. This was July 14th, and the wheat was being harvested around Kabul. In the following few weeks, it would be harvest time at the higher elevations. A family of Hazarahs makes a contract to cut and thrash a field for a price, or to work as day laborers. They were all wiry and dark-complexioned with high cheekbones. As we passed a group, Aslam would invariably stick his head out of the window and shout the Afghan greeting, "*Staray mashy.*" That greeting—"May you never be tired"—reflects the friendliness one feels along the Afghan highways. We were to experience it in a vivid sense on many stages of our rough journey.

We stopped at the small village of Chardeh Ghorband for lunch. We chose a teahouse on the shady side of the road and parked the station wagon in a small open courtyard next door. This small restaurant, which faced south, was in the shade of huge mulberry trees. Six long steps led up to the open porch where people sat on Afghan rugs. The kitchen with its large round brazier and grill and steaming samovar was below the porch. Three Pathans greeted us with slight formal bowings and the Persian "*Salaam aleikum.*" The oldest one, with a mustache, was the owner; the young man was his son; the thirty-year-old Pathan was the waiter.

The teahouse food smelled good. But Mrs. Mills had put up a delicious lunch of cold roast beef sandwiches, hard-boiled eggs, cold chicken, and cookies. All we needed was tea. So *chai* was our order; and we reordered it three times before the meal ended. All the time Aslam engaged the proprietor in conversation about religion, politics, and women. While we ate, two tank trucks pulled into the courtyard and the drivers joined us. One truck was a diesel from Russia; the other, an International Harvester gasoline truck.

Aslam had a long conversation with the drivers. Russian gasoline was ruining American trucks; the engines knocked; it was necessary to clean the fuel line every few weeks and to change the carburetor often; the engine had to be overhauled twice a year.

"This Russian gasoline," Aslam said, turning to me, "is full of resin or some sticky substance that ruins the American motors. That's why the Russian diesels are so popular here."

It came time to go. The twelve cups of tea we drank came to eight afghanis or sixteen cents.

"*Staray mashy* [May you never be tired]," was the farewell.

"*Kwar mashy* [May you never be poor]," was the reply.

Beyond Chardeh Ghorband the road narrows; and in an hour we were in a winding defile. Even here, land was being cultivated. Now the houses moved up the canyon wall, leaving thin, irregular strips along the river to be cultivated. Soon we came to the head of the narrow canyon. A group of mud teahouses and merchandise stalls were on the right. Not a bush, not a tree was in sight. This was bleak, barren country. Several samovars in the teahouses gave off steam. When we stopped, Pathans left their *chai* to gather round and urchins popped up from nowhere to peer into the car. We filled the radiator and took pictures. Then on we went. In a hundred yards the river turns north through an eye of the needle-like break in the canyon wall, while the road goes west up horseshoe turns to Shibar Pass. The teahouse is probably 8000 feet; the road climbs steeply to Shibar, which is 9800 feet. We stayed in low and did not stop until we reached the flat open saddle that marks the summit. Before turning off the motor, we faced the car into the wind to cool it.

Shibar is a historic pass. Hsüan Tsang, the kindly Chinese Buddhist pilgrim, crossed here in the seventh century A.D. Genghis Khan, the cruel Mongol, followed six hundred years later to apply his sword and torch to every town that showed resistance.

Over this crossing, or somewhere near, came the Moroccan Ibn Battuta in A.D. 1325. He traveled by camel in springtime when the snow was still thick. So his entourage spread "felt cloths in front of the camels for them to tread on so they should not sink."

Hindu Kush means Killer of Hindus. For the raiders who came down from the north left the low southland with large numbers of captives. These Hindu slaves died like flies crossing this cold, cruel mountain range. Hence its name.

Perpetual snow lies at 13,000 feet. We could see it not far above us. And the wind off the snow fields was chill and strong. It was so strong I could hardly hold the tripod steady, as I took moving pictures of Russian trucks starting their journey down the pass and of Afghan sheep and goats crossing the saddle. High above, two black and white vultures, which I first mistook for eagles, soared. Their wings were motionless as they caught streams of air that carried them hundreds of feet up and then down in long graceful sweeps.

Here on the northern slopes of the Shibar are many partridges and pheasants; higher up are ibex and markhor. Here in the saddle peasants had plowed rocky ground to grow a few bushels of wheat per acre. The miserable crop they had raised would soon be harvested; and the rough rocky fields looked as if they had more weeds than wheat in them. The crop was so spindly as to be pitiful.

Great snow-packed peaks, now blue in the haze that had settled over the Hindu Kush, were to the north and south. We saw them off and on for some minutes as we dropped off the Shibar. Soon we were once more in a deep defile, a canyon that finally opened into two canyons. The one on the right we were to follow the next day to Pul-i-Khumri. The one to the left leads to Bamian. It is indeed the canyon down which the main fork of the Bamian River flows. At this Y we turned left and crossed a tributary of the river on a narrow, one-way bridge made by toppling two large logs across the stream. After entering the Bamian River canyon we soon crossed another one-way log bridge. After that we kept the angry Bamian on our left all the way to the ancient city.

Not far up the Bamian River and across it to the left are the ruins of ancient Shahr-i-Zohak, a city that stood on a cliff overlooking the entrance to the Bamian Valley. It's a fascinating location, for it sat on the corner of a volcanic hill of red rock. The city, whose origins are in question, excites interest. Not much is known of it. It antedated Genghis Khan and was destroyed by him. It has some connection in legend with the King Snake, Zohak, whom the Persian poet Ferdowsi describes in *Shah Nameh.* All that the people of Bamian can say is that the town was built by a Persian King.

Bamian today is a small village of several dozen mud huts in a valley rimmed east, south, and north by snow-flecked peaks of the Hindu Kush. It is a peaceful valley—green, quiet, and pleasant. Cereals, beans, Persian clover, and milk cows are its chief products. Poplar and willow trees, thickly planted, line its streets. Mud walls divide the fields. Bamian has a mosque, a school for boys, a bazaar about two blocks long, and a caravanserai. On the west side of the river up on a hill is a two-story hotel owned by the government. From a distance it looks like a hostel in Switzerland or northern Italy. Its attractiveness somewhat lessens as one draws nearer. It is not in good repair. While its rooms are clean, they are barren of everything except cots and bedding; there is running water but it is not reliable; there is no regular dining-room service; one must order meals and they are cooked on the outside and brought in.

Knowing these things from my earlier visit, I instructed Aslam to leave us in the village with our camera equipment and go at once to the hotel, reserve three rooms, and order dinner. We had perhaps two hours of daylight left; and I wanted to use them in and around the ruins of the ancient Buddhist shrine.

Bamian was once a great center of Buddhist learning. When Hsüan Tsang came down from the north and visited Bamian he found 10 monasteries and 1000 monks and a village filled with people who had "the utmost devotion of heart." These monasteries were built around a shrine carved from a sandstone cliff on the opposite side of the valley from the present hotel. It's a straight up-and-down cliff about two hundred feet high. Into its face have been carved three figures—Buddha, Buddha's wife, and Buddha's child. They are huge figures, the one of Buddha being 53 meters or about 175 feet high. The cliffs into which these statues were carved are dotted with caves, most of which were rooms where Buddhist monks lived or to which they retreated for meditation. It was these caves and the main Buddha figure that we wanted to photograph in the afternoon sun; and before darkness fell we also wanted to climb to the head of the Buddha.

After we had dispatched Aslam on his mission, we picked a guide from among the villagers, who had gathered around looking for the job, and started the climb up the cliff. This guide, like most of the villagers of Bamian, was a Hazarah, a descendant of Genghis Khan's hordes. He was slightly Mongol in appearance and tall, thin, and emaciated.

The Buddhists had been here many centuries before they were destroyed. The flourishing Buddhist community that Hsüan Tsang found here was destroyed by the Moslems who crossed the Shibar on a holy war in the eighth century, reducing Bamian and disfiguring the features of the noble Buddha. But the Moslems were in turn destroyed in A.D. 1220 by Genghis Khan, who ordered that every living thing in Bamian be killed and burned. Bamian was reduced to ashes and the sword of Genghis Khan moved on. But those who stayed behind and remnants of his forces who returned from India settled here. They are the ancestors of the miserable people who eke out a living there today.

One gets to the head of the Buddha by following a steep path that eventually ends in a dark tunnel. The tunnel passes over the head of the Buddha and empties into a deep void a few paces beyond it. We stopped on the Buddha's head, photographing not only the valley but the remains of the frescoes that once adorned the dome above the Buddha; Mary said that they have a strange combination of Indian and Chinese traits. Some of these frescoes have been removed and are to be found intact in the Kabul Museum. There are still colorful remnants left. They are in blue, yellow, green, white, and black, most of the colors having been made locally. The paintings are on plaster of paris glued on smooth clay with an animal mucilage. Lying on my back in thick droppings from the starlings who inhabit this place, and using my strobe flash equipment, I photographed these frescoes.

This Buddha once was beautifully decorated. Hsüan Tsang reported, "Its golden hues sparkle on every side, and its precious ornaments dazzle the eyes by their brightness." I marveled at the delicate vital colors left even after the wear and tear and the vandalism of the ages.

After photographing the frescoes, I took pictures of Bamian below us and the beautiful Koh-i-Baba spur of the Hindu Kush beyond it to the south. Then we dropped off the Buddha and explored many of the caves dug into the face of the cliff and took interior flash shots of them. Each is a one-room affair. Charred floor and walls show where small fires were once built. It takes no great imagination to visualize devout men in meditation here, searching in the depths of their souls for the mystery of life.

It was dusk when we got back to the bazaar, a straggling stretch of shops dealing in cheap merchandise. I paid our guide fifty cents (twenty-five afghanis) and almost got kissed for my generosity. It was almost dark by the time we reached the hotel. An attendant was waiting for us at the door with a lantern. We took out our overnight bags and were relieved to find a garage with a lock where we could leave the car all night. While these country people are friendly, they are also tempted by articles which, though commonplace to us, are sheer luxury that would take a lifetime of savings to buy.

The hallways of the hotel were empty corridors; and the wide, creaky staircase leading to our rooms on the second floor was without a carpet. The place echoed with our footsteps; and in the dark gloom even the rustle of Mercedes' dress had a ghostly sound.

There were kerosene lamps in our bedrooms and a trickle of water from the tap at the washbowl. A cold wind came up out of the north, fairly rattling the windows on the exposed side. Our shadows made eerie forms as we went down the dark corridor to dinner. In the dining room a lone candle flickered in the draft from the high wind. Plates, cups, forks, and spoons were set on a soiled and grimy tablecloth. But the food did not come for over an hour. During that interval Aslam went on various missions to inquire what was wrong. He had no success; this Afghan kitchen, like an Afghan burro, was taking its own time.

The meal when it came was not tempting: the mutton was

tough, the rice was too heavy with saffron, the eggplant was too deep in grease. But the *chai* and *nan,* as always, were good; and I settled for them.

The wind died down by morning and at daybreak the sky was clear and calm. I had thought the evening sun at Bamian was superb; but this morning's sun brought beauty I had never seen. Left and right, as I faced the west, were spurs of the Hindu Kush, purple below white peaks. To the west was a small range of mountains that at sunrise was first red and then orange, then copper. To the east along the ridge where the hotel sits was the ancient city of Bamian—Shahr-i-Ghulgulla, the City of Noise. Like the present hotel, the old city was far enough away from the monasteries not to disturb their peace and quiet. This morning the green of the valley below me was dark and rich. Opposite were the Buddhas in the red sandstone. This valley, soaked in colors, was still and quiet—no roar of motors, no whistle of trains not even the call of a bird. I had been greatly impressed both at Taxila and at Swat by the selections of sites the Buddhists had made for their monasteries. But of all the places for quiet and meditation, Bamian heads the list. These were my thoughts as I stood in the dazzling sun that soon dried up a heavy dew. I was lost in my thoughts when a turbaned hunter passed by, his black dog at heel and an ugly falcon on his wrist.

After an early breakfast of tea, *nan,* cucumbers, and goat cheese, we packed and left the hotel. The sky was so beautiful, the sun so radiant we could not resist the temptation to take more pictures. This time we worked around the base of the Buddhas. One foot alone was as big as several couches and about six feet high. On the body we could see holes that once held some jewels or decoration. They had been torn off; the feet had been hacked by swords; the nose and one side of the face had been mutilated. But the noble figure still stands—reinforced by scaffolds—as a reminder of men's faith long before the machine sent us hurtling through space looking for happiness.

The road due west of Bamian leads into beautiful high lake country. We wanted to visit it. But that would take two more days; and Herat, Tehran, Baghdad, and Istanbul beckoned. So we turned east to backtrack to the main road leading north to Pul-i-Khumri.

I had two more stops to make before leaving Bamian. The school was open and I wanted pictures. Teacher and students were co-operative. At first one boy stood between me and the class, shouting, "Go away, foreigner." But boys are boys the world around, always tolerant of distractions from class work; and the crowd shouted him down. After a while I got them back to their routine; and it was then I used my Leica. The routine is for them to recite the Koran in unison. Verse after verse, page after page is recited, not in Pushtu nor in Persian but in Arabic, the language in which the holy book, dictated by Mohammed, was written. Arabic is to the Koran what Latin is to the Catholic Mass. These Afghan boys did not know the meaning of what they were reciting. In later grades they would get instruction on that. As youngsters they were learning the ritual language that would make them at home anywhere in the far-flung Moslem empire—Karachi, Mecca, or Rabat.

The other thing I wanted to find in Bamian was a singing shepherd. On my earlier Afghan journey, I had come across a shepherd high in a poplar tree singing at the top of his lungs. I know of no other country where one can find a soloist in a treetop.

CHAPTER 6

THE GARAGEMAN AT KARACHI CATCHES UP WITH US

The main road north to Pul-i-Khumri winds through a deep, barren canyon for miles and miles. It's a canyon that has no sign of habitation, no mark of cultivation. This is the route of the Bamian River, dark with sediment, as it pushes its way north to the Oxus. The stream is a turbulent one, for the drop off the northern slopes of the Hindu Kush is precipitous. We soon felt the change. For while Bamian was cool, we fast lost elevation and with the lower altitude and the rocky canyon walls, the heat began to mount.

This canyon would have been entirely desolate, like some of ours in Utah, except for one huge fortress perched high on a ledge that commands one section of the defile. It had no sign of life and apparently was a castle and fortification built by some invader in ancient days who wanted a lookout to guard his rear. For the gorge of the Bamian was perhaps the main route of the invaders.

This Bamian River gorge had other resemblances to the canyons of our Southwest. It is gaily painted in pinks, browns, greens, purple, and copper. What metallic ingredients have given it these many hues, I do not know. They are there in quantity and extend for miles. The changing lights produce new shadows. The effect is kaleidoscopic. Moreover, the rocks have strange exotic forms and shapes. They do not appear to be sedimentary, for they are not laid down with precision or symmetry. They appear to be granitic and volcanic. Some walls have great swirls in them. It seems as if some gigantic finger played in the molten rock, shaping it in fantastic shapes. These gorges of the Hindu Kush are the most colorful I know apart from our own Southwest.

We had a late start from Bamian so the noon hour came when we had not been on the road more than two hours. As we still had some of Mrs. Mills' delicious luncheon left, we decided as we jogged along on this rough dirt road to look for a pleasant teahouse at Doabi, the first village which appeared on our map. The sun was high and we were now low enough to feel its intensity. The car needed water and we needed shade.

Doabi is a small village of mud huts on the Bamian River. The road entering from the south makes a sharp left turn into the one and only street of the village. We all had been so engrossed in looking to the left, we had almost missed a startling view to the right that appeared as we cleared the canyon. There in great majesty was an unnamed peak of the Hindu Kush, a little indistinct in the heat haze but draped with snow over purple shoulders. Though miles away, it seemed to stand at the very end of Main Street in Doabi. This beautiful mountain transformed an ugly, dusty, hot, wind-blown village into a thing of beauty.

Our selection of a teahouse for lunch was dictated not by signs of cleanliness nor by marks of modernity, but by the depth of the shade. We chose one on the left-hand side that the sun had not yet touched, parking the car by the platform where lunch was being served.

Most of the assembled Afghans, with their turbaned heads and loose flowing trousers, sat on their haunches eating rice and lamb with the aid of *nan* from a plate that rested on the carpeted floor of the platform. The proprietor—a small, wiry man, with an indigo coat, red plaid trousers and shirt, and a tall skullcap—came running with two rope-bottomed beds, spread them with rugs, and with much salaaming bade us sit down. We ordered tea and unwrapped the lunch. As we did so, a street crowd gathered.

They were interested first in a Swiss pocket knife of mine which has two blades, a screw driver, leather punch, scissors, etc. I used it to slice some tomatoes and passed it around so these friendly Afghans could have a glimpse of a Western gadget. They were also fascinated with the mildly fragrant cleansing papers called "Wash-'n-Dri" now commonly found on American planes. Mary had brought a supply with her; and we found them most useful along the roadside, for they take the place of soap, water, and a towel.

The *chai* was so delicious we ordered several cups and the genial proprietor obliged by posing for pictures by his samovar and with a tray of small glasses set in metal holders with handles —the cup in which *chai* is usually served in the Middle East.

Not far from the teahouse was an irrigation canal bringing water to the farms of Doabi. It had a fast current and was about twelve feet wide. From the teahouse it looked blue. But when I reached it with a canvas bag for radiator water, I saw it was extremely dirty. As I was filling the water bag, a young boy came down with a bucket. I recognized him as the son—or at least the assistant—of the teahouse proprietor. I followed him back to the shop and my worst fears were realized. The water from the dirty ditch went into the samover to make more of the delicious tea we had just enjoyed. The water boy at Doabi made me suspicious of every drink I was to get on this Middle East journey.

Down, down, down the Bamian we went in a northerly direction through sun-baked valleys. This part is hot country that reminded me of southern Idaho. Like Idaho, it too is irrigated and grows sugar beets and corn. But it also grows cotton; and it lacks the green gardenlike appearance of southern Idaho. There were few trees in this blistering stretch and the dust, fine as face powder, kept swirling up in our faces.

I began to wonder about a place to stay this night. Our destination was Pul-i-Khumri. Aslam was supposed to have called from Kabul to make a reservation. At Bamian I had asked him about it and he said he had not telephoned but for me not to worry. But I worried nonetheless. Bamian was a backwash, off the main track. But Pul-i-Khumri was on the highway; and accommodations are not numerous. There is always one hostel in a sizable Afghan town; but outside of places like Kabul seldom more than one. They fill up early in the summer months, for this is a busy road. Over a hundred tank trucks travel this road every day, going to the Oxus for Russian gasoline and coming down with their tanks filled. Though they usually travel all night, there are breakdowns and the crew often has to lay over. Moreover, the Russian technicians I have mentioned need places to stay. We always found the hotels filled with them. So I pressed Aslam on the matter until he agreed to stop at Doshi, the last large village south of Pul-i-Khumri, and telephone. My friend the Foreign Minister, Prince Naim, had said in Kabul, "Be sure to contact the Governor if you need help." So I directed Aslam to phone that official in Pul-i-Khumri.

While Aslam went for a phone, the three of us had tea under a huge mulberry tree on the bank of a tributary of the Bamian River. It was so hot that every living thing was in the shade, but for a few boys splashing in the creek and an old man doing his washing there. Mercedes decided to join them and bathe her hot feet in the water. Mary had tea in the shade. I poked along the main street of this mud village, looking for photogenic faces. In a half hour Aslam appeared reflecting the frustration he had experienced. The connection with Pul-i-Khumri was poor; he had shouted himself hoarse; the Governor was not in town; he only hoped for the best.

So on we went, carefully preserving the last half pint of cool water in the thermos for the heat of the valleys ahead of us. After Doshi, the Bamian River becomes the Surkhab, and after Pul-i-Khumri, the Kunduz. As it changed its name, it grew in size from the tributaries that joined it and also became muddier. Beyond Doshi it was, indeed, darker than I had ever seen our own Missouri. We had not gone far out of Doshi before we met our first dust storm. The valleys began to open up more and more; the road seemed to be filled with powdered dust; the movement of the car caused us to be enveloped; a hot wind came from the rear, pushing our own dust ahead of us so we could not see the road. Aslam reduced our speed to a few miles an hour as we scraped through the first real ruts we had experienced. The oncoming traffic seemed to increase. The tank trucks bore down on us ominously, giving no quarter. We could only pull off to the side and suffer their dust. It was so hot that the interior was insufferable when the windows of the car were closed. The dust was so thick that the interior was also insufferable when the windows were open. Mercedes and Mary solved the problem by closing their windows. I solved it by opening mine.

The dust got worse rather than better. The dust, indeed, proved treacherous for our low-hung car. What appeared to be only a shallow ridge in the center of the road often turned out to be high and rough. For the shallow-appearing ruts were actually a foot or more deep in fine dust. The result was that we scraped the bottom over and again, sometimes ominously. It happened repeatedly in spite of the fine advice Aslam was getting from the ladies in the rear seat.

In a few miles we had to leave the road because of construction work. The detour seemed a better highway, for the truck wheels had not yet pounded out the ruts. But the improvement was more illusory than real; these detours had lateral ditches so deep that no matter how slowly we proceeded, we scraped bottom. We came abreast of a construction crew, the first we had seen. They were boys in the Afghan Army and we were to see them day after day. They were the labor force; the Russians were the supervising engineers; the earth-moving machines and the rollers were Russian-made. This treacherous detour paralleled the road for nearly five miles. Once we got back onto the highway we were again in deep ruts. We rode the center strip when we could. But oncoming trucks forced us over; and every time we moved to the right we hit bottom. We came to a fairly decent stretch where Afghan soldiers were using Russian pneumatic drills to pry off slabs of rock from a huge elbow in the road. They greeted us with grins and salutations; and we had no sooner passed from sight around the bend than there was a tremendous clatter and bang under the car. We were to get used to that noise as the weeks passed. This first time we got out, worried and puzzled, to find the muffler had dropped off. Aslam seemed fully capable of retrieving it; but Mercedes went under the car like a terrier looking for her prey. And the muffler was so hot to handle that I was able to get some nice pictures of her feet sticking out before she retrieved it.

We cooled it with some water from a canvas bag and put it inside the car. We did not know at the time that there it was to stay throughout our Afghan journey. Not until we reached

Meshed in Iran could we find a garage that could weld the muffler back on properly.

We soon got used to the roar. But as the car started without the muffler, the noise was startling. From now on we entered villages not quietly and discreetly, but with a noisy proclamation of our coming.

On the outskirts of Pul-i-Khumri we came to one of the worst roads of our journey. We were on and off the highway as we met detour after detour. Finally we dropped off a steep shoulder on the right and came down to a field that the trucks had pounded heavily. There was no good choice to make; high centers seemed everywhere. Aslam unfortunately chose the worst of the lot and in a minute we were hung in the center and the wheels were churning the fine dust in great clouds. The three of us got out and when I stepped into the rut at the rear of the car to give a push, the dust came up eighteen inches on my legs. We shoveled and backed and pulled until Aslam got clear; and he was able to get to high ground before getting stuck again.

I opened the car door, waiting for the ladies to catch up. They were walking rather gingerly to avoid the deep dust holes, when a gust of wind enveloped them in a cloud of dust. I did not have time for a light reading, but making a guess, I went to work with the Leica getting pictures of the two ghostlike creatures emerging from the foggy dust. Instead of being complimented for my industry, I got severely criticized. The screaming that emanated from both of them had nothing to do with any lack of chivalry in letting them come unassisted down the treacherous road. Not at all. The screaming was in protest at keeping the car doors open, as if by now another inch of dust could possibly make a difference.

It was six o'clock before we finished our 150-mile journey from Bamian to Pul-i-Khumri; and there were no rooms left at the hotel. So we crossed the bridge over the Surkhab River where the dam marks a hydroelectric project (installed by the Germans twenty years ago) and went to another hostel. This one was owned by the textile mill at Pul-i-Khumri. Aslam was gone what seemed an interminably long time and my heart was heavy. We were equipped to camp out. But the heat and dust had been grim; what we needed was a shower and cool drinks. We were to be rewarded beyond our expectations. Aslam returned with a grin. My friend Prince Naim had telephoned the manager of the mill and rooms had been reserved.

This guesthouse was the best we were to experience for many days. It was set back a hundred feet or so in a shady garden. Its veranda had comfortable chairs. The hallways were adorned with beautiful Afghan rugs. There were two nicely appointed rooms and an excellent shower and toilet. The steward appeared with electric fans for the rooms and with the news that all water was boiled and that even the ice was made of boiled water. He had a big bowl of ice with him and, taking him at his word, I put some in a pitcher and drained a quart of ice water without stopping. We appreciated the shower too. But we had not been long on the road the next day until we were as dirty as we were when we reached Pul-i-Khumri. The ice, however, served us longer. It gave us cool drinking water all the way to Mazar-i-Sharif.

I had no sooner cleaned up than two gentlemen called. They were Afghans in their late thirties dressed in Western clothes, well versed in English, and most affable. One was Mohammed Ibrahim Afifi and the other Gholam Omar Neksad, both officials of the textile mill at Pul-i-Khumri. They stayed not more than a half hour. Like all Afghans, they had a keen sense of protocol and propriety, leaving early because they knew we were tired from our long journey. Before going they discussed the problem of our car. I told them of the muffler; and they advised me there was no welding equipment in this town of 20,000 people. Mr. Neksad expressed concern about leaving our car all night on this Afghan street. We could possibly get all the stuff on the rack inside the car. But it would take a lot of time to unload and re-pack in the morning. He offered his own garage at home. But Aslam, who measured our clearance, decided we were two inches too high. Neksad and Afifi had a conference which ended in calling the head of the gendarmes. The result was that gendarmes stood guard over the car all night, taking turns at two-hour shifts. This was the first of many acts of kindness the gendarmes were to extend us across the Middle East.

Of a sudden Mercedes got dreadfully sick, turning first white, then pink. All food was distasteful; so she went to bed. When

Mary and I answered the dinner call, we faced a table that had on it twelve courses, all served at once. I settled for scallions, roast chicken, *mawst* (curds), *nan, chai,* and a very sweet cantaloupe.

Mercedes was no better in the morning but insistent on being on the road. So I rose at five o'clock to get an early start. When I took the bags out to the car, I found a merchant at the gate. Pul-i-Khumri is a town of Turkmen, Uzbeks, Tadjiks, and Hazarahs. But the merchant who called on me this morning was a Hindu, literally bedecked with merchandise. He had shawls, prayer rugs, jewelry, coins, mirrors, combs, face powder, hair oil, and colored handkerchiefs. He must have known of my presence or he would not have appeared at this early hour. He acted as if I had invited him to come. He would not take no or the shake of a head for an answer. He kept pulling out divers articles from his pockets, from under his coat, from his belt. I could not get rid of him. He followed me everywhere. Finally I bowed to the inevitable and bought two ugly colored handkerchiefs with prints of Afghan scenery on them. He bowed and grinned as he took the afghanis, showing betel-stained teeth.

This Hindu had so distracted my attention that I had failed to notice that the left rear tire was flat. Aslam and I jacked up the car and unpacked the rear end to get the spare. It was then I discovered that the spare had no inner tube. The picture of the garageman in Karachi came back in memory. He was bowing and saying, "Yes, Sahib," as I asked whether the spare had twenty-eight pounds of air.

"He outfoxed you, as we Afghans say," Aslam added.

We both laughed quite inappropriately. For now we had two tubes to fill with air. There is no pressurized air in Afghanistan. Tires are filled by hand pump. Aslam and I were left with the chore. We discovered it took twenty pumps to produce one pound of air pressure.

CHAPTER 7

A KEROSENE STOVE COMES IN HANDY

As we left Pul-i-Khumri, the textile mill was on our right. We did not stop to visit it as we were pressed for time. The houses for the thousand men and women who work there looked neat, tidy, and modern. The company, privately owned, builds the houses and sells them to the workers on easy terms. The price is so moderate that the tenants get title in seven years. These houses are gaily painted; and each had an attractive garden. There is plenty of water from the Surkhab River and it is plentifully used to make Pul-i-Khumri a pleasant, though very hot, garden spot. When the hydroelectric project and textile mill were built, this town was plagued with malaria. Thousands died from it during the construction. But today, thanks to spraying, there is little malaria here.

Beyond the mill we passed fields of melons, cucumbers, and maize and then came to a fork in the road. The right-hand one that goes almost due north leads to Baghlan, where there is a sugar beet factory, to Kunduz, and on to the Russian border. We took the left-hand fork that bears northwest to Mazar-i-Sharif. Now we were in cotton country; and here and there I saw thin stands of wheat. But the farther we went the more desolate and dry the country became. For the Surkhab had turned north at Pul-i-Khumri, leaving us in dusty, barren country that is sparsely settled all the way to Mazar-i-Sharif. We stopped for lunch at Robatak. The teahouse, though shady, was not attractive. It was built around a very dirty tank of water that I suspected was used to make tea. We had for lunch a small roast chicken that we had ordered the night before at Pul-i-Khumri. That plus a melon and *nan* from the guesthouse were our meal. We had *chai* heavily sweetened and, as we ate, two Russian diesels heavy with gasoline rolled in from Mazar-i-Sharif. The road ahead was good, they assured Aslam. They also twitted him about driving in the middle of the day.

"We'll stay here until four o'clock," one of the truck drivers said. "When the heat of the day is gone, we'll head south. Only fools travel at this hour."

"But you travel all night," Aslam rejoined. And so the bantering continued during the entire meal.

In a half hour after our departure from Robatak, we were sorry we had not followed the advice of the truck drivers and waited until the cool of the afternoon. For we entered a series of small defiles that were as hot and desolate as anything I have ever seen. There was nothing but rocks, scrub, and camel's-thorn to be seen. The heat from the low canyons walls was like a furnace. I cannot imagine a worse place for a blowout, and without warning it came with a bang. It was the right rear. I pointed out to Mercedes what unique quality a Kodachrome taken of her changing a tire in this fierce canyon would have. Later she was to respond to the challenge. But this day she was still ill. So Aslam and I went to work. Mercedes did, however, make a distinctive contribution to the photographic record of the trip. She took one of the straw mats we had brought for seat covers and she and Mary held it as a canopy over Aslam and me while we worked on the tire. The nuts on the wheel were too hot to touch; I had to use gloves. The rocks that we used to keep the car from rolling were also too hot to touch. We had to push them under with our feet. We had perspired so much that, when we finished, my tongue stuck to the roof of my mouth. I handed Aslam the water bag first; and he practically drained it before giving it back.

I picked up the blown-out tire and threw it to the side of the road. Aslam retrieved it with a grin.

"Will you let me sell it?" he asked.

"Certainly. But to whom?"

"You wait and see," he answered.

And sure enough he found a buyer in Mazar-i-Sharif who paid him forty afghanis or eighty cents.

"How come?" I asked.

"You see," answered Aslam, "in Afghanistan the fabric of a tire makes excellent soles for shoes. The man I sold the tire to is a cobbler."

The blowout was only the beginning of a day of hard work under a searing sun. We had not gone a dozen miles more when the canyon opened up into a broad valley perhaps ten miles across. Barren mountains with easy slopes rose a couple thousand feet on each side to form a huge bowl. One of the ladies shouted and, looking ahead, I saw hundreds upon hundreds of camels and thousands upon thousands of sheep.

As soon as we stopped and went to work with the cameras, the camels turned away, the whole herd heading south to a basin. First a curious lad of eight appeared, then a man of forty, than one of sixty, each with a turban, a dirty patched coat, and loose flowing trousers. I did not see where they came from. Suddenly from nowhere they were there.

Aslam engaged the oldest one in earnest conversation. Would he send the boy to turn the camels around and herd them toward our cameras? The old man agreed instantly and shouted commands to the boy that sent the lad running.

Would he agree to have his picture taken?

He was all smiles and ready to comply.

Would he have the sheep (that must have numbered several thousand) turned our way so that I could get good pictures?

The old man gave commands to the younger one, who went running.

After these errands were run and we had our pictures, we prepared to leave. Now the old man engaged Aslam in further conversation. He wanted us to visit his camp.

I had seen no camp. But when the old man pointed north, I climbed a small knoll above the car and saw the black tents numbering a dozen or more a half mile away.

It was blistering hot and Mercedes was still weak in the knees. But she agreed we should accept the invitation. So up the knoll we went with our cameras and across a treeless slope that burned under the fierce sun.

I learned as we started that the old man was Malik Zi, head of a tribe of nomads who wander the plains and hills of northern Afghanistan. He and I led the way to the encampment; and all the while he kept shouting commands ahead to the women who collected at one tent. Aslam said he was directing them not to hide, that he was coming with friends. But knowing the shyness of Afghan women and the tradition that segregates them from men who are not members of their immediate family, I let Malik Zi go on alone, while I turned to a group of tents where the men were gathered.

These men, all barefoot and dressed in flowing trousers with long coats over dirty shirts, shook hands and ushered me into the shade of a black wool tent whose sides were rolled up so that every breath of air would pass. I sat on an Afghan rug facing them and talking with them through Aslam. They brought out a pan of water which they offered me for drinking. It was so dirty, I passed it by, only to notice that Aslam drained it to the last drop—and as a result was deathly sick a day later. We talked with these primitive nomads of sheep and camels, of horses and donkeys.

They had mostly burros and camels for transport and only a few horses and donkeys. A good horse in northern Afghanistan—one we would call a first-rate Turkmen horse—costs 80,000 afghanis ($1600) these days. This tribe had no such horse. That quality horse is owned only by the rich man. The man who rides that kind of horse compares with the one of us who drives a Cadillac, or, better still, who flies a Beechcraft Bonanza. Camels vary in price depending on age, health, build, teeth, etc. The top price for a camel in this area is 30,000 afghanis ($600). A good donkey costs 700 afghanis ($14). A good burro sells for 400 afghanis ($8). That price, however, is only average in the Kabul market. We had seen below Pul-i-Khumri herds of burros being driven by herders on foot to the Kabul market. They were young burros in their prime; and these herders expected to get anywhere from 1000 afghanis ($20) to 5000 afghanis ($100) for the animals. But up north the burros' market price was less.

By the value of inventory these nomads were rich, wealthier by far than the average Afghan peasant. They had no community life except what they themselves provided. There were no movies to see, no concerts to attend, no schools for the children, no doctors or medicines. Their babies were born in black tents and a midwife attended the birth. And they had no bazaars for shopping. Sometimes a member of the tribe would hitchhike rides to town on one of the big oil trucks that came lumbering through. Yet few of them had ever seen a bazaar. They had no radio to catch news and music from the air. They were all illiterate and wholly unaware of what went on in Afghanistan, let alone the world. They were not carefree, for they had the problems of birth and death, ill-health and disease, hunger and sorrow. They were not emaciated or sickly-looking. Since they had no sugar, their teeth were beautiful. They had patches of wheat and patches of melons in some valleys. The wheat gave them enough *nan;* the melons were their only fruit. They made their winter clothes, their blankets, rugs, and tents from wool. Their milk and cheese came from the camels and sheep. They would drive sheep to market when they needed tea, cotton cloth, and decorations for their ladies' headdress.

I felt a warm glow of friendliness in this circle of men. I changed film as we talked; and they were fascinated with the interior of the camera, for it was the first they had ever seen. They had among them a few talented musicians. One brought out a primitive guitar, obviously handmade, and played plaintive music. Two other men sang; and their theme was the loneliness of people in a hot, barren land.

They were all Moslems and said that they prayed five times a day. But they could not obey the command of the Koran to bathe their hands and feet before prayer because in this blistering valley there was no water. Their own supply was from a spring high up, a source that the sheep kept very muddy. They asked me if I were a Moslem and I said no, that I was a Christian. They said that Islam was superior to Christianity and I asked why. So far the conversation had gone back and forth between myself and a half dozen of the herdsmen. Now Malik Zi spoke up and said:

"Once a Christian and a Moslem had an argument that the Moslem brought to a *mullah*. The Christian had claimed that

Christ was higher and more important than the Prophet because Christ was in the sky while the Prophet walked the earth. The *mullah* called for scales and put enough gold on one side to bring it way down."

"I do not understand," I replied.

"You see," the old man said with a twinkle, "what goes up in the air is not always the best."

We all laughed and I got up to leave. Malik Zi bowed graciously but insisted we stay all night. He wanted to kill a sheep and roast it for us. His people would put on a dance and entertain us. No foreigner, no Christian had ever visited them before.

There is nothing I would rather have done. But Mercedes felt miserable and our timetable was tight. Moreover, Afghan officials would worry if we delayed. We were getting close to the area where Peter Winant disappeared in 1956, never to be heard from or seen again. For these reasons I reluctantly declined Malik Zi's invitation and shook his hand in farewell, saying:

"I'll come again and visit you."

"Inshallah," he answered. *"Inshallah* [God willing]."

"Inshallah," I added as I turned to go.

But I was not to leave for some time. I saw that the women of the tribe had Mercedes and Mary completely surrounded.

Most of the women were dressed in red dresses with black capes over their shoulders and black scarves over their heads. The wife of the Khan wore a specially fine red dress. A blue scarf was tied tightly around her head. A string of silver coins hung from each ear, reaching her knees. Women are women the world around. What these women were interested in were strictly feminine things. They wanted to see lipstick and face powder and pocket mirrors. Each article had to be passed around. They wanted to know how American women cooked, what they ate, how they dressed their children, what was good for eye swellings, for earaches, for pains in the stomach, for diarrhea. Aslam had been shuttling back and forth between their tent and mine, doing double duty as an interpreter. When he returned to me the last time, the nomad women started a minute examination of the clothes that Mercedes and Mary wore. Soon I heard a scream; then the whole crowd of women surrounding Mercedes and Mary broke into laughter. It appeared that several of the women had got down on their knees to get under the skirts which our two ladies wore to see what was underneath. The nomad women were consumed with curiosity about what kind of undergarments these strange women wore.

It took Mercedes and Mary much longer to get disentangled than it had me. The result was that we spent two hours with these wonderfully friendly nomads and once more were far behind schedule.

The hills were rolling but barren in the stretch that lay ahead. We climbed for a while and soon came to canyons sparsely covered by wild pistachio trees. These trees produce well. They are owned by the Afghan government, which for a fee of ten afghanis (twenty cents) issues an annual permit for their picking. The local peasant—the nomad too—finds this a ready source of cash. For pistachios bring a good price in the bazaar at Mazar-i-Sharif.

Now we picked up a small river, fed in the spring by many small tributaries now long dry, and by 3:30 P.M. came to a green garden spot known as Tushkurgan. Like all Afghan cities, this too has houses of mud, each surrounded by walls of mud and each having behind the walls a green and respectable garden. The gardens of Tushkurgan are distinguished in one respect. They are thick with fig trees; and the figs of Tushkurgan are famous throughout Afghanistan. When we stopped for gas, I peeked over a few walls only to find the figs still green. So after filling up the gas tank, we drove the car into a shaded courtyard behind the gas station to slice a melon and quench our thirst. It turned out to be the unhappiest stop we made on our long journey. For no sooner had we carved the melon than a host of yellow jackets appeared, quickly appropriating the melon to themselves.

Mazar-i-Sharif is about forty miles from Tushkurgan. But the roads were so badly rutted in some sections and so deeply filled with washboards in others that it took us over two hours to reach that ancient city.

This town of 20,000 people is nondescript except for the shrine I will mention. Its streets are dirt or cobblestone, lined by chenar and willow, and the city has an extensive bazaar. This bazaar has one feature that distinguishes it from other Afghan bazaars. It stays open until nine o'clock every night. There are no movies or concerts in Mazar-i-Sharif. The bazaar furnishes the entertainment. Here people assemble after dark for the greatest social event I saw in Afghanistan.

We hoped after the delightful stay in the de luxe guesthouse at Pul-i-Khumri that we would have like quarters at Mazar-i-Sharif. Mercedes' spirits were high as she thought of another spick-and-span room, a good shower, and some more clean ice cubes. Her dreams were soon shattered. For when Aslam stopped at the Governor's mansion in Mazar-i-Sharif, he was informed that the Governor had made reservations for us at the hotel.

This hotel was one of the worst. It was gloomy, having long hallways unlighted, with rough cement floors. The rooms had high ceilings and tall windows that swung inward. It had electricity; but the power was off during our two-day visit there. The beds were iron cots; and we had not been in the rooms many minutes before we discovered that the mattresses and bedding had bedbugs. There was a tub and a washbowl and a toilet in the bathroom. There even was a big wood-burning heater by the bathtub. But the heater did not work, for there was no circulating water. All taps were indeed dry. I spoke to the dark, swarthy man who wore slippers and a loose brown gown and he instantly bowed, saying he would get water for bathing and water for drinking. I emphasized in my best Persian that the drinking water had to be *"ab jush"*—i.e., boiled water.

"Bali, bali, ab jush," was his reply as he disappeared down the dark corridor.

Shortly I heard him pouring water into the tub. I looked and saw the dirtiest water imaginable filling the tub. But it was cool and the bath was refreshing. When I finished, I found that a bottle of water had been placed on the table. I put several halazone tablets in it and went to work fumigating the beds and wallboards with our DDT bomb. When I finished, I noticed that the bottle of drinking water was collecting a big deposit of dirt in the bottom. I called the man in the brown grown and again demanded *ab jush*. Pointing to the bottle, he said, *"Ab jush, ab jush."*

I took it and poured it out in his presence and then handed it back to him, saying, *"Ab jush."*

He had a puzzled look on his face as he took the bottle and

went down the dark corridor. I went outside to stretch my legs and get a breath of air. On the veranda of the hotel, facing a small lawn watered from an irrigation ditch, sat a young man in his thirties with a thin, scraggly beard. He wore shorts and a shirt with short sleeves, an attire plainly marking him as European or American. He was an Austrian stationed in northern Afghanistan on an engineering mission which he was anxious to keep to himself. But he spoke English and we finally got around to "*ab jush.*"

"I would never believe an Afghan if he said the water was boiled," he said.

I asked what precautions he took. He said that amoebic dysentery was so common up here that he never drank any water unless he himself drew it from the samovar. Then he set it aside to cool and settle. Several drawings a day kept him supplied. I asked about other drinks. He drank tea of course. But beer and wine are banned throughout all Afghanistan and not available. Soft drinks are sometimes found but they are untrustworthy.

The Austrian gave me quite a lecture on health, saying that we should abjure buttermilk, fresh vegetables, and ice cream. All fruit must be peeled. Melons—especially watermelons—are dubious items if bought in a market. Merchants, to increase the weight of the melons, sometimes use a syringe to fill them with dirty ditch water.

The words of the Austrian inspired me to renewed research of the *ab jush* of the hotel at Mazar-i-Sharif. During our two days I followed the servant many times as he went with my bottle for *ab jush*. But he was a cagy man and would always disappear to out-wait me. Once I caught him in an outbuilding pouring water from a big earthen jug into my bottle.

"*Ab jush?*" I inquired.

"*Bali, bali,*" he said with a grin.

But finally I got to the truth of the matter. I eventually found the man filling the earthen jug from the dirty irrigation ditch that ran through the bazaar of Mazar-i-Sharif before it reached the hotel on the western edge of the city. Our *ab jush* had been unboiled ditch water.

The night of our arrival was oppressively hot; and Mercedes, even after a bath, felt worse than ever. The thought of food was repulsive. So I brought in the kerosene two-burner stove and set it up in the bathroom. We soon had boiling water. The dried chicken soup smelled appetizing and tasted good. But the hot powdered milk and crackers tasted better. For two days we used the battered stove in our own bathroom-kitchen. It spelled the difference between comfort and despair to an invalid in a bug-ridden, ill-smelling hotel sitting on the hot wind-blown plain that runs flat as a pancake to the Russian border.

CHAPTER 8

WHITE PIGEONS, PISTACHIO ICE CREAM, AND LOVE

While the July days at Mazar-i-Sharif are oppressively hot, the nights are cool. By nine o'clock each night a cool northwest wind was blowing. The stars seemed close enough to touch. The whine of the wind made sleep restful.

The early morning hours too are refreshing. When I went out shortly after sunrise, the man who kept me supplied with *ab jush* was lifting water from the irrigation ditch by a deep pan attached to a pole and scattering it on the lawn. He watered the morning glories that lined the lawn on three sides with water from a goatskin over his shoulder. Burros loaded with vegetables were coming into town. A few turbaned men with bright-colored shirts rode fast-stepping saddle ponies down the street. A few bicyclists pumped by. Then came the tongas. I had seen them all the way from Karachi, drawn by scrawny horses whose ribs were protruding, whose bodies were covered with lather, whose feet were sore, whose joints were swollen. In Mazar-i-Sharif I saw beautiful healthy horses pulling the tongas, usually in a team of two. And these tongas, unlike any others I had seen, had a distinctive bell. It was a multiple bell in two tones, as unusual as the chimes we sometimes use as doorbells.

Mazar-i-Sharif means Noble Shrine. We had decided to spend the cool of the morning photographing the famous shrine where

Ali is said to be buried. Mercedes, though still woozy, was game for it. But once again our schedule was delayed. When we arrived at the shrine, we were turned back at the gate by the white-bearded, white-turbaned gatekeeper, who had a gendarme with a rifle as an ally.

"No foreigners are permitted," he told us in a tone that sounded final.

I knew they were sometimes allowed. For friends of ours—Franc and Jean Shor of the National Geographic Society—had once visited it; and I had read of other travelers who had been inside the walls.

There was nothing to do but see the Governor. Aslam returned us to the hotel while he went seeking a permit. He was gone an interminable length of time. But he was smiling and happy when he returned.

When we arrived at the gate with the permit, the white-bearded gatekeeper was grim and silent like a person who was taking orders he did not like; but he bowed and took our shoes, explaining as he did so that the permit was good only for the outer court, not for the inner one where the body of Ali is supposed to rest. Why this barrier, I do not know. Perhaps it was drawn on account of the women in our party. Moslem women never are allowed into the holy of holies. Perhaps if I had been alone, I could have entered. For the inner court was filled with men who, first washing in a tiled pool, said their prayers by the tomb. But the trip to the outer court was well worth the time we took.

The shrine has four main gates with archways ornamented by verses from the Koran. The tilework of the building which houses the tomb is almost as lovely as the best tilework we saw in Meshed and Isfahan, Iran. The blues and turquoises are exquisite; and the mosaic has grace as well as power. The minarets are graceful and well proportioned. They give a startling effect when one lies on his back looking at them against a blue sky dotted with fleecy clouds.

Mary talked about the breath-taking combination of blue tile and the intensely blue sky. The absence of red in the color scheme gives a cool, serene feeling. What in the subconscious prompted this? Was it the heat of the surrounding desert? Was it to soothe highly volatile passions? Was it an instinctive choice of spiritual qualities? These were Mary's questions.

The other main attraction of the outer court was the white pigeons. I heard people in Mazar-i-Sharif call them pests. They shuttle back and forth between the bazaar and the shrine. They are untouchable because they are an attachment of a holy place. They are fed by everyone and banned by none. Perhaps to merchants in the bazaar they are nosy, dirty, and destructive. But at the shrine they are a thing of beauty. They are so numerous that they are very difficult to count. I got high enough in an actual count to estimate they number about five hundred. To the rear of the outer court on the right is a feeding platform about five feet high with bowls of water. One man has been hired by the shrine to do the feeding. The feed is the best wheat that Mazar-i-Sharif can produce. It is bought by the bag and stored in locked rooms opening into the courtyard from the wall that encloses it. I suspect that year in and year out the grain costs the shrine little or nothing. Perhaps they make a profit on the pigeons. For we spent a hundred afghanis (two dollars) buying grain from the affable warden of the pigeons so that I could get pictures of Mercedes feeding them. We had to maneuver to do this, especially to get the pigeons on her shoulders and hands and to get the body of them in flight. The pigeon warden was a great help. The pigeons knew his voice, which came out in great bellows. And when it seemed the flock would take off for the bazaar, the leather-lunged warden would call them back.

Once while I waited for the pigeons to perform, I studied the wall of the courtyard where the warden kept the grain. He occupied but one room. There were other cell-like rooms the length of this wall. They were about six feet wide. Some had doors whose hinges were on the side. Other doors had hinges at the top so that they opened by lifting the bottom. One such door was propped open about two feet by a stick. I looked in and there in the doorway on his haunches was a *mullah* reading the Koran out loud. He had a long white beard and turban and was dressed in white. He wore steel-rimmed glasses. He was a professorial type—studious and intent. He looked up and returned a weak smile.

"Is Ali really buried here?" I asked.

"Yes, certainly," he replied.

"But Ali died in Iraq," I answered.

"Yes. But the faithful brought him here so that the criminals would not desecrate his grave," he answered while his blue eyes pierced me.

He returned to his Koran and I to the pigeons. Word of the burial of Ali in this place came about, so legend says, in a strange way. A manuscript acquired in India made the assertion. The rumor reached Balkh, where others swore they had a dream to the same effect. A *mullah* denounced these dreamers. The next night Ali appeared in a dream to the *mullah* and reprimanded him for denying the report. The *mullah* told the Governor of his dream. The Governor had a grave opened and there was the body of Ali in perfect preservation. Sultan Sanjar thereupon ordered that a mausoleum be built over the grave. This was in A.D. 1136. But Genghis Khan destroyed the shrine; and the present one was not finished until A.D. 1481.

Weeks later when I told the story of Ali's shrine to a *mullah* in Iraq, he scoffed at the idea. According to him, the shrine in Mazar-i-Sharif is, indeed, a holy place. But Ali is buried at Najaf, Iraq.

Balkh—the ancient city of Alexander—is only twenty miles from Mazar-i-Sharif. It's on one of the roads west. But since that is the poorer of the two, we decided to go over to Balkh and back rather than include it on our trip to Shibarghan and Andkhui. Mercedes was too weak for any further exploits this day. So when four o'clock came, Mary, Aslam, and I took off in the station wagon.

The land around Mazar-i-Sharif runs flat to Russia on the north; it's like a vast delta, only quite dry. There is an escarpment of cliffs and hills to the south and a meager supply of creek and well water for irrigation. This is cotton country. Figs, melons, grapes, tomatoes, and cucumbers also grow here. In the old days Mazar-i-Sharif was a big center on the Silk Road from China. Great caravans came down from Samarkand and from there went on to Tabriz in the west or Kabul in the south and east.

Today Mazar-i-Sharif is also a caravan center. Some camel trains come through. But most of the traffic is made up of the gas tank trucks that come down to this city from two of the three ports the Russians have built on the Oxus River. They were roaring into Mazar-i-Sharif, night and day, during our two-day visit. But we missed them all on our short trip to Balkh, which lies west of the point where the roads lead down from Russia.

When I stood at Balkh I remembered a conversation I had had with my friend, M. A. Shakur, of the Peshawar Museum. I could still see his eyes light up as he spoke of the unexplored mounds of Balkh. To an archaeologist this rubble would doubtless be inspiring. To me it was only depressing. Part of the trouble was the heat. It was over 120°F. when we arrived. The ground was so hot it soon burned through the soles of my shoes. Moreover, Balkh today is nothing but rubble. I have seen mounds of dirt that suggest the existence of a fort, a dwelling, a courtyard. But the mounds of dirt at Balkh suggest nothing. They are formless, barren, and without beauty. Balkh, the mother of cities, once had mud walls about seven miles in circumference. There are pieces of old mud walls there today. But these are remnants of the Moslems who came in the eighth century. The broken archways that are often seen in pictures are also recent, dating back to the ninth century. They are a half mile or so south of the ancient city. The ruined gateway that one sees in pictures was a part of a *medresse* or religious school built by a descendant of Timur in the sixteenth century. The city that Alexander the Great knew, the one that still flourished in the seventh century as recorded by Hsüan Tsang, has moldered and disappeared. Today there are patches of grass between mounds of rubble where young girls herd brown cattle. It was impossible for me to recreate in my mind's eye the ancient thriving city of Balkh.

Balkh was once a Zoroastrian city and by 500 B.C. was part of Persia. In the days of Alexander the Great, Balkh was then in Bactria. He marched north from Kabul, crossing the Hindu Kush in wintertime, and surprised Bessus, murderer of Darius III of Persia, who ruled Bactria in those days. The result of this surprise move was that he took Balkh without a struggle. It was then an ancient city and Bactria, the province of which Balkh was the capital, was known as the Garden of Asia. It had, indeed, a beautiful irrigation system from the Oxus River. Alexander made Bactria a Greek province and settled many Greek mercenaries at Balkh. And the Greeks ruled there for nearly two centuries.

After the Greeks came the Kushans, who made Balkh their capital and who became protectors of Buddhism. They ruled in Balkh until the White Huns came in the fifth century. Then came the Turks.

Since Balkh rests on a flat plain where the ancient crossroads of Central Asia met, it needed good fortifications. Hsüan Tsang noted that, though the town was thinly populated, it was strongly fortified. At that time it was still a Buddhist center with some 100 monasteries and 3000 monks. One of the convents outside the city walls had a famous figure of Buddha which was richly studded with gems. So were the walls of the room in which it stood. "That is the reason," wrote Hsüan Tsang in his notebook, "why it has often been robbed by chieftains of neighboring countries, covetous of gain."

The Arabs and the sword of Islam took Balkh from the Turks and liquidated the Buddhists. Genghis Khan laid Balkh low and destroyed the Islamic civilization. Later that century, when Marco Polo visited the city, he found many of the buildings partly demolished. Yet he called it "a large and magnificent city," occupied by Moslems and situated on a plain noted for "the predatory attacks of lawless marauders." But the constant Mongol raids destroyed the city. By 1333, when Ibn Battuta passed that way, he found Balkh in ruins and deserted. Balkh revived to be sacked by Timur. And while it has changed hands many times since then, it never has known a renaissance. People live there on the edge of the ancient ruins. It's a town of 500 people with a Jewish minority, a moth-eaten bazaar, and a caravanserai where I saw long camel trains packing for trips east. A mosque known as Masjed-i-Sabz in fair condition of repair stands in the middle of the present city. The city that once rivaled Babylon and Nineveh is an administrative unit of the province known as Mazar-i-Sharif. At Balkh today there is what is known as the little or subgovernor, who is the agent of the Governor of the province. He is the *Farmandar*.

On reaching Balkh, I had called on this official and he had assigned a guide to me. When I finished the tour, I went back to thank him. His office is in a two-story brick building that has high stone steps leading up to a veranda where many colorful Afghan characters were gathered, some out of curiosity, some on business. I found more inside, standing in line to see the *Farmandar*. I was ushered in ahead of the rest. We walked on Afghan rugs laid on a rough stone floor down a long corridor and turned into a rather barren room which was an anteroom to the *Farmandar's* office. Though the anteroom had a dozen or more Afghans wanting to see the *Farmandar,* we had only a minute to wait. The *Farmandar* is Mohammed Sidiq, an energetic, enterprising man in his thirties who greeted us with a broad smile. The room had high ceilings and tall windows that were open. It was unadorned except for an Afghan rug on the floor and a picture of the King behind the *Farmandar.* The furniture was plain, the chairs overstuffed but hard. An electric fan moved the air across our feet but left the room stifling hot.

Sidiq was in his shirt sleeves; and so was I. He is affable and well educated; and he speaks English beautifully. So I excused Aslam, and Sidiq and I settled down to a half hour of interesting talk.

Balkh has much malaria. The Afghan government has taken measures to stamp it out. All the way from Kabul I had seen signs indicating the dates when the various buildings had been sprayed with DDT. But the malaria control program has not been too successful in Balkh. Moreover, the town lies low on the plain and suffocates in the heat. These two reasons led Mr. Sidiq to settle about ten miles from Balkh on a height of land where there is no malaria and where the wind blows. He lives at Takhta Pal, a city built last century to avoid the mosquitoes of Balkh. We talked of courts and crops, of Alexander the Great, Buddhists, and Genghis Khan, of *mullahs* and schools, doctors and public health. We had not talked long before a servant appeared with a tray of huge dishes filled with ice cream.

"It's pistachio ice cream," Sidiq said. "Please have some."

Never in my Asian journeys had I eaten ice cream. I remembered the advice of a friend in Delhi: "One teaspoon of delicious ice cream may give you five years of undulant fever." I knew that Afghan milk, like Indian milk, was seldom if ever pasteurized.

I remembered the advice of a Tehran friend: "A dish of ice cream is an excellent source of amoebic dysentery. Never—let me repeat, never—eat ice cream."

I remembered what the Austrian at the hotel in Mazar-i-Sharif had said about ice cream. He too had it on the taboo list.

These memories had made me hesitate; and the *Farmandar,* noticing it, said, "I want you to taste our pistachio ice cream. It's especially nice."

I could not bring myself to ask if the milk had been boiled. That might insult my host. My choice was either complete rejection or complete acceptance of the dish.

I weakened and accepted. It was partly my confidence in this genial host. It was partly the agonizing thirst for something cool. We had had nothing but hot drinks at Mazar-i-Sharif. This day had been especially hot. The indoor temperature was over 100°F.

I must have gulped the ice cream, for it was down in a jiffy. It was, as I told the *Farmandar,* the best I ever did taste. And I thought as I told him that, though this pistachio ice cream contained thousands of amoebic cysts, the relief it brought seemed worth it. I gambled and won. For this dish was wholesome as well as cool. But having won, I never touched ice cream again on this journey. For the law of averages was now against me.

Coming back from Balkh, Aslam's memories turned to love. In Afghanistan the country people believe in love potions. Frogs are baked back to back until they are reduced to ashes. The ashes are put surreptitiously into a man's drink by the woman who covets him. The frog ashes assure his love. If she can obtain pieces of the man's fingernails, she will bake them and put the ashes in his drink. Some men follow the same practice by cremating three hairs from a lady's head and impregnating her drink with the ashes. Still another pertains to rabbit's blood. A man who can kill a rabbit and drink its blood when warm assures his popularity with the ladies.

"Have you tried any of these potions?" I asked Aslam.

He was noncommittal in his reply and finally said almost absent-mindedly:

"If you spot a rabbit, let me know."

CHAPTER 9

THE LOESS DUST DEPOSIT

We had unpacked the top of the station wagon our first night in Mazar-i-Sharif and put everything in the car so we could lock it against thieves. But we had to plan differently the second night, for we wanted to leave Mazar-i-Sharif by four o'clock in the morning. That meant loading the car the night before. Aslam solved that problem by agreeing to put his cot on the porch next to the car and sleep there.

The food at Mazar-i-Sharif had been quite a problem. The hotel has no kitchen; all food is brought in from the bazaar. And the anonymous chef who cooked our meals was not ordained to be superior. All his food was unpalatable except the chicken. So we ordered one small roasting chicken for dinner and another small one to take with us for lunch the next day.

Mercedes was still too ill to come to the table. Her activity in the heat of the day at the shrine had been too much. She had a bursting headache and sipped only some soup that we made over the kerosene stove. By bedtime her head was still splitting; and aspirin did not seem to help. Aslam and I had a conference. It turned out there was no ice in Mazar-i-Sharif sold in blocks or cubes. Some ice is cut from ponds and stored in sawdust. But there are few, if any, iceboxes to make it; and no place in the bazaar to buy it. I had seen, however, a merchant in the bazaar selling cold soft drinks, mostly orange or lemon. He had a piece of ice in his two-wheeled pushcart; and with each purchase he would shave some ice off and put a handful in the glass before pouring the drink for some male customer wearing an embroidered skullcap or for some Turkmen woman with a bright shawl. I asked Aslam to take our rubberized bag used for an ice pack and ask the vendor, should he find him, to fill it with shaved ice. Not more than fifteen minutes passed before I heard the roar of the station wagon coming from the bazaar. Aslam pulled up with a grin and the ice pack crammed with shaved ice—all for five afghanis (ten cents). Mercedes had a good night; and all her fever and symptoms were gone when the alarm went off at 3:30 A.M.

Two sleepy servants with unshaven faces, baggy brown trousers, and soiled white shirts stood quietly by while we sipped hot *chai* before departing. They had served us well, according to their lights. We had fought bedbugs and had ditch water instead of *ab jush*. But these men had been attentive to every request we made and received generous tips, partly in gratitude for the low bill that was rendered. It cost each of us fifty afghanis (one dollar) for the two nights we stayed there; and that price included all the meals and all the extra *chai* we ordered, as well as the rooms.

We were off in a cloud of dust and with a roar of our open exhaust at 4:20 A.M. We rode in silence on a dark, bumpy, dusty highway until the sun came up about an hour later. Our destination that day was Andkhui, which is only about twenty miles from the Russian border. The midway point is Shibarghan where we planned to have breakfast. The road from there to Andkhui was said to be the worst piece in all Afghanistan; and we wanted to pass it before the heat of the day. The sun rose red and flaming behind us and shortly after the sunrise came the grasshoppers. We had seen other waves of grasshoppers on our journey but none as big as these. Some that flew in the window were over three inches long. Not long after the grasshoppers came flocks of birds that Aslam called the *sachs*. They had a yellowish-white body and black wings. They are liked by the Afghans because they attack grasshoppers, which in this region assume proportions of a pestilence. These *sachs* apparently had been feeding on grasshoppers. But when the station wagon appeared they left the hunt and joined us. It was an amazing performance. For mile on mile a flock of these birds, numbering at least a hundred, kept in front of our car and only a few feet higher than it. When the road turned, the flock turned. These birds acted as a pilot plane guiding us across this dry, desiccated country. Aslam was delighted, almost jumping up and down behind the steering wheel.

"Good luck, good luck," he cried, pointing to the birds. "The *sachs* always bring good luck to the Afghans."

We were to have a harrowing day. But we had good luck that Aslam always credited to the *sachs*.

We reached Shibarghan by nine o'clock and went at once to the hotel. From Balkh to Shibarghan we were on the trail of Marco Polo. We were not to follow in his footsteps again until we reached northwestern Iran. For Marco Polo came to Shibarghan from the south while we were headed west; and after Balkh he turned north to Soviet Central Asia while we reached Balkh from the south. Marco Polo had fine things to say about Shibarghan. It was, he reported, "plentifully supplied with every kind of provision, and is particularly celebrated for producing the best melons in the world." "They preserve them," he wrote, "by paring them round into strips, and drying them in the sun. When dry they are sweeter than honey and are carried off for sale all over the country."

It does, indeed, have a bountiful bazaar. The day we reached there—July 18, 1957—was a Thursday; and Thursday in Afghanistan is market day. The Moslem Sunday is Friday; so Thursday is comparable to our Saturday. Once the sun was up we began to see people going to town. Aq Chah is a town to the east of Shibarghan. On both sides of Aq Chah we had seen them by twos, threes, and by the dozens, traipsing toward town. The people going into Aq Chah were Turkmen and Uzbeks. Some were dressed in their best bibs and tuckers. Others carried produce on their heads as they plodded along barefooted. Some had burros loaded with vegetables. Some had chickens tied to donkeys' saddles or loaded in crates lashed on the side. There were camels bringing rugs. Sheep chosen for slaughter were headed for auction. Goats, similarly doomed, stepped gingerly along. Two donkeys had milk cans lashed to their packs. Most of the people were men and boys. A few women were also in the procession.

They were filling the bazaar at Aq Chah when we passed. None of the women we met were veiled. Like country women who work the fields of Afghanistan, they reject the *chadhri* out of necessity if nothing else, for no one could cut grain or hoe cotton in a costume of those Halloween proportions. These women wore only scarves around their heads, presumably to keep dust from their hair. Legend, however, has it that this is a style or fad that goes back to Ali Sher Beg, a sixteenth-century Afghan poet who one day tied a kerchief around his head because of an earache. Suddenly that became a style among the ladies.

"We should stop at Aq Chah for the day," Aslam said. "Market day in Aq Chah is the best in all Afghanistan."

I was sorely tempted. But Istanbul was still a long way off, our schedule was a tight one, and we had not many spare days left over. So we pressed on. Had we stayed either at Aq Chah or Shibarghan for the day we would have seen not only a busy bazaar and colorful hawkers of merchandise, but also singing and dancing in the streets at nighttime. Our night was destined for dedication in another venture: crawling over washboard roads at a speed of five miles an hour.

The hotel at Shibarghan had a special interest for me. It is where Peter Winant was last seen. Peter Winant, the young American, traveled north from Kabul in 1956 with his Swedish fiancée. They stayed at the hotel at Shibarghan one night, had breakfast, paid their bill, and left presumably for Andkhui and Herat, our own destination. They were never seen after they left the hotel; and their bodies were never found. The mystery of their disappearance still stirred Kabul on our visit and gave Shibarghan a special interest.

The two servants at the Shibarghan hotel were neatly dressed, Western style, and got us a nice breakfast in a jiffy. They brought a melon that lived up to Marco Polo's claim for Shibarghan, *nan* that was slightly leavened, round and still warm, fresh fried eggs, and *chai*. It was the best breakfast we had had in weeks. When we finished, I talked to the servants to see if they had any clues as to Winant. They were not too eager to talk to strangers. I was to learn later that practically everyone between Shibarghan and Herat had been shaken by the collar, as the gendarmes worked hard to find this American and his fiancée. Everyone was on edge when this subject came up. I left the hotel knowing only that the servants thought young Winant a fine man.

I left the ladies there while I went to pay my respects to the *Farmandar*. This turned out to be the smartest thing I did all summer long. The office on the edge of town is a two-story brick affair, rather run down and ancient, like the one at Balkh. But the *Farmandar,* Mohammed Omar, is as fine a person as my friend at Balkh. I went unannounced. Though there was a great crowd waiting to see the *Farmandar,* he sent for me at once. He's a middle-aged man, slightly gray, with warm brown eyes, soft-spoken, and heavy-set. When he learned of our itinerary, he told me through Aslam:

"You must not go to Andkhui alone. An ordinary car cannot get through. I'll give you a jeep escort for half the distance and arrange for the *Farmandar* of Andkhui to meet you with a jeep escort for the other half."

He moved at once into action, putting in a telephone call and buzzing for secretaries who came running.

He said goodbye to me solicitously as if I were a brother going on a long and dangerous journey.

In half an hour the jeep escort appeared at the hotel. It was in charge of a captain of the gendarmes; and it had in it six assistants in addition to the driver. The captain was about thirty, neat, tidy, and all business. He told us to go ahead and he would follow.

We no sooner got to the edge of town than we hit the loess dust. This is the same deposit we had difficulty with east of Pul-i-Khumri.

Loess is a fine-grained loam formation that forms soil of high fertility. Farmland belts of Europe have it. It covers a large part of our own Middle West. In Asia it starts in northwest China and sweeps toward the Middle East in a southwesterly direction. The loess of Central Asia is in the main a wind-blown deposit formed under arid conditions. The deserts of northwest China have been scoured for ages by the wind. And they carry this dust that is fine as face powder hundreds of miles, depositing it over a vast domain. It is often deposited on the lee of rocks and ridges and is shaped like fine snow after a blizzard. I've seen it in Central

Asia whipped along the ground by a fierce wind, the whole earth seeming to move as the fine dust swirls at ankle level. The wind takes this loess and forms hills. The lines of the hills follow a jet stream and have indeed wind-swept curves. For years a low mound accumulates loess, catching a bit more than it loses, until it grows several hundred feet in height. Desert plants take hold and the surface and the hill stop moving. These centuries of work involve gales without number, thousands of tons of earth moved on the wings of the wind, the delicate shaping of mounds into hillocks and hillocks into small ranges. Then a slight change in the course of the wind or a fracture in the loess deposit produces a weak spot where the wind picks up the deposit and the loess goes whining on south to leave a lone pinnacle.

We were to see many of these exotic forms of loess deposits between Shibarghan and Bala Murghab to the west. But our immediate interest was not the geological oddities created by this wind but the deep loose loess on the road before us. In a mile our wheels were slipping and spinning in dust six inches deep. Soon we were in loess dust up to a foot deep. The road was wide, showing the endeavors of many drivers to escape the slippery loess by turning out from a deep hole or making a new track on the side. The result was a dust road four lanes wide, each one as treacherous and as slippery as the others. Aslam was always steering to a far side where desert scrub was catching hold, in an attempt to find traction. Sometimes it was successful; more often it was not. Over and again we had to back up a few yards to keep out of a dangerous drift and make a new start. All the while we were weaving, as the rear wheels caught the slippery dust just right and skidded.

Since there was a strong head wind blowing, I noticed the jeep stayed a mile behind to be free of our dust. We could be free of it by moving. Yet once we slowed down or stopped, we were enveloped. The dust created quite a problem apart from the difficulty of driving. We found that it penetrated every package, every suitcase. It sifted through zippers and drifted into camera cases. It even penetrated the lenses of our cameras and got into the working mechanism. We fought loess dust on the road and in our baggage all the way across northern Afghanistan.

We drove for perhaps an hour on the dusty plain northwest

of Shibarghan. We averaged not over fifteen miles an hour; but apart from backing and filling we never stopped and never got stuck. There are a few small rivers that run off the northern slopes of the distant mountains to the south—the western spur of the Hindu Kush known as the Paropamisus. Their meager waters irrigate Shibarghan. For miles we saw nothing but melons and cucumbers flourishing in the rich loess. Then we climbed a bit and came to rougher country. The farming now was in winter wheat presently being harvested with hand sickles. We had come to a large stretch of it extending on both sides of us when the road narrowed to one lane. Here the ground was full of hummocks and it was impossible to detour. The oil trucks had pounded this one lane fiercely. They had dug ruts that measured eighteen inches deep. We stopped to survey the situation and knew that this stretch could be negotiated by the car Ali only if it rode the edge of the road and the center strip. I suggested that we all walk but Aslam, and then abandoned the idea when I saw that these ruts stretched as far as I could see.

We backed up a bit to get a good run at the high center strip. The start was propitious, for we rode the two high strips easily. But we soon realized we had to go at a fast speed to keep on them. Once we slowed down the wheels started to slip sidewise in the dust. That meant holding the car close to thirty miles an hour. Aslam did the best he could. But it was a cruel, rough ride. The two high strips had potholes of their own. We rocked back and forth, up and down as we raced along; and it seemed the station wagon would shake to pieces.

It was obvious we could not do this mile on end. It was sheer luck to get over some sections. At points the high center strip narrowed to a few inches. Here we always slithered to one side and rescued ourselves only by gunning the motor. Once we slithered too far and in a flash were astride the center pieces, our wheels spinning.

We waited for the jeep escort. The shovel we bought in Kabul came into use as the seven men from the jeep went to work. By digging away the obstruction of the center piece and lifting and pushing, they got the car up on the side of the road. It took nearly an hour. But the impossible was achieved. Aslam now drove the car along the side of the road for a few yards until he found a depression where once more he got it back onto the center strip. Again we started down this treacherous road of deep loess dust. We raced the motor to keep our speed close to thirty miles an hour. Our narrow escapes were too numerous to count. The dust seemed to be getting more and more slippery. Now the ruts were two and even three feet deep. We fairly flew over them, Aslam hanging onto the wheel for dear life and shouting, "Grease pit, grease pit." We were indeed on the rim of a grease pit; and in less than a half hour we were in the grease pit again. This time we were badly stuck, the car being almost crosswise of the highway.

My seven good Afghan friends from the jeep piled out and went to work once more. They tried to use the jeep as a rescue car. But that idea did not work. The solution was in the muscles of the Afghan crew whom the *Farmandar* had sent with me. They had to dig the car out and move it by lifting—inch by inch. It took over an hour to get it pushed and lifted back onto the center strip.

By this time the sun was high and it was well over 120°F. Mercedes, Mary, and I sought refuge for a while in the jeep. But that was too warm. So I put on my straw sombrero to investigate a field of wheat running up to a mud house. The wheat was being cut by hand sickles in this searing sun and taken in bundles to a thrashing floor where cattle, driven by a boy, were pulling a sled around and around the floor to separate the wheat. As I started across the field, a man in his twenties came down to meet me, carrying a small bundle of wheat in his arms. He had distinct Mongol features; he wore a tall brimless felt hat; his clothes were a brown garment that he slipped over his head. He beamed at me and bowed, holding out the bundle of grain. I had learned that it is an old Afghan custom to offer tokens of the grain harvest to travelers in expectation of a gratuity. I was not able to discover its origin. I conformed to custom and gave this chap five afghanis (ten cents), which made his eyes dance. We talked briefly in Persian and he returned to the field, apparently unimpressed by the efforts of eight men to get the station wagon out of the ruts.

Once more we had the slippery center piece to travel. But we had not gone more than two miles before the road leveled out and we took such wide detours as we chose to avoid ruts and potholes.

We came to a height of land where a mud house stood on the left. Here we stopped, for this was the gendarme station of Andkhui. It was here our jeep escort turned back and we picked up a new one, this time a truck. I shook hands with each of the eight men in the jeep, thanking them for their great help. The rest of the trip to Andkhui was an anticlimax. The loess roads were treacherous; but we had seen the worst. We skidded and weaved back and forth. But we never got stuck and arrived in windblown Andkhui about 3:30 P.M.

The people in Andkhui live in a constant dust storm during the summer months. It shows in their faces and clothes. The town is grimy. Even the leaves of the trees do not show bright green, for they are loaded with silt. The town has the feeling of grimness about it. There are only a few trees. It's a town of perhaps 10,000 people housed in very unattractive mud homes. The people are mostly Turkmen. They wear the tall, black karakul hat even in the heat of summer. They are kin to the Turkmen I saw in Ashkabad when I visited Soviet Central Asia in 1955. Some speak Persian; most of them speak Turki. They are Moslems; they have Turkish ancestors; they have the dark, swarthy complexion of the Turks; and they are mostly tall and angular.

There is some cotton and winter wheat grown in Andkhui. But the main crop is karakul. Andkhui is the karakul center of Afghanistan. This species of sheep produce lambs who are slaughtered within thirty days of their birth for their curly skins. These skins, which cost (uncured) thirty-six to forty dollars each in America, sell for about five dollars each in the bazaar at Andkhui. And a skillful merchant can, if he is honest, quickly sort through great burlap bags of these skins, picking out three dozen that will match when made up into a lady's coat.

Andkhui for its dust, dryness, and heat reminded me much of the Columbia River basin above McNary Dam. Our plan was to spend a day there. But we were to be deprived of that pleasure by a strange occurrence.

When we reached Andkhui, all bazaars were closed as this was the hour of the siesta. We looked and looked to find anyone whom we could ask about the hotel. We finally saw, coming into town on his burro, one forlorn Turkman who gave us the direction. From a distance the hotel looks like a two-story building. When we reached it, we found that the hotel was built on a mound of dirt, the edifice being raised high in order to catch the breeze. As we drove into the yard, I saw a pool to the left surrounded by green grass and trees. I asked Aslam to find out if we could go for a swim. He inquired of the servant who came running on our approach and, when the servant answered, Aslam laughed.

"That pool is the cistern where water is caught in the rainy season. It's all they have to drink."

The hotel has a small orchard of quince and figs where we parked the car in the shade. It has thirty-eight steps leading up to the entrance. A balcony runs completely around the building; and every room opens onto the balcony. There is no running water. The toilet is a hole in the floor with gigantic molds of footprints in concrete showing where the feet are to rest. A servant poured cool water over our hands into a basin as we washed. And we were served in a half hour a nice luncheon of rice *pilau,* eggplant, *nan,* melon, and *chai.*

Then we stretched out for a nap.

This was to my thinking a delightful place. The town of Andkhui was a mile to the northeast. A brisk northeast wind blew. It had been beastly hot in the sun. But here in the shade it was cool. I took off my shoes, shirt, and trousers, pulled my cot over by the door that opened on the balcony, and settled down for a nap.

I had been asleep perhaps five minutes when I was awakened by loud knocking on the door. The head servant was there, talking to me in Turki. Obviously something important was brewing, for he was agitated. All sorts of thoughts ran through my mind. Perhaps the excitement of the servant had something to do with the disappearance of Peter Winant. Some thought he had been killed by Turkmen in and around Andkhui. Perhaps the servant had received a threat. These were my thoughts as I dressed hurriedly to find Aslam. I hated to wake him, for he was sleeping well. But I took him at once to the office of the hotel where three servants were jabbering. Aslam turned to me and said:

"There's a telephone call for you."

"From whom?"

"The Governor; that's why these men are excited."

I waited a moment while a servant jiggled the phone. Finally he handed the receiver to me and everyone very politely left the room.

The Governor of Maimana, the next province to the west, was on the phone. His name is Gholam Haider Adalat; and he speaks English well. He started by introducing himself and welcoming me to Andkhui. Then he said with a voice full of concern:

"You must not stay in Andkhui tonight."

"But we are most comfortable," I added. "We like the hotel here."

"You must not stay there all night," he repeated.

"But, Governor, the place looks fine to me."

"I know but please believe me. Do not stay all night."

"Where shall we go?" I asked.

"Come to Maimana," he said. "It's only eighty-eight miles." And then he added quickly:

"But I want you to come at once. It's a four-hour drive. If you leave at once you can be here at eight-thirty or nine o'clock. I'll meet you halfway. I do not want you at Andkhui tonight or on the highway either. I want you with me."

I explained that we were tired. We had come 141 miles over miserable roads since morning. I told him that Mercedes had been ill. I said we were all worn out.

"Can't we see you tomorrow, Governor?" I asked.

"Tonight. You must come now."

"All right, we'll come," I replied.

"I'll meet you at seven o'clock at Faizabad with a guard," he answered.

The ladies were in rebellion when I broke the news. They too liked Andkhui and wanted to explore it. But Peter Winant had disappeared somewhere near here; and Governor Adalat was concerned. His concern set us a bit on edge as we repacked the car and prepared to head south to Maimana, long known on the ancient Silk Route as Joez-jon.

We first had to get gasoline. We had seen a station on the outskirts of town so we went there. But it was closed. Aslam saw a gendarme and hailed him. Off they went in a jeep to return in five minutes with the sleepy Turkmen proprietor, who unlocked the pump. These Afghan pumps are different from any I have seen. There are two glass containers at the top of the pump. The operator fills one by working the pump handle back and forth. When it is filled, he turns an iron handle which allows the full container to drain into the hose. By the time that container is empty the other one is full; the handle then is turned back so the gas can drain, and so on. This takes time; and there is no automatic count of the gallons dispensed. The proprietor and the car owner usually chant the number together.

We were in the midst of the chant when a bus drew up for gas, showering us with dust. Afghan busses are usually painted as gaily as those in our circus parades. This one was blue and white with fancy designs and a parrot painted on the back. They are always filled inside. A rack about four feet high runs around the top where the baggage is carried. And it is common to see the top also filled with people.

While we waited for gas, an oil tank truck went by. It was a Russian diesel headed south. There must have been twenty Afghans riding it. They sat precariously on the rounded tank top, hanging on as best they could as the truck hit deep ruts in the road. We had seen many trucks so loaded.

Through Aslam I asked the Turkmen gas pump owner who the travelers were.

"People traveling to Kabul," he replied.

"Why don't they take the bus?"

"It only runs once or twice every week. The tankers run every day."

"But here's a bus heading south. It looks more comfortable than a gas truck."

The Turkman grinned, showing lovely teeth.

"Yes, but it costs very little to ride the trucks—fifty afghanis (one dollar) at the most. Maybe twenty-five afghanis. If you know the truck driver it may cost nothing."

"Why do the bus companies allow this kind of competition?"

He shrugged his shoulders, saying, "What can they do? The money goes to the truck driver. He may lose his job, yes. But probably not. You see, there are not many truck drivers in our country."

CHAPTER 10

AN ENTERPRISING AND FRIENDLY GOVERNOR

For the first two hours out of Andkhui the road was so rough we never once got above five miles an hour. This was the worst washboard road I ever did see. It was loess and rocks. The wind kept up. It was now in our rear, enveloping us in clouds of dust. There were green patches by a creek where a few karakul sheep grazed. A few black tents dotted the horizon. Now and then an irrigated melon patch showed up. But the greenery had been overwhelmed by loess dust. Then night fell. I have no idea of this sixty-mile stretch we covered in the dark except the potholes, the ruts, the washboard, and the loess dust.

We were an hour and a half late reaching Faizabad. It was indeed after eight o'clock when we saw a flashlight ahead waving us down. This was the Governor and a gendarme, who had been waiting for us since dusk.

Governor Adalat greeted me like a long-lost brother. I asked him if trouble had been brewing in Andkhui. I inquired if he had delivered us from a trouble spot. He merely grinned and squeezed my hand, saying:

"It's better that you folks stay with me."

He later talked with me about Peter Winant. He had investigated the case at length and made his report. His conclusion was that Peter Winant had crossed the Russian border and disappeared. But press him as I did, I never learned the cause of his anxiety about our staying in Andkhui all night.

Governor Adalat was a perfect host, a symbol of the best in Afghan hospitality. He would not lead the way to Maimana. He insisted that we go first so that we would be free of his dust. He, of course, offered us tea at Faizabad. But we preferred to get to our beds in Maimana. So we went on without stopping, arriving there about ten o'clock.

The Governor's house at Maimana is a huge two-story residence with a spacious walled garden as big as several city lots. In the dark we could not see the pinks, geraniums, and morning glories that lined the walks. All we saw was the corner of the garden under a huge plane tree where beautiful Afghan rugs had been laid on the lawn. A table was laden with food; there were comfortable chairs and sofas; and the entire corner was brilliantly illuminated by electric bulbs.

We washed up in a lavatory in the house and joined the Governor on the lawn. The servants brought pitchers of ice water, all previously boiled, according to the Governor. So we drank literally quarts of it. We were too tired to do more than nibble on the delicious fried chicken which was served. And we excused ourselves almost at once, for we had had a long hard day.

The hotel is in a compound next to the Governor's home. It is commodious, airy, and clean. A cool wind was blowing; and this night we slept nearly nine hours without waking.

We sat for several hours after breakfast in the Governor's garden, visiting with him, meeting his wife and children, and two other ladies who were relatives, and taking photographs. These ladies are of course in *purdah* like all Afghan women.

In Afghanistan *purdah* extends to every public appearance of a woman. As I have said, on the streets they all wear *chadhris*. According to the Afghan women I met, *chadhris* are very uncomfortable and very awkward for shopping. As a result, most Afghan men do the shopping in the bazaar for food. That was Aslam's main complaint against *purdah*. Throughout the trip he kept saying, "I wish *purdah* would end so my wife could do the shopping." Women do not of course wear the *chadhri* in their homes or gardens. But even there, they put it on if strange men are present. So it was a privilege—a rare one—for us to meet Afghan women socially without the *chadhri.*

But after Governor Adalat had introduced his ladies, he added, "Would you forgive me if I ask you not to use any photographs you take of my wife?"

I promised.

He went on to say, "You see, our people would not understand. Some might think improper things about my wife. Some might even demand that I be removed from office."

Adalat brought out a Polaroid camera that he had never used and could not work. He had but one roll of film; and without an instruction book I did not dare risk spoiling it. We worked a half hour on it without solving the mystery. He would have to await the instruction book I later sent by air.

Adalat sent to the bazaar for a merchant and ordered several dozen matched karakul skins. The merchant was honest, he assured me, so we made a selection and settled with the Governor in dollars for what we owed the merchant in afghanis.

Adalat brought out three karakul skins for each of us—skins suitable for making the Afghan brimless hat that is so comfortable in winter and exotic in appearance.

Adalat is an enterprising official, doing heroic work in perhaps the remotest of Afghanistan's ten provinces. This is mostly an agricultural province—corn, wheat, a soybean type of vegetable, birdseed, and karakul skins. The Governor is a man of action. His roads are the best I saw in Afghanistan. He is building good bridges and culverts. His road scrapers are everywhere. He has built a fine hospital in Maimana and two schools for girls through the twelfth grade. He has established stonemasonry as a trade in his prisons, bringing marble from the Paropamisus for the prisoners to work. The articles he showed us were quite nice. He is trying to develop cottage industries in Maimana. The Governor had only high praise for the Russian road machinery and for the Russian trucks and jeeps. His prize was the jeep he met us in at Faizabad, a Russian model. And after breakfast he suggested we take a ride in it.

Adalat's idea was to show us a village where rugs are handwoven. It was Shakh, which is off the main road we were to follow to Bala Murghab, our next night's stand. We would follow the Governor in his jeep and leave our car on the main road and travel twenty miles to Shakh, which lies in the foothills of the Paropamisus.

We did not leave Maimana until ten o'clock. I rode with Adalat and his young sons in his jeep. Mercedes, Mary, and Aslam followed in Ali.

Unknown to us, the Governor had telephoned ahead, ordering lunch at the village of Qaisar, thirty-seven miles west of Maimana. We stopped at the gate of the *Farmandar's* residence and walked through a garden deep in the shade of tall willows to a rug on the lawn, set for a luncheon.

There was broiled chicken, *mawst,* rice, lamb, *nan,* and *chai.* There was also *doogh,* a dish formed by mixing water with *mawst.* This day the cook had added a few chopped cucumbers; and I almost disgraced myself drinking *doogh,* for it was very tasty and refreshing. The Governor's four young sons were with us; and they wanted to learn English. So I gave them a few elementary lessons that they absorbed quickly. The others, knowing I was a lawyer and judge, brought the conversation around to law. We discussed the law of the Koran, civil law, common law. Finally an aide to the Governor—a serious young man—asked:

"What would happen in the United States if one Siamese twin committed a crime? Could the other be punished?"

Treating the question as a joke, I replied that I did not have any lawbooks with me.

"But, being a judge, you know all the answers."

"The case has never arisen in America so far as I know."

"That's no excuse. In Afghanistan every *mullah* knows the answer to any legal problem no matter if it has never arisen," was the reply.

So, not to be outdone by the *mullahs,* I answered:

"Guilt is personal in the United States. In case of imprisonment both would of necessity have to go to jail. But if a sentence could be devised (such as a fine) that could be imposed on the guilty one alone, that would be the remedy."

By this time the Governor's face was beaming. "That's the law of the Koran," he said. And he went on to emphasize that doubtless Afghanistan and America were much closer together than people ever dreamed.

The luncheon and the lessons in English and in law consumed about two hours. Leaving the Governor's sons there, we hurried on to the crossroad leading to Shakh and parked our car on a village street lined with trees that touched in the middle. Then we all got in the jeep and went pell-mell over roads our car never could have negotiated. The great peaks of the Paropamisus were in the distance. None of these were snow-capped but they were rich in foliage and slightly purple in the haze. They are the home of grouse, deer, and ibex. Lower down are gazelle and antelope. In the valley around Shakh are wild boar and partridge. The lowlands are irrigated by innumerable streams coming off the mountains.

We crossed a low range of hills through a V-shaped pass and came at once on the green valley of Shakh. Poplar and white willow of great proportions lined the roads. The air was filled with black birds that swooped and chattered the entire hour of our visit there.

Our host was Mohammed Yusoff, an elderly turbaned man with a black Vandyke beard. He is a large landowner with the largest house in Shakh—a two-story stone house with an upstairs balcony. We went there first to have tea. Coming into the courtyard, I saw an arbor heavy with golden grapes. We had not been long on the balcony before I saw a servant washing these grapes in a ditch, not realizing that the grapes were more sanitary before rather than afterward. They came to us dripping wet and were as sweet as Afghanistan produces.

Shakh, like most Asian villages, has its farmland separate from the houses. The farmers live together in the village, not on their separate tracts. After tea and much photographing, we walked across the village to the courtyard of a farm family where rugs were being made. Shakh is famous for the *maimouri* rug—not the best that Afghanistan produces but excellent in quality. The women do the weaving. The skill is passed down on the mother's side of the family. The loom lies flat on a porch. The weavers sit at one end, making the innumerable knots that add up to a rug. The women spin the yarn. Men dye it. The rug patterns are not many. But each is faithful to a master design that rests in cardboard on the porch. This afternoon two young girls did the weaving. They were rather gaily dressed, one in red and one in blue and each wearing an embroidered skullcap. Their mother was not present; only men filled the courtyard. The head man—the one who apparently was the father of the girls—was dressed in loose white trousers and shirt over which he wore a striped coat open at the front. He wore a scraggly black beard and a small black skullcap. The two young girls wove with great speed, their eyes never looking up once. I suspected they had been drafted for the occasion and did not enjoy the flash pictures I took. For they never smiled or relaxed. They acted as if they were doing a command performance against their will.

The women and girls keep at this work in all their spare time the year around. There is no maximum-hour law that stands in the way. These rugs are the chief cash crop of Shakh. They sell up to 2400 afghanis ($48) per square meter.

CHAPTER 11

BATS IN THE DINING ROOM

By the time we got back to the highway from Shakh it was six o'clock and we had close to a hundred miles to go to reach Bala Murghab. We had before us another stretch of night driving that I did not look forward to with any pleasure. We were, indeed, to get plenty of excitement from it before the night was over, and rich dividends too.

There is some irrigated land in this part of Afghanistan. The water is not piped across the highways; there are no neatly covered culverts; there is only an open ditch. We inched across a few of them, scraping bottom. Then we came to one that was too deep for that kind of maneuvering. We got out and built runways of flat rocks and sent Aslam over them with the car. The front wheels made the crossing but the rear wheels slithered off into the ditch. Mercedes got out the jack and after raising the rear end we rebuilt the runway and finally made the crossing.

This stretch of land in western Maimana is mostly sheep country. Some who live in villages during the winter move to the country in the summer and set up tents and plant melons, growing them by dry-farming methods. We saw many of the melon patches, as we headed for Bala Murghab. Most of the people, however, run sheep. Their tents are mostly the round *yurt*, either black or brown, though some have the traditional black tent. Fires were glowing in front of these *yurts* and tents as we drove by. Each band of sheep has several dogs. They stand as high as a

German shepherd but they are heavier and longer. In appearance they look like a gigantic husky. They are a ferocious dog, as we were to discover. They invariably charged the car with a frenzy I had never before seen. Until darkness came we saw dozens of *yurts* and many, many dogs. While the people waved, the dogs barked. We made no stops as it was too dark for pictures and I dreaded this night on Afghan roads.

As we traveled west we gradually climbed. The pull on the motor was noticeable. The poor quality of the Russian gasoline was beginning to be apparent, for the motor now had a great knock. The engine was heating up. Finally we decided we should pull over to the side of the road, turn the car into the wind, cool the engine, and fill the radiator. We hated to do it, for we had worked hard to pass two trucks. We did not want to eat their dust again. But we stopped anyway; and in a few minutes the two trucks passed.

It was now eight o'clock and dark. The trucks no sooner passed than they were swallowed up. But we could hear them in the distance shift gears and begin to labor hard. I could barely make out the dim outline of an escarpment or low hill ahead. The trucks seemed to take an endless time to get up it. Our turn came next; and we no sooner started than we were sorry the two trucks were not behind us. Once more we hit deep, slippery loess dust. The escarpment was, indeed, a hill of loess. A one-lane road had been dug through it. There were only two or three feet of clearance on each side. The pounding of the trucks had worn deep ruts in the road. Aslam tried to ride the center strip as we did east of Andkhui. But there was not enough clearance on the side. We were doomed to the ruts. Soon the axle began to scrape. In a few seconds we were hung high, our wheels spinning.

The three of us got out and by pushing we got the car back a few feet. Aslam started again without the passengers. He got stuck at the same place. He got out and we all had a conference. The only thing to do was to unload the car completely, take the empty car up the narrow canyon, and carry the baggage to the top. How long a carry it would be, no one knew.

Before unloading, I took the portable spotlight we had, turned it on, and sat it on a ledge of the canyon wall so that it pointed into the valley behind us. This spotlight was given us by our friend Abe Fortas of Washington, D.C. At the time we received it, it looked like a real excess luxury to carry to Asia. Tonight I could have hugged Abe for it. This spotlight was not only strong; it also had a unique feature. An auxiliary red light on it was worked by a flasher. So we had a red flashing light as well as a white spotlight working for us in this remote dark, dusty Afghan canyon.

It was difficult finding ledges for all of our equipment—safe places where our things would not roll. As I worked, I thought of the Americans killed in Iran in 1957 by the famous bandit, Dadshah. Kevin M. Carroll and Brewster A. Wilson had been shot down in cold blood as they traveled by jeep. Carroll's pretty wife, Anita, had been captured by Dadshah and later killed. These were some of the thoughts in my mind as I unloaded the station wagon in the dark. I also thought of Peter Winant. At whose cruel hands did he perish? I thought of the uniform advice I had received. *Never travel at night.* Criminals are in every country; and those who travel by night flout needed protection in the Middle East.

I felt uneasy and derelict, especially on account of the women. So when I turned to find myself surrounded by men—two, four, six, eight—my heart missed a beat. I had no idea where they had come from. They had appeared silently and swiftly and without any warning. I was certain that this was the end; that bandits, much publicized since the murder of the Carrolls and Wilson in Iran, had finally caught up with us.

Acting as coolly as I could, I took the spotlight from the ledge and very impolitely shoved it in the faces of these men. They were grimy, dusty, grinning Afghans—all eight of them.

"Salaam," they said in greeting.

They had arrived out of the dark road without Aslam seeing them. So I called him. They greeted Aslam as an old friend.

"They are the crews from the two trucks up ahead," Aslam said. "They've come to help us."

The eight Afghans went to work at once, finishing the unloading and piling the baggage on the side of the road. Then they got behind the car and invoked the aid of the Imam said to be buried at the shrine at Mazar-i-Sharif. Crying, "Ali, Ali, Ali," they pushed while Aslam steered. After several false starts, Ali the car got going and disappeared in great clouds of dust around a bend up the narrow canyon.

Mercedes, Mary, and I were left with the eight Afghans. They silently loaded most of the baggage on their shoulders and started up the canyon. The youngest had the heaviest package of all, the box of tools and spare parts (weighing eighty pounds) and a duffel bag. Each man had at least two parcels or bags. They all disappeared up the canyon; the ladies followed with smaller parcels; and I brought up the rear. Before we reached the top, which was a half mile off, the Afghans returned for a second trip. I returned with them; and this time we got everything. They insisted on loading the car and helping us lash the baggage on the rack on top.

Then they stood around laughing and joking with Aslam. I was overwhelmed by this act of kindness and rummaged through my jacket looking for afghanis to pay these men. I assembled fifty afghanis (one dollar) each for them and started to hand it out. Each and every one of them refused. I said:

"In America I would expect to pay for this road service. I want to pay in Afghanistan."

The oldest of the eight, the driver of one truck, spoke up. He had high cheekbones and a small mustache.

"In our country," he said, "we take care of each other. Every truck stops at the top of a hill to see if anyone is coming. If someone is coming, we wait to see if he needs help. We cannot take pay for it. We saw your lights and waited for you. That's all. We all do it for each other. If we got stuck, you'd help us."

I remonstrated, saying we were strangers and most grateful.

He replied, "All the more reason we should help you."

Once more I tendered the money. Once again each refused. Finally I said, "Here are a hundred afghanis. There is a teahouse ahead. Will you for me stop and drink *chai* for Afghan-American friendship?"

They broke into cheers as I gave the money to the young man who had carried the heaviest box up the dusty canyon. Then they waited for us to pull out ahead of them.

This episode set me thinking. We of the West have grown impersonal in our relations. Apartment houses, big cities, corporations, automobiles have made us that way. We tend to turn our backs on neighbors and live apart. When we settled the West we had house-raising and barn-raising bees. We chipped in and helped each other in emergencies. Civilization, so called, has carried us beyond these amenities. We are, of course, very dependent one on another. But we live aloof and remote from each other, except as we meet *en masse* on TV, radio, at a sports stadium, or in the subway. People are closer to each other in Afghanistan. Their survival depends on it. The countryside is friendlier than anything we have known for a century. Friendly Afghanistan, though backward in some respects, is far advanced in others.

"*Staray mashy* [May you never be tired]" and "*Kwar mashy* [May you never be poor]" had new meaning for me tonight.

There was dust from the tail wind all the way to Bala Murghab and so many ruts that our speed was cut down. But we had no more difficulty and pulled into the yard of the hotel close to midnight. Three bareheaded unshaven men, dressed in brown and green gowns tied at the waist with a sash, met us with lanterns at the door. A gendarme had been assigned to watch the car. We took in at first only our overnight bags. But once I examined the rooms, I returned for the sleeping bags. The bedding crawled with vermin. We dumped it unceremoniously in the hall, blew up air mattresses, and placed them and our sleeping bags on the iron cots.

The toilet at Andkhui had been a slit in the floor. Here it was a wooden box set in the middle of the room. The wash water was in a big metal tank, filled by hand, that emptied by faucet into a tin bathtub. The chairs were decrepit. The flies were thick even in lamplight. The dining room was a gloomy place with a tablecloth badly soiled. Two candles furnished the light, as lamb, rice, *mawst, nan,* and *chai* were served. Soon Mercedes gave a scream. What I thought was a shadow caused by the flickering candlelight was a bat circling the room. Soon the dining room was filled with bats. The women ducked as a bat came by, holding their hands over their hair. I excused myself and got the spotlight with the red light. Turning on the flasher, I set the light on the table. The flashing red light kept the bats away while the ladies raced through dinner.

The bats took their appetites away and they retired early. But

I sat up late, talking with a *mullah* who appeared as dinner was served. His name is Asadullah and he's a judge of a trial court in Bala Murghab. He is in his thirties. He was turbaned and wore a short beard. He speaks a little English.

Like Shafik Kamawi, whom I met in Kabul, this *mullah* is bright, earnest, and dedicated. Both he and Shafik are progressive men who know that the Koran, to be ageless, must have a great degree of adaptability, that literalness kills the spirit.

This night in the gloomy dining room of Bala Murghab, I got new insight into the Moslem dream of justice. It's a dream that differs in form and detail from our own. But it has common ground with us in the essentials. While the bats filled the room, Asadullah completed Shafik's account and showed me the golden threads that run through the fabrics of his system of justice and our own.

This day, July 19, 1957, though long and dusty and wearing, was one continuous adventure in friendship.

CHAPTER 12

WE ARE ATTACKED

It was cool and bright the next morning. Bala Murghab by daylight is more attractive than the bat-filled dining room made it seem the night before. It's a village of mud huts located on the Chichaktu River which runs through a rather deep loess gorge near the city. I walked along this gorge while Aslam went looking for gasoline and met many early risers among the natives. Veiled women came down in numbers to get water from the river in their earthen jars. At one point along the embankment I saw some ladies washing the huge baggy trousers Afghan men wear. They had waistlines wide enough to encompass several men. I was reminded of Marco Polo's description of women's dress when he passed this way:

"A peculiar fashion of dress prevails among the women of the superior class, who wear below their waists, in the manner of drawers, a kind of garment, in the making of which they employ, according to their means, an hundred, eighty, or sixty ells of fine cotton cloth; which they also gather or plait, in order to increase the apparent size of their hips; those being accounted the most handsome who are the most bulky in that part."

If an ell is taken conservatively at thirty inches, these dresses Marco Polo described would stretch out a hundred and fifty feet. While he might have exaggerated, as the Venetians thought, he was describing dresses that have vast proportions compared with anything we know, even to this day. How wide a woman's dress might be, I do not know. But I measured men's trousers which, when doubled, extended twelve feet at the waist.

Men sat high on the bank of the Chichaktu, singing. Some sang solos. When I stopped to photograph one, a small crowd gathered. Soon several men joined the singer and gave me a rousing Afghan song that had Turkmen overtones. Bala Murghab is only a few miles from Turkmenistan in Soviet Russia. The Turkish cultural influence here is still strong. But as I scanned the faces of the men who lined the bluff this bright morning, I saw more than Turkmen; I saw Uzbeks, Kazakhs, and other Mongol influences too. The Hindu Kush had long separated this part of Afghanistan from Kabul's influence. This was country which for centuries had been beholden either to those who lived in the Russian zone or to the Persians.

Bala Murghab has an elevation of about 2000 feet. Our next stop, Qal'eh Nau, is about 4000 feet. The road between follows a winding valley, narrowing at points to canyons and climbing all the way. Up this canyon we saw dozens of *yurts* and black tents. There were many sheep, some goats, and a few camels. Every sheep camp had big vicious Afghan dogs to guard the herd; and invariably these dogs chased the car. I worked hard to get a good picture of a dog lunging at us. I stepped up the speed of my lens and leaned out the window, trying to get the charging beast in focus. Sometimes a cloud of fine loess dust enveloped me or the dog at the wrong time. Once the dog got perilously close when Aslam, looking over his shoulder, shouted from the front seat:

"Look out the dog does not grab you."

He went on to tell how these dogs sometimes grabbed elbows that protruded from moving car windows. They are trained to do battle with the enemy. The chief enemy is the wolf that lives in northern Afghanistan and raids the sheep at nighttime. These dogs, they say, can whip a wolf. But these dogs do not differentiate between men and wolves. They come at strangers with a vengeance and can easily kill a man. They have, indeed, an instinct for the jugular. They are trained to be mean. Their ears are cut when they are young. The ears are not clipped for style, they are cut down to the quick to remove a hold a wolf might get on the animal in a fight. And the ear that is cut off is fed to the young pup in the hope that the animal will realize that the world into which it was born is a cruel one, demanding viciousness above all else. The dogs we saw exuded ferocity. They chased the car when it first appeared on a rise in the road, running a mile or more to catch us. Even after we passed, the dogs stayed in pursuit sometimes for a half mile. I never got close enough to one of these animals to pat him. But I often wondered as they came roaring alongside the car how much time and kindness it would take to tame their wild character. Not far out from Qal'eh Nau we got stuck again. We were going up a steep hill made up primarily of loess dust. Two roads were available; we chose the one on the left. It was smooth travel for half the way. Then the deep ruts started. Aslam was doing well behind the wheel, riding the center strip. But the ground was so bumpy, he had to slow his speed. That was fatal, for the wheels at once sideslipped; and we ended in the ruts, the axle resting on the center strip.

We got out the shovel and went to work, our only hope being to back the car down and start over. We were still hard at it when a truck came over the brow of the hill toward us. It took the other road and soon was opposite us. Then it stopped and six men piled out.

These Afghan trucks have at least two helpers, sometimes more. Each helper has a great wedge-shaped block of wood about two feet long and fifteen inches deep at the thick end. This wedge is usually on a handle. The helpers slip the wedges under the wheels of the truck when it stops. Busses too have the same device. Brakes are not trusted to hold heavy vehicles on Afghan hills.

Two men slipped wedges under the wheels of the truck that had stopped and all six men came to us, laughing and joking. They had great fun with Aslam as they teased him about his predicament. But they went to work at once. First they took off their shoes and coats and piled them neatly by the side of the road. Then, using our shovel, they got the axle off the high center strip; and with much pushing and much invocation of the help of Ali, they got the car moving. Soon Aslam had good traction and away he went without stopping to the brow of the hill, a mile distant.

I tried to pay these goodhearted men, as they put on their shoes and coats. But they turned down my offering with smiles and thanks. Once more I was overwhelmed by the helpfulness of the people who travel the highways of Afghanistan. We had been warned that we would meet bandits. Instead we had met only good Samaritans.

Qal'eh Nau had been our destination for the night before; but the long visit with Governor Adalat had put us behind schedule, with the result that instead of spending the night at Qal'eh Nau we had lunch there.

The town is a neat and tidy place; the streets, though paved, are in pleasant shade from trim trees that line the avenues; the gardens behind the mud walls are well maintained. The town is indeed lush and green from the plentiful water supply coming down from the Paropamisus. The hotel is as nice a place as any we saw except the one at Pul-i-Khumri. It's a two-story affair with a balcony off the upper rooms. The garden behind the courtyard walls has pine trees for shade; and cannas, nasturtiums, morning glories, and goldenrod adorn the beds. The rooms were clean and pleasant and the bathroom so attractive I decided on a bath with special emphasis on a shampoo to rid my hair of the pounds of dust that seemed to have gathered there. Lunch of chicken, *mawst, nan,* and *chai* was served on the balcony. We ordered an extra roast chicken to eat along the way, for a study of the road map strongly suggested we take our own food for dinner. To reach Herat by dinnertime we would have had to leave Qal'eh Nau by nine o'clock. It was now 1 P.M.

I was anxious to move on as soon as we had eaten. But Aslam brought word that the *Farmandar,* Abdul Baki, of Qal'eh Nau was anxious to meet us; that he had indeed sent word to detain us until he could come. He had been high in the hills on some mission and did not arrive until close to three o'clock. He is a young man about thirty, quite dapper and efficient and typical of the fine public servant Afghanistan is developing these days.

There was a note of concern in Baki's voice. He was worried about our safety. I pressed him for a reason; and at the mention of Peter Winant his face clouded with anxiety. What end he thought Peter Winant met I could not discover. He was most solicitous that no harm befall us. So he advised me that a jeep would follow us all that day until we reached the summit of Zarmast Pass of the Paropamisus. From there on he thought we would be in no danger.

We left at once and had no sooner quit the city and reached the countryside than we saw a Turkmen family on donkeys going our way. The women were not veiled and they were gaily dressed with blue coats and colorful headdress. We felt we had been cheated of Turkmen pictures along Afghan highways. We never photographed a person without his consent; and each Turkmen had invariably refused. Why, I did not know. They were friendly people. In Soviet Turkmenistan they were eager and co-operative. Here they had been shy and almost panicky. The same pattern reappeared as soon as Mercedes left the car with a camera to photograph this group. Up to then the family had been riding parallel with the road. Now they turned at an angle and went away from us. Mercedes ran after them across a field of stubble, shouting for them to wait. The faster she went the more they urged on their donkeys.

The guards in the jeep caught up with us while Mercedes was still in the field. I asked them why the Turkmen ran. Aslam, interpreting for me, said:

"These days all Turkmen run."

I asked why and the answer, though vague, again related to Peter Winant.

"Ask the guards what Peter Winant's disappearance has to do with the nervousness of the Turkmen," I said to Aslam.

He conversed with them for a few moments and then joined me to walk back to the car.

"They do not like to talk much about it. But in the search for Peter Winant most of these Turkmen were arrested and questioned. That's why they are so nervous and unfriendly."

We were still on a 4000-foot plateau running south of Qal'eh Nau. The Paropamisus loomed closer ahead. But we were still not in them. The *yurts* and black wool tents literally covered the valley and produced innumerable dogs that chased us.

As we rounded a hillock a very strange thing happened. Ahead of us a quarter mile was a sheep camp on the left. Other tents were scattered the length and width of the valley; but this was the closest one to the road. On the right were a few trees where some sheepherders were loafing. We no sooner rounded the hillock than a big red Afghan sheep dog came running toward us. He was coming in fast on the driver's side, not quite head on. I saw the animal leaping with the power of a lion as he cleared brush and ditches. As he reached the road he must have been going thirty miles an hour. He did not break his pace for any obstacle. Not even the steep pitch of the road's embankment seemed to slow him up. Now he was on the road itself. He did not stop like other dogs to bark at the wheels. He was not distracted for a second from his mission. When he was a half dozen feet from the car he lunged for Aslam, who was at the wheel. He came hurtling like a tiger through the air. His timing was perfect; his aim was excellent. But for one circumstance, Aslam today might be dead. For the last I saw, the dog was within inches of being in the car. At the last instant the ventilating window intervened. By happenstance it was open just far enough to form a small shield for the open window. The vicious dog hit that with his shoulder, shattering it into hundreds of pieces. That slight deflection broke the trajectory of the lunge. The body of the dog hit the side of the car just below Aslam's left elbow. The impact caused a tremendous thud. Aslam, visibly shaken, slowed down; and as the dust cleared I saw the red dog slinking away with a decided limp. If the dog had been killed, I would have stopped. For I had traveled Afghanistan enough to know that a sheepherder values his dog next to his family and his flock. These dogs are so valuable they are not for sale. Litters are distributed among friends. One must find his way to an Afghan's heart, not his pocket, to get one of these dogs.

"Kill an Afghan's dog," a friend had once told me in Kabul, "and he will follow you to the end of the earth."

We slowed down just long enough to discover that the dog was alive and then speeded up. After we had gone a quarter mile, I asked Aslam to stop.

"What about our water bags?"

Three of them, freshly filled at Qal'eh Nau with *ab jush,* hung on the side-view mirror on the left front door. When we looked, the side-view mirror and the water bags were gone. The ventilator window had deflected the lunge of the dog, causing his shoulder to hit the mirror. The power of the blow was so great that the mirror had been ripped completely off. It and the three water bags had dropped to the ground.

In a few moments the jeep caught up with us and I told the

gendarmes what had happened. Aslam and I got into the jeep and returned to the scene of the accident. Several Turkmen were gathered around under the trees. They disclaimed any knowledge of the water bags. The gendarmes went to the nearest tent and started their interrogation. They had interviewed three men, each of whom shook his head and proclaimed his innocence, when a bearded Turkman came out of the tent with one water bag. Getting the other two was like pulling teeth. He disclaimed all knowledge of the mirror. We went back to the road but could find no trace of it. Finally the gendarme in charge of the jeep shook his fist in the faces of the Turkmen and shouted:

"The man who owned this dog will be prosecuted for letting a dangerous animal run loose."

That pronouncement produced the mirror. A small girl came with it from around a black wool tent and gave it to the gendarme.

We were to have the ventilator window repaired and the rear-view mirror reinstated in Tehran. The damage to them was minor. But I could not get from my mind the picture of this fierce dog lunging for our window. Now every dog became a genuine hazard. We not only pulled in our elbows; we also rolled up our windows on every charge.

Finally that day the mystery of Peter Winant's disappearance was solved for me. This is theory only; and I have no evidence on which a verdict could be rendered. But I am convinced the young man and his fiancée were killed by dogs. They were on foot, hitchhiking their way across Afghanistan. Strangers who walk a road of northern Afghanistan are exposed to the full fury of these Afghan sheep dogs. They are powerful enough to kill a man. When Peter Winant and his fiancée were killed by dogs and the owner discovered the tragedy, he was panic-stricken. Murder is a heinous offense in Afghanistan. He would have difficulty proving he did not do it. Having a dog so ferocious as to kill a man was enough to send him to prison. In his panic the sheepherder, therefore, buried the bodies in a shallow grave. Perhaps others shared the secret; perhaps he alone. But no matter how long the gendarmes looked, no trace could be found. These two young people, walking Afghanistan with carefree hearts, lie in graves that never will be marked.

I cannot prove this. But I left Afghanistan convinced of it.

CHAPTER 13

"WHAT YOU LADIES DOING HERE?"

We climbed steeply and steadily, so much so that every five miles or so we turned the car into the wind, stopped the engine, lifted the hood, and cooled the motor. We were coming close to Zarmast Pass. *Yurts* and black tents were still numerous. The slopes were greener. Once in a while a few patches of cedar trees appeared.

The engine was not only heating up; it had a severe knock. I took the wheel for a short stretch and found that we had practically no power except in low gear. Even in low, we could barely make a horseshoe turn. The pitch was not severe, though the upgrade pull was steady. The roadbed had surprisingly improved. We were now on good dirt roads. Our difficulty was with the Russian gasoline. The octane was so low, we got little power from it. Moreover, we had been in Afghanistan for two weeks and our points and plugs were gumming up. After a trial run by one of the gendarmes, the prospect of the station wagon making Zarmast Pass with us as passengers seemed dim. He proposed that Aslam take the car up alone and the three of us ride the jeep.

We waited for two huge Russian diesel trucks, loaded with wool and headed east, to pass. Then we got Aslam off, and away he went for the five-mile run to the top. After picture taking in the long shadows of late afternoon, we followed in the jeep. This gendarme who took us was a daredevil at the wheel. I have never had a wilder ride in all my life.

When we got to the top we said goodbye and joined Aslam for sunset pictures. Zarmast Pass, which is 7774 feet high, means "a little green." This is an apt description, for it is not heavily wooded. It's open country dotted here and there with cedars. There are some springs and some slopes of grass. The rest is made up of shrubs and plants, the most conspicuous being edelweiss. Hundreds of acres of blue edelweiss were at our feet. There were still several dozen species of wild flowers left even though this was late July. I liked especially one with a tall yellow cone, one that the natives called the "foxtail." We took a few botanical specimens and a number of pictures of this vast expanse of alpine meadows. Now the sun was down and a bitter north wind was blowing. It was so cold that for the first time we had to keep all windows closed. I actually shivered and had to look for a coat.

It was still dusk when we came to a pleasant basin on the west slope of the pass, where we stopped to put on warmer clothes, wash up, and stretch our legs before the long pull to Herat. As I washed, I heard partridge calling, the bird the Afghans call the *coupk*. They are gray with red feet and a delicious white meat. I followed their call and climbed several hundred feet up the mountain. They went out ahead of me, never flying and always resuming their call when I stopped. There are white-tailed deer in the Paropamisus, and rabbits and wolves. Since there are not many people who can afford ammunition, game thrives here. Partridge are indeed in great abundance, not only the one I heard but also a bigger variety called *coupk-dere*.

The *yurts* and black tents increased in numbers as we dropped down from the pass. It was not yet dark when we came to a group of twenty to thirty, pitched to form a small village for the night. Each tent had a fire going. The people had seen us coming and they lined the road—men, women, and children. There must have been over a hundred gathered there to greet us. I asked Aslam to slow down; and everyone waved. Dogs that started out were called back. Greetings were shouted. I had a strong desire to stop the car and spend the night with these people. I had slept with mountain people before, sharing their camp and their food. They were always friendly and outgoing. Big copper bowls full of *mawst* were by the fire. Lamb was on skewers. Fires were dancing; the wind was high; the stars were beginning to come out. If I had been alone, the decision would have been easy. But I decided that the introduction, unannounced, of two Western women to an Afghan sheep camp might create great confusion. So I waved Aslam on and regret to this day that I did so.

Farther down there were camels grazing in open slopes.

Still farther down and just before darkness enveloped us, we came to another black-tent settlement. Women and boys had apparently spent the day collecting thistles for the livestock. All day long we had seen people bringing this fodder to camp, carrying it in huge bundles on their heads. In this camp it was piled twenty feet or more high in a crude frame made of poles. The camels were feeding at the top of the stack. Donkeys were feeding at the mid-point. Burros were feeding at the bottom. There was no crowding or pushing. It was a well-behaved collection of animals, united in a common cause. Beyond the stack of thistles were the camps. Fires were burning brightly. A musical instrument was playing. Shrill voices of children could be heard.

The picture of this black-tent settlement and the other one up the road were pastoral scenes of lasting beauty.

We had hoped to get to a teahouse so that we could order *chai* and have the cold chicken we had brought from Qal'eh Nau. But we had passed through several villages and each was dark. So by eight o'clock we decided to have dinner in the car. We pulled over by the side of the road next to a roaring creek.

Across the creek was another big sheepherders' camp. But its fires were so dim I judged it was a mile away. Our presence attracted the dogs, which came part way down to the creek and never ceased barking. The spotlight Abe Fortas had given me picked up sheep bedded down a half mile up the opposite slope.

Mercedes and Mary prepared dinner inside the car. The wind was howling and piercing cold. It was so cold that the water in the canvas bags was getting icy. The icy water suggested iced coffee. We mixed the powder and sugar with the water, added powdered milk, and had as nice a drink as I can remember. The cold chicken was delicious. We finished a can of asparagus. We had tinned crackers with marmalade; and for dessert we had a few malted milk tablets. The darkness, the isolation, and the cold wind produced a camaraderie inside the car. Aslam, who never thought he had eaten unless he had lamb and rice, boasted that this was the best meal he ever had eaten, adding at the end:

"Of course my wife will never believe me."

That afternoon at one stop, Mercedes had met a co-operative Afghan woman who invited her into her *yurt*. Mercedes got some pictures of the lady baking *nan* and making *mawst*. The *yurt*, she said, was as neat as a pin with a cat thrown in. And now she added that preparing a meal in a Chevrolet was like living in a *yurt*—both were so small. It was a nice dinner—one of the best on the long journey.

I went out to hang up the water bags. The stars were all out; and they seemed to hang low. The Big Dipper was close to the horizon; and, finding the North Star, I learned we were headed west. Now the wind had shifted and was coming from the east. That meant we would have a tail wind into Herat. That was bad luck, for it meant we would be enveloped the whole way by our own dust.

We had dropped nearly 2000 feet from the pass, and were still on a plateau between 4000 and 5000 feet in elevation, when we reached Karrukh. It was eleven o'clock at night and still quite chilly. We had met two trucks since dinner. But there was no other traffic on the road. And none of the villages we had passed showed even a faint candle glow. Suddenly on rounding a curve we saw a lantern waving. A group of men stood in the middle of the road. I could see a few rifles. But the faces and the attire of the men were indistinct.

"Is this a road block?" I asked Aslam.

He remained silent.

"Some of these Afghan bandits we've heard about?" I asked.

No answer. And then we stopped.

I took the spotlight and turned it on the group, as I got out of the car.

A young man, speaking perfect English, stepped forward and extended his hand.

"I am Mohammed Yusuf, the *Farmandar* of Karrukh. We've

been expecting you since dusk. We were beginning to be worried."

More Afghan hospitality was proffered us. We entered a courtyard and followed a gravel walk through a well-kept garden into a stone house. A room on the ground floor was lighted and laid with rich-colored Afghan rugs. We sat on the floor leaning against round pillows and drinking *chai*. Yusuff was insistent we stay all night. His invitation was tempting, for the day had been long. But once again we refused, preferring to stay on schedule. We lingered an hour, however, in Karrukh, having several cups of *chai* and discussing Afghan affairs with this young enterprising official. Karrukh has no schools for girls, only schools for boys. And the boys' school goes only through six grades. Karrukh has no hospital and no first-aid centers. There are midwives in Karrukh but no doctors. Health-wise and education-wise, Karrukh is about average so far as Asia goes.

We made our parting from these friends in Karrukh about midnight. Now the road dropped steadily to the basin of Herat, which lies at 3000 feet. The road was so winding and pock-marked that we made poor time. Though it is only a bit more than fifty miles, we did not arrive at Herat until two o'clock in the morning. Once more we were flagged down by a lantern. Now we were on the outskirts of the town of Herat. A jeep was there to guide us to the hotel.

"Your reservations are all in order," the gendarme told me.

But when we were unpacked, a sad-looking, sleepy manager appeared.

"Four of you?" he stammered. "I expected only one."

We saw the room he had reserved. It had a single bed. We learned later that he had held our space until about one o'clock when, figuring we would stay at Karrukh, he released our space to some Russian engineers.

Aslam was easy to dispose of; he could stay with the servants. I suggested we blow up air mattresses and sleep on the porch. Mercedes, however, came up with the suggestion that won out. I would take the single bed; she and Mary would sleep on sofas in the lobby.

The manager, when he heard the news, was fit to be tied.

"Impossible. Impossible," he snorted. And that was the inflexible viewpoint of a man who knew women only in *purdah*. They used my room, preparing for bed; and they laid their sleeping bags on the sofas in the lobby. Soon we were all in bed. I turned out the electric light and turned over once, noting how the wind did howl and whine. Then I was sound asleep. It seemed that I had slept only a few minutes. I awoke, startled, to hear two women scream. I sat up in bed. The sun was streaming in the window; and in a second here came Mercedes and Mary in great disarray.

"What's wrong?" I asked.

"What's wrong?" Mercedes said. "We were sound asleep when a man—a Russian—came by and shook us, saying in English, 'What you ladies doing here?' That's what's wrong!"

CHAPTER 14

GIFTS OF KIND WORDS AND DEEDS

Though this was my first visit to Herat and though we stayed only a short time, the city becamc one of my favorites the world around.

Herat, a city with 80,000 population, lies in a huge bowl rimmed on two sides by low hills. It is green, in the California, not the New England, sense. Herat lies in a dry belt. It gets its water from the Hari Rud, which runs off the western slopes of the Paropamisus, flows west a hundred miles or more, then turns north to form the boundary between Afghanistan and Iran, and eventually ends up in Russia. There are tall tales in Herat of the floodwaters from melting snows that sweep down the Hari Rud in springtime. When we were there, it was a calm purling river, heavily drawn upon for irrigation. Irrigation water is also obtained through elaborate *qanats* or tunnels that go high on a slope to tap underground streams and bring the water down to the valley. These *qanats,* extensively used in Persia as well as in Herat, are marked on the surface by miles of piles of dirt beside the series of manholes that were used to excavate the tunnel by hand.

Herat does not have many marks of distinction, since the buildings with few exceptions are low, flat mud houses. But the streets, though dirt and cobblestone, are very wide; each has a center strip; the sides are lined with pine and tamarisk; and the avenues extend far into the outskirts. The bazaars are mostly open, not covered; the streets clean and tidy, with open *jubes.* Pieces of the mud walls of the old city are still in evidence. We inspected them with Shamsuddin Suljoqi Matin, Inspector of Schools in Herat, who speaks English fluently. The earthworks on which the mud walls rested were about 250 feet wide and 50 feet high, the wall being on top of them. This wall was built and rebuilt so often no one knows who built what remnant. It and its five gates are mostly in ruins. Some sections of the old walls are said to have been built by Alexander the Great, though Matin relegated those accounts to legend.

Near the center of the town stands a high mound where the King's castle stood. Remnants of the castle are there as reminders. At the base of the mound is one section of the bazaar. Every shop has a door trimmed in blue. From a distance they look like decorated caves in the base of this hill.

Herat was once the glorious center of Khorasan, the easternmost province of Persia. There is an Eastern proverb, "Khorasan is the oyster of the world and Herat is its pearl." It is so strategically located that every uprising, every invasion, every war seemed to touch it. It was leveled time and again, only to be rebuilt. Only a few dozen people survived the attack which Genghis Khan made on it in A.D. 1222. It was to be sacked a half dozen times after that, only to revive again. It was long claimed by Persia; it was long independent of Kabul. It was not firmly incorporated into Afghanistan until 1863.

To the north and west of the city are remains of a civilized community that looked as if it had been razed by bulldozers and leveled out. Pieces of pottery, bricks, and friezes are there without number. Here once stood a former city of Herat.

On the edge of the present city sits a huge mosque with a great courtyard about 465 feet by 275 feet. It has cupolas, windows, and pillars too numerous to count. Its name is Masjed Jameh and it was built by Timur's descendants, near the end of the fifteenth century. It is rich to this day in mosaics of colored tile; and in the central courtyard stands an alabaster throne where the King used to hold audiences. It has on it some marks of decay and depreciation. To remedy that, an active group of artisans was busy at work the day of our visit, making tiles to replace broken panels. I photographed them in color with my flash equipment and sensed that my subjects were men of great skills and artistic talents. Apart from these artisans, what caught my fancy was a huge bronze bowl that stood in the courtyard of the mosque. It was about five feet tall, and nearly as wide. It was highly decorated with symbolic figures. It is known in Herat as the Sherbet Bowl. The man who built the mosque was Shah Sultan Hussein. It was his custom once a year on a holy day—Eid-Al-Adha, I believe—to summon the poor and feed them. The food would be placed in this great bowl and ladled out as the line moved by. On festive occasions celebrated by the court, the Shah would have the bowl filled with sherbet—a sweet, cold drink that we of the West later froze into a dessert. This massive sherbet bowl today is only a showpiece in the courtyard of the famous mosque.

To the northeast of the present city stands the ruins of a *medresse* or religious university built by Queen Goharshad in A.D. 1417. It was flanked by six beautiful minarets covered with blue tile. The Queen's mausoleum was placed in the corner of the *medresse*. It is a square chamber with a low dome. The walls are decorated with gold and with blue and red pigments in delicate designs. This mausoleum is the resting place of several princes as well as the Queen herself. But the minarets—standing in splendid isolation—and the mausoleum are all that remain of the great building. The building was razed in 1885 to give the garrison at Herat a clear field of fire in case the city was attacked.

Higher up on the hills overlooking Herat from the northeast is the beautiful shrine of Kazergah, where the famous Persian poet, Abdullah Ansari, rests. It stands in a grove of pines that reminded me of the Mediterranean species. The inner court is sparkling, most of the tombs being in white marble. This shrine is filled with many of Afghanistan's great, including Dost Mohammed. It was Dost Mohammed, a great-grandfather of Mohammed Zahir Shah, the present King, who won the First Afghan War (1838–42) against the British. From the heights of Kazergah one gets a beautiful view of Herat. From here the town looks like a rich green bowl. The faint suggestion of desert on the horizon accentuates the effect of an oasis. The sky was blue with only specks of white clouds. A faint haze hung in the distance. This view perhaps summoned memories of boyhood days in eastern Washington, where deserts also bloom. That may have been one reason Herat had such a strong appeal.

Another was the strong wind coming down from the north. The wind blows 120 days during the summer almost without stop. It sometimes howls at night. It is always cool and fresh and keeps Herat from wallowing in the heat.

This wind, the suggestion of the oasis in the desert, and the friendly people endeared Herat to me.

One of the friendliest was Mohammed Ismail Mayar, middle-aged Governor of Herat. He invited us to tea in his garden. The walks are fine gravel, the flower beds sunken and filled with geraniums in elaborate patterns. Inside the high walls that shelter the garden are fine stands of pine. The Governor is a high-quality public servant who has worked many years for his country in various posts. This day his wife was in Kabul with some of their nine children. Four boys—bright and friendly—were present for tea and two of them, like their father, spoke good English.

Lemon squash was served, then regular Afghan *chai*. After the *chai*, bowls of peaches were passed. Some of these peaches were small white ones, most delicious. There was also a red variety that looked more like a plum. Yet it is a true peach, and very delicate. They are so delicious and so perishable, they are called "sweet water" (*shaftalou*).

We got from Governor Mayar a vision of the Afghanistan of tomorrow, when there will be schools and hospitals for all, good roads, flourishing bazaars, and a rising standard of living through industrialization.

He urged us to stay some days in Herat; and as we left he had presents for the ladies. During our visit many fine compliments had been paid the red peach. When we reached the car, a servant had a bowl of them for us. We had also praised Afghan *mawst*. Another servant had a bowl of *mawst*, which was indeed the best we ever tasted.

Another friend we made in Herat was Gholam Nidur, who writes after his name "Meer of Kazergah." He is, indeed, the learned man who lives at the shrine and honors by his life and deeds the memory of the poet, Ansari, who is buried there.

We called on him one morning and he gave us tea. He served good *chai*, lemon squash, and fine cold water. He also served apples, peaches, and grapes. This tea was in a house on the hillside below the shrine and on the second floor, which we reached by climbing spiral stone stairs.

Nidur is a *mullah,* lame in one leg. He has a gray beard and warm gray eyes. He wears a white turban, a white flowing gown, and a long black coat. He uses snuff and writes poetry of his own. He greeted us by asking if we knew of the link Amanullah, Afghanistan's progressive King, had established with America. I told him I knew of Amanullah but did not know the link he meant.

"That link," he said, "is the abolition of slavery. He followed the example of your Lincoln, whom we Afghans honor. Amanullah abolished all slavery in our country in 1925. By that act he forged an enduring tie with your nation."

Nidur asked if I knew Ansari and I admitted I did not. I added that I knew Iqbal, having once delivered an Iqbal memorial address. Nidur asked for a copy, which I later sent. Most of our talk was about Ansari, who was born in A.D. 1005 and died an octogenarian. He was a prolific poet, having written 100,000 verses in Persian and 6000 in Arabic. He was a devout man who believed that the law of life requires (a) sincerity to God, (b) severity to self, (c) justice to all people, (d) service to elders, (e) kindness to the young, (f) generosity to the poor, (g) good counsel to friends, (h) forbearance with enemies, (i) indifference to fools, (j) respect for the learned.

His poems were mostly short, homely verses:

> If thou wouldst become a
> Pilgrim on the path
> Of love
> The first condition is
> That thou become as
> Humble as dust
> And ashes.

Matin, the school inspector, changed the subject from Ansari to Nidur, saying our host was a poet in his own right. I urged him to give us some recitations. He speaks only a little English. His languages are Persian and Arabic; and the poems he recited were in Persian and translated by Matin. They were beautiful to hear, each having a musical quality lost in translation. But the thoughts were universal and worth repeating.

1. *The money man.* He who wants only money has a knot in his heart. To untie the knot one has to use kindness and generosity.

2. *The poet.* The poet should not use words that fly over the heads of men. He should use words that reach their minds and stay in their hearts forever.

3. *The beggar.* Do not be harsh with the beggar. Remember that some of the finest things man has to give are kind words.

Kind words and kind deeds had been bestowed on us all the way across Afghanistan. We were to leave in the morning for Meshed, our first stop in Persia. We hated to leave the ancient land of Afghanistan. Its people had been more than kind to us. The two weeks there had been filled with adventures in friendship.

PART 3

IRAN

CHAPTER 1

WE LOSE THE WAY TO IRAN

We left Herat in the early morning of July 22, before dawn. The wind was blowing and the air was chill. The corridors of the Park Hotel resounded with snores from Russian engineers whose hall doors had been left open. These were the men who kept studiously to themselves and who were always gathered around the radio in the lobby at 6 P.M. to get the Moscow news. They never stirred until about eight o'clock in the morning. We left quietly at four-thirty, having packed the car the night before and arranged for the gendarmes to watch it while we slept.

The sleepy manager brought us *chai* for breakfast and a chicken he had roasted for our lunch. We also had the Governor's peaches, some melons, and a large piece of *nan*. I had given Aslam his air ticket, which would take him from Herat to Kabul. He had an aunt in Herat with whom he would visit while he waited for the plane. He was still ailing from the pan of dirty water he had drunk in the nomad's camp several days earlier. We gave him medication and Mercedes bottled a supply of pills to last him until he got back to Kabul.

It was hard parting with Aslam. We had shared many happy and sad moments together and had become close friends. He had indeed asked to go with us at least to Tehran. I took the matter up with Governor Mayar, who said it would take the approval of the central government as passports were issued only in Kabul. Days if not weeks would pass before any decision would be reached. So it was a forlorn Aslam whom we let out at a corner of the dark and empty bazaar in Herat. We said goodbye several times while he stood in the street. But I almost forgot to find out the directions to Meshed. The border town in Afghanistan is Islam Qal'eh. So when I asked Aslam he said:

"Go to the end of the bazaar. Islam Qal'eh is straight ahead."

The directions sounded simple enough. We continued through the bazaar and kept straight ahead. Once the city was behind us, I had doubts that we were on the right road. It did not seem sufficiently well traveled to be the main highway west to Iran. Moreover, it bore too much south to our liking. It was getting light when I saw a man on a burro coming toward us. I stopped the car and, pointing the direction we were going, asked:

"Islam Qal'eh?"

"Bali, bali," was the reply. So on we went.

In a few miles we met another man headed toward Herat and asked the same question. He too nodded and answered in the affirmative. We met another and still another and each one answered the same. In perhaps twenty miles we came to a fork in the road. One road bore west, the other sharply south. The map counseled the former and we took it. But in a few miles we were on a bullock trail, crossing culverts too precarious for a car. With great difficulty I managed to turn around without ending in irrigation ditches that crowded the edge of this trail and slowly and cautiously got back over the fragile culverts, finally reaching the fork. This time we turned south and had gone a mile or so when we met a boy on foot.

"Islam Qal'eh?" I asked, pointing down the road.

He shook his head and pointed back to Herat.

"Someone is crazy," I suggested. Being undecided what to do, we went forward until in five miles we were on another bullock trail headed for a dead end in a small village. There was only one thing to do and that was to return to Herat.

The sun was up when we got to Herat. But no traffic policemen were in their stalls at the street intersections. I tried my luck with one or two pedestrians but the expression *"Islam Qal'eh kojast* [Where is Islam Qal'eh]?" brought no response.

So we decided to return to the hotel. The place was still quiet, the snores of Russian engineers filling the corridors. No one was up. On the second floor I finally found the manager, who, when he saw me, started as if he'd seen a ghost. For he, who had bid me farewell at four-thirty in the dark, now was seeing me in the flesh two hours later. I explained to him our predicament. He dressed hurriedly and went with us as an escort. We learned that Aslam had been technically correct in telling us to go to the end of the bazaar. But he had failed to add that there we should turn right, for the road straight ahead, while going to Islam Qal'eh, was only in the end a bullock and camel trail. Having found the way, we said goodbye a second time to the hotel manager, leaving him enough money to take a tonga back home. It was now seven o'clock; we had wasted two and a half hours being lost; but we were now headed in cool, bright sunshine west to Iran, a country I had visited so often it was a second home to me.

We met no traffic all the way to the border. Afghanistan's traffic—tragically, I think—is predominantly north and south with Russia, not east with Pakistan and west with Iran. The western border with Iran is at this point a large unbroken plateau averaging a little under 4000 feet in elevation. It is dry, unirrigated land except for strips along the Hari Rud, which the road more or less parallels for almost a hundred miles. The plateau is grazing land. There are small pieces of mountains both north and south—the last of the western fingers of the Hindu Kush. The rest is barren land with sheep and camels and black tents occasionally in view. Before nine o'clock we crossed the Hari Rud, which at this point turns north, forms a boundary between Iran and Soviet Turkmenistan, and then goes on to Russia —one of the rivers on which Russia and Iran have agreed to erect hydroelectric projects. We paralleled the Hari Rud for a few miles and then, bearing west, came to the border outpost called Islam Qal'eh. We had come 1225 miles from Kabul and had 239 miles to go to reach Meshed before dark.

Islam Qal'eh has but three buildings, one for administration, one for immigration, and one for customs. We delivered our passports, exit permits, and "triptyque" to immigration and waited in the main reception room for the formalities to be finished. An Afghan official soon brought *chai*. A young Britisher came up for advice. He was going by bus from Meshed to Kabul. The roads in Iran he found to be terrible and he asked about Afghan roads. I did not have the heart to tell him the whole truth. I made my answers vague, for he was already discouraged. He was about ready to turn back because of the Asian flu. It had reached Iran in epidemic proportions and Afghan officials at this border post had not yet received permission from Kabul to clear the bus. The young Britisher had been in Islam Qal'eh a day and was ready on the slightest encouragement to return west with us, provided of course he could take his partner with him. But I tried to stir the coals of adventure in him and steadfastly pointed him to the east.

I was interrupted by Mercedes. There was no gasoline to purchase at Islam Qal'eh. So she planned to fill our tank from a jerry can. On the Chevrolet the cap to the tank is reached by turning a catch above the left rear light and dropping the light down. This catch had somehow caught and she could not turn it. Neither could I. Finally a big, husky, lumbering Sikh with his customary beard and turban appeared. I asked him if he could help. The giant went to work and in a jiffy turned the catch and released the cap. In gratitude I made him a gift of the last remaining ten-gallon gas coupon I had. It was good only in Afghanistan and we were now within a few yards of Iran.

When I finished with the Sikh, I found Mercedes on a rice mat under the car. As I have said, the muffler was inside the car. But the exhaust pipe was still in place. It had, however, worked loose and part of it was beginning to hit the higher ridges in the road. She was hard at work with baling wire, fastening the exhaust pipe to the frame so that it would neither rattle nor drag.

She had hardly finished, when our papers were returned and immigration waved us on. We passed through a wire fence and were soon on the barren plains of Khorasan, famous in Persian history. A few miles ahead was an adobe building which turned out to be an Iranian military post. A large pole resting on two stumps lay across the road. We gave our passports to a sentry who disappeared with them and then quickly returned, waving us on as he moved the pole long enough to let us through. We were now headed for Yusofabad, the first Persian town where we would clear customs.

A few gray partridge flew up. A dozen gazelles were grazing a hundred yards away. There was no other sign of life in the dozen miles to Yusofabad. The roads were good, noticeably better than Afghanistan's; and I stepped on the gas as we for the first time today held our speed at a little over thirty miles an hour. But as we picked up speed, the motor knocked badly. Also, we would lose speed, then gain it again. We talked about the motor and all agreed that Russian gasoline had taken its toll. We had no idea, however, that it would cough, sputter, and die on us before the sun was much higher.

Yusofabad is a pleasant village with tall locust trees shading a broad dirt main street. The customs and immigration building is the largest one in the city. We turned into its courtyard, parked the car in the shade, and gave our papers to a uniformed official who appeared. I also handed him a letter written in Persian by the Iranian Ambassador to Kabul and given me at the luncheon he and his wife gave us. The English translation, also furnished by the Ambassador, reads as follows:

THE IMPERIAL IRANIAN EMBASSY

KABUL

No. 869 July 14, 1957

To the Iran-Afghanistan Border Officers:

Mr. Justice William Douglas of the United States Supreme Court, accompanied by his wife and another lady, is arriving in Iranian territory from Afghanistan via Yusofabad, by his own civil Chevrolet Automobile.

In view of Mr. Douglas' personality, it is proper and expedient that necessary facilities and guidance be accorded to him. Mr. Douglas has also made other journeys to Iran.

Mohammed Shayesteh

AMBASSADOR

Though Persian customs officials had always been most polite, this letter produced quick results. We were ushered at once upstairs to a large, nicely furnished waiting room, and served piping-hot *chai*. Then started a parade of officials—the chief of customs, the head of the gendarmes, the principal of the schools, a judge, and the Mayor. They all were solicitous of our needs. I could not think of anything I needed except Iranian currency. I had a supply of afghanis left over and, showing them to the Mayor, asked if I could exchange them for rials. He shouted a command to a servant who went running. In ten minutes a heavy-set man entered, holding his hat over his chest and bowing. He, it appeared, was the banker. He took my afghanis and gave me rials with the same dispatch one expects at the cashier's cage. I later learned that the rate of exchange he gave me was as favorable as I would have got at the American Embassy in Tehran.

We were urged to stay for lunch; but we resisted the temptation, knowing the road to Meshed was long. It would be inappropriate, the Mayor said, that we should leave town alone. After all, Ambassador Shayesteh had said we needed "guidance." He, the Mayor, would therefore give us a jeep escort to the next town. By this gesture he rendered us the finest favor possible, for we had not yet reached Keriz, a village less than ten miles from Yusofabad, when our car coughed, sputtered, and stopped.

The jeep returned and its agile chauffeur went to work on our car. He turned out to be an expert mechanic, trained by an American military mission. In a few minutes he had filed and adjusted the points and worked with Mercedes on the carburetor, cleaning it. He grinned as he started the engine. Now it purred again. But before we left, he told me in Persian and by gestures that the carburetor had been practically ruined by Russian gasoline and we might have more trouble.

The jeep stayed with us through Keriz and as we were in no apparent difficulty turned back at that point, after fulsome farewells. We had not passed through the next small village before we were flagged down by a gendarme on a motorcycle. When I stopped he came to the car window, greeted me with a "Salaam," and handed me a letter written in ink:

"DEAR SIR—VILYOM DUCLAC—

I got information that you short of Torbat and will reach to Torbat jame at noon for this reason my duty told me to come to Hasanabad for you. I am sorry you did not come yet, for this reason I am going balk to racol to my gonderme to stay nove the town and guide you. Anyhow this proud for me that to serve my duty in the best way.

CAPTAIN ARAD
CHIEF OF JEMDARMRY IN TORBAT-JAM

Sincerely yours
ARAD

We were an hour or so from Torbat-e Sheykh Jam where Captain Arad was located. We passed many villages, all small, and saw many sheep grazing and quite a few stands of wheat almost ready to be cut. The road was straight, the country open and rolling like South Dakota, the dirt road in fine repair. Motorcycles appeared by the dozens, a sign indicating that not only were the roads of Iran better than those of Afghanistan, but the standard of living was higher too.

The gendarmes were waiting for us at Torbat, a pleasant town of 10,000 people, and escorted us first to a filling station and then to Captain Arad's home. The Torbat filling station was typical of many across Iran. It was no more than a small warehouse filled with four-liter cans of petrol and a few barrels of oil. We ordered four tins, emptying out the rest of our Russian gasoline from the jerry cans into a ditch and finding in the bottom so much sand and other sediment we had to flush the cans several times to get them clean. Gasoline in Iran was easy to purchase; no coupons were necessary; it was in bountiful supply from Iran's own wells; it cost about thirty cents a gallon; and it had a golden hue in contrast to the darkish cast of Russian petrol.

Captain Arad greeted us at his garden gate. He speaks English a bit and is an enthusiastic student of it. He spent one exciting year in America, studying police methods, and became enamored of us and our free institutions. He brought his wife and daughter from the kitchen and introduced them. We washed in a pool fed by a fountain in the courtyard and sat down to a table, heavily set with food. The cold chicken, *doogh,* and *nan* were the main course and for dessert we had cake, cookies, melons, plums, cherries, and grapes. The cherries were those for which Khorasan and Meshed in particular are famous.

The Captain wanted us to stay for dinner, if only that he might practice his English. We had good-natured banter about it. I explained that Robert Schott, American Consul at Meshed, and Mrs. Schott expected us for dinner and that we must be on our way. It was now midafternoon and we had five hard hours' driving ahead of us.

Once we left Torbat we paralleled a low mountain range on our left. These were barren, broken mountains with sharp peaks, deep canyons, and high crags. They were purple in the distance. At times the dark green of trees showed in ravines, marking creeks or springs. Mostly it was desertlike country, strongly reminiscent of the mountains southeast of Tucson, Arizona. One peak had a startling resemblance to Baboquivari near the Arizona-Mexican border, which I like to climb.

We stopped once more for gasoline at a village called Sangbast and bought eight liters. The engine seemed hungry for benzine, our mileage per gallon being very low. It was almost dusk when we came out on the new highway that has recently been put in from Tehran to Meshed. We had been practically free from traffic except for motorcycles and jeeps. Now the trucks and busses loomed up. They were all heavily loaded whichever way they were moving. The surface of this new road was marked with noses of protruding rocks. So our speed was somewhat reduced. The engine seemed to be losing power with every mile. I had driven all day and noticed that now I had to keep the car in second even on level ground.

Meshed loomed up in the dusk, its houses lighted. We came to black asphalt and for a few seconds got the car Ali up to the remarkable speed of fifty miles an hour. But it was too great a strain for the engine and for us. When we reached Meshed, we stopped every block or so to ask a traffic policeman directions to the American Consulate. Finally we were in mid-town caught up in Meshed's heavy traffic—camels, donkeys, burros, autos, trucks, busses, porters with huge packing boxes on their backs, boys on bicycles, teen-agers on motorcycles, veiled ladies with packages under one arm and babies under the other, peddlers, and ordinary pedestrians. People filled the streets as well as the sidewalks. Somewhere along the way we had lost the chrome ring around the center of the steering wheel that makes the horn work. Now I had to find the exact spot in the center of the wheel to sound a warning. I kept fumbling with the horn block after block. Our speed was so slow we just crawled along; and every time we stopped the motor stalled. Each time it seemed to take longer to start it and I wondered if Ali would have to be pushed or pulled the last mile. At one stop where I asked directions from a policeman, a young boy wheeled up on a bicycle and asked in good English what my question was. When I told him, he shouted:

"Follow me."

And so we were escorted through a labyrinth of alleys into the oldest part of town. The passageway was so narrow, I sometimes had difficulty turning the corners. In a mile or so we pulled up in front of a lighted portico where Bob Schott stood awaiting us. We had been coming since 4:30 A.M. and it was now 8 P.M. Unknown to us, the Persian gendarmes had kept the Schotts advised of our progress.

I parked Ali in a courtyard opposite the Consulate. As I turned off the motor it gave an ominous cough. It was the last wheeze left. For in the morning Ali, badly mutilated by Russian gasoline, had to be towed to a garage.

CHAPTER 2

A GOLDEN SHRINE

Meshed is on a broad plain about 4000 feet in elevation with a range of mountains to the northeast and another to the southwest. It is a large city of 250,000 with paved streets, shaded parks, mosques, bazaars, and mud huts. It has more of the touch of the East than the West on it. It has recently been connected with Tehran by rail; and it boasts of a new $4,000,000 railway station. But its point of greatest charm is the Golden Shrine which rises above a mass of poplar trees near the center of the city.

It is the burial place of the famous Arab Caliph, Harun al-Rashid, who died in Khorasan in 809 and who walks through the pages of *The Arabian Nights*. This shrine is also the burial place of Imam Reza, the eighth Imam in the line of holy men whom the Moslems of the Shiite sect revere.

Ali al-Reza died suddenly after eating grapes. The Shiites refuse to believe his death was natural, but are convinced that he had been poisoned. The place where he is buried takes its name from that circumstance. For Meshed means the Place of Martyrdom.

The people come to pay homage to the memory of the Imam, not to Rashid. The legend is that they kick the tomb of Rashid and bless the Imam, for Rashid is not honored as a holy man.

That is not quite true. It is a fact, however, that nobody enters the shrine to visit Rashid's tomb. He is not considered the equal of Reza. Most pilgrims, indeed, curse Rashid and salute Reza when visiting the shrine. For it is believed that Rashid imprisoned and poisoned Reza's father, the seventh Imam, and that Rashid's son, Mamun, poisoned Reza.

The dome of gold is brilliant in July sunshine and can be seen for miles. Next to the Golden Shrine is the Mosque of Goharshad, built by the Queen of that name, already mentioned, who built the beautiful *medresse* in Herat whose minarets still stand in solitary splendor.

Shah Abbas, who lived in the sixteenth and seventeenth centuries, popularized a pilgrimage to the Golden Shrine at Meshed. He, himself, traveled by foot from Isfahan to Meshed to visit the Golden Shrine. Anyone who did likewise was entitled to be called a Meshedi and wear a green turban.

Under the shrine is a flat stone, in which grooves have been cut, the stone where the Imam was laid for washing before burial. Childless women pour water over the stone and catch it in a bowl as it drips from the grooves. Then they drink it to insure pregnancy.

The Golden Shrine is generally closed to foreigners, as was the Shrine of Ali at Mazar-i-Sharif. But Mr. Taheri, administrator of the mosque, gave me permission to climb one of the minarets and take photographs.

It was noon when I reached the top and men were entering the mosque for prayers. A large square pool lies in the center of the courtyard and here they were washing their hands and feet before prayer. As I watched the people gathered about the pool, I remembered what one of my interpreters on an earlier visit to Iran had said about this washing and praying.

"There's no special value in praying and washing oneself five times a day," he observed. "Yet they are important. One who prays that often and keeps his body washed is apt never to forget either God or cleanliness."

The mosaic work on the walls of the shrine and the mosque show the best of Persian tile in delicate shades of blue, turquoise, and green.

From this minaret, little of the town of Meshed can be seen

because of the thick carpet of treetops. Here and there a mosque protrudes, but more often chimneys and factories.

The principal street of Meshed is the Khiyaban, built by Shah Abbas about A.D. 1600. It is the thoroughfare leading to the Golden Shrine. A canal runs through this avenue, bringing water from a lake forty-five miles distant. By the time the water reaches the city it is polluted but used for drinking, washing, and religious ablutions.

The upper part of Khiyaban in the vicinity of the Golden Shrine is known as the Bast, which can be entered only on foot. It is open only to Moslems. The Golden Shrine owns all the property in the Bast; and 10 per cent of its revenues go to the Shah.

The main entrance is the Bala gateway beyond which runs a street about 250 yards long filled with shops. All around the shrine are busy bazaars, religious schools, hostels, caravanseries, and public baths. A large part of the annual business of Meshed is catering to the needs of pilgrims. The greatest shortage in Meshed is in first-class hotels; only third-class hostels are available. As I said, Meshed has a population of 250,000 people; and at least twice that number come there each year on pilgrimages to the Golden Shrine, paying a tax of twenty rials (twenty-six cents) each for the privilege.

Curzon in his book on Persia called Meshed the most immoral city in Asia, basing his denunciation on the practice that prevails here of the *mut'a* or contract marriage. It is a nuptial arrangement for the convenience of a pilgrim. A contract marriage can last for a few days or for years, depending on its terms. A *mullah* approves the contract for a fee; and the temporary marriage becomes lawful. Curzon concluded that these short-term wives were prostitutes. But the *mut'a* is a wholly lawful arrangement; children of the union are legitimate; and the wife may not marry again for one hundred days after this marriage is dissolved, so as to protect the paternity of any children subsequently born. The *mut'a* was once common in the Moslem world. Later the orthodox Moslems barred it. But the Shiites of Persia persisted in the practice. Though the lawbooks of the Shiites now ban the *mut'a,* it still persists.

The Meshedis told me that, though the *mut'a* is frowned upon these days, it is still used by many pilgrims to the Golden Shrine —perhaps thirty thousand a year.

"Some of these pilgrims are gone for weeks," one said. "Would you have them leave fatherless and abandoned children?"

I commented that it was a system of dubious social value. "But the system of European mistresses is much worse," one of them added.

I met Mercedes and Mary in the museum of the shrine, which sits in a garden of petunias and cannas. It is the most beautiful and the best cared for of any museum we saw on the trip. It has one of the most valuable collections of Islamic manuscripts and scrolls in the world. Rare pottery, carvings in ivory and turquoise, gold plate, rugs, and paintings crowd its showcases and walls. The museum has probably the finest collection there is of miniatures, including those of the famous Behzad of Herat, who lived in the sixteenth century. We could find none of his work in Herat. But many of his miniatures rest in Meshed at this museum.

Meshed has a small but flourishing Presbyterian Hospital run by Dr. and Mrs. J. P. Cochran, whom I visited in their home. The flu was raging in Meshed and the Cochrans were still weak from it. But they left their beds to serve me cool sherbet and chocolate cookies. Dr. Cochran was born in Meshed, returned to this country to study medicine, and returned at once to Meshed where he has lived for nearly forty years. A man who could have made a fortune at home sets bones, injects penicillin, and removes gall bladders for a bare living in Meshed. As I moved among the people of this city, I found that they, mostly Moslems, had nothing but praise for the Cochrans, good Christians.

Nadir Shah brought one hundred Jewish familes to Meshed in the eighteenth century. They suffered a great massacre in 1839. The story is that a native doctor had advised a Jewess, who had an eruption on her hand, to kill a dog and put her hand into its bowels. She did so on a public street during a Moslem holy day. The Moslems, who look on dogs as unclean, considered her act an insult to their religious observances and fell upon the Jewish quarters.

Many embraced Islam to escape certain death. They are known in Meshed as the Marrano Community. They number about 3500. They are rich merchants who control the pearl trade.

Many are also rug and shawl merchants. To this day they carefully observe the rituals and practices of the Islamic faith. But there is reason to think they cling to Judaism as a way of life.

Landlordism is rampant in Khorasan. Most farmers are tenants. Their nominal rent may not exceed 50 per cent of the crop. But in practice the portion the landlord gets far exceeds that amount. For there is interest as well as rent to pay—exorbitant usury on loans the landlord makes to the tenants. The landlord is the chief source of agricultural credit; and he charges what the traffic will bear, 400 per cent interest a year being not uncommon. Some provinces in Iran are taking steps to alleviate the plight of these sharecroppers. But Khorasan brings up the rear, being under the control of an unholy combination—church and landlords. The church is in fact the biggest single landlord in Khorasan. The Golden Shrine owns about one ninth of all the agricultural land of that province and most of the choice land. It owns many blocks of the bazaar and rents the stalls to shopkeepers. It has so many commercial interests that it employs 1700 people to take care of them. The administrator is Dr. Fakhreddin Shademan, a noted writer, novelist, and essayist. He, and his wife emancipated from *purdah* like most women among the intelligentsia, gave us a tea at Malekbad, the headquarters of the shrine outside Meshed. This is a garden containing about 220 acres. Some of it is in fruit trees; some in corn; part of it in gardens. The fruit includes cherries and peaches, for which Meshed is famous. The gardens are formal and watered by hand. They are so elaborate that it takes forty full-time gardeners to care for them. They are lined with graceful poplars; and petunias, dahlias, phlox, and gladioli line the gravel walks. A huge pool is the center of one garden. It is used for swimming; and when dinner parties are held, Mrs. Shademan has hundreds of lighted candles floating on it. The Shademans are Western in outlook and attitudes but deeply attached to the Islamic faith.

Meshed is noted for its religious fanaticism. The burial of the two holy men in the Golden Shrine perhaps ignites the flames. In 1935 Meshed was the center of resistance to the reforms of Reza Shah, father of the present Shah. Reza Shah, following the example of Ataturk in Turkey, put on a campaign to abolish the use of the veil by women. He gave orders to the police to tear them from the heads of passers-by. The *mullahs* were furious and put on a big protest meeting in the square outside the Golden Shrine. Word of the protest meeting was telephoned to the Shah. He ordered the Governor to go to the shrine with machine guns and direct the crowd to disperse. He said to announce that the people had ten minutes to leave. He directed the Governor to tell them that the machine guns would open fire if the square had not been cleared in that time. The Governor appeared with soldiers as directed and made the announcement. He pulled out his watch and waited for ten minutes to pass. All the time the *mullahs* were shouting to the people to remain, not to be frightened, to resist this armed invasion of a holy place. At the end of ten minutes the Governor gave the command to the soldiers to open fire. They swept the square, killing two hundred people. That episode, more than any other single event, put an end to *purdah* among the upper classes of Iran.

Every year the Shiite Moslems celebrate Moharram, which in Arabic means "sacred." It comes in the first month of the Arab lunar year. It is the period of mourning for al-Hossein, son of Ali, who was murdered by Ubaidallah in Iraq in A.D. 680. The period of mourning lasts about ten days; but there are three days of deep mourning. These three days are anniversaries of the day before his death, the day he died, and the day after. A devout Shiite believes that, should he die on any of these three days, his entry into heaven is guaranteed.

Moharram was only a week away when we visited Meshed. I talked at tea with the anxious Governor of Khorasan, Reza Jafari. He told me how in other years the Moslems of Meshed had worked themselves into a frenzy over Moharram. Hossein had a brother, Hasan, who was poisoned by his wife. The crowd adds his name to the wailing list. Hundreds of people spend the night beating their breasts and shouting, "Hasan Hossein! Hasan Hossein!" They wail in cadence and pass their frenzy on to others until a mob forms. Sometimes the mob whirls aimlessly. At other times processions form and parade for hours. Men beat each other's bare chests and backs with chains until they bleed. Some men, running berserk, cut their foreheads and cheeks with sharp knives and go howling through the streets to show their anguish over the murder of Hossein. Men in that emotional state are dangerous and disrupt the peace of a city. These were the worries of the Governor as he gave orders to the police to arrest any man bent on mutilating himself and to break up any crowds gathered to observe any demonstration of that kind.

Reza Shah had banned Moharram. The present government wants to do it but hesitates, because of the political power of the *mullahs.*

CHAPTER 3

THE BEST TOWN

There was a United States Army sergeant in Meshed, Sergeant C. M. Johnson by name, who volunteered to work on our car; and he turned out to be one of the finest mechanics who ever touched a Chevrolet. His commanding officer, Maj. M. E. McCollum, said that Johnson could build a brand-new car if he had enough baling wire and pieces of scrap iron.

He discarded our muffler as unworthy of repair; and in the bazaar we bought a new one that the Sergeant welded into place. He fastened the exhaust pipe to the frame, tightened all nuts under the car, adjusted the brakes, and checked the springs and shock absorbers. We had new points for the distributor with us and he installed them. He also put in new spark plugs. The main problem was the carburetor. The Russian gasoline had been so poor that the carburetor was ruined. It was so gummed up, it would have to be taken completely apart, cleansed, and reassembled. We decided against that course and gave the Sergeant a new carburetor we had brought from the States. The repair work was about done when the Sergeant left the car on the street for only a few moments. When he came back he discovered that someone had stolen the key. There was no way of changing switches in Meshed. Our only recourse was to leave town.

The next morning we left Meshed for Bojnurd, Gorgan, and

Babol Sar on the Caspian Sea. Almost eighteen miles west of the city we turned off the main highway for a mile or so to visit the tomb of Ferdowsi, one of the greatest epic poets in world literature. Persia honors her poets more than her generals. Ferdowsi, who died in A.D. 1020, is among the great. He rewrote early Persian legends in the book *Shah Nameh* and many of the scenes from that book are carved in marble on the walls surrounding his tomb. The small square building over the tomb is in a dignified, quiet garden adorned by a huge reflecting pool. These grounds are maintained by a trust at the head of which sits the Shah. The tomb has an aesthetic-looking manager about forty years old by the name of Seifi Qaem-Magami, who served us tea and spoke sparingly.

Not far beyond Ferdowsi's tomb the gearshift stuck. We could not shift into first or high. A rock had hit the connections underneath the car, making it impossible to shift into these other positions. So we went in second for ten miles until we reached a gendarme station. We got temporary repairs there. But the gearshift was to plague us for some hours.

The country west of Meshed to Bojnurd is somewhat reminiscent of eastern Oregon, except the hills are barer. Natives told us that this was wooded country thick with oak and chestnut a hundred and fifty years ago. But the trees were cut for charcoal and the goats ate the saplings. Now the slopes are mostly bare except for green canyons where willow and poplar still grow. The passing of the trees in Khorasan has marked the beginning of the end of the use of charcoal except what can be shipped in. Iran's oil fields mean an abundance of kerosene; and today it is supplanting charcoal at a rapid rate.

As the crow flies, this piece of Khorasan is not very far from Ashkabad, capital of Soviet Turkmenistan where I visited in 1955. Yet this country is greener and more fertile by far than Ashkabad. This is wheat country with cotton and rice being grown alternately where there is irrigation.

About noon we reached Quchan—a bleak-looking town that might well sit on the plains of western Nebraska. It is, however, the center of a great grape industry. We stopped to pay our respects to Masud Shakeri, the *Farmandar,* and were ushered into his reception room. This room, like most reception rooms in Iran, was barren but for a picture of the Shah on the wall, Persian carpets on the floor, and heavy, high-backed chairs all identical and crowded shoulder to shoulder around three sides of the room. While we sipped tea, he told us with pride of the Quchan distillery, whose products are very popular. The vodka manufactured there is called *Shad,* which means Happy. The volume of sales is so great and the municipal tax so high that Quchan finances most of its municipal activities through the tax revenues from the distillery.

Another source of revenue is a tax on all raisins exported from the town. Some cities have taxes on exports, others on imports, some on both. The other main source of municipal revenue in Quchan is the tax placed on every truck and bus that passes through the city. Meshed has a similar tax on every passenger who leaves by rail, by bus, or by plane. Real estate taxes in Iran all go to the central government. Municipalities reach avidly for revenues from all sorts of excise taxes. The tax on busses and trucks takes one back to medieval Europe, where each feudal lord was sovereign and levied a tax on everything that came his way.

The Atrak River rises west of Quchan and runs northwest to Russia and eventually the Caspian Sea. It is the source of many irrigation projects; and Russia and Iran have recently agreed on a hydroelectric development of it. It also has swampy areas where the wild boar is found. In Iran it irrigates some land that raises seven crops of alfalfa a year.

We reached Bojnurd, watered by the Atrak, in midafternoon. This is country where Bob Schott, American Consul in Meshed, comes hunting partridge. He was with us on this part of our journey and took us to meet his hunting friends, the Shadlus.

The Shadlus are Kurds. They are descendants of the tribe of Kurds moved by Shah Abbas from northwestern Iran to Khorasan in the sixteenth century to serve as border patrol. In those days the Uzbeks of present-day Russia were constantly raiding Khorasan. The Kurds, known for their excellence as soldiers, became armed settlers on Persia's frontier. Years passed and these Kurds became unpopular with the central government. A quarter century ago, Reza Shah banished them from Khorasan, sent them into exile in southern Iran, and confiscated all their property. After World War II they returned north, repossessed their property, and now are the most influential people in the area. Today they number about 150,000 and represent four tribes—the Za'aferanlu, Shadlu, Picheranlu, and Tupkanlu.

One, Aslam Khan Shadlu, is Mayor of Bojnurd. The others run sheep, goats, and beef cattle and engage in farming. The one we called upon was Khanlar Khan Shadlu, who has a lovely home in Bojnurd, surrounded by a high brick wall. It is here the Shah stops when he travels Khorasan. We, indeed, had the room of honor reserved for him.

We stopped for tea but stayed on for dinner. These Shadlus are Westernized in their dress, cosmopolitan in their outlook, and modern in their approach to problems. Firouz Khan Shadlu, a cousin, speaks some English. They are religious but not sticklers to the Word. They pray and go to the mosque; but they also serve vodka made from raisins at Quchan and mixed with Pepsi-Cola. This day they were talking about the new road from Meshed, the one we had traveled. This road, down to a year earlier, had been a track and a trail, not a highway. Now that it was finished, trucks could move easily. That meant beef cattle could now be shipped to Tehran for slaughtering. Without the road, that was impossible. For cattle driven on the hoof that far would not sell high enough for a profit. Now that the road was in, the beef cattle industry in Khorasan was increasing. The Shadlus had in mind as the next improvement a packing plant somewhere near Bojnurd.

They had interesting things to say about Soviet Russia. Under Stalin a Kurdish sheepherder who let his sheep stray over the Russian border (which is about forty miles from Bojnurd) was in serious trouble. The Russian border guard would invariably arrest him, round up his sheep, and take one out of every ten as an unofficial fine for the trespass. These trespasses were hard to avoid, as the Soviet-Iranian border had not been definitely determined. Sheepherders continuously crossed the unmarked frontier and suffered the penalty. Now that Khrushchev has Stalin's place the Soviet border patrol is lenient. They no longer bother the Kurdish sheepherders who cross over and graze Soviet lands. Yet their error has less justification, for in 1957 the two countries finally agreed on the boundary.

The Shadlus took us to a shrine ten miles from town called Besh Qardash or Five Brothers. It has a blue-tiled dome and four minarets. Here five springs pour ice-cold water from the ground. A pool several acres in size has been formed and carp planted in it. They are sacred and never touched. The Persians feed them bread; and we saw two-footers come to the surface for it. In World War II, when Russia occupied Khorasan, Soviet troops stationed in Bojnurd dynamited the pool, killing most of the carp and cooking them. The Persians protested this desecration. The commanding Russian general finally put a stop to the practice.

The origin of these carp is lost in history. So is any precise account of the shrine. In this part of the world a remote spring marked by a small stand of trees is commonly called a sacred place. Even a single tree may be looked on as sacred—a *jin* tree protected by a spirit. How else could it have survived the ravages of men and goats? Five Brothers has a huge chenar tree that puts practically the entire pool in shade. It is therefore a sacred tree possessed of some *jin* or spirit. People had tied pieces of cloth to the branches, each shred representing a promise—that if the supplicant has a child, he will feed the poor; that if his wife is cured, he will endow the shrine.

The shrine is used as a vault for the Shadlu family. Here the grandfather of these Shadlus is buried. He is said to have had thirty-two wives. It has on its walls an inscription of another Shadlu ancestor who had six wives and eighty-two children, who was never sick, and who died an octogenarian. The inscription thanked God for all those blessings.

We met the Shadlu women and enjoyed their cooking. Persians know how to cook rice better than any others. The rice at Bojnurd was white and fluffy; the lamb slowly turned over charcoal was tender; and the *doogh,* like some we had in Afghanistan, was mixed with chopped cucumbers.

We arose at four-thirty to leave and found the Shadlus up ahead of us with sweet melons and soft-boiled eggs for breakfast.

Bojnurd is on the same high plane as Meshed; and, like Meshed, it has low mountains on each side. Though the country is sparsely settled, each ravine has water and a clump of trees. Here in splendor and isolation are small villages of mud huts.

The habitations have the mark of poverty on them. But their locations are a realtor's dream. Their views command broad vistas with distant mountains in the background. The Khorasan skies are blue, the waters cold. One who lies on his back under Persian poplars, watching wisps of white clouds go by, knows why this brilliant land produces poets and philosophers.

A few hours out of Bojnurd brought us to the edge of the plateau. Passing through the northeastern spurs of the Elburz Mountains, we dropped down and down through stands of deciduous trees until we reached the low hot basin that runs to the Caspian. Now we were in semitropical country where rice, sugar cane, and tobacco predominate.

This is Turkmen country that gets hotter the farther west one goes. The women are not veiled; and the men wear the tall karakul hat even in hot weather. The plateau is dotted with mounds from twenty to a hundred feet high. Some are small, covering an acre or so; others cover ten acres. The local people sometimes say they were signal towers used in ancient days to transmit messages by code. Others say they are the locations of ancient villages, now reduced to the mud out of which they were built. They looked to me more like ruins of ancient villages, for they did not form the chain one would expect of signal towers.

After passing an unusually large number of these mounds, we reached Gunbad-e-Qabus. This is such bleak, dry, and windblown country that an old-fashioned swimming pool on the edge of town gave a refreshing touch. Here children splashed as women washed rugs in the hot sun.

The city Gunbad-e-Qabus is named in memory of King Qabus, who was the contemporary of Ferdowsi and the benefactor and protector of many learned men.

A rather severe fluted shaft of brick marks his grave. It's an ugly ten-sided tower with one door facing to the southeast and a dark interior filled with bat dung. It has the mark of neglect and defacement on it.

This city of great heat and little shade had for me only one redeeming feature. The smell of ripe melons was tempting as we passed through the bazaar; but we kept going. Now we were in wheat, tobacco, and cotton country where we saw much modern farm machinery—thrashers, reapers, tractors. We also began to see houses with tile roofs and substantial in appearance. Shortly after noon we reached Gorgan, the center of a vast wheat belt where the farms are mostly mechanized.

The streets of Gorgan were like an oven in the searing sun. Gorgan is a dusty, wind-blown place, without much shade. We went around a circle in mid-town twice, looking for a restaurant and a garage. We first saw a theater where Robert Taylor was playing in the movie *Ivanhoe.* Next we saw the Park Hotel. We stopped and went upstairs to find a Greek proprietor. He told us of a garage. After leaving the car there to have the brakes tightened and the gearshift rods adjusted, we returned to the Park for lunch.

Upstairs in the restaurant it was cool. Cross ventilation provided a brisk breeze. We had ice-cold beer while we waited lunch. The lunch served was rice, *dolmeh, nan,* and *mawst.* It was one of the best luncheons we had on our journey. *Dolmeh* in Persia can mean many different kinds of stuffed dishes. This one was (eggplant stuffed with rice and chopped beef.) It was an appetizing dish that we reordered, without the same success, all across Iran.

Bob Schott had come all the way to Gorgan with us, bringing his own car. He had official business there. So after lunch we parted, our aim being to reach Babol Sar on the Caspian before dark. It seemed simple, for we had only a hundred and fifty miles to go and Iranian roads usually allowed us to average nearly thirty miles an hour.

We had not gone far from Gorgan when we ran into road construction. There would be one-way construction for several miles at a stretch. This slowed us up. So did the traffic, made up mostly of trucks and busses. This traffic hugged the narrow, dusty road, unwilling to let a car pass. Each driver, anxious to keep clear of the dust, stayed in the center no matter how loudly we sounded the horn. For miles on end we would hang on to him, eating his dust, until a wide space in the road allowed us to pass. Victory would be only short-lived, for another truck or bus was always ahead.

These were two reasons why we were delayed in getting to Babol Sar. The main reason, however, was near disaster at Behshahr. We were taking turns driving and my turn came on the outskirts of this town of 10,000 people. I had no sooner entered the city than I noticed the gas-tank needle dropping. I looked once and it was below the half mark; in a minute I looked again and it was close to empty. It had been an erratic indicator for some days but never so neurotic as this. At that instant I spied a gas station with pumps and pulled into it, telling the attendant to fill the tank.

He had no sooner started than he called me excitedly. The gas tank was punctured; the gasoline was running out in a fast stream. I got in the car and drove it hurriedly across the street and parked it by a garage just before the last drop drained out.

The garageman—a lean, wiry Persian, middle-aged and dressed in Western clothes—came out. The filling station owner, Mansour Sepehri, who was with me, spoke English and Persian. He gave my message to the garageman, who summoned three assistants and went to work at once. While a motley crowd of old men and young boys gathered around, the mechanics jacked the car up, resting the rear axle on wooden blocks, removed the springs, and took off the gas tank. Then they cleaned the tank, and welded it with an acetylene torch and reassembled the rear end.

This took four hours. During that time we were deluged with hospitality. Mr. Sepehri's house is in the rear of his filling station. He invited us into it, turned on a huge electric fan, placed ice-cold Pepsi-Cola on the table, and bowed out. Mercedes and Mary napped. I went back to the garage to watch the repair work. As I was standing there, a jeep driven by an Iranian pulled up. He introduced himself as Moussa Ashrafi, an agricultural expert connected with our Point IV program. He speaks English fluently. He suggested that we go with him on a tour of the city. The ladies were willing; so we piled into his jeep and climbed a precipitous road to a bluff about three hundred feet above the valley. There sits a palace and castle built three hundred years ago and called Saffiabad. It sits in a garden lined with cypress trees. Here and there are isolated palm trees. Great hedges of arborvitae surround the palace. This was the home of the last King of this region. It's a high-ceilinged, roomy castle, so empty that it filled with echoes of our footsteps. We took pictures and bathed our arms and faces in a pool of cool clear water in the garden. A dozen or so Iranians also were sight-seeing. A lady, unveiled, with three charming children allowed me to photograph them against rambler roses along a fence.

Below us stretched a green fertile valley of cotton, tobacco, and wheat. A new textile mill and a tobacco processing plant looked spick and span from the high bluff.

On returning to town we went with Mr. Ashrafi to the home of an Iranian engineer for tea. The engineer, whose name did not get into my notebook and whose wife was on vacation in Isfahan, was a private entrepreneur, an enterprising chap in his late thirties. His four-room house was completely modern; but it had the Persian touch. A garden newly planted was enclosed by brick walls. The rooms were screened. A huge American icebox stood in one corner of the kitchen; and when our host opened the door we saw that it was filled with freshly cut watermelons and cantaloupe. We had tea too. But the chilled melon caught our fancy and we ate practically the whole supply.

We returned to the garage to find the car just about ready. All they had to do was to get it off the wooden blocks. The four mechanics pushed against the rear, rocking the car. As they rocked they shouted the name of the son-in-law of the Prophet. "Alee, Alee," they chanted. Down came the car with a crash. And when I came to pay the bill, I discovered that the total cost of four men working four hours was $1.65.

It was now nearly seven-thirty P.M. Before starting, I thought we should get air in the tires. In Iran few filling stations have compressed air. The Behshahr station was no exception. Mr. Ashrafi, however, knew a shop where a man kept tanks of compressed air. We drove there in the deep dusk but found the shop closed. Ashrafi sent a boy on a bicycle to find the proprietor. He came running in about ten minutes; but he did not have a key. It took him another ten minutes to return with a key. His shop, which was locked by board doors flush with the sidewalk, was finally opened and the owner and a bystander carried out a large tank of compressed air. They carted it from tire to tire and put twenty-eight pounds of pressure in each. His charge was ten rials (thirteen cents).

By the time the tires had been filled, it was 8:30 P.M. and a crowd had gathered around. I shook hands with Mr. Ashrafi and Mr. Sepehri. They had been kind to us. We were complete strangers when we arrived five hours earlier; and they still did not know who we were except that we were Americans. We had enjoyed the hospitality of their homes; they had taken us in off the street and treated us as friends. A welcome from my friend the Shah could not have been more warmhearted. As I said goodbye to them I remarked how wonderfully friendly Behshahr had been.

"Behshahr," said Ashrafi, "has a great meaning."

"What is it?" I asked.

"Behshahr means 'the best town,' " he added.

As we headed our car down the dark, dusty road that leads to Babol Sar and the Caspian Sea, we all agreed that, of all the strange and faraway places we had visited, Behshahr was indeed the best so far as friendliness was concerned.

CHAPTER 4

THE CASPIAN

It is only seventy-three miles from Behshahr to Babol Sar; but we took three hours to negotiate it. Road construction had turned this section into a one-way highway. The dust was heavy. We were able after much persistence to pass the trucks, but I never could get by a Russian-made car—a Muscovitz—which was lightly loaded and took the bumps with ease. When we speeded up, it stepped out in front; when we slowed, it dropped to our speed. We stayed for nearly three hours in a cloud of frustrating dust.

I have not mentioned Major Mohammed Beigzadeh of the Iranian Army, who joined us at Meshed. He reported to me there, saying the army had assigned him as our guide and interpreter. He was slight, dapper, and unused to country travel. While the Major spoke English fluently, it was plain that he had never served in the field. He hated the highway and the dust. At every stop I noticed that he was dusting his shoes and, when possible, standing in front of a mirror preening himself. He had stood the trip to Gorgan fairly well. But with the thickening dust out of Gorgan, he had become very unhappy. Now he never said a word, as he sat with a handkerchief over his nose and mouth. The road was not clearly marked; and once in a while we reached a puzzling fork. In Iran the road signs are almost always in Arabic, which I cannot read. I would stop at one of these signs to let the Major read the directions. Several times he misread it and put us off onto wrong roads, after which he was always sullen and quiet. The night drive from Behshahr to Babol Sar was particularly unnerving to him. He sat with me up front; and I found him almost standing up in the car, filled with fright, and nervously shouting orders. Finally I stopped the car and moved Mercedes up front and the Major to the rear. There he sat in silence, his handkerchief half covering his face, until we reached the hotel in Babol Sar at 11:30 P.M. I had asked the Major at Behshahr to telephone Babol Sar and advise the hotel manager that we would be late and wanted dinner held. He promised faithfully he would do it. I appreciated the importance of the call, for I had visited Babol Sar before and knew that the kitchen closed early. But when we pulled into the gravel driveway of the hotel, the manager received the first word of our coming. The kitchen was closed until morning. The result was that we had for dinner only what the icebox held—beer, cheese, bread, and jam.

I saw the Major briefly after breakfast. Though we stayed in Babol Sar two days, he never showed up again. Nor did he leave a message or send one. He completely disappeared. The result was that we spent a week on the Caspian without an interpreter. It was, however, a happy week. Though the days were warm, the nights were cool. The meals at Babol Sar were good. The evening meal was served in the garden by a small, tiled dance floor where a three-man band played American jazz.

The three-story stucco hotel at Babol Sar is set in a large spacious garden. Tall stately cypress dominate the landscape. There are a few palm and citrus trees. And when we were there the oleander bushes—the species we had seen all the way from Swat—were in full bloom.

Babol Sar has two main attractions—a caviar plant and a beach. The caviar industry flourishes from October to May. In July no caviar fish, the principal one being a hooked-nose species new to me, are caught. Fishing boats ply the Caspian year around and bring to the market several fish, the most important being sturgeon, a fish as popular in Marco Polo's time as now. But practically no fish were caught during our visit there. The other attraction at Babol Sar is the hard, sand beach that runs for five miles or more. It's about a mile and a half from town. Deep loose sand, a quarter of a mile wide, stretches between the edge of the city and the beach. This strip can be traversed only by a jeep. An American Point IV team, headed by Kurt M. Falk of Florida, sent a jeep and a driver; and we used a Point IV tent, pitched behind the beach, for dressing. We spent hours on the beach. Our first day there was Friday, the Moslem Sabbath; and people for miles around packed the beach. Families, each with a bit of canvas stretched on poles for shade, were camped for miles along the sea. Many had brought their own samovars for tea. Hawkers went up and down, selling toys. The most popular merchants were those with melons and roasting ears. The melons, iced in great tubs, were sold by the hundreds; and their rinds soon covered the place. The roasting ears, turned over charcoal in large flat iron pans, were tough. But dipped in a mixture of salt and cooking oil, they were quite palatable.

For the first hundred feet or so the water is ankle-high, and therefore dirty. But beyond that, it is pure blue to the horizon. The bottom is sandy, with no rocks or seaweed. There is good wading against a fine surf for about a hundred yards. Then it is deep-water swimming. The salt water of the Caspian is warmer than the water at Hyannis or Nantucket. But it still leaves a bracing effect, especially in its deeper parts. A life guard sits on a high platform. No life needed saving during our visit; and the life guard always appeared to be sound asleep.

Sailboats ply the southern end of the Caspian, anchoring in a yacht basin near Babol Sar. Men bring their saddle ponies down to the sea for washing and scrubbing. Children by the score run and splash on the edges. No Moslem women, except a few of the sophisticated, don bathing suits. A few, however, fully clothed, went for a dip in their *chadors*. Never have I had a deeper feeling of guilt than when I stalked those timid souls for a photograph.

Our arrival at the beach was an occasion. Boys thronged around me as if I were indeed the Pied Piper. Hundreds followed me wherever I went. They made the task of taking pictures always difficult and sometimes impossible. Just as I was about to get a striking profile, an urchin would interpose his leering face. I could not bribe them or persuade them to leave me alone. Once in a while I got a respite when a policeman came down the beach.

But the rest of the time I was the victim of curiosity, finally resigning myself to my fate and putting up my camera.

One day at Babol Sar Governor Abraham Mahdavi of Mazandaran Province called. The capital is Sari, not far from Babol Sar. The Governor proposed a luncheon at Babol Sar. He and his wife and two daughters were present. This is a strictly modern family who might pass as American even in our Midwest. All members speak English. The older daughter, Sherin, is doing graduate work at the London School of Economics. Her field is sociology; and she was starting in Iran a few days later a field study of education and living conditions in the villages. Here was a family well educated and dedicated to the welfare of their country.

The Governor is promoting a program of industrialization of his province; and the new mills—particularly textile mills—which are going up are a monument to his industry. But industry in Iran is, in modern terms, only beginning. Trade unions are lawful; but they are greatly feared, and so strictly supervised under a regulatory law, that they amount to little more than company unions. One night in Meshed I had met in the lovely garden of the Schott home a group of Iran's labor leaders. This was the story they told me. And Mahdavi confirmed it at Babol Sar.

One night when we were dining in the garden at Babol Sar two Persians came to our table and introduced themselves. They spoke some English and at my invitation joined us for dessert. One was an engineer, one a manager of a new textile mill in the Caspian area. They sought me out because they thought I was an American official disbursing financial aid in Iran. But they stayed on to answer many questions I had on my mind about Persia.

There is much graft in Iran. There is an income tax from which, of course, the royal family is exempt. But many a wealthy man does not pay this tax. He settles for a small amount with an official, and goes his way. There is a tax on real estate, also collected by the central government. But this tax, too, is discriminatory in its application. For those strong enough and rich enough evade it through one tax-evasion device or another or through graft.

At one point the textile man climaxed a point by saying:

"Here in Iran, the wealthier the man is, the fewer taxes he pays."

The Parliament, or Majlis, is made up of these wealthy groups. They are either wealthy in their own right or spokesmen for the powers-that-be. The Majlis has no sharecropper in it. It is a landlord and industrial group. That group is not interested in basic reforms, but in maintenance of the *status quo*. Maintenance of the *status quo* means that the load of taxes remains on the poor, that the rich are practically tax-exempt, that the villages lie deep in poverty, sickness, and misery, while fortunes pile high in foreign bank accounts.

The account I got that evening I heard throughout Iran. Widespread corruption, tax exemption of the rich, the increasing tax load on the poor—these were the complaints I heard from hotel servants, barbers and bazaar owners the length of Iran.

Ramsar, three hours west of Babol Sar, was built by Reza Shah as a tourist attraction. It is much more impressive than Babol Sar. It sits back over a mile from the sea. Between it and the beach are huge formal gardens with a statue of Reza Shah in the center. Cypress trees dominate the garden. There are palm trees too—and crepe myrtle. And when we were there the white lilacs that line the walks were in full bloom. On the beach is a pleasant building, surrounded by cypress, that has a restaurant and dance floor in the middle and dressing rooms in each wing. A large tiled uncovered porch set with tables is popular for tea.

This resort was very quiet the two days we spent there. Moharram had started; the Baghdad Trio that furnished music for this resort had gone its way. For during the fifteen-day period of mourning for Hossein, no music is tolerated; and all dancing is banned.

The beach at Ramsar has a long pier for the loading and unloading of small boats. But the surf churns up so much mud that swimming in front of the resort is not pleasant. The crowd congregates to the east. One can rent chairs and an umbrella from an attendant. The Ramsar beach is more pleasing to the eye than the one at Babol Sar, for it is not strewn with melon rinds and the other debris that comes with heavy usage. Yet the beach at best is a bit on the rocky side and even far out from shore one gets entangled with seaweed. The food at Ramsar is excellent, its service superb. The rooms overlooking the Caspian give a view of beauty and serenity; and the high winds make them restful places for sleep. Ramsar, much more magnificent than Babol Sar, lacks the beach to make it as popular a resort.

As one goes east to west along the Caspian there is a change in economy. Wheat and cotton predominate around Babol Sar. Rice production increases as one moves west. At Ramsar some rice fields—the most beautiful I have seen—are planted right next to the Caspian. The deep green of Persian rice against the sapphire blue of the Caspian Sea gives a richer color picture than any scene I know.

West of Ramsar around Lahijan are many tea plantations with a few tea factories, lying against the green mountains to the south. Here are also many mulberry trees. The Caspian, indeed, has quite a silk industry. Marco Polo commented on it. He called the silk *ghelle*. Today that silk industry is centered at Chalus.

We visited the factory at Chalus. I had seen it before; but I wanted Mercedes and Mary to see it. We were anxious to get colored pictures of the weaving operations. The place was open and the looms were going full speed when we arrived. The director, unfortunately, was away. I had no government official with me to make the arrangements for the visit. So I negotiated them on my own. It was a frustrating experience, the kind that often turns the foreigner against the Persian. The deputy was filled with excuses. Finally he said:

"I can grant you permission only if I have authority from Tehran."

I asked him if he would put in a call to Tehran. He shook his head. I said I would pay for the call. He shook his head. I said that telephonic authority was as good as any authority.

He smiled, shaking his head and saying:

"You see, the authority I need is written authority. If you go to Tehran you may get the written authority. If so, please come back because I would be delighted to show you the weaving."

"There are no military secrets involved," I rejoined. "I took black and white shots when I was here before. All I want are color shots."

"But you see, sir, I do not make the rules; I only enforce them." Though smiling and courteous, the deputy was also getting satisfaction out of my frustration. It was natural that he do so.

For centuries Persia has been tramped on by the foreigner.

For years the foreigner has been the overlord. The great resentment in modern Persian history has been toward the Britisher who pulled concealed wires behind the scenes and made Prime Ministers, Cabinet officers, and even Shahs perform like puppets. The Persian has been so beset, befuddled, and enraged at foreign manipulations that the sense of joy at the foreigner's frustration comes naturally. Knowing the powerful forces piled up in the emotions of these fine people, I did not feel offended; and I left in good humor. But I sadly missed the color photographs of the silk weaving.

I had another disappointment on the Caspian. A 1957 earthquake had badly shaken the northern slopes of the Caspian and caused so much damage and suffering that the Shah cut short a vacation in Europe to return home. The damage was done in a series of settlements high in the mountains. The official figure of dead and missing was 1000. The earth opened in great yawning gaps, swallowing entire villages.

Mahdavi had been up there on inspection trips and wanted me to go. We did not have time to go on our own, as it is an eight-hour muleback journey after one parks the car high in the hills. That would require a minimum of three days from the Caspian. Mahdavi suggested an airplane, a two-seater that would pick me up at Ramsar and return me the same day. The plan suited me perfectly. Every morning we scanned the skies; and each day, though the valley was clear, the top of the Elburz was deep in clouds. The Elburz rise 20,000 feet and catch the moisture from the Caspian on their northern slopes. The Caspian is the world's largest inland sea, covering 170,000 square miles. This huge body of water changes the character of the Elburz. Their northern slopes are thick in undergrowth and deciduous trees. When we were there, moisture was catching along the slopes and hanging there in dark clouds. We waited four days but no plane could get clearance for the ridges. So we never saw the earthquake area of the high Elburz.

We did, however, have an interesting visit to Pahlavi. The road down from Ramsar, like all Caspian Sea roads, is gravel and very dusty. It's a hard three-hour drive, for the road is washboard for miles on end; and there are many villages and small settlements to pass, making slow speed necessary.

We went at a relaxed rate, for we were out to get a few photographs. We found women washing rice mats in streams that come off the Elburz. Some were cultivating rows of tea bushes. Others were picking the tender green leaves. Some were rocking babies on porches of thatched huts that stood high on stilts. Others were carrying water in earthen jars on their heads. Whatever they were doing, they were gaily dressed in blues, yellows, and reds. And each one had a scarf tied around her head, for this day the wind was brisk from the north.

Pahlavi is Iran's big port on the Caspian. It has several hotels, the oldest being the Grand where I had stayed in 1955 when I caught the Russian boat to Baku. The Grand, though very decrepit and run down, has a wonderful cook; and the food is among Persia's best. This noon we had a rich *borsch* soup and some nicely turned, delicate *shish kabab*. Then we went down to the water front and hired a wooden boat with a white canopy that was rowed from the stern by a swarthy, silent Iranian.

The beaches at Pahlavi are the dirtiest along the Caspian; and the water off the beaches is muddy. But the harbor, protected from the surf by a sea wall, is calm and clear. We traveled up and down the length and width of it, getting pictures. At one end are fish-packing plants. Salt fish is packed in large flat boxes. Caviar is packed in tins that rest in the middle of wooden barrels, filled with ice. Some of the fish goes to Iranian markets. Most of it goes to Russia under a trade agreement. Persian caviar is almost a staple in Soviet Russia. It's so highly prized it could as easily be the cause of war as coffee could be with us. Iran sells most of its caviar and most of its tea and cotton to Russia. In exchange she gets from Russia many manufactured products, including automobiles and steel products for building materials.

This day a Russian ship was in port. For sentimental reasons, I hoped it was the *Pioneer,* which I had taken to Baku. But it was not. This combination passenger and freighter was the *Baksovet.* It was unloading when we came alongside. The Russian crew gathered on deck to cheer and jeer as we photographed them. One, more serious than the others, took off his straw hat and held it over his face so he would not be recorded in "a spy's film." When they were finished shouting us away, they went back to the task of unloading the freighter. What they were unloading were Western-type toilets made in Russia. I had counted two hundred before Mercedes' insistent call turned me back to the car.

CHAPTER 5

MISHAPS ON THE TEHRAN ROAD

It's a six-hour drive from Chalus over the Elburz Mountains to Tehran. The road is dirt practically all the way. It was surveyed and constructed by German engineers in the 1930s during the reign of Reza Shah. The grade is easy; the shoulders wide; the bridges and culverts excellent. It's a pleasure to drive this road.

The northern slopes are thick with foliage; the southern slopes barren. The views en route to the top from the Caspian are often startling. The top itself, like our own Continental Divide, is not dramatic. One needs extra water on this trip. For while the Elburz canyons have plenty, the climb down from the road is anywhere from two hundred to a thousand feet.

Our crossing was uneventful except for two circumstances. We were not more than an hour out of Chalus when we heard the muffler hit the ground with its familiar bang. I pulled to the side of the road and stopped. Mercedes got out a straw mat and lay on it, trying to fasten the muffler so that it would not drag. Soon a bus loaded with people caught up with us. These busses, like the Afghan ones, have helpers hanging on the sides. Women in Iran have only recently been emancipated. Few ever drive a car, let alone repair one. The sight of a woman under a car was apparently too much for this driver. He stopped, ordered his helper to give us assistance, and moved on, knowing we would bring the helper with us. With the aid of baling wire and the helper, Mercedes fastened the muffler; and the helper traveled with us until we caught up with the bus. On we went, climbing steadily. We had gone hardly twenty miles more when the muffler came loose again, this time with an ominous bang. Once more Mercedes got under the car and went to work. This time her verdict was that the muffler could not be refastened securely, that the only thing to do was to take it off. It was a difficult job to do because the muffler was practically red hot. When she was close to success, the worst happened; the muffler fell on her left hand and arm, burning her severely on the palm and fingers and above the wrist to the elbow. Now we had not only a car to repair but a mechanic to get back to health.

We bandaged her hand and arm as best we could, put the muffler in the car, and headed up the Elburz to the 6958-foot pass we had to cross. We had left all timber and now were in barren land. There was no cover for the slopes except grass and weeds. The Elburz have the reputation of flowering in rare beauty, come springtime. Now the wild flowers had all gone at this elevation except the lupine, mostly blue, that painted streaks along the slopes. Near the top, a truck going our way was stalled in the middle of the road. A half dozen other trucks were piled up on each side of the stalled one. The truck drivers were all talking at once and no one was doing anything about clearing the highway.

The stalled truck was out of gas. Plainly it could have been rolled backward so as to be parked on the roadside. Then traffic could move and an emissary could be sent for gasoline. But the truck driver was a smart person. The nearest gasoline station was at Gach Sar, over twenty miles south. Iranians are highly individualistic. They had to be in order to survive all their invasions. They know a strategic position when they see it. This truck driver knew he was in the best possible position. He was astride the highway so that no one could pass. In that position everyone had an interest in helping him get gasoline. If he were parked on the side of the road, the list of those willing to help would get shorter.

When I joined the group, the discussion concerned ways and means of siphoning gasoline from some of the trucks. No one had a hose. No one had a funnel. Only one man had a bucket. The men coming up from Gach Sar did not want to turn their trucks around and go down for the gasoline. No one else could do so because the road was blocked.

After listening for a while, I said that I had a can of gasoline and a funnel. The whole crowd, over a dozen men, followed me to the rear of our car. The truck driver who was stalled was instantly filled with joy. He eagerly took the jerry can containing five gallons and the funnel and poured my gasoline into his truck. Soon the engine was roaring. As he pulled out he bowed graciously and shouted over and again:

"Kheyli mamnoonum," or "Thank you very much."

He did not offer to pay me; and I was glad he did not. For, over the years, the Persians have been so kind to me it is only in these ways I can ever hope to catch up.

We practically coasted down to Gach Sar where we got gasoline and oil and ate luncheon in the car. We had crackers and cheese and a tin of cherries that had been canned in India. Then we rolled down the Karaj River Canyon, past the huge hydroelectric project American engineers are building—the one that has been severely criticized as improvident but that is going ahead to completion. At the town of Karaj we picked up black asphalt pavement and continued to drop to the warm, rather barren plains where Tehran sits. The city was now only ten miles or so distant. The airport was off to the right. A Pepsi-Cola bottling plant was straight ahead. Far in the distance the dome and minarets of a mosque pierced upward from mud roofs. It was five o'clock and I could almost feel the cold shower I was headed for. At that moment the left rear tire went down and I pulled off the busy highway.

The traffic was so thick and the road so narrow that it was dangerous to change the tire. The passenger cars and trucks whizzed by perilously close. Mercedes' hand and arm were giving her great pain. Nevertheless, in spite of all the handicaps Mercedes, Mary, and I changed tires in ten minutes flat, Mercedes doing most of the work while I got some wonderful pictures.

CHAPTER 6

AN AUGURY

Though Tehran lies at an elevation of nearly 4000 feet, it is a hot sticky town in summertime. Those who can move out to Shemiran, which is a suburb nearly 6000 feet high on the lower skirts of the Elburz. Tehran is moving that way. New houses, each with a walled garden and most of them built of brick, are spreading in that direction. Some of Tehran's oldest and loveliest homes are also there. Nowhere in all the East do I know of any spot where more beautiful walled gardens can be found. Ice-cold pools, tall pines, rock gardens, winding paths, roses, phlox, geraniums, hollyhocks are there in designs and patterns as intricate as the personality of the owner.

We stayed at the Darband Hotel in Shemiran, a fine modern hostel owned by the Shah himself. Breakfast is served in one's room. There is an inside dining room where lunch is served. Dinner is on a tiled terrace around a large pool frequented by a lonesome male swan. There is a covered stage where an eight-piece orchestra usually plays at night. But this was Moharram and the orchestra was absent. It was so delightfully cool at the Darband that we slept ten hours the first night without waking up.

Our first order of business in Tehran was getting the car fixed. The list of repairs and adjustments was a long one, beginning with the muffler, the ventilator window and side-view mirror broken by the Afghan dog, and the missing chrome ring of the horn. There are many garages in Tehran, and all the spare parts an American car would ever need. Iran has no foreign exchange problem when it comes to dollars. The markets are filled with imported articles, many from America. Shopping in Tehran is like shopping in Des Moines or in Paris. It now has a Western-type department store, called the Ferdowsi, with fixed prices and all signs printed in English as well as in German. There is a wide choice and an infinite variety of consumer goods in the shops. Tehran is more of a Western than an Eastern town. Its mosques, its covered bazaar, and its walled gardens give it the imprint of the East. But the architecture is mostly Western, as are its broad avenues of modern shops.

The garage problem in Tehran is the same as our own—finding the most reliable and the most competent one. The Ford garage was recommended and there is where I went. Its mechanics did excellent work; and at the end of five days we drove out a car that from all appearances and from the hum of the motor was brand new.

During the interlude we flew to Shiraz and Isfahan by Iranian Airways.

Shiraz in southern Iran is one of the oldest and yet most modern cities in Asia. Sa'di, who lies buried in Shiraz, spoke in eloquent verse of Shiraz:

> Pleasant is the New Year's entry, especially in
> Shiraz,
> Which turns aside the heart of the wanderer from
> his native land.

Hafiz, also buried in Shiraz, loved the place beyond all others.

> The Kazvinis steal our hearts, the
> Tabrizis have lips like sugar,
> Beautiful are the Isfahanis, but I am
> the slave of Shiraz.

It was to him a "site without peer."

Shiraz lies 5000 feet high, nearly the elevation of Denver, Colorado. It rests on a well-watered plain about seven miles wide. The plain is surrounded by hills that are purple in summer. The valley is broad and green. Dark shade marks the stately cypress trees that adorn the gardens; there are lighter shades of green from fields, and lawns, and orchards. The streets are wide; turquoise domes rise above groves of trees; slender minarets stand in splendor.

On this landing the plane came down low and we barely skimmed the tops of the cypress trees of the famous Garden of Heaven. My heart sank. When I last saw this place, it was a pre-eminent establishment occupied by the Khans of the Ghashghai tribe as a winter home. The mansion is a lovely building with well-proportioned rooms and hallways of delicate tiles. A small creek runs through the living room over a series of small falls that produce music lovelier than a stringed trio. The garden was beautifully manicured when I saw it last. Now the whole place looked as if it were in ruins. A huge stack of hay had been piled in the garden. The lawn was untouched. The flower beds were shriveled. Only the tall cypress seemed to have survived the ordeal.

The Ghashghai Khans were now in disfavor. They had been banished from Shiraz. These Ghashghais were old friends of mine. I had been with them for a week one fall when they moved 300,000 men and women and children on foot, on donkeys, and on camels three hundred miles to their winter quarters on the Persian Gulf. I had hunted and ridden with the men over the Namdan Plain and lain out with them in the Zagros Mountains. They were old friends who had once rendered a fine service to the United States and the cause of freedom.

In 1946 the Ghashghais had helped save Persia from the Communists. The Russians, who had been in occupation of parts of Iran during World War II, left behind many people to do their bidding. One who was susceptible was Qavam-os-Saltaneh, who was Prime Minister. On August 2, 1946, apparently reacting to the pressure of Soviet power, he added to his Cabinet men who were sympathetic with the Tudeh Party and members of it. Moreover, in southern Persia along the Gulf and in Shiraz, the Communists had heavily infiltrated the army and local units of government.

On September 23, 1946, the four Ghashghai Khans sent a telegram to Qavam demanding that certain reforms be made and that the Communists be eliminated from the government.

Their ultimatum was not met. The Ghashghais, some 50,000 strong, moved into action. They had only cavalry equipped with rifles. They had to face tanks. They set fire to the tanks with bottles of gasoline. The battle raged at Bushire on the Persian Gulf for one day. When that town fell, the Ghashghais moved on Shiraz. As the attack on Shiraz started, the Qavam government negotiated with the Ghashghai Khans through the commander of the Shiraz garrison. The demands of the Ghashghais were largely met. Qavam resigned and all of the Tudeh members and sympathizers were dismissed from the government.

In 1953 the Ghashghais helped American interests even more directly. On April 16, a mob wrecked the Point IV office in Shiraz. The Communists had started the slogan "Yankee Go Home" and the rioters responded. The local authorities in Shiraz made no effort to halt the attack.

The American hero of the event was E. C. Bryant, head of Point IV in Shiraz, who got the women and children out only a few blocks ahead of a mob of 500 rioters.

The Persian heroes were the Ghashghais. Bibi Ghashghai, mother of the four Khans, was at the Garden of Heaven. This remarkable woman, on hearing of the Communist threat, sent word to the Americans to make her home their haven. And she sent word to the tribe to send armed tribesmen forthwith. The tribe was on its northern migration, not far from Shiraz. Nasser Khan and Malek Mansour, the oldest of the four Khans, were with the tribe. Meanwhile, Bibi took fifty Ghashghai boys out of school in Shiraz and brought them to the Garden of Heaven, and armed them, together with fifteen servants, with clubs and put them outside as guards of the palace.

Bibi's courier reached the tribe that night. The Khans summoned their tribesmen, who are always armed on the migration and who ride beautiful Arabian horses. Sixty of them rode all night and reached Shiraz before dawn. On their way to Shiraz they met other Ghashghais and told them to spread the word and bring more armed tribesmen and to join them.

When the sixty Ghashghai cavalry arrived, the rioters were burning and looting. These armed Ghashghais held off the mob. By noon they were joined by 1000 more Ghashghais. By midafternoon 10,000 armed Ghashghais had arrived. The Ghashghais put out a proclamation that the Communists were fighting Ghashghais, not Americans. The opposition quickly melted away; and the third day after the rioting started, Shiraz was once more peaceful.

Those were my thoughts as the wheels of the plane put down at Shiraz.

Many officials were there to greet us, Americans as well as Iranians. And it was a warm reception we received. But I kept scanning the crowd for the telltale sign of a Ghashghai. Gashghai friendship is enduring; and I knew there would be one to meet me if they had heard of my coming. While I had sent no word to them, I felt sure they would know of it. For news travels fast in Iran. It's known as the *giveh* telegraph, *giveh* being a moccasin made of webbing and worn by all peasants in Iran. Soon I saw a Ghashghai on the edge of the crowd—a young man with the typical Ghashghai headdress—a round felt hat with flaps fore and aft. I had never seen him before. He greeted me warmly on behalf of his people and then slipped away as mysteriously as he had appeared.

Two of the Americans who met us were Mr. and Mrs. Donald W. Gilfillan. Mr. Gilfillan heads an important Point IV program in Shiraz, the one that the Communists in 1953 inveighed against.

We went to the Gilfillans' for lunch. We went to the Nemazee Hospital to have Mercedes' burns dressed and to take a tour of it. Mohammed Nemazee, a wealthy Iranian who has a keen sense of public duty, first installed a public water system in Shiraz. He drilled for water and found artesian wells. He laid water mains and brought the water to every house in Shiraz. It took some years to complete the project. As Iran had no plumbers adequate for the task, they first had to be trained. Finally in 1951 Shiraz became the first town in Persia to have pure cold water from taps in every house. Then Mr. Nemazee donated $6,000,000 to build a hospital there. It's as fine as any I have seen in America. Its rooms are clean and modern. Its operating tables, laundries, kitchens, and laboratories are up to the minute. It's a hospital that serves poor patients as well as paying patients. About 50 per cent of its patients are admitted free or virtually free. The day we were there several beggars from the bazaar were being cared for. It's a bright spot in a bleak medical environment.

The doctors are excellent. The director, A. T. Mehra, is a dynamo of energy, as well as a good physician.

The main problem of the hospital concerns nurses. Women in *purdah* were never allowed to be nurses. The lifting of *purdah* has lifted the taboo. But habits are hard to change. Iranian parents still turn their daughters away from nursing, as it is too intimate a relation with men. The consequence is that the Nemazee Hospital has great difficulty in obtaining nurses. There is a fine medical school in Shiraz that turns out fifty doctors a year. The nursing school in 1956 turned out only four graduate nurses. I met them, and they are bright-eyed and ambitious. Beginning in 1958, the nursing school will turn out fifteen nurses a year, still far too few for the needs of the hospital.

We stood at the entrance of the hospital, saying farewell to the staff. There in the distance across the valley was a line of hills. Actually two hills form the sky line, though from this point they seem to be one. Their profile shows the head, nose, chin, and throat of a man lying flat on his back with a protruding belly. This profile is called Kuh Mostasghi, which means the Dropsical Mountain. Dr. Mehra joked about it.

"Even the mountains of Shiraz are a medical challenge," he commented as we drove off.

There is much to see in Shiraz and we saw far from all of it. But we did include two historic sites—the tomb of Hafiz and the tomb of Sa'di, both poets of Shiraz.

Sa'di was born in Shiraz in 1184 and died there in 1291 at the age of a hundred and seven.

Sa'di was a writer of didactic verse. He was also a coiner of epigrams:

> He knows the value of health who lost his strength in fever.
>
> Take a new wife each spring, O friend, for last year's
> almanac serves no purpose.
>
> He who worships grandeur is the slave of pride.
>
> Prison is preferable to a house full of frowns.
>
> That poor man is a king whose wife is obedient and chaste.
>
> Utter not slander before a wall—oft may it happen
> that behind are listening ears.
>
> He whose stomach is full is void of wisdom.

Sa'di was not only a maker of epigrams; he was also a philosopher who wrote:

> The sons of Adam are members one of another, for in their creation they have a common origin. If the vicissitudes of fortune involve one member in pain, all the other members will feel a sympathy. Thou who art indifferent to other men's infliction, if they call thee a man, art unworthy of the name.

He has a pretty tomb set behind cypress, pine, and orange trees with vineyards in the distance. It's a rather somber place, the tomb being marked by a tall tower in blue tile. When I first saw the tomb in 1950 it was being repaired. In 1957 the dome over the tomb was cracking and falling and in new need of repair. The truth is that though Sa'di is highly respected as a great poet, he is not held in the same respect as Hafiz. The reason, I think, is that Sa'di was a Sunni or orthodox Moslem, while Hafiz was a Shiite. Sa'di is too heavy for a regular diet. Hafiz reflects more the Persian soul.

Every Persian has a real affection for Hafiz. He was born in 1300 and died in 1388; also a product of Shiraz, Hafiz means "one who remembers," a term applied to one who has learned the Koran by heart. The Persians have a lovely spot for his tomb. It lies in a quiet garden that one enters by climbing eight steps. The tomb is in the middle of this garden, dominated by pine and cypress. It's made of marble and rests under a canopy with a hexagonal roof supported at the corners by eight stone pillars. There is a narrow ledge around the base of the tomb where people kneel in prayer. It is indeed customary for Persians to take an augury there, some coming from many miles to do so. They bring with them the Diwan—one volume of Hafiz' poems. The book may be a pocket edition or it may be de luxe, with pages eighteen inches long. The suppliant kneels at the tomb and prays. At the end he slips his (or her) finger into the volume, opening it at random. Sometimes I have seen a servant sprinkle the open pages with rose petals before the text is read, the owner then brushing them aside to read the augury. Usually the suppliant merely opens and reads, seeking from the verses in the open pages some clue to his perplexity, some comfort to his sorrow.

A word should be said about this practice of taking an augury.

In Persia it is done with only one of two books, the Koran or the Diwan of Hafiz. It is generally believed that, if one has doubts as to what he should do, clues may be obtained by saying a prayer and then opening the Diwan at random. The clue is to be found either in the passage that first meets the eye or the last ode on the open page plus the first line of the succeeding ode. The bazaar of Shiraz is filled with stories of auguries. Browne, *Literary History of Persia,* gives an account of some of the most famous ones in history. The one I witnessed is repeated dozens of times a week in Shiraz.

On this visit, only one man was praying, a bareheaded man about forty years of age in Western clothes. He had no coat or necktie; his sleeves were rolled up. He had a small volume of the Diwan that would fit his rear pocket. He prayed for some time. And when he opened the book he read as follows:

> Mine enemies have persecuted me,
> My love has turned and fled from out my door—
> God counts our tears and knows our misery;
> Ah, weep not! He has heard thy weeping sore.
> And chained in poverty and plunged in night,
> O Hafiz, take thy Koran and recite
> Litanies infinite, and weep no more!

The man had been very morose. Now his eyes lighted up.

"Is this good news?" I asked.

"Yes," he replied. "I lost my job. But now things look better for me."

CHAPTER 7

GOD IS MOST GREAT

An old friend had accompanied us from Tehran to Shiraz—M. Kazemi of the Seven Year Plan. He was with us the day we visited Persepolis.

We left Shiraz by car, climbing to the northeast through a low chain of hills and coming out on a vast plain known as Marv Dasht. This is irrigated country, growing mostly sugar beets for a factory near Shiraz. Point IV has the Baghjah Experimental Farm and Livestock Station on this plain where alfalfa, melons, and other agricultural produce are grown and developed. Also prominent are several prize bulls and a large collection of roosters and hens. The bulls are used for artificial insemination; the chickens for crossbreeding with native stock.

Our Point IV people have a diesel engine that pumps water from deep wells for extensive irrigation. I talked with Kazi, whose family has long been in agriculture, about the economics of this system as compared with the *qanat* or underground tunnel, extensively used in all Iran.

I have already referred to the *qanat*. It taps underground reservoirs of water in a land where the surface streams are scarce and the run-offs quick and wasteful. Iran is covered with *qanats*, there being at least 20,000 of them. I use the word "covered" because one sees these *qanats* from the air as a long line of craters stretching for miles. Sometimes two lines of craters meet, forming a Y. They start on a high slope and empty into a valley for irrigation purposes. One who comes to the mouth of a *qanat* has a source of drinking water as pure as an artesian well.

These craters one sees from the air are piles of dirt from sunken wells. The wells, all dug by hand, start with a mother well up the slope. The mother well may be a hundred feet deep. Once water is struck the direction of its flow is estimated and the diggers go downhill a few rods to dig another well. The two wells are then connected by a tunnel. The dirt from these excavations is piled in low cones around the well openings so as to keep surface drainage from entering. As wells are dug in succession and connecting tunnels made, an underground waterway is constructed. The task is delicate, for the grade of this underground waterway must be so slight that it will not cause erosion in the tunnel. The *qanat* digging is a skill handed down from father to son. The tools are simple—pick and shovel, a level, compass, and buckets. The buckets are usually leather and hauled to the surface by a hand-operated windlass. Most of the tunnel walls are unlined. But when the underground waterway passes through soft dirt or loose gravel prone to cave-ins, shoring is used. These are U-shaped, made of baked clay. Since the tunnel of the *qanat* is only about two feet wide and three and a half feet high, these U-shaped clay bracings are a standardized product made by brickmakers.

Landlords and tenants alike swear by the *qanat*. Since it produces more water in the winter than in the summer, it may not be considered efficient by Western standards. But it works, and is cheap to operate—much cheaper than diesel oil for a pump, according to Kazi. And the digging of the *qanat* certainly costs no more than the digging of an artesian well and the installation of a pump. Kazi maintains that the installation of a *qanat* is in fact cheaper than an artesian well.

"Why go in for technological advances when they reduce your profits?" Kazi asked with a grin.

I was to be convinced more than once on this trip that many "outmoded" methods of ancient vintage were better suited to Asian needs than the "modern" methods of the West.

Some farmers we saw kept water costs at a miserably low level. They got water from dug wells in an ancient way: a goatskin was tied to a rope and the rope run over a wooden cylinder or pulley above the center of the well; a horse backed up to lower the goatskin into the well and walked forward to pull it up. When the goatskin full of water was clear of the ground, a boy pulled a cord that lowered the small end of the skin so that the water ran out into a trough leading to the irrigation system. A covered runway had been erected for the horse, as this was a long day's operation beginning at sunup and continuing until dark. But it is a system that works, one well watering forty acres or more of sugar beets.

Persepolis is a small village with perhaps a dozen mud huts. Beyond the huts is the Apadana Hotel. It's a rambling one-story building with a dozen bedrooms. The place is modern and well maintained; and the food is good. The presence of the hotel adds to the pleasure of Persepolis. Now one can stay for days and do his sight-seeing leisurely. And if he comes at the time of the full moon, he can see the stately ruins under romantic conditions.

When we were there, Persepolis was guarded by gendarmes from Baluchistan. They were short, dark, and wiry; each boasted a heavy black mustache; and each wore a white pith helmet.

Persepolis sits on a terrace of many acres. On the east is the Mountain of Mercy; on the other three sides are immense stone retaining walls 14 to 50 feet high and as much as 29 feet wide. The terrace is over 300 yards wide and 500 yards long.

Two staircases in two sections, each with 110 steps, reach the terrace. At one time they were the only access to Persepolis. They are so wide that the story is that ten horsemen can ride up them abreast. This I doubt. But they are wide and very low, not more than four inches or so high. At the head of the stairway is the Propylaea or the Entrance Hall of the Apadana Palace. It is often called the Gate of Xerxes since the inscriptions on it show that he erected, or at least completed, it.

The empire of Darius (521–485 B.C.), the King who started Persepolis and made it capital of Persia, included many nations, the most western being Greece. It was through the Propylaea they all came to pay homage to the King. A pair of bulls eighteen feet high carved on the stone doorways guard the western entrance and winged man-bulls are at the eastern doorway. These figures have been defaced over the years by tourists who carve or scratch their names there; and it came as a shock to me to find that Curzon, the distinguished Britisher, was in the group.

A third doorway opens to the south—to the Apadana—Darius' palace of audience. Of its seventy columns, thirteen remain standing and are the most photographed part of all Persepolis. To the south of the Apadana is the Tachara or the private palace of Darius the Great. Beyond is the Hadish (a dwelling place)—the private palace of Xerxes.

The Apadana has two flights of steps leading up to its level, one on the north and one on the east side. These staircases are among the unique and priceless masterpieces of art of Achaemenian times. They show the representatives of the countries throughout the empire bringing gifts and offerings to the King. They have broad low steps. One who walks up does so slowly and meekly, not quickly and boldly. He must take short steps that go better with humility and obeisance than with arrogance. One morning when we walked up the eastern steps they were sharply reflected in the sun as men were washing the friezes with water, then polishing them with wax to bring out each detail. The curator has erected a wooden roof over this stairway to help preserve these friezes.

The largest palace is the Hall of the Hundred Columns, sometimes called the Throne Hall since another section with a hundred columns had been unearthed to the south next to the Treasury, the storehouse of the Achaemenian wealth. This largest palace lies between the Apadana and the Mountain of Mercy. Its columns are no longer standing but its tremendous stone doorways facing the four points of the compass show marvelous carvings with the bearded King Darius seated on his throne.

There is also the Central Palace, which is approached from the southern end of the eastern staircase to the Apadana. It has three doorways known as the Tripylon, and just beyond it lies the Harem or the Queen's apartments. This has been restored and is used as a museum and office for the staff of the Archaeological Institute of Persepolis.

On the slope of the Mountain of Mercy, which borders the terrace of Persepolis on the east, are three tombs, one unfinished and two supposed to be the tombs of Artaxerxes II and Artaxerxes III. One morning I climbed to these sepulchres to get pictures of Persepolis in the soft morning light. I stopped first at a well, high on the hill, where Darius got water for Persepolis. The well is still being used. A servant of the curator was drawing water from it with a bucket. I was thirsty from my exertion and waited anxiously for the bucket to come up. But when it got close to my face, I found it had a repulsive odor. The servant told me of the fast flow of the well and assured me it could be pumped free and clear of all pollution.

I climbed higher to the tombs and saw the whole great terrace below me. A lonely-looking Persian sat on a low stone wall. I solicited his help in getting a good picture of Persepolis. For such a long-distance view, one needs a face or figure in the near foreground. I proffered him some coins as a reward; and he pocketed them eagerly. After posing for a few pictures, he suddenly took my coins out of his pocket, handed them to me with an oath, angrily vaulted the low wall, and disappeared among the limestone rocks on the hillside below the tombs. Why, I never knew.

Darius was a Zoroastrian and Ahura Mazda was his god. On the southern façade of the terrace, Darius inscribed: "On this spot, by the grace of Ahura Mazda, I built a fortress where no fortress had ever stood before."

Along the stairway leading to the Apadana Palace of Darius, Xerxes, who finished the structure his father began, inscribed:

"By the will of Ahura Mazda, I added to that which had been built and built additional. May Ahura Mazda along with the gods protect me and my Kingdom."

One who sees the ruins from above can recreate the magnificence of this ancient capital. There was plenty of water to keep the terrace green. This is arid country, needing irrigation. In the ancient days the plain of Marv Dasht was green with crops as it is today. Irrigated valleys against parched hills that lie purple in the distance make a picture of contrasts that spell beauty to one who loves the desert. Never have I seen a picture of desert splendor more overwhelming than that of Persepolis. This is a place one needs days to see. As the light changes, the ancient ruins take on a different mood. In the fullness of early morning light, it's a palace. In midday it's a welcome oasis. With the lengthening shadows of evening it becomes a fortress. In the moonlight it's half built, but soon to ring out with laughter and music.

We went eight miles north by car to Naqsh-i-Rustam where four tombs are cut high on a sheer rock wall. These are the burial places of Darius I, Xerxes I, Artaxerxes I, and Darius II. One reaches them by a wobbly ladder about sixty feet high which leads to a shelf in the cliff off which a low doorway opens with a long, narrow gallery where four tombs have been hewn out of the rock.

As one faces the tombs he sees crosses cut out of the rock, the surface having been deeply chipped away. The arms of the crosses are of equal length; and each is about half as wide as it is long. There is one for each of the four rock sepulchres. They are roughly seventy feet high and sixty feet wide. Each is a façade for one of the tombs.

Each doorway is marked by two columns capped by heads of bulls. The upper limb of each cross is elaborately sculptured. Two rows of vassal subjects in bas-relief support the King, who thus makes them his footstool. The King is shown in worship before the sacred fire over which is the winged effigy of Ahura Mazda.

Seven panels are carved along the base of the rock below the tombs. One is a royal group. Two are equestrian sculptures representing two stages of a battle in which the King triumphs. A fourth shows the surrender of the Roman Emperor Valerian. A fifth shows a lively battle on horseback. The sixth shows a royal group. The seventh shows Ardashir on horseback trampling his Parthian adversaries.

Naqsh-i-Rustam is a misleading name for the place. That means "Rustam's Picture"; and it acquired that name on the mistaken belief that the equestrian statues represented Rustam and his famous horse.

This is a blistering hot spot on a summer day, for the rock wall gives off heat like a furnace.

There is no tree one can sit under to enjoy the scene. The gendarmes have a hut there. And next to the hut is an edifice most interesting of all. It's a square structure built of rock and standing perhaps forty feet high. It can be climbed inside. It is probably contemporary with Darius I. For it is a fire temple, called the Shrine of Zoroaster by the natives.

One night in a quarter moon we walked Persepolis. It seemed much larger in the moonlight. In the dim golden glow it took on new character. The ruins seemed to shape themselves into a half-built edifice of great splendor. One could almost recreate, in this shadowy moonlight, the palace as it was before Alexander destroyed it.

This destruction of Persepolis was an awful thing. It fell to Alexander without opposition, for Alexander had defeated Darius III in a decisive battle near Erbil in modern Iraq. The race was now on to reach the treasure cities of Persia before others looted them or secreted their wealth. Persepolis was one of these; and Alexander by a forced march of three hundred miles in wintertime reached it in thirty days to find its wealth, mostly in gold, intact. The gold and silver of Persepolis was estimated at 4500 tons. There was so much loot at Persepolis that it took 20,000 mules and 5000 camels to carry it away. In the celebration that ensued, many people were slaughtered; but Persepolis remained intact. Various legends of its burning are extant. Plutarch created an Athenian woman, Thais, as the instigator. By that story she egged Alexander on to the deed at a drinking party. The truth probably is that, since Xerxes destroyed the Acropolis when he conquered Greece, Alexander exacted repayment when he took Persepolis. The burning was symbolic of his power to undo all the wrongs the Persians had inflicted on the Greeks.

On our return to Shiraz, we saw the city in some of the views that Hafiz liked best. First we reached the stream Ruknabad which the poet said was lovelier than any in Paradise. Then we reached a turning of the road where Shiraz comes into view. When one first sees Shiraz from this point, Hafiz wrote, he is so overwhelmed with the beauty of the view that he will say "*Allahu Akbar* [God is most great]." The distant valley is dark green against purple hills. Above the distant trees are dozens of minarets from about fifty mosques, pointed like colored fingers to the sky. Soon we reached an arch over the highway. It is called the Arch of the Koran. In a chamber in the arch is preserved a gigantic Koran—a book so heavy with gold that it weighs over fifty pounds. Below the Koran arch is Isfahan Gate through the city wall.

As we passed through the gate to the rose gardens, Judas trees, sycamores, and cypress trees of Shiraz, I felt at one with Hafiz about the place. I had an advantage over him. He saw only the beauty of the city. I saw more. For I saw a city that he had romanticized and helped make into a sanctuary. Not Hafiz alone. Sa'di too. And in addition to them, the Bab. This man, Mirza Ali Mohammed, was born in Shiraz in 1820, and became the founder of the Bahai faith—a religion that recognizes all prophets—Zoroaster and Mohammed, as well as Christ, and opens its arms to those of all faiths. It was the Bab who wrote, "No one is to be slain for unbelief, for the slaying of a soul is outside the religion of God . . . no sin can be greater for him than this."

Shiraz is a home of culture, poetry, and philosophy. It joins my small list of choice cities the world around.

CHAPTER 8

A CITY OF MONUMENTS AND ARTISANS

When the Iranian Airways plane was approaching Isfahan, the pilot sent word for me to come to the cockpit. He said he would go off course, if I liked, and bank the plane against the sun so that I could get a color picture of the famous blue mosque known as Masjed-e-Shah. I opened the cockpit window on the pilot's side, braced myself, and as the plane turned, took several shots of the splendid edifice. Its dome is 145 feet high. The walls and dome are tile over brick. And on this bright July day, the tile of Masjed-e-Shah was as blue as the sky itself. From the sky it looked like a massive jewel set in dark green.

Some two hundred and fifty miles to the west as the crow flies were the Zagros Range of mountains running north and south and separating Iran from Iraq. Its high peaks were snow-flecked. They were dark blue in the distance. The sight of them brought back memories crowded with many events. For there I had hiked, ridden, and hunted with the Bakhtiari tribe. Like the Ghashghais, they were now adopted brothers. They too were in trouble. Bahman Samsam, a young Khan in his late forties, had been jailed for four months. There was no charge against him. The powers-that-be merely feared that he would be elected to office. I did not know if Bahman had been released from prison. But I knew that the Bakhtiari would have someone meeting me if they knew I was coming. Though I had not sent word, news of this sort, as I have said, travels quicker than airplanes in Iran.

Gordon King, American Consul, and his wife, were the first to greet us. Then came the Governor, Mohammed Zolfaghari, whom I had met in Tehran on early visits; the Mayor, Habib Eshraghi, newly arrived on the political horizon; and an old friend, General Jehanbeglu of the Isfahan Brigade. And behind them, grinning from ear to ear, was Bahman Samsam, with the message that his father, now an invalid, was in Isfahan and anxious to see me. This landing was for me a homecoming, and for Mercedes and Mary it was, I think, an introduction to a fascinating city.

Isfahan has been under many rulers. Its history is long and bloody. Timur, who conquered it in the mid-1300s, slaughtered 200,000 people. It has many scars of disaster on it. It was Shah Abbas who constructed the beautiful Isfahan we know today. His work started about 1598, when he mobilized architects and artisans to make Isfahan a beautiful city. Shah Abbas decided it would be his capital. This man, noted for his cruelty, made it one of the loveliest cities the East has known.

Isfahan, unlike Tehran, has no mark of the West on it. There are streets of quaint shops; and the main bazaar is covered with vaulted roofs. Every house, no matter how small, has a walled garden, and every garden has a rose. The city has a collection of mosques and shrines it would take weeks to explore.

The oldest and the most popular is Friday Mosque, which to some seems the least artistic and beautiful of all. It was built about A.D. 1089. But there are units in it that go back to Zoroastrian days. One section with low arched ceilings and alabaster windows has its floor covered with mats where people pray. Thousands gather here every Friday. In the center court is a wooden throne where the *mullah* preaches. It rests on four pillars rising from a pool of water. It is therefore a symbol of the earth. Friday Mosque, in great need of repair, is probably the holiest place in Isfahan. One goes quietly, for at all hours someone is there for prayer. The walls are covered with interesting inscriptions that contain decrees of ancient Shahs: one prohibited soldiers from entering homes on foraging expeditions; a second prohibited the use of alcoholic drinks; a third abolished tolls and certain obnoxious taxes.

There are also many Islamic religious schools in Isfahan. One we visited was the Madresseh-e-Mader-e-Shah, built about 1706. It lies on Chahar Bagh, a broad promenade, lined with sycamores. This boulevard, built by Shah Abbas, leads to the famous Allahverdi Khan Bridge. The name Chahar Bagh means Four Gardens; and its origin is interesting. Shah Abbas wanted a majestic approach to the city. But four vineyards were in the way. So he took the four vineyards and converted them into Chahar Bagh.

The Madresseh has a quiet garden with a pool. It is decorated with cypress trees and arbor vitae; and when we were there the zinnias, cannas, and dahlias were in bloom. This school has some hundred rooms for study. Two minarets rise above a blue-domed mosque. I climbed one and Gordon King the other; and we took each other's pictures looking over the railing against blue and green tile.

Not far off Chahar Bagh is the Hall of Forty Pillars, also built by Shah Abbas. Here is a throne room, heavily carved and rather ostentatiously painted and overlooking a large garden. The Hall has only twenty pillars; but the name comes from the fact that in front of the veranda is a large rectangular pool where the twenty pillars are reflected.

The center of the city is Maidan-e-Shah or Royal Square. This is 560 yards long and 174 yards wide. In its middle is a huge rectangular pool with spouting fountains. It was used as a polo ground by Shah Abbas; and the goal posts still stand.

At the south end of the square stands Masjed-e-Shah, adorned with blue tile, which I photographed from the air.

The entrance to this mosque faces the square; but the courtyard and the chamber of the main dome are almost at right angles to it. The reason for this strange design was the desire to align the mosque with the square and to orient it toward Mecca. The double effect adds, I think, to the architectural achievement. The acoustics under the great dome are marvelous. One taps a pencil or snaps his fingers and the echo is instant. It is repeated a dozen times or more before it fades away.

The blue of the tiles and the intensity of the sky were a spectacular combination. Mary especially commented on it. I remember her saying that it took her back to a small chapel in South France that had been designed by Pierre Matisse. His painting, she said, has been strongly influenced by Persian miniaturists; and he used windows of the same color range as this beautiful mosque at Isfahan.

"I always remember," she said, "the effect of the stained glass in that chapel—yellow, green, and blue with no red or orange at all."

On the west of the square is Ali Qapu, the palace of Shah Abbas. It's a huge biulding cut up into many rooms and once housing a valued collection of chinaware. On the top floor is the Porcelain Room, lined with thin wood panels with niches shaped to hold special vases or jars. The rooms are decorated with gold. Delicate miniatures in various colors are on the walls. The arches are richly colored. Numerous figures of men and women with cups of wine in their hands fill the lower portions of some walls. The suggestion involves both Bacchus and Venus; but these frescoes close to the floor are getting indistinct these days.

The upstairs rooms have balconies where the King and his entourage sat to watch polo games. For the entire block the ground floor was made up of so-called box seats for the nobility. The gate to the palace had a sill of porphyry too sacred to be touched by the foot. It had to be stepped over. The gate was also considered sacred. People kissed it in honor of the King and the King himself always dismounted before passing it. At least this is what our guide, a learned Persian, said.

Opposite the palace on the east side of the square is Masjed-e-Sheikh Lotfollah, also built by Shah Abbas in honor of his father-in-law. Here is the most delicate, the most colorful tilework in all of Asia. Persian tile is famous anywhere, for each piece is hand-baked by an artist. But the tile in this mosque has the finest quality of all; and the mosaic the most intricate, most artistic designs I have seen anywhere. The dome has a soft green-yellow hue; and at dusk it fairly glows. The base of the dome is a peacock with a tail almost lost in formal tilework. The inner rooms have tile set in flowing patterns. Square yards of wall space have finer textures than any cloisonné I know. The interior walls have the effect of faïence. The blue-domed chamber has a quiet that is spiritual. In this serene place time seems to stop and man is at peace with the world. For one on the search for man-made beauty, this mosque is the end of the trail. I know nothing more beautiful that man has created. The whole building has the delicacy of the miniatures of Herat, so finely chiseled are the tiles, so perfectly blended the colors. We went by it time and again after sunset to see the dome glow in the dusk as though it had an inner radiance.

At the north end of the square, opposite Masjed-e-Shah, is Naqar Khaneh—the Drum Tower—which forms the main entrance to the bazaar. This tower bears that name because in the time of Shah Abbas an orchestra of drums and woodwinds played on top of the tower every evening at sunset until the sun had dropped below the horizon. This custom of "drumming down the sun" is no longer practiced in Isfahan; but it's a custom that still prevails in other parts of Iran. This bazaar is not surpassed anywhere in Asia. It is the most colorful of any market place I know. Tongas drawn by single horses are lined up outside the main entrance looking for customers. One has the feeling of entering a high semi-dark tunnel when he steps into the bazaar. As I have said, its high roofs are vaulted. Tiny windows let in light that shines down in grimy shafts. The avenues are wide enough for animal transport. These avenues go off at various angles, forming a labyrinth for one who does not know his way. Once in a while one comes to a courtyard off the avenue. These courtyards empty on the far side into the city. They are freight depots, so to speak, where camels and donkeys unload and load.

There are sections in the bazaar for various commodities.

We saw the famous *gaz* candy (a type of toffee) being made in the bazaar with egg whites and syrup, being whipped and beaten in large earthen bowls by a half dozen men.

We visited sections where the din of hammers on copper and bronze was so great we could not hear each other talk. Here large trays and samovars were being made by hand.

In a quieter section men were making pipe fittings, faucets, and all the plumbing fixtures a modern house would need.

In the woodworking section barefooted men held boards with their toes as they sat on their haunches sawing, chiseling, and hammering.

The long avenue housing cobblers showed a wide variety of lasts and heels for men, women, and children.

Soccer balls were being made in several stalls.

In a few others files were being cut and nails being made—all by hand.

Down another avenue called the Street of Gold and Silver delicate jewelry was being manufactured by long-fingered artisans. Silver vases were polished—silver trays, samovars glistened on display as far as the eye could see.

Blacksmiths in another area hammered out shoes for donkeys and burros.

Tinsmiths made gutters of galvanized iron and buckets, funnels, baking pans too.

Potters whirled clay and shaped vessels.

Merchants sat behind burlap sacks that were open to show their contents—spices, sugar, dried fruits, beans, potatoes, hard candies, tobacco.

Other merchants had racks of secondhand suits made in New York, Toledo, Seattle, London—all repaired and pressed and offered at bargain prices.

The section of the bazaar we enjoyed most was the one where cloth was being hand block-printed. The cloth is known as Ghalam Kar (Pen Work). I photographed artisans carving the designs by hand in wooden blocks which are then dipped in a pan of dye. The work is done by men sitting on the floor with low platforms before them. The first one blocks on the basic design in one color. The piece is passed on to another who stamps another design on in another color. It goes from man to man, each adding a piece of the design until the pattern is complete. The cloth may be the size of a napkin, tablecloth, bedspread, or curtain. Once stamped, it is dried, folded, and put on the shelf of the owner in the bazaar.

Collateral activities attach to these block-printing shops. There are men who mix dyes. There are vats where cloth is dipped before stamping and then taken outdoors and dried.

What we are accustomed to do by machinery is all done by hand in the Isfahan bazaar.

In one section of the bazaar are cottonseed oil presses. There is a large stone, set at an angle on a huge flat millstone, from which a wooden axle protrudes. The cottonseed is placed on the millstone and a camel is hitched to the wooden axle. He is blindfolded and walks in a circle, pushing the axle which turns the stone that grinds the cottonseed. The camel carries a bell which rings as he walks. He walks two hours and then is replaced by another camel. In the off periods the camel's blindfold is removed and he is taken to another room where he is fed the husks of the cottonseed. When the seed has been sufficiently pulverized, it is scooped up and put in a huge press. There is a wooden handle to the press that extends high into the vaulted ceiling. Four men climb a wall, grab the handle, and bring it down with their weight. In that way the ground cottonseed is squeezed of its precious fluid.

I talked to the amiable proprietor of the cottonseed press. His eyes twinkled as he told me a story. One day a Shirazi visited the place and, after watching the camel walking the circle, asked the proprietor:

"Why is the camel blindfolded?"

"Because when he's blindfolded, he thinks he's walking in a straight line."

"What difference does that make?" the Shirazi asked.

"Because then the camel thinks he's walking away from the cottonseed and is not tempted to eat it."

"Why," asked the Shirazi, "do you hang a bell on the camel?"

"Because then we know, even when we are not in the room, that the camel is walking and not eating the cottonseed."

The Shirazi went into deep meditation. Finally he said, "Now suppose the camel does not walk but gets down on his knees and eats the cottonseed. As he eats, he keeps waggling his head so that the bell rings."

"What did you say to that?" I asked the manager.

He replied, "I turned to the man and I said, 'Get out of here. My camel has none of the tricks of a Shirazi.' "

We found miniaturists at work in their studios, painting biblical scenes of Joseph and Mary and legendary scenes from *Shah Nameh*.

I visited a shop I had first seen in 1950, a shop where delicate enamel is hand-painted on silver articles. The proprietor, small, wiry, and dark, is an artist of great talent. He paints his own designs, sitting barefooted on the floor with his back to the wall. In each of his small shops he has another room where apprentices work and learn the trade sitting on their haunches as they do delicate miniatures on silver. I took colored flash pictures of these men at work. The proprietor showed us great trays of his finished products—pins, rings, cigarette boxes, candelabra, jewel boxes, earrings, vases. Each piece is a work of art, delicately executed. He makes the patterns, fashions the jewelry, and bakes the design all in this small place.

I found out on this trip that this artist is a dervish. There are many kinds of dervishes in Iran. The ones I had known about were the dancing dervishes and the howling dervishes. These dancing and howling dervishes are usually marked by four external signs: they carry a weapon (ax) for protection; they carry a gourd for receipt of alms; they wear a felt cap; and they keep their hair long. But this is not the attire of many dervishes. I learned from this man that there are about thirty more sedate orders of the dervishes. He belongs to one that has about twenty members. They meet weekly in the home of a member. They have passwords and rituals that reminded me somewhat of Freemasonry in this country. They are strictly religious orders under lay leadership. Here men repent of their sins and enter upon a "path" of conduct and advance through various "stations" of spiritual life. This devout Isfahani spoke with pride of his order of dervishes, as a Rotarian or Mason might speak of his club or lodge.

The Zayandeh Rud runs through Isfahan and we crossed it on the Allahverdi Khan Bridge, built by Shah Abbas. This bridge is nearly 1000 feet long and 40 feet wide. It has thirty-three graceful arches and is therefore popularly known as the See-o-Seh or Bridge of the Thirty-three. There are seats on the abutments at bridge level where pedestrians can rest. In these niches I often found old men reciting the Koran in a singsong voice. This bridge is a fancy one. It has flanking galleries that are much used by picnickers. There are rooms or alcoves beneath the roadway where young folks gather at nighttime. The bridge has foot passages at three levels. There is a foot passage on each side of the roadway. Stairs lead to the top of the balustrade where there is also foot passage. Other stairs lead down to the river level where one can cross the river on large steppingstones under a series of arches cut through the stone piers of the bridge.

Below the bridge by the waterside is where the rug beaters work. Early every summer morning four or six can be found there. They work on a contract basis for householders who need rugs cleaned. The men beat them with sticks, causing great clouds of dust to rise. Then they carry them into the river and wash them. After washing they are laid out flat on the rocks to dry. Isfahan, which lies at about 4500 feet elevation, has cool summer nights but bright warm summer days. As there is little humidity, clothes dry fast. The rug beaters try to get their rugs washed by mid-morning so that they will have the hot hours for drying. At dusk each day, or before, these men fold up the rugs, load them on burros, and take them back to the owners.

Isfahan does not make the best rugs in Persia; but they are of high quality. We visited a factory that I had seen on an earlier visit. It is in a corner of the bazaar. One or two women supervise the looms; but the work is done mostly by young girls from five to sixteen. By American standards, the factory is a sweatshop. By Persian standards, it is a place where children eke out enough to help buy a meal a day for their parents.

The looms, unlike the ones we saw in Afghanistan, are vertical. The girls sit on a board, working first on the bottom edge of the rug. As they progress the board is raised until on the last strip they are high in the air. The little fingers of the girls moved as fast as spindles the day we were there. Their faces were pressed to the loom as they tied the tiny knots with lightning speed. A girl who starts at five years of age to work on a loom and works twelve hours a day is often blind when she reaches twenty-one. The work is that close and exacting. A large rug, with three girls working, may take three years to finish. The few cents a day that goes to their wages, when added up for three years, amount to little compared with the value of the rug. The venture is capitalism in a rugged exploitive form. The Persians have an expression, "You may walk on my eyes." It is an offer of hospitality to a guest or an expression of appreciation to a friend. In Persian parlance it is only a figure of speech. But one who walks the delicate rugs does sometimes walk on eyes of little girls that were lost in these sweatshops from too close work and too long hours.

Isfahan probably has the greatest artisans of all Asia. Various nationalities are represented there—Armenians, Jews, Mongols, Tajiks, Turks, and Persians. Their faces are wonderfully photogenic; and they usually are willing to pose.

There are many tales about the astuteness of these bazaar merchants and their capacity to pinch rials. When one wants to attach the extreme opprobrium of stinginess, he says:

"As mean as the merchants of Isfahan who put their cheese in bottles and rub their bread on the outside to give it a flavor."

The movement of the crowd through the bazaar has endless variety. *Mullahs* in white turbans and black gowns, Ghashghais with felt hats having brims in front and behind, Bakhtiari with the tall, brimless black felt hat, turbaned camel drivers, merchants wearing sandals, flowing trousers, and Western shirts, old men with long black coats, young men in slacks and open shirts, barefooted urchins darting in and out.

A camel comes through, ready to be loaded with freight. Donkeys and burros heavy with baggage plod down the avenues, nudging passers-by with the corners of their packs. Porters, with huge bales and packing cases on their backs held by a strap over their foreheads, plod along crying out for people to beware and make room.

Apart from the movement of the crowd is the medley of voices and noises. Apart from them are the odors. We of the West have shut up all our odors in tin cans. The East has preserved them for the nostrils. Spices, tobacco, candies, camel dung, burros, people fill the bazaar with a pungent odor. This smell comes back in memory more frequently than the sights themselves. It's a powerful force pulling one toward the East over and again and making the attraction of Asia irresistible. Of all these pulls, the bazaar of Isfahan has the strongest.

Bazaars invite discussions and debates, as well as trade. They are social centers as well as markets. Strange things happen there. One day in the Isfahan bazaar a man recognized me from my pictures in the Persian press. He ran after our party, calling Kazemi, my Harvard-graduate interpreter. He kept Kazi in animated discussion for perhaps fifteen minutes. When Kazi rejoined us, I asked what was up. Kazi replied:

"He wants you to speak to President Eisenhower and advise him that America has foisted a corrupt government on Iran."

CHAPTER 9

ISFAHANIS AND THEIR GARDENS

In Persian legend, Isfahan was Gai, the home of Kaveh, the blacksmith who led a revolt against the Snake King named Zohak. Zohak had two serpents growing out from his shoulders, and they had to be fed the brains of children. When Zohak took the children of Kaveh to feed the serpents, Kaveh went on a warpath. His flag was his leather apron on a spear—an ensign that was to become the national standard of Iran. For Kaveh and Feridun destroyed Zohak, all as related by Ferdowsi in *Shah Nameh*.

Isfahan is watered by the Zayandeh Rud; and as a result of Persian engineering, these waters have recently been augmented. The Karun River, which runs off the western slopes of the Zagros Mountains into the Persian Gulf near Abadan, has been linked with the Zayandeh Rud. Water is gold in this part of the world; and much of the Karun's flow went wastefully into the Gulf. The engineering achievement was the construction of a tunnel—known as the Kuhrana—which reached the headwaters of the Karun and diverted them to the Zayandeh Rud. As a result, many thousands of cubic feet that once were wasted now irrigate hundreds of acres around Isfahan. The irrigated lands are so large and the demand for water so great that practically the entire flow of the Zayandeh Rud is consumed in irrigation. The river ends in a low depression southeast of town. The time was when that depression was a swampy expanse. But these days very little water ever escapes an economic use. Even with the additional irrigation coming through the new tunnel, Isfahan is a food-deficit area.

From the air, however, it's a rich garden. And when one walks the city he can find gardens as beautiful as any in the world. The walls lining the streets and isolating the homes are a dozen feet or more tall, made of stone or brick. There are ponds and pools inside the walls; flowers grow in abundance; lawns lie deep in shade; mulberry and quince trees flourish. These walls give the great advantage of privacy. But they have one disadvantage. They radiate heat, which is so high during the summer months that vegetable gardens next to the walls suffer. But the shade of Isfahan, like its nights, is cool and refreshing; and grass and other greenery flourishes there.

We went swimming in the pools. They are fed by well water which is not safe to drink but not so badly polluted as to be a risk to swimmers. But they fill with algae that grows fast in this climate and makes desirable the use of copper sulphate.

We spent delightful hours in these Isfahan gardens whose walls are so high and so thick that when one shuts the gate he steps into another world, a world marked by its peace and serenity. In one garden we visited with Morteza Gholi Khan Samsam, head of the Bakhtiari tribe, and one of his wives, who is a Ghashghai. Morteza is about eighty-five years old. He is a short, stocky man with a round head and face and a half beard. He is hale and hearty to meet; and his heart has a great capacity for friendship. I first met him in 1949 when my son Bill and I visited Bakhtiari country, west of Isfahan. I had seen him on other trips and been his guest at his village of Shalamzar several times. He was a prominent character in my book *Strange Lands and Friendly People*. When my daughter Millie was married, Morteza put the women of Shalamzar to work making her a wedding present. It was a rug 17 feet by 21 feet that it took them two years to make. It is one of the loveliest Persian rugs I ever saw. I mention these things to show how close he and I had been and to explain why our reunion in Isfahan was a sentimental occasion. Tears almost came when I saw the old man. For now he is crippled, unable to use his legs. But his mind is active and his health is good; and the hug with which he embraced me was hearty and vigorous. We talked for over an hour of old times and of today, of ancient Persia, and of modern problems. It was Morteza Gholi Khan Samsam who helped save the Constitution of Persia in 1909 by marching Bakhtiari cavalry against Tehran when the Shah abolished the Parliament and put the Prime Minister in jail. Tears came to his eyes when he recounted the story again and deplored the fact that he could no longer sit a saddle. We took many flash pictures of him and his wife; and Mercedes took some of him and me. We had tea and fresh peaches.

Bahman had stood for election to the Majlis. But he was opposed by a man who had strong influence with the gendarmes. The gendarmes arrested Bahman and held him four months until the election was over—an act which was possible only because Persia has no truly independent judiciary nor a remedy comparable to our *habeas corpus*. Bahman, who was prevented from campaigning and held incommunicado, naturally lost the election. We talked of corruption in government and the oppressive practices of gendarmes who blackmail the tribesmen and exact levies from them. It was hard to leave Morteza Gholi Khan, for I feared we might not meet again.

On another occasion in still a different garden, we met Helen Bakhtiar, mother of Jamshid Bakhtiar, famous football player at the University of Virginia. Helen is an American who married a Bakhtiari. He studied medicine here and went to Abadan to practice. He still practices there, his office being in the bazaar as a convenience to his patients. Helen has a clinic for the training of midwives in Isfahan. In Persia 98 per cent of the women have no doctor at childbirth. Part of the difficulty is the great shortage of doctors; part is the prejudice, born in *purdah,* in favor of midwives. Midwives, especially well-trained ones, are not numerous. There are women who perform the service. But not many have received any education in sanitation and in the art of delivery.

The Bakhtiari, immortalized in the movie *Grass,* still migrate, south to north, with their flocks in springtime, returning to the basin of the Persian Gulf in the fall. On these marches the Bakhtiari women have babies. Sometimes when the tribe is busy with cattle or flocks, a mother must make the delivery alone under a tree. Usually another woman tries to stay with her and help but that is not always possible. A Bakhtiari woman who is expecting a baby always carries in her pocket a sharp-edged stone with which she can cut the umbilical cord. After delivery the mother does not stay quiet. She is on the move again, not in a few days, but in a few hours. Cattle and sheep do not bed down for long. They keep on the move; and the job of the mother after delivery, as well as before, is to keep up with them. The newborn babe is sometimes carried on his mother's back in a cradle. More often than not, the cradle is fastened to the back of a cow. The baby is tied down so that his hands and feet cannot move and so that his eyes are out of the sun. Babies sleep all day long on the back of a cow, as the great migration moves on.

To tribal women and to city women alike, Helen Bakhtiar is trying to bring simple skills and ideas of sanitation that can be used under primitive conditions. Her clinic gives instruction to several hundred women a year.

We met another Bakhtiari in Isfahan, Yahya Khan, a young man in his thirties, nephew to Morteza. Some of the younger Khans drift away from the tribe and live in cities. Yahya is different. He is one of the tribe. He lives with them and takes the long migration twice a year. He has introduced a new rug for the Bakhtiari women to make. The wool of sheep and goats is brown, white, gray, or black. He has this wool spun in its natural color and has the women weave rugs out of it. The colors are therefore fast; and the rug, made by fine technicians, is certain to have great appeal when it reaches the markets.

Yahya urged us to come with him to the tribal country. There was nothing I would have liked to do more. But it would have taken a minimum of three days and Istanbul was a long way off yet. So we declined the invitation. Yahya, however, partially made up for our disappointment. He sent a Bakhtiari woman to the Gordon Kings' home, where we stayed, and had her measure us for the beautiful full trousers of the Bakhtiari style.

In another garden we ate small sweet plums while a British doctor from the British Mission Hospital in Isfahan dressed Mercedes' hand and arm for the burns she had sustained.

Governor and Mrs. Mohammed Zolfaghari gave us a luncheon, most of the dishes being cooked by her.

The Governor of Isfahan, like Governor Mahdavi of Manzandaran, is concerned with the problems of industrialization. Iran, rich in oil and having only 18,000,000 population, is one of the richest countries in the world per capita. These responsible Governors believe that the proceeds of oil production should be treated as capital, not income, and put into improvements that will benefit everyone.

"We have not yet learned the discipline we need to keep our wealth from being dissipated," the Governor said.

The Mayor of Isfahan, Habib Eshraghi, was also at the luncheon. He's a young enterprising man with modern ideas. Up until recently the people (women do not vote) elected a city council which chose a Mayor. Under a new reform, the people elect the Mayor. The financial worry of Isfahan, like that of other municipalities the world around, centers on the search for revenues. As I have said, the land tax and the income tax in Iran are national taxes; municipalities are relegated to various types of excise taxes. The taxes of Isfahan include not only taxes on the stalls of the merchants in the bazaar, but also taxes on all trucks or busses entering or leaving the city. Like Quchan up north, it taxes commerce in a way which we prohibit under our Commerce Clause.

One day we went with the Gordon Kings on a picnic out of Isfahan. We had the use of a country place owned by the Gahreman family about fifteen miles from the city. This is a medium-sized house in a spacious garden enclosed by a high brick wall and known as Sahraye Charom. On the way out we saw a fire temple on a barren hill high above the shaded highway. This was a Zoroastrian *ateshgah*. Here the flame sacred to Ahura Mazda was kept burning year in and year out. The priests, whom we of the West called the *magis,* attended the flame; the multitude sang and prayed from a distance.

Down to A.D. 640 when the Arabs started their invasion of Iran, fire temples dotted Iran throughout its length and breadth. They symbolized the fight between Ahura Mazda, god of light and wisdom, and Ahriman, god of darkness and evil. It was there the Persians once sang the songs and said the prayers of the Avesta:

These, Lord, Thou'lt give and through that Spirit bounteous
By Fire for good to strivers twain 'gainst wrong,
Through growth of Zeal and Truth, O Mazda,
For Zeal instructeth her beseeching throng!

On this picnic we saw the Shaking Minarets known as Minar Jonban. A small tiled mosque has a minaret on each side of its dome. Like all minarets, these have an interior circular staircase leading to the small balcony under the roof, where the *mullah* calls the faithful to prayer. It was discovered that if a man put his back against the wall at the top of a minaret, braced his feet against the other, and rocked back and forth, he would cause the opposite minaret to shake.

Gordon King got a local Iranian to climb one minaret and start the rocking motion. Sure enough, in a minute or so the opposite minaret started to rock, the top moving back and forth in a small arc.

There are two minority groups of consequence in Isfahan—Jews and Armenians. The Jews number about 6000. They live by and large in a poor section of Isfahan called Jubareh, which is near the Friday Mosque. In their neighborhood is a small mosque, rather moth-eaten, at least five hundred years old. It is interesting only in its history: the *mullah* who long presided there served in his spare time as public executioner. The story is that the first Jewish settlers came as exiles from Jerusalem at the time of Nebuchadnezzar and contemporaneous with the transportation of other Jews to Babylon.

Most of the Isfahan Jews are either peddlers or merchants in the bazaar. They are rugmakers, hand-loom weavers, antique dealers, tailors. A few are physicians. They have the better linen shops and the better brass and copper stores. They have two synagogues in Isfahan. They practice their faith without hindrance. Their shops are closed on Saturdays; and they observe the Passover and other Jewish religious holidays. About 60 per cent read and speak Hebrew. They have their own schools; and recently they opened a health clinic. It's a hustling institution; and the day it was dedicated the entire official and VIP community turned out *en masse*.

The Armenians live across the Zayandeh Rud in the part of Isfahan called Julfa, the name of the town from which they were deported. The Armenians were brought here in A.D. 1603 by Shah Abbas—50,000 Armenians who made up 12,000 families. These Armenians were deported from what is now southwest Russia and then northwest Persia when Shah Abbas retreated from the Turks and desired to leave behind a worthless, desolate country. It was a forcible deportation. Shah Abbas wanted artisans for his realm. But he also wanted business middlemen. The business of the East was mostly in the hands of Christians. Shah Abbas wanted middlemen to deal with them. At this time Armenian colonies were established not only in Persia but in India and Ceylon. Shah Abbas pledged the Armenians who came to Isfahan the right to practice their own religion. I saw the charter which Shah Abbas executed, guaranteeing them religious freedom. I saw the charters executed by every succeeding Shah who redeemed the pledge of Shah Abbas.

We went to Julfa and visited the Armenian cathedral—Church of St. Saviour—built in A.D. 1606. At that time there were 50,000 Armenians in Iran. Today there are about the same number. Five thousand belong to this church. Many are still artisans. But most of the Armenian artisans in Isfahan have moved to Tehran. The bulk of the Isfahan Armenians are farmers.

On earlier trips I had visited their villages west of Isfahan. Most of them are sharecroppers; a few own their own lands. They all follow their ancient rites. Quite a few were induced to go to Armenia SSR, which Russia created out of a part of ancient Armenia. Many prefer their freedom in Iran rather than the regimentation in Russia, even though in Russia their standard of living would be five or six times what it is in Iran.

Their cathedral in Isfahan is in a compound about a block square. There is a museum on the left, a church on the right, and living quarters for the clergy in the back. The mid-portion is a garden beautifully arranged and well preserved.

We met two of the clergy, Father Khoren Kirakos and Father Terdad Hovagemian, both bearded and dressed in their clerical garb; and Mercedes took pictures of me conversing with them. Father Kirakos speaks English and we covered much ground as we talked.

The church is a beautiful edifice, combining features of both the East and the West. Like Moslem churches, this cathedral has carpet laid on stone floors and a rounded dome. Like Western churches, the dome and the walls are highly decorated with Biblical scenes. It has a cross on top of the dome and bell towers.

The museum is rich in paintings and carvings of theological personages and events. Here are ancient Bibles, priceless brochures and manuscripts, the dress of the clergy, the history of the race. One room has pictures of Armenians buried here. The pictures show the tools they used. Some had axes, chisels, files, hammers, saws, scissors, or the various tools of tinsmiths or silversmiths. The one I like was the picture of the headstone which showed a stonecutter using a wet wooden wedge to split rock.

Outside Julfa is the Christian cemetery. One famous grave is that of a watchmaker who was put to death three hundred years ago by the *mullahs* for killing a Moslem in self-defense. The Shah offered a pardon if he would embrace Islam. The Armenian refused and was executed.

Here too are Bahai graves—the King of Martyrs (Haji Mirza Hasan) and the Beloved of Martyrs (Haji Mirza Hossein). These men were brothers who operated a shop in the Isfahan bazaar. They had a debtor who owed them 10,000 tomans and who conceived of a devilish way to avoid payment. The debtor went to a *mullah,* saying these brothers were Bahais who did not believe Mohammed was the last prophet. That belief was apostasy, carrying the death penalty. A person executed for apostasy had a deep stain. In that event his wealth could be appropriated by the church.

This clever way of avoiding payment of the debt to the two Bahais was accepted by the *mullahs,* who received permission from the Governor to proceed with the prosecution. *Mullahs* were assembled and a court constituted. A trial was had and the brothers were convicted of apostasy and sentenced to death. The Shah gave a reprieve but the Governor held back its announcement until after the men were executed. Their throats were slashed by the executioner and their bodies dragged through the streets and cast out of the city. The bodies were retrieved by a servant and buried. This happened last century. These graves have been holy places to the Bahais ever since.

This cemetery is also the resting place of a friend of mine, J. Hall Paxton, who died in Isfahan while serving as American Consul. He was an heroic figure. He was serving in remote Tihwa of Sinkiang (Chinese Turkestan) when the Communists took over. He brought thirty-one Americans safely over five hundred miles of trail in the treacherous Himalayas and escaped the Red Army. This act of heroism is one of the greatest in the records of our foreign service. Paxton loved Isfahan. The Christmas card he and his wife sent me in 1951 read: "Isfahan is half the world."

I returned to the cathedral to say goodbye to Father Kirakos. I congratulated him on the flourishing church, the beautiful garden, the enterprising Armenians I had met in Isfahan. As I left I gave him a small donation for his church. In reply he bowed and thanked me by saying, "May your kindness be increased"—a Persian expression that gives thanks for what has been received and looks forward hopefully to future generosities.

CHAPTER 10

THE JEWELS, THE BAHAIS, AND MOHARRAM

One evening at dinner in Tehran, Dr. Manouchehr Eghbal, Iran's Prime Minister, suggested to Mercedes that she might like to see the Crown Jewels, estimated to be worth $60,000,000. And so we photographed them. It took the Chief of Protocol several days to arrange it. There is difficulty in seeing them because the keys to the vault, where they have been deposited, are held by six men. Not one but six keys are necessary to unlock the vault. Important personages in Tehran have those keys, including the Chief Justice of the Supreme Court. Each must be there for an opening of the vault or have a deputy to represent him.

One of the six could not be present but another had his key. Five were present when we entered the antechamber to the vault and the five were with us during the hour's visit. The vault is a small room perhaps 40 feet long and 20 feet wide. The jewels are all behind glass, carefully polished. Low tables with their tops enclosed in glass cases, stretching down the middle of the room, show a large variety of small items—unset jewels, thick pocket watches, rings, bracelets, earrings, medals, watch fobs, brooches, necklaces, and multitudes of unset precious stones. The item in these cases which excited my interest the most was a snuffbox made of solid emerald and about the shape and twice the size of one of our safety-match boxes. It was among the loot which Nadir Shah, King of Persia, brought back from India following his conquest of Delhi in 1739.

There is an interesting story about this emerald snuffbox. Its existence was well known; but when Nadir Shah's men had collected all the loot from the Mogul dynasty that then ruled India, the snuffbox was missing.

A servant of Mohammed Shah, the Mogul King, revealed the secret of its whereabouts. It appeared that Mohammed Shah, who prized the box highly, kept it hidden in the great turban he wore. This posed a delicate problem for Nadir Shah. Mohammed Shah was King and entitled to respect. Nadir Shah could not with propriety seize and search the person of a King. So Nadir Shah put his mind at work on the polite and proper way of getting the emerald box from Mohammed Shah. He finally hit upon a plan, based on the Asian custom of pledging friendship by exchanging hats. One day when he was talking with the Mogul he said:

"You and I fought; but we are now friends. It is the custom of friends in Persia to exchange hats as a mark of their friendship."

Reaching over, he removed Mohammed Shah's turban and put it on his head; then he placed his own hat on the Mogul's head. Mohammed Shah, boiling inside, had no protest he could with propriety make.

The curator of the Crown Jewels told me the story and then added a moral of his own:

"You see, Mr. Justice, life consists in changing hats."

I did not get the point.

"You mean that life consists in making new friends?" I asked.

"No," he said, "the best hats always end up on the heads of the strongest men."

The walls of the vault are lined with glass cases whose doors are sealed by twine locked in wax seals. Here are swords, belts, and helmets studded with jewels. Vases and goblets are be-jeweled. There are strings of precious pearls and beautiful tiaras heavy with diamonds that the Queen wears on state occasions.

In separate cases in the center of the room are two large crowns, both rich with precious stones. There is a heavy one with a short tassel that is a hundred and eighty years old. It is from the Kajar dynasty. A smaller one is the crown of the Pahlevi dynasty, of which the present Shah is the existing member.

We took flash pictures with my strobe of this valuable collection and drank Pepsi-Colas tendered by the curator. When we left, the curator turned out the lights and closed the vault; and the deputies turned their keys in the complicated lock that guards this treasure.

Tehran was crowded with activities. There were luncheons, teas, and dinners with many old friends and happy hours spent in gardens whose beauty is almost beyond the reach of words.

One night we dined at a restaurant, the Golden Cock, with Abbas Aram, who was attached for some years to the Iranian Embassy in Washington, D.C., and another old friend, Dr. A. H. Radji, Minister of Health. It had been a very hot day in Tehran and the evening was humid. But branches of trees hung low over the garden where we ate and the fountains that played in a pool created at least the illusion of coolness. Mr. Aram presented Mercedes with a small pewter samovar that holds three cups of water—a type so rare these days that they never appear in the bazaar. Over shrimp, chicken, and rice we talked for a couple of hours. We talked of Persepolis and Alexander the Great; the influence of Islam on the culture of Spain, Portugal, and South America; the artisans of Isfahan; and the common ground Americans and Persians have in their sense of humor. Radji talked of his dream for Iran—nurses, doctors, hospitals. Iran has a great distance to go. There are in the entire nation only two good public health centers—one in Tehran and the other in Shiraz. In all of Iran there are only four nurses trained in public health. Much progress has been made in preventive medicine. In some areas of Iran, notably the Caspian, the percentage of people having malaria was 90 per cent or more a few years ago. The anti-malaria program is so far advanced that less than 2 per cent of the people have malaria today. Every inside wall of every mud hut is sprayed these days. Villagers are organized to do it; and they take pride in their work.

The Minister of Foreign Affairs and Mrs. Ali Gholi Ardalan gave us a dinner in the garden of their new home in Elahieh Shemiran. The house is modern in design and air-conditioned.

The garden, too young to have tall trees and shrubs, is planned and planted with an eye to exotic beauty. There are pools and fountains; flowers and shrubs that bloom the round of spring and summer; and this night jasmine that filled the air with fragrance.

The dinner was formal dress and buffet. We sat at tables for four placed throughout the vast garden. The garden was bright with electric lights; the night air was cool.

The conversation, table by table, covered a wide range. I went to quite a few, greeting old friends, and found Alexander the Great, the unveiling of women, the miniaturists of Isfahan, the rule of Mossadegh, all being discussed. In one group I caught up with new stories about Mullah Nasr-ed-Din. He was a twelfth-century legendary humorist who would have been at home with Mark Twain and Will Rogers. He had wisdom in his jokes. His pranks never had sharp edges; they only illustrated the weakness of humans.

It appeared that a friend of Mullah had a belief in sorcerers and magicians. One day he fell under the spell of a sorcerer who convinced him that if he bought some of his pills and took them—three at night and three in the morning—he would become invisible. The gullible man bought the pills, went to Mullah, and told him the secret.

"Tomorrow," he said to Mullah, "I will come to your house. No one will see me enter. I will come to your room; you will hear my voice. But you will not see me."

Mullah humored his friend and encouraged him in the project. Mullah also told the servants to pretend not to see his friend when he came to the house in the morning. All went as planned. The friend took three pills at night and three in the morning. Then he started for Mullah's home. He was delighted when he entered the gate, for the watchman did not notice him at all. The same happened at the door. A servant, whom he knew, never looked up from his scrubbing when he stepped into the hall. He went upstairs to Mullah's room and entered without knocking. Neither Mullah nor a servant pretended to notice.

"You can't see me," the man said to Mullah. "It's the pills of the sorcerer."

"I never would have believed it," replied Mullah.

Then Mullah clapped his hands and by prearrangement two servants came running.

"There's an invisible man in the room," said Mullah. "Get your sticks and see if you can hit him."

The servants went after the man, raining blow after blow on him while he jumped and whirled to elude them.

Finally he shouted, "Mullah, Mullah, if I'm invisible, why do the servants never miss?"

Then there was the story of Mullah and his lazy donkey. The day was hot and the donkey was slow. Mullah was anxious to get the donkey moving fast down the road, for he had a long journey to make. So Mullah took some ginger and put it under the donkey's tail. The ginger burned so badly that the donkey raced like mad down the highway. He went so fast Mullah could not keep up. Finally in desperation Mullah put some ginger on himself. Soon Mullah got going so fast he passed the donkey. Both of them raced down the street of a village. The villagers, wanting to be helpful, rushed out and stopped the donkey.

"Don't stop the donkey," cried Mullah. "Stop me."

Later in the evening the talk in my corner of the garden turned to superstitions. A lady told of an old—a very old—religious custom that antedates Islam. It concerns the eclipse of the moon. When that happens the villagers beat copper vessels frantically. The aim is to frighten away the dragon who is supposed to swallow the moon.

"The nice thing about it," she said, "is that it always works. For here in a few seconds comes the moon again."

We went home to the Darband in a full Persian moon over Mount Damavand, which looks down on Tehran from 18,600 feet.

In Tehran, we had several visits with the Prime Minister, Dr. Eghbal. He is a physician by profession and one of the best in all Asia. He was drawn into politics from a sense of public duty and is an outstanding official of our time. I first met Eghbal in 1950 in Tabriz when he was Governor of Azerbaijan. The luncheon he tendered me then was the beginning of a warm friendship, renewed by his visits to America. He is a large, well-built man about middle age. He speaks English adequately but with hesitation; so he prefers French, in which he is fluent. As Prime

Minister he is the busiest man in Iran. But he was not too busy to look at Mercedes' badly burned arm and give medical advice. He is also a most tolerant man of a forgiving nature. Our appointment with him was at four o'clock. The Iranian chauffeur took us to his home. It was not until five o'clock that we arrived at his office where the appointment was supposed to be. At that late hour, he held off the Ministers who had assembled for a Cabinet meeting and had tea with us, teasing me about my Persian and belittling Mercedes' burn. He was a happy, carefree man during an interlude in a harassing day.

We saw the Bahais in Tehran. The one who was our host was Habib Sabet, a prominent businessman in Iran. I do not know what all his business interests may be. One of them, however, is Pepsi-Cola, which has become a very popular drink in Iran. The Bahais have many businessmen among their numbers. They enjoy a fine reputation as merchants. The reason is that they maintain a high ethical standard in all their dealings. Merchants in the bazaar are quick to take advantage; they will cheat and palm off false or inferior goods. Never the Bahais. They are scrupulous in their dealings; and as a result they grow in prestige.

The Bahais have the Pepsi-Cola bottling and distributing business in Iran and make a good thing of it. The *mullahs,* who have strong feelings against this dissident religious sect, subtly campaign against the Bahais in an endeavor to have Moslems boycott the business. A bottle of Pepsi-Cola costs ten rials (thirteen cents). It is common for a *mullah* to say, "Don't drink Pepsi-Cola. Two rials are for Pepsi-Cola; eight are for the Bahais." Some *mullahs* take a subtler approach. The Persian word for hat is "cola." The Persians have also made an idiom out of "cola." We use "to pull the wool over the eyes" to describe an act of deception. The Persians use "to pull the hat over the eyes." And "cola" used as an idiom means just that. So the *mullahs* often speak of Pepsi-Cola in these words: "Two rials are for Pepsi, eight rials are for Cola."

The Moslems have strong feelings against the Bahais, not because of their wealth and reputation but because of their faith. The Moslems have a doctrine known as "Seal of the Prophets," which means that Mohammed was the last and final prophet. The Bahais recognize Mohammed as a prophet; but they claim others in succession too, including the Bab of Shiraz, whom I have mentioned. It is this doctrine that arouses the fanatical Moslems. Their fanaticism is increased in intensity, I think, because the Bahais are Persian in origin and therefore are like kinsmen who have become traitors. Every once in a while they retaliate against the Bahais for their faith. In 1954 they persuaded the government to have the Iranian Army seize the Bahai temple in Tehran. Some Bahais were arrested. Others were dismissed from government service. Many Bahai shops had to be closed. Some Bahais were killed.

Knowing many Persians, some Moslems and some Bahais, and feeling a deep attachment to Iran, I wrote the Iranian government in protest. I said in effect that the greatness of a nation was in its tolerance for religious minorities, that America had gone through a period of intolerance and discrimination and finally ended it with our Bill of Rights, that those who loved Iran hoped and prayed that she too would cast off religion as a test and welcome all men equally into her community.

The discrimination against the Bahais hung on for a year or so but then ended. When we reached Tehran, the temple had been restored and the Bahais were once more on an equal footing with Moslems. Word of my intervention on their behalf had apparently reached them. Hence the tea they tendered us at the Darband Hotel.

At five o'clock on the morning of our departure from Tehran, Mr. Sabet appeared at the hotel with a portable ice chest, filled with ice and soft drinks. Mercedes at first did not know where to put it. But we managed a spot on the rear seat. And all the way to Turkey we blessed the Bahais for this gift. We were to experience around Baghdad and Mosul temperatures of 130°F. Cool drinks from the Bahai icebox saved our parched throats.

We stayed close to the hotel for three days in Tehran while Moharram was in progress. Moharram, which I mentioned earlier, is looked down upon by the Persian elite and by the government. Reza Shah tried to ban its celebration. But the fanatical fringe of Moslems still observe it by parades and by loud public mourning for the slain Hossein. We saw parades forming beneath the Darband Hotel. Men with short chains marched four or six abreast and twelve or more deep. They beat the men in front of them and then occasionally threw the chains over their own shoulders to take a wicked bite from their own flesh.

Kurish Shahbaz, my interpreter on several Persian journeys and political adviser to the American Embassy, stood with me on a wall looking down into the street where the religious procession was in progress.

Shahbaz, who is an Assyrian, not a Moslem, but highly regarded by the Shah, asked:

"What do you think of it?"

"I'd prefer to be the man in the rear ranks," I answered.

"Why so?" he inquired.

"Then there would be no one to hit me but myself and I could go easy."

We both laughed and returned to our table in the garden of the Darband to munch pistachio nuts and drink *abjo* (beer). Soon the wailing of the crowd started. The procession had stopped and the crowd, led by a *mullah,* was crying in a sort of a chant, "Hossein, Hossein."

The procession had caught me by surprise, and I had no camera. Though now I had time to get one to take a picture of the street meeting, Shahbaz restrained me. These mobs, made up of fanatics, act violently and without reason. They might tear a man limb from limb and certainly they would destroy his camera.

For this reason Mercedes, Mary, and I stayed close to the hotel for three days of our visit in Tehran. On one of these days John Bowling of the American Embassy took us into the Elburz Mountains for an outing. Mr. Qarib of the Protocol Staff joined us. The two cars quickly left the city and followed a dirt road up a barren canyon. The south slopes of the Elburz have no trees. The snowfall is heavy in winter. By early spring these open slopes are ideal for skiing. We passed several favorite ski spots on our climb, and saw one ski lift. Below us was a clear, blue creek lined with willow and poplar. These Persian creeks, so beautiful as to invite one to stoop and drink deeply, are deceptive. We of the West collect our sewage in pipes and carry it to the nearest river for dumping. The Persian mountain people act in the same way, though more directly. They use the streams as outhouses, even in the highest reaches of a tributary in the remotest part of a mountain range. So no Persian stream has water safe for consumption.

We soon came to Darband-Sar, a village located on the banks of this creek. We stopped at the upper end where a small teahouse is located. This is a favorite spot of John Bowling, who loves the mountains. Here he leaves his car and takes to trails that lead around mighty Damavand. He showed us the garden of the teahouse. It is set in apple and quince trees on the edge of a creek. Nearby is the home of the owner, Abdul, who lives there with his wife and daughter. Abdul laid rugs on the grass in the garden; and I followed him to his kitchen to take pictures while he prepared tea. His daughter, aged ten, broke into tears and was filled with sheer fright when I pointed the camera toward her. But Abdul was more amiable and gladly consented. So did his customers, who were men from the village, dropping in to pass the time of day. In summer this is a delightfully cool village about 7000 feet in elevation. In winter it is bitterly cold. For months the snow lies three feet or more in depth and cold winds whine down from the north. I asked Abdul how he kept warm.

He brought out what the Persians call a *corsi*. It is a brazier that is filled with charcoal and placed under a low, flat table. The table is then covered with blankets. The entire family sleeps there—some on top, some on the floor, putting their shoulders or their feet to the heat as the need dictates.

We had almost quit the village on our return trip when I asked the driver to stop. An old man was on the edge of the road sawing wood with a crosscut. He had a splendid face; and though the light was low, the sun streamed through the poplars onto him. I asked his permission for a photograph and he gladly gave it. I took my light reading and stepped back a few paces for a picture. At that moment a young man in his twenties appeared. He had come in from a side trail, riding a burro. He jumped off the animal and came running toward me, screaming. His language was plainly vile. In a flash he was between me and the woodcutter, shaking his fist. He lunged at me, trying to grab the camera. It took Mr. Qarib, with all the prestige of his office, and John Bowling, with all his persuasiveness, to halt him.

"Foreigners have no business taking our pictures," he screamed.

"Foreigners always take pictures of poor people. Take pictures of the Shah's palace," he shouted.

"Go home, Yankee," he demanded.

The eyes of this young man were burning like coals as I took my pictures and put the camera away. His jaw was still set and his fists clenched as I got back in the car. When we started up he shouted a dirty epithet.

We were riding along in silence when Mr. Qarib spoke up.

"I do not know the young man, and I apologize for his action. He is voicing the sentiments of the Communists."

He was acting in a way that was responsive to the party line. But the party line was adapted to play up to the prejudices of the people. The anti-foreign prejudice is one of the deepest of the area. Because of the long rule by the Greeks and the Arabs and the interventionist policies of Russia and England, it is easy in Persia to get the people united *against* the foreigner. That is indeed the single secret of Mossadegh's great power and continuing popularity.

CHAPTER 11

THE SHAH

One morning I spent an hour with the Shah at his summer palace in Shemiran, known as Saad Abad.

Mohammed Pahlevi is about forty years old, pleasant, gracious, and greatly interested in the world. He speaks English fluently; and his voice is always low and well modulated. Today he was dressed in a gray suit and a blue tie. He was happy and relaxed and generous with his time.

Mohammed Pahlevi is the son of Reza Shah, who took Iran by the neck in the thirties and shook it. Following the example of Ataturk in Turkey, Reza Shah sought to reduce the control of the state by the church, to unveil women and free them from *purdah,* to rid Iran of many of the traditions of the East and bring it an industrial era.

The son's role is to guide the nation in the period of transition, to free it of foreign domination, and to safeguard it from Communist infiltration. It is a difficult role for the Shah. A group of corrupt men have their fingers in politics in Iran. Iran and Russia have an 800-mile border in common. Iran, though bordering the Persian Gulf, is an interior country, far removed from outside sources of help. It's a four-hour non-stop flight in a DC-6 from Beirut to Tehran, which means that Iran is as deep in the interior of the Middle East as Nebraska is in this country.

The Shah talked of this fact and the geographical propinquity of Russia. The Soviets are an immediate threat, as much as Canada would be to us were she to become Communist. The Shah talked of his recent state visit to Russia. He reminded the Russians, when they made overtures of peace, that they had to live down the history of their aggressions.

Historians, such as Toynbee, often write that Russia through the century has been the victim of aggressors. In that way they explain Russia's passion for the defensive block of satellites between herself and Europe. But in Central Asia, Russia has been the aggressor, last century sweeping south until she gobbled up most of Central Asia. In this process, she bit off great chunks of Persia which a hundred and fifty years ago extended as far north as Baku. Several millions of people in Russia's domain today are Persians.

"When Khrushchev started to reprimand me for joining the Baghdad Pact," the Shah said, "I interrupted to say that I did so only as a safeguard against Russian aggression."

We talked of the problem of Russia in the modern world. The Shah mentioned the value of NATO as a check on Russian moves in Europe. The news of the day, which carried suggestions of a weakening of NATO, had sent a shudder through the Middle East; and the Shah reflected the general apprehension that was felt.

"Russia would gobble Europe as she gobbled us if there is a weakening of NATO without real disarmament by the Soviets," he said.

Ice-cold rose water was brought in as our talk turned to America. The Shah, extremely friendly to this country, wants domination by none. For a century, England cruelly controlled and exploited Persia, as partially told in Shuster, *The Strangling of Persia.* The feeling of the Persians against England came out in the Shah's story about a British contractor who had a construction project for five years and did very little on it.

"The contractor bled us as the British did in the old days," the Shah said.

The Shah wants to spread foreign influence thinly in Persia. Americans feel upset that the Shah should give oil-drilling contracts to the Italians and favorable business contracts to the Germans. The Shah explained to me that he welcomes many foreign countries into Iran's development program. Shortly after this interview he announced the grant to Russia of a contract for the construction of hydroelectric projects, on several rivers up north—the Aras, the Atrak, and the Hari Rud. And I had not been home very long before the Shah announced that Russia was also going to build numerous silos throughout Persia. This desire to escape the domination by any one country has led to diffuse and perhaps improvident arrangements. But the desire to stay independent is as strong as any single influence in Middle East thinking these days.

At this point in our discussion Mercedes joined us; and while the Shah and I talked, she sat on the floor taking pictures of him with the strobe flash equipment. Now we talked of domestic affairs—of his sale of the royal lands to villagers and the building of modern communities around these projects. Actually they are only important symbolically, as they involve but a small fraction of Iran's lands. The bulk of the farming lands are closely held by rather greedy landlords who have nightmares when they think of bringing schools and first-aid centers to the villages. They feel more secure if they can maintain the *status quo* and keep the peasant illiterate and ignorant.

The Shah knows this and hopes to set them an example by his model communities.

Our talk turned to Communism in Iran and the much-debated figure of Mossadegh. The Shah had named him Prime Minister; and Mossadegh overnight became the most popular of all Persians by ousting the British and nationalizing the oil. From there Mossadegh went on to other reforms. He started a vast agricultural reform. But the one that triggered the explosion leading to Mossadegh's downfall was a constitutional argument with the Shah. The Shah both reigns and rules, appointing Prime Ministers as he chooses. Mossadegh wanted the Shah to follow the example of the British monarch and reign but not rule. Mossadegh's bid was for parliamentary control and the transformation of the Shah into a constitutional monarch.

Mossadegh played politics with extremists. One was an Islamic religious leader, Seyed Abdal Ayatallah Kashani, who had many hoodlums at his beck and call, and who often produced them *en masse* on the streets of Tehran. The Communists joined forces;

and Mossadegh, who encouraged the rioters, soon became their tool. In his last days the country was so divided and the authority was so weak, it seemed that the Communists might accomplish a *coup d'état*. Yet in spite of the fact that the Shah and Mossadegh had been locked in a bitter struggle, the Shah bears no malice. He spoke of Mossadegh in soft words.

"Of course," he said, "Mossadegh was not a Communist. He and I disagreed. But he was a loyal Persian and unhappily a tool of the Communists."

The matter of the Iranian Army was different. The Communists had infiltrated the army in force, occupying many strategic posts. The Shah told me in dramatic terms of the plots within his own army and how near to success they were.

"It's a good army, now," he said proudly.

I believed him, for I had seen a different brand of soldier than I had first seen in 1949. American military missions have had a potent effect. Iranian privates now step along the roads with life and zest. They are probably as good foot soldiers as any in the world.

"And the officers?" I asked.

He answered that too many officers were still fat and flabby but that the quality had increased on the average.

We talked of mutual friends in America and places we both liked, particularly California. Then the time came to go.

He held my hand in a friendly clasp and, turning to Mercedes, paid me the finest compliment an American can expect abroad. I felt a blush as he said:

"You are one of the few foreigners who understand us."

CHAPTER 12

FREEDOM OF EXPRESSION

Iran's press law was the subject of several conversations I had with Tehran lawyers. One lawyer broached the subject at the garden dinner given by the Minister of Foreign Affairs and Mrs. Ali Gholi Ardalan. Another joined me for tea at the Darband Hotel where we reviewed censorship in Iran and the Middle East.

The Iranian press is licensed. To get a license a publisher must show, *inter alia,* that he has never been indicted or "incarcerated for lunacy."

Criminal penalties are freely provided:

(1) One to three years' imprisonment for publishing "an article contrary to the Islamic religions."

(2) One to three years for "the offense of libel" against the Shah or the Queen.

(3) One to three years for publishing "anything insulting or false or libelous against the Head of the Moslem religion or the recognized religious authorities."

(4) Two to six months for the publication of anything "liable to injure the honor" of a person.

(5) One to six months for publishing anything against "the recognized religious or racial minorities or with a view to create differences or hatred, or social or religious strife."

These press offenses are tried by a court composed of three

judges and a jury of twelve. The jury is drawn from a panel of seventy-five made up of twenty-five from each of the following classes:

(1) writers, scientists, teachers, attorneys, and notaries;
(2) merchants, landlords, farmers;
(3) workers and shopkeepers.

There are also broad provisions governing the suspension of publications, exercisable either alone or in connection with criminal prosecutions. Suspension is made by an interdepartmental committee consisting of representatives of the Ministries of Education, Justice, and Interior. A paper suspended can appeal the order to the courts.

On paper the press law looks horrendous. In practice it is gently used. As one attorney, who preferred to remain anonymous, put it, the law is "honored more in the breach than in the observance."

In recent years there were comparatively few papers that felt the squeeze of suspension. In 1956 six were suspended for publishing pictures of women in bathing suits and other scant attire. These were appealed and in two instances the courts ruled against the censor.

There were four short suspensions of papers for making insulting remarks about foreign countries. In each case the country was Russia or Egypt. One was a large weekly which was suspended for one week for publishing a photo showing Nasser's head resting on the body of a belly-dancer.

During 1956 there was only one suspension for internal political reasons. *Bamshad,* a daily, was suspended for three months for criticizing the Shah. It published a photo of the Shah as a child wearing a hat and riding horseback. Underneath was a cynical proverb to the effect that a man who sits on a horse while wearing a hat is not fit to rule.

One other episode bearing on political censorship occurred in 1956. A column in one paper was suspended for one week for criticizing the government.

But these episodes are not typical. The Iranian press criticizes and even insults with impunity all high officials (except the Shah) and all ex-officials. Criticism of government is more severe in Iran than in most countries. And it is tolerated. The Iranian press is not the victim of coercion. It may be bought by the government, by politicians, by advertisers, or by other powerful groups. In that sense it is not free. But the press law in practice does not provide a terroristic supervision over the newspapers.

The tolerance shown by the government toward criticism is subtly shown in a recent story about Mullah Nasr-ed-Din which has been widely printed in the Persian press. Mullah, while passing a cemetery spied an empty tomb and decided to lie in it to see how it felt to be dead. He felt wonderfully relaxed and contented in the tomb. Soon he heard a noise. Raising his head, he saw a mule train loaded with glassware passing the cemetery. His movement in the tomb frightened the animals who bolted, breaking all the glassware. The owners came at Mullah with sticks, beating him and causing his face to bleed. When Mullah reached home, his wife dressed his wounds and asked what happened. Mullah answered,

"These days, my dear, you must watch out and not irritate anyone. Things are so bad that you must mind your own business, even though you are dead."

Any damper on such freedom of expression as now exists in Iran is of the intangible sort. It goes back to the Zahedi coup against Mossadegh in August, 1953, when there was repression. Before long martial law was lifted. General Zahedi was replaced by Hossein Ala, former Ambassador to the United States, who restored civilian government. The appointment of Manouchehr Eghbal, who is a progressive, contributed further to relaxation of tension in the field of literature proper, as well as journalism.

During the decade preceding the fall of Mossadegh there was a tremendous renaissance in Persian literature. It was a flowering of letters unparalleled in almost five hundred years of history.

I learned more about this from Dr. Sidney Glazer on my return to Washington, D.C. Dr. Glazer, one of our foremost Persian experts, told me how this literary flowering had been in preparation for over seventy-five years. It started with the influence of Western culture on Persian and Arabic thought. Along with new ideas, the Persians gained a new style of writing. Theretofore all literature worthy of the name was in poetry. It was designed for the elite and ruling classes. It concentrated on romantic, moralistic, and mystical themes—in conscious imitation of such great medieval poets as Sa'di and Hafiz.

From Europe the Persians learned about the ideas of freedom and democracy. The leading thinkers also came to realize that, if they were to gain mass support, they had first to arouse mass interest and understanding. The intricate rhymes and meters of poetry, the elegance of language, and idealistic themes, while delighting the ears and sense of the Persians, were not suited to express fighting ideas with social content. So those who at the beginning of the century directed the struggle for a Constitution began to write in a simple prose language. This was the language of ordinary people. And it marked the beginning of the era of pamphlets and newspapers in Iran. Those pamphlets and newspapers contributed greatly to the successful battle for the Constitution in the early 1900s. Since then a large number of talented Persian writers has emerged.

In the opinion of Dr. Glazer, this literature—for its social sensitivity, wit, style, and intrinsic interest—has few equals in the Middle East and, so far as the work of its top men is concerned, is entitled to respect by Western standards.

Accession of the present Shah to the throne in 1941 liberated the energies of the writers. A stream of novels, short stories, essays, and poetry began to pour off the nation's presses. Some were Communist; most were not. They described the misery of the masses, the various manifestations of social injustice, the evils of bureaucracy and corruption in high places with keen insight and unerring aim in the racy idiom of the common man. They fought a rear-guard action against the traditionalists who, backed by political conservatives, yearned for the only "true" literature —poetry describing the immortal rose and nightingale, mystical and physical love, and lavishing encomia on the rulers of the day.

The increasing stability of the country and the slow but sure benefits from the various vast development projects now under way are producing the atmosphere in which writers can flourish. My lawyer friends in Tehran and Dr. Glazer all agreed that it will not be long before Hejazi, the Persian Maugham, Chubak, the Persian Hemingway, Jamalzadeh, Dashti, and Shademan will be writing in translation for the world the stories that have delighted their fellow countrymen.

Those who know Persian literature are convinced that its thousand-year-old unfinished carpet will in due time have golden strands reflecting the genius of twentieth-century men of letters.

One night at the Darband Hotel, I asked a Tehran lawyer about book-burning; and I referred to some "leftist" writers who had been imprisoned. He made no effort to avoid the fact that some writers have suffered or that there have been random instances of book-burning in Iran's long history. But he stoutly maintained that such acts were extremely rare and untypical.

"We Persians might in a fit of passion execute an author for some outrageous deed," he said with evident sincerity. "But book-burning is different. Our respect for the creative works of man is so deep we would consider such an act irreverent."

He spoke the truth, I think. For in these ways the Persians are more civilized than some in the West.

CHAPTER 13

THE ROAD TO HAMADAN

It was on the road to Hamadan that I met the farmer Ali, to whom this book is dedicated. We left Tehran with a smooth-running car. The side-view mirror on the door and the ventilator window had been fixed. We had new tires, new spark plugs, new points. The muffler was once more hitched on. The car was gassed up and lubricated. Even the horn was fixed.

We had a new interpreter with us—Jamshid Kashi, a Persian, a grand person, and the owner of a rug shop in Baghdad. This short, soft-spoken man is proficient in Arabic as well as Persian; and he met us in Tehran to be with us for our Iraqi journey.

It should be an easy day's drive to Hamadan. The distance is not much over two hundred miles. The road at one time was a black-surfaced highway. It had been built during World War II, when our Persian Gulf Command had the job of moving thousands of tons of Lend-Lease material from the Persian Gulf across Iran into Russia. Many roads were paved by the American Army to expedite that program. One of these was the road to Hamadan via Gazvin that we took.

This road today is one of the worst in all Iran—far worse than a poor dirt road. Apparently no repair work has been done on it since the American Army left in 1946. The black top is so badly pock-marked that it is difficult to average twenty miles an hour.

Though we left Tehran at seven o'clock we had not gone much over a hundred miles by noon when we reached Takestan.

This is a small village about a block long on the main highway. A row of shops and a couple of teahouses are set back a hundred feet from the road. There were trees planted in this space and tables placed there for travelers. Many besides us had also stopped for lunch. Large families occupied the tables under the trees. So we picked out a teahouse with tables at its door and ordered lunch. It was a dingy and rather dirty-looking kitchen. But the proprietor was affable and eager to please. When I asked what he had for lunch, he took out of a case pieces of freshly killed lamb that looked most attractive. He cut it and put it on skewers and then turned it over charcoal. He served it with raw sliced onions that were quite sharp. He also served *chai* and *nan*. This bread was about the best we had all summer long. It was soft, thin unleavened bread which one could easily use to pick up food. The flies were a bit thick; and a strong wind blew dirt from the street into our faces. But the meal cost twenty rials (twenty-six cents) each and was one of the best of our journey.

Not far out of Takestan we met the locusts. Whole clouds of them swirled through a barren valley. They were so thick that they caused a heavy shadow, like that of an airplane, on the ground beneath them. The locust of northern Iran is an invader, not a permanent inhabitant. It has its permanent abode in Africa, southeastern Iran, and the southwestern fringe of West Pakistan. It has two broods a year. The eggs of the first brood are laid in early spring and the fliers develop by early summer. The second brood turns to fliers in the fall. The locusts are a great pest in Iran. Both the Iranian government and our Point IV have locust control programs. Planes are now used extensively for spraying DDT. Once in a while the Russians furnish spray planes for this work in Iran.

The people try to keep locusts from their fields by waving cloths and beating gongs. On cold nights in the fall, the adult locust fastens on bushes and becomes somewhat lethargic. The farmers sometimes shake them into bags and use them for cattle feed. This day the locusts were so thick, they soon collected by the dozens in our car. Some measured over three inches.

It was not long after we cleared the locusts that I met Ali. We came to a flat valley stretching for miles, where wheat was being harvested. This was the ninth of August, and the harvest was about over. There is not much farm machinery in Iran. Most of the wheat is cut by hand sickles, and the wheat is tied in sheaves or bundles and stacked in the field. These are loaded on donkeys and taken to a central thrashing floor. The floor is usually a flat place in the field with no covering. The sheaves are untied here and the wheat stalks scattered on the floor. Some farmers hitch cattle or donkeys, or cattle and donkeys together shoulder to shoulder and drive them around and around the floor, depending on the beat of the hoofs to dislodge the wheat from the head. More often, they use a heavy sled to help thrash the wheat. Frequently the animals draw a crude drag that has one or more large drumlike wheels that pound the heads of the wheat. Women and children usually drive the animals. Round and round they go for days until the wheat is separated. Then men use a fork (usually a wooden one) to toss the residue into the air. The wind catches the chaff and blows it to one side. Sometimes a large round wooden traylike vessel is used to pick up the residue. A man shakes it until the kernels are at the bottom. Then, tipping the tray, he blows the chaff away. After many backbreaking days, the golden kernels lie in piles and are transferred by hand into burlap sacks. The landlord comes to the thrashing floor and takes his half or three fifth or four fifths—whatever the rental arrangements may be.

I had pictures of every phase of this operation from Swat to Tehran. My picture series was complete; and since the process is about the same across the Middle East, I no longer kept an eye out for harvesting scenes. But on this stretch, when Mercedes was driving, I saw so striking a picture I asked her to stop. Though this was a conventional thrashing floor, the cows were being driven by an unveiled Persian woman, dressed in gay colors.

It is my custom when photographing to get permission first, for I always assume that any person, no matter how lowly, has the same sensibilities as I do. And when a man was present I always asked him if I could photograph his lady.

An old man was separating wheat at a thrashing floor next to the lady's. He looked nearly seventy. He was tall and spare. He had the long oval head of the Persian and a patrician nose.

Though living in poverty, he had an aristocratic look and bearing.

"May I take your wife's photograph?" I asked.

"Bali, bali," he said without hesitation.

When I had finished, I returned to the man to thank him. He wanted to know if I were American or British. When I told him I was American, he asked me to sit down. It was a very warm day and we were now in the heat of three o'clock. So I sought the shade of a stack of chaff and talked to the old man, while Mercedes and Mary fumed in the car.

His name was Ali. There is no doctor in Ali's village. There's not even a first-aid center. No medicines are available for distribution, not even aspirin. The people resort to sorcery and old wives' cures. Ali's wife wore an agate to fend off evil. She eats figs to cure hemorrhoids; she makes a powder out of the wood of the *zegul* tree to remove warts; she uses the gum of the wild olive on wounds or sores; she cures diarrhea by putting charred peach stones on the navel; she uses garlic to drive off cholera and mulberry leaves to cure carbuncles; she uses oleander to keep fleas away. There is a yellow herb called the rue whose seeds have medicinal values. Ali's wife keeps a pod of the seed for good luck; and she burns the rue seeds over hot coals and uses the smoke to ward off evil. The blood of a sheep may be spread across the road leading to the village to keep out a plague. Or a piece of a looking glass may be put there to deflect the evil eye.

Ali was a sharecropper. He was born and raised near Hamadan and, like 95 per cent of the farmers, is illiterate. He has farmed the same tract as his father and grandfather before him, and has inherited some of the debts that those ancestors incurred. They were loans from the father and grandfather of the present landlord—loans that often go down from generation to generation.

Mossadegh was a hero to Ali, partly because he took stern measures against the British. Beyond that, Mossadegh had Ali's welfare in mind. I asked him why he felt that way. He mentioned the "20 per cent" law which Mossadegh got the Parliament to enact.

This "20 per cent" law provided that 20 per cent of the annual crop should be set aside and divided into two equal parts. One part was to be returned to the tenant; the other part was to be used for village development. The reduction in rent was a simple operation. Village development, however, was a different matter. That necessitated an organization within the village that would manage the fund. Iranian villages have no political organization—no village council, no town meeting, no Mayor. The landlords who own the village determine and direct policy. They have never been interested in plowing profits in schools and hospitals. Historically, they have merely drained the village of every available rial.

The Mossadegh law was a push in the direction of forming a political organization, at village level, to spend the 10 per cent in village development. For the first time in Iranian history institutions of self-government were introduced at the grass-roots level. It was indeed the beginning of a vast democratic revolution. During Mossadegh's regime, some villages actually got under way with village councils elected by the people. I had talked with some of these councils and seen their development programs on earlier visits to Iran. But the village council did not spread far. Ali's village never had one. And Mossadegh soon was out of office.

When Mossadegh fell, the "20 per cent" law was repealed. It was anathema to most landlords; and they controlled the new government. But the law reform that Mossadegh started was too popular to be suppressed. There was a ground swell for action. Men like Ali, though illiterate, are intelligent and articulate. They demanded reform. Finally the Mossadegh law was re-enacted in a modified form: (1) it is applicable only where the tenant's share of the crop is 50 per cent or less; (2) when applicable, 5 per cent of the crop is set aside for village developments.

"What happened to you under the new law?" I asked Ali.

"My share of the crop had been 50 per cent," Ali replied. "When the new law was passed, the landlord increased my share so the new law would not apply."

I asked him by how much his rent had been decreased. After some computations between Ali and Kashi, it appeared that the rent had been decreased to 49.9 per cent of the crop. The reduction in rent by a tenth of 1 per cent had evaded the application of the new law. This evasive tactic, I was to learn, was used the length and breadth of Iran. There were exceptions. But Ali's experience was typical.

This friendly farmer did not know who I was except that I was an American. But, like most Iranians along the countryside, he was hospitable. I was at once a friend. I was hot and dusty from my travels; and by reason of my stop in the shade of his haystack I had become his guest. When we had finished talking of Mossadegh, he reached into the straw and pulled out a jug of water.

"It is cold and you are thirsty," he said, handing me the jug.

This simple gesture carried my mind back to countless deeds of kindness done in my honor along the byways of the Middle East. Now I was once more befriended in a strange land. My benefactor was illiterate, grimy, and destitute. Yet he had a noble bearing; and he was by instinct hospitable. He and his like had been tramped upon by countless invaders and adventurers; and their faces had been ground into the earth by avaricious landlords. But somehow he had retained human warmth and the bright spark of friendliness. In these few minutes with Ali in the shade of the strawstack, he became somehow the symbol of thousands of Persians who shape the character of their country and make it for me a second home. As I returned to the car, I decided that Ali, whose last name I never knew, should occupy the honored place in this book.

Hamadan, a city of about 100,000 people, lies in a flat rolling valley pressed against low mountains on the south that are snow-capped many months of the year. Hamadan is the ancient Ecbatana where Darius III, after being defeated by Alexander the Great in the battle of Gaugamela (near Erbil in northern Iraq), retreated and gathered his forces. Hamadan is where Alexander, after his conquest of Asia, spent some months in preparation for an expedition into Arabia that was forestalled by his death in Babylon. Hamadan is a delightful town both scenically and weather-wise. It has by reason of its altitude and nearness to the mountains some qualities of a summer resort. In the early days of Persia during the rule of the Achaemenian dynasty (559–331 B.C.), Hamadan was, indeed, a summer capital. A new hotel, the Buali, has been built to meet some of the current demands for accommodations by those seeking to escape the heat of the plains.

This hotel takes up a whole square block. Its back faces the main street. Its rooms have porches opening into a great garden on the far side. The rooms are neat and modern. The garden, when we were there, was fragrant with carnations in bloom. There were many pools in the garden; and its gravel walks are lined with intricate flower beds. The service is excellent; and the cuisine, run by a Frenchman, is very superior.

We were met at the hotel by the Governor, Ashraf Pizishkpur, the Mayor, Hosein Bat'ha'i, and the head of the gendarmes, Colonel Mofi. The Colonel speaks excellent English and explained that the Governor, realizing we were tired from our journey, did not want to burden us with a dinner or entertainment. It would be better, he thought, to let us have our rest; and he would meet us in the morning. For this we blessed the Governor, and repaired to the garden where we sipped cold drinks and ate the largest, sweetest pistachio nuts I ever did see.

In the morning we saw the sights of Hamadan.

Avicenna is buried in Hamadan. The tomb, set in a massive garden, has an entrance porch supported by ten huge white pillars. The tomb is set back from several reception rooms filled with mementos of Avicenna. The building is topped by a ten-pillared tower which in turn is capped by a solid piece of stone in the shape of a rocket's nose. This tower, which can be seen for miles, looks indeed like a miniature launching frame for a rocket.

Avicenna died in Hamadan in A.D. 1037. He has been claimed by several races, including the Arabs and Kurds. But he was Persian, and spent his youth in Bukhara, now in Soviet Central Asia. His identification with Central Asia persists. For the Russian medical school at Stalinabad is named for him. Avicenna is, indeed, one of the most illustrious names in medicine. He wrote an encyclopedic medical treatise called the *Canon* which became the leading textbook for medical education in Europe. Sir William Osler once remarked that this book by Avicenna remained "a medical bible for a longer period than any other work."

Avicenna was also a philosopher and, while living at Hamadan, wrote commentaries on the works of Aristotle and helped recover for the West the scientific learning of the Greek. He wrote treatises on metaphysics, psychology, and religion, and contributed to an understanding of musical technique. Avicenna got into trouble with the orthodox theologians. He did not believe in personal immortality and the resurrection of the body. That was heretical by the theology of the time, for it was at war with the Koran. Avicenna was so unpopular with the orthodox that some of his books were burned. His own library was seized and deposited in a library which later burned.

He is today a symbol of opposition to conformity. For that trait he appeals to the Persians, who escaped the orthodoxy of the Koran and developed their own school of Islamic thought.

The visit to the Jewish quarters was the highlight of our stay in Hamadan. There are a few thousand Jews in Hamadan today. They first came there about the fifth century B.C. They suffered many persecutions; and both Timur and Shah Abbas slaughtered them. But during the last century they have lived in relative peace, and now are a rather thriving community, as Persian communities go.

It is claimed that Esther and her cousin Mordecai who, according to the Book of Esther, became a minister to Xerxes I, are buried in Hamadan. A domed mausoleum, situated in the center of town, has been erected over their alleged graves. In this mausoleum is a copy of the Old Testament written on parchment made of doeskin. Whether Esther and Mordecai rest in this mausoleum is not known for certain.

The Jewish woodworkers are not legendary. They occupy a section of the bazaar and are famous throughout Iran for their inlay work. Their stalls are flush with the street, being boarded up at night with large removable doors. The shop where we bought some articles was owned by Movla Mughterae, a slight, bearded man near sixty. A friend of President Eisenhower once purchased a box from Movla and presented it to the President, who in turn wrote a letter of appreciation. That letter is framed and hangs on the wall in Movla's shop. Next to it there now hangs a letter from me. I too appreciated Movla's work. It is very delicate work, showing mixtures of various types of wood. We bought small matchbox holders, a cigarette box, and a coffee table with a secret drawer. The tools Movla uses are simple. All he has by way of machinery is a lathe. The wood he uses is mostly old stumps, which produce the wonderful burled effects in the inlay.

Some of his wood is pear, some walnut. But I never did learn all the pieces in my beautiful coffee table.

Movla, a respected member of the Hamadan community, was filled with joy at our arrival and sad on our departure. We meant America to him; and America in his eyes was the great refuge of the oppressed of all lands.

Though he had followed the example of some of the Meshedi Jews and become a Moslem, Judaism was still his driving force.

CHAPTER 14

POINT IV AND A MOONLIGHT PORCH

We had a peck of trouble from Hamadan to Kermanshah. The black-top road was heavily pockmarked. Our speed was necessarily slow. But once in a while there would be an inviting stretch of pavement where we would get up to thirty-five miles an hour for a quarter or half mile. That almost invariably led to disaster when some deep break in the pavement would loom up, Then we would either brake so hard that the baggage in the rear ended up on top of us, or we would hit with a thud, rattling the whole car. These thuds did more damage than we realized at the time. It was not until we got to Baghdad that we learned they had broken three leaves in our rear springs. But we were not far out of Hamadan when we discovered that the left front shock absorber was broken. For some miles there seemed to be something suspiciously wrong with the left front of the car. When I stopped to get a picture of men loading thistles on donkeys for the winter feed supply, Mercedes did some exploring under the car. The bracket that held the shock absorber in the front coil spring was broken, and the shock absorber was nearly dragging on the ground. We had no spare parts for this repair job.

We stopped at every gendarme station to inquire where we might find a blacksmith or a garage. We had no luck at three villages. But at one stop we got wonderful pictures of women flattening cattle dung into large cakes and laying them out in the sun to dry.

Some were laying them flat on the ground. Others were plastering them on the sides of buildings. A few young girls were collecting those that had dried and placing them in stacks. These cakes were to be used for cooking, come winter. They would be piled in a small stack shaped like a beehive and lighted. Little other fuel, except the kindling of tumbleweeds, would be available. This dung is also used as cement: it seals the mud roof; it patches walls made of reeds; it is used as mortar between rocks.

This dung—collected by women only—is considered unclean and not touched by the men.

When I finished taking the pictures and returned to the car, we were advised that the gendarmes had a garage we could use at Kangavar on the Kashkan River, to try to repair the shock absorber.

This garage had a pit over which I drove the car. Two mechanics went to work diagnosing the problem. They took measurements of the broken bracket and consulted a blacksmith. He did not hold any hope of being able to finish making the part this day. So the mechanics, under Mercedes' supervision, wired up the shock absorber, saying it would last until we got to Kermanshah. They were optimists. In twenty miles the shock absorber was down and every bump was a heavy knock on the frame. We were creeping along in this crippled condition when a jeep approached and flagged us down. It was Mehdi Raaufy, Mayor of Kermanshah, out to greet us. He said the Governor and some Americans were awaiting our arrival for a luncheon in our honor. The Mayor of Hamadan had phoned them of our departure and these friendly Iranian officials had arranged a luncheon and invited all the Americans in Kermanshah.

But we wanted first to stop at the village of Bisotun, which sits at the foot of a 1700-foot rock cliff, and see (the bas-reliefs of Darius.)

At the base of this cliff is a bas-relief of the triumph of Gotarzes (A.D. 46–51) over Meherdates, two Parthians struggling for the throne of Persia. There are three figures of heroic size; a mounted warrior pursues another with a spear; over one of these an angel holds the victory garland. Most of the sculpture was mutilated many years ago by a curious kind of vandalism. The story is that a Persian overlord, Sheikh Ali Khan Zanganah, cut an arch-shaped panel directly in the middle of the sculpture in order to record, in an Arabic inscription, a gift of the income of two villages, which he donated for keeping up a caravanserai he had built at Bisotun. This inscription is quite plainly seen from the road.

The more interesting bas-relief is about three hundred feet high on a cliff to the left of this Parthian sculpture. Darius, followed by his two ministers, has his foot on the prostrate body of one vanquished King. Nine other captive Kings are in front of him. Their hands are bound behind them and each has a rope around his neck. Above them is a winged figure representing Ahura Mazda, god of the Zoroastrians. At the sides and beneath this monument are fourteen columns of writing, recording the accomplishments of Darius in three different languages—Old Persian, Elamite, and Babylonian. Near the middle of the base of the cliff is a huge surface—500 feet by 100 feet—that had been cleared for sculpturing by stonecutters. But the project was dropped; and the smooth stone wall has no inscriptions on it.

Twenty miles farther on (and only four miles from Kermanshah) we came to another historic stone cliff known as Taq-e Bostan or Arch of the Garden; which I mentioned earlier in giving the reason for calling the car Ali. It was an ancient hunting lodge. There is a garden at the base of this cliff, a garden with a large pool, well watered and shaded by willows. The place gets its name from the arched recesses that were carved into the base of the mountain. Here are three separate sets of bas-reliefs.

The lowest relief shows two Kings, a religious figure, and a prostrate figure trampled under the feet of the two Kings.

A second relief is in a cave about 20 feet wide, 17 feet high, and 12 feet deep. King Sapor II and King Sapor III are shown life size standing side by side.

The third relief is in a second cave, almost twice as large as the other. The outer edge of the arch has beadwork of a lotus pattern. The base of the arch has floral designs. Above are two winged Victories bearing coronets and cups. On the right is the King Firuz (who built Taq-e Bostan) pursuing a deer; on the left his pursuit of a boar. The rear wall shows the King mounted on a war horse, known in history as Black as Night. Above this scene is the King receiving by the right hand a wreath from a bearded figure and by the other a garland of victory from a woman who pours a libation from a vessel in her left hand.

The story is that the lady is Shirin, immortalized by Nizami, the Persian poet who died in A.D. 1203. One of his famous poems is entitled *Khosru and Shirin,* which the Russians dramatize on the stage in Soviet Central Asia. Taq-e Bostan is, indeed, one of the most sentimental spots in Iran, linked with the love of Shirin for Farhad, who built Taq-e Bostan and who was deceitfully deprived of the fair lady. Farhad was the sculptor of Taq-e Bostan and had been promised by the King the hand of Shirin, if he would cut a channel through the rock cliff which would bring water to the garden. The King, who thought this was an impossible task, was surprised to learn that Farhad had about succeeded. He was anxious to be relieved of his promise and consulted a sorcerer. She, for a fine fee, promised to free the King of his obligation. The King paid her and she proceeded to the high cliff where Farhad was working and brought him the false news of Shirin's death. Nizami put the ending scene in great poetry:

"Cease, idle youth, to waste thy days," she said,
"By empty hopes a visionary made;
Why in vain toil thy fleeting life consume
To frame a palace?—Rather hew a tomb.
Even like sere leaves that autumn winds have shed,
Perish thy labours, for—Shireen is dead!"
He heard the fatal news—no word, no groan;
He spoke not, moved not,—stood transfixed to stone.
Then, with a frenzied start, he raised on high
His arms, and wildly tossed them towards the sky;
Far in the wide expanse his axe he flung,
And from the precipice at once he sprung.
The rocks, the sculptured caves, the valleys green,
Sent back his dying cry—"Alas! Shireen."

I sat in the garden looking at the cliff and thinking of Shirin and Farhad. I also thought of another Kermanshah tragedy. It related to a famous Jew, Solomon Chayyim, who lived in Kermanshah about thirty years ago. He came to the Persian Majlis or Parliament under Reza Shah after the King broke the hold of the *mullahs* over the state. Chayyim had a newspaper, sponsored Zionism, and was active in all Jewish affairs. He did not long survive public life. When an attempt on Reza Shah's life was made, Chayyim was accused by his enemies, including the *mullahs*. Though he was never tried, though no proof of his guilt was ever established, he was executed. In the midst of these thoughts I was interrupted. The Governor, Nahi Ardallan, had arrived to welcome us. He and the Mayor had a wreath of freshly picked flowers for us which they tendered as they bowed from the waist. When we had not arrived by noon, the Governor became concerned and came to find us. It was now 1:15 P.M.

So we left Taq-e Bostan at once and followed the Governor and the Mayor into the city. When we stopped at the hotel, Mr. and Mrs. Rolla L. Amsberry, head of our Point IV program, were at the door to greet us. Mr. Aziz Rais Rohani, the Iranian who was assistant area development adviser, went with Mercedes to take the car to a garage to have the shock absorber fixed while we ate. I went into the hotel to meet the other guests. There were seven Americans there from our Point IV program and our military mission. None was an old friend; but we seemed to have so much in common that greeting them was like going to a college reunion. There were five Persians present, three being associated with the Point IV program, the other two being the Mayor and the Governor, Nahi Ardallan.

It was an informal friendly luncheon. Both the Governor and the Mayor made speeches which touched on my former visits to Iran and my 1950 visit to Kermanshah. There were toasts to the Shah and toasts to President Eisenhower; and there were toasts to the continued friendship between America and Iran.

It was close to three o'clock when the luncheon ended. Though Kermanshah is nearly 5000 feet in elevation, the midday sun can be hot. We had been cool under the overhead fans of the hotel; but outside the cobblestone street was warm. We drove with the Amsberrys in their jeep to the garage. Two expert mechanics —both Persians and both working for our Point IV mission— had enlisted the aid of a blacksmith and repaired the shock absorber. After paying them, we went to the Amsberrys' home for a visit. Two Americans—Anna K. Garietson and C. E. Rhoad, both of the Point IV program—were also present. In the hour of our stay in the Amsberry home we learned more about Point IV than we had known before. Or perhaps it would be more accurate to say that the conversation in the Amsberry home put into clearer focus many impressions of Point IV that we had obtained in several countries.

First is the problem of getting the various ministries of an Asian country to work together. It was customary in some lands for one minister to work in isolation from the others. He might get letters inquiring about locust control or some other agricultural pest. If the matter was not in his jurisdiction, the letter would go unanswered; or he would reply that he had no information of value. The letter would never be referred to the proper minister. Moreover, one minister would never call at the office of another minister to discuss a problem. For him to do that would mean a loss of face. The result was that the government was never co-ordinated, ministries often worked at cross-purposes, a recurring problem often went unsolved even though the government had the skill and resources to resolve it. One important role of Point IV has been to bring officials at the same level of government together and to inculcate patterns of co-operative work. This has been initiated by the Point IV official's calling a meeting at which all common problems could be discussed.

Second are the problems of improving breeding stock and of pest control. In Kermanshah as in other parts of the Middle East one of the important roles of Point IV has been to provide demonstration farms with high-grade bulls and roosters for cross-breeding.

One of the first steps in livestock improvement in Iran was taken by Point IV in 1952. Good jackass stock from Cypress was brought in for breeding purposes. The Communist press started an uproar. "The people are hungry and what does imperialistic America send them? Jackasses!" But the country people and the Iranian Army knew the value of this breeding stock. So the braying of the Communist press was futile. Moreover, our agricultural experts have introduced the use of fertilizers, sprays, crop rotation, and other methods of scientific farming.

Point IV shows films that tell how to prevent diseases from spreading, what causes dysentery, what causes malaria. Demonstrations of new fertilizers and sprays are shown to farmers. William E. Warne, who headed Point IV in Iran for a few years, shows in his book *Mission for Peace* how Point IV spray increased the pistachio crop tenfold; how improved seed increased cereal and fiber production by 40 per cent.

Third is the teacher-training program. The aim is to develop and train local teachers who in a few years can carry on without outside assistance. In agriculture this means training teachers of modern agricultural methods. Only a small percentage of students will ever go to any agricultural school. If scientific agriculture is to be introduced, it must be through secondary schools where farm children will be reached. The program of teacher training in agriculture is a three-year one. At the end of the three years the graduate is qualified to teach the elements of scientific agriculture needed for the area where his school will be located. The teacher-training program does not end with agriculture. The aim is to provide teachers for the new public school systems of the Middle East. Until recently, there have been few schools. With the spread and growth of schools the greatest demand is for teachers. Point IV usually provides, as it does in Kermanshah, a two-year teacher-training program. These teachers' colleges are designed to operate long after the Americans leave and to be a continuing adjunct to the educational system of each country.

Point IV in Kermanshah has started many new projects and helped co-ordinate many others.

I had visited Varamin Plain, near Tehran, in 1954 and had seen new villages being constructed under the impetus of those ideas. Paul Maris of the Ford Foundation was with me. So were William E. Warne and John McCauley of Point IV. And I marveled at the progress they were making.

A recent meeting of Kermanshah officials called by Point IV discussed a wide variety of subjects: spray for fruit trees, locust control, results from new vegetable seeds, the problems of a veterinary among livestock, adult education in literacy, student camps, teacher-training problems, road repair, snow clearance, road construction, malaria control, baby clinics, training of midwives, maternity wards, establishment of new health clinics, public health education, smallpox vaccinations, purifying drinking water, village development programs, construction of village bathhouses, the digging of wells, the construction of new schools, sewage disposal projects, introduction of swimming pools in parks, irrigation system for city lawns, and repairs to the city slaughterhouse.

As Amsberry talked, my mind carried back to January 20, 1949, when President Truman was giving his Inaugural Address, the speech that launched Point IV:

"We must embark on a bold, new program for making the benefits of our scientific advancements and industrial progress available for improvement and growth to underdeveloped areas. . . . I believe that we should make available to peace-loving peoples the benefits of our store of technical knowledge in order to help them realize their aspirations for a better life."

The Point IV program brings new ideas, practical know-how, and scientific attitudes to the solution of all village problems in the Middle East. This is what the area needs more than anything else.

Each region is hungrier for ideas on reconstruction than for guns or even for dollars. No group I ever saw better vitalized this idea than Amsberry and his staff in Kermanshah.

We left Kermanshah at four o'clock accompanied by a jeep full of gendarmes. We were continuously slowed down by the broken black-top pavement. We had a flat tire not far out of Kermanshah which Mercedes, with the help of a gendarme, fixed in less than ten minutes. And when we reached Shahabad, a green oasis in a rather dry valley, the gendarme jeep led us to a gendarme station where a hot patch was put on the tube and the tire pumped up by hand to twenty-eight pounds—all in twenty minutes. Our destination was Gasr-e Shirin near the Iraqi border. But the long luncheon and visit in Kermanshah and the flat tire had detained us. We were now headed for more night driving.

Shortly out of Shahabad the black-top pavement smoothed out and for the first time in weeks we reached fifty miles an hour. We were now climbing sharply up a winding road that led through a narrow ravine of the Zagros Range. The engine worked well in the cool of the evening.

We occasionally saw patches of forests on the eastern slopes of the Zagros. Once the whole mountain chain had been covered with chestnut and oak. Only occasional forests remain. Fires were burning in the ones we saw, for charcoal is still the favorite fuel. The discovery of oil and the scarcity of forests is gradually transferring Iran over to a kerosene regime. Unless that transfer takes place quickly, Iran will be completely denuded except for the north slopes of the Elburz, which get the wet air of the Caspian Sea. We passed in the dusk great stretches of mountain slopes where oak and chestnut trees were struggling to take hold. But it will take several generations of careful conservation to bring back the forests.

By the time we had reached Karand a full moon was showing. It was deep dusk, the air was wonderfully cool, and the electric lights of Karand marched gracefully down a beautiful hillside. Karand did, indeed, look like a garden. There is no hotel there or we would have stayed all night. Kashi said that, if I desired, he would go to the gendarmes and ask for lodgings for the four of us. Friends in Tehran had suggested they make forward arrangements for us to stay there with a private family. But no arrangements had been made, and it seemed better to go on to certain reservations at Gasr-e Shirin than waste an hour or more in Karand. In twenty miles or so we reached the top of the Zagros Range. There on the highest point of the ridge stood a lonely teahouse. It was now close to nine o'clock; and we pulled in for dinner.

Mrs. Amsberry had put up some nice sandwiches for us. She had added to the carton a large can of tomato juice and some homemade cookies. We bought *chai* in the teahouse; and for dessert we opened a tin of fruit and served it with the cookies. We sat at tables in a small garden, actually shivering as we ate. Two stray dogs, lean and emaciated, came by begging for morsels. The proprietor stood at a respectful distance, a white apron around his waist and a towel over his shoulders. We were his only patrons and we received his undivided attention.

After the teahouse we dropped fast to Gasr-e Shirin. The distance was probably not over twenty miles. Yet while we had been shivering at the teahouse, we were soon uncomfortably warm even in a moving car. We were nearing the plains of the Tigris and Euphrates, which give off great heat in summer months.

We reached Gasr-e Shirin in moonlight at ten o'clock. We

checked into customs to find what reservations had been made for us. The chief of customs—Mr. Jalechin—had given us up and gone home to bed. While a courier went for him, polite and thoughtful Persian servants brought us iced rose water and offered us chairs on the porch of the rambling customs headquarters. Soon Jalechin appeared—a forty-year-old, pleasant, energetic official. We followed his jeep across town to a huge walled-in building. A gendarme swung open a great iron gate and we wheeled up in front of a massive public building set in a garden of palm trees. It was the Public Health Building of the district. It had no toilet. In one room an iron tank supplied a bowl with water in the fashion of a very old commode or washstand. Gendarmes brought iron cots and bedding. Jalechin said we could sleep indoors or on the porch. I went inside to examine the rooms. They were truly like ovens, even with the windows open. So we had the cots put on the porch. Five gendarmes stood guard as we slept. I counted them every time I woke. I awakened five times to move my bed back into the shadow of a pillar on the high vaulted unscreened porch. Finally I dropped into a deep sleep and awoke only after much shaking at 5:30 A.M.

Jalechin had appeared early, as he wanted us to have the cool of the morning for our journey. His servants brought hot water for washing and shaving, and a delicious breakfast—watermelon, boiled eggs, *nan,* coffee, and a sweet marmalade made out of green pistachios.

The arrival of breakfast so early caught us all in bed. But with the politeness that is deep in the bones of all Persians the gendarmes and the servants turned their backs until our toilets were completed.

PART 4

IRAQ

CHAPTER 1

THE ROAD TO BAGHDAD

We left Gasr-e Shirin at six-thirty. For the twenty miles or so to Khosrowi, the border town of Iran, we stayed on a rolling plateau about 2000 feet in elevation. We had left all remnants of forests and were now in a barren expanse with the canyons and defiles showing the work of severe erosion.

A Lur boy was grazing sheep; and for a small coin he threw off his shyness and posed for pictures. The gendarmes' jeep which was following us to the border had a flat tire. We stopped and helped repair it. Two cars parked on an Iranian highway always cause curiosity. In this region we excited the utmost interest, for every truck, every motorcycle stopped.

We were in what is known as the northern limits of Luristan, which I had first visited in 1950. Luristan is the ancient home of the Lurs, one of the four major tribes in Persia. They once had Khans and a tribal government. That day is passed. Under Reza Shah they were crushed. They are today unorganized, illiterate, and miserable people. Once they were victims of the Khans; today they are victims of oppressive landlords. One can travel all of Luristan and find no schools for girls and only a few schools for boys. Even the latter stop at the fourth grade.

My surprise this morning was to find every truck, every motorcycle packed with Lurs. They were employed by the government or by business and were emerging from the misery of the villages of Luristan to some kind of competence as employees. Their faces were all new to me; but their headdress was familiar. It was the large loose circular turban of black and white cloth. I talked with probably a dozen of them this morning. Each had an infectious smile. His teeth were always excellent, for he was so poor he could not afford the soft drinks and the sweets that destroy the enamel. His face always lit up when I said I had been with the Lurs on an earlier trip. The saying is "as poor as a Lur." But one can also say, "Once a Lur, always a Lur." There is pride in tribe and ancestry. And one who befriends a Lur makes friends with an entire community.

Lur women also walked the highway this morning. A group of three were first frightened by Mercedes and me with our cameras. Kashi tried to calm them down. But it was only after he and I retired that these three Lur women would allow their pictures to be taken. They had metal pots which had carried milk and *mawst* to the market at Khosrowi. They were dressed in loose black gowns and black turbans so loosely wound that their stringy hair showed around their faces.

Khosrowi is a small town devoted mostly to border business. It has a fine-appearing administration building and a nondescript bazaar. One building along the main road is a huge restaurant roofed over but open on the street side. There are charcoal burners in the rear where the cooking is done; and several large samovars constantly bubbling. The rotund, bald-headed proprietor also boasted of an electric refrigerator and a tub full of ice and Pepsi-Cola. He had tables by the dozens set up in this restaurant; and most of them were occupied. For here was the greatest gathering of travelers—around two hundred—we had encountered on our journey. Six busses had come up from Iraq loaded with pilgrims to Meshed and the Golden Mosque, which, as I said earlier, has become sacred to the Moslems. These were Arabs—all men—dressed in the flowing headdress, the *kafeyah,* that covers the side of the face and the back of the neck and is wonderful protection against the sun. Some wore long gowns; others were dressed in shirts and trousers with the baggy or drooping crotch. They looked grim but were in a holiday mood. For when Mercedes approached them with a camera, they were all grins and ready to pose.

There were six busses and a few loaded trucks headed from Iran to Iraq. These passengers and crews were also lounging in the shade of the restaurant, waiting for border clearance. Some were curled up on blankets sound asleep; others drank *chai;* a few sipped Pepsi-Cola. We called the five gendarmes who had come with us in the jeep and bought them cold drinks. Kashi went to the telegraph office to send messages for me. This took time; but even so, Kashi returned before Jalechin came back with our customs and immigration clearance.

The road drops sharply after leaving Khosrowi for Baghdad; and on a summer day the heat is searing. The Iraqi border town is Muntheria. There's nothing there but a square adobe building flying the Iraqi flag. There was no shade when we stopped, for the sun was high. No tree marks the place. No touch of green. We heard that in spring these hot, barren slopes are alive with color. Now they were brown.

I went inside with Kashi to present the passports. We passed through a hot, barren courtyard brilliant in sunshine, where a peasant packed a small burro train. An official sat in a darkened room. The only light came from the doorway. Outside sat a bedraggled man on his haunches, pulling a rope that worked a *punkah* or overhead fan in the dark room. A dozen men lounged there waiting their turn for customs. The floor of the darkened room had been freshly dampened with water and the air smelled something like a wet dog. So I chose the heat and the sunlight. Soon the head of customs arrived by car—Mahmood Majid Agha. He is round-faced, baldish, and plump—a good natured forty-year-old Arab to whom courtesy comes by instinct. There is Pepsi-Cola on the Iraqi side of the border too; and after each of us had a bottle with this amiable official, we were off to Khanaqin. Muntheria turned out to be only a check post for immigration. At Khanaqin customs was in full operation.

This is a small town with shady streets. On the outskirts a camel train, recently unloaded, was resting on the ground, the camels chewing their cuds. These camels were bedded down for the day. For in the East men know that the time for travel is by night. The sun has taught the lesson—a sun that sears everything green, that dries up water, that strikes down men. In the cool of the evenings the camel trains make up and head for distant market places. The way is beset with many dangers. The saying from an old religious play is "Men travel by night and their destinies travel towards them." But the dangers of night travel are not as great as the awful hazards of the sun.

Next we spotted a gasoline station where we filled our tank with gasoline. This station, like the better ones in Iran, had automatic pumps. But, like all other service stations in the Middle East, it had no auxiliary services. One checks his own oil and wipes his windshield. From there we went to the low, flat customs building where dozens of trucks were parked. The place was a beehive of activity. Officials were unloading some trucks to take a look at every parcel. They were climbing over others to make a token search. Kashi and I sat in a dark room under a lazy electric fan waiting our turn. Soon an official offered us lukewarm Pepsi-Cola. Then there was an interminable wait. After a while he returned to the darkened room and sat at his desk fumbling papers. Finally he looked up and asked in Arabic:

"Do you have any Persian rugs?"

I had none and told Kashi so, who passed the word on to the official. He stamped a customs sheet with three large bangs and out we went. I asked Kashi why they were specifically interested in rugs, not other items. He said there was very heavy duty on rugs.

"What is the duty on Persian rugs brought into Iraq?" I asked.

"About 30 per cent of the value," he replied.

"Are there no exceptions?" I inquired.

"Yes. A person is entitled to one free rug a year, provided it is a prayer rug."

"Why the exception?" I asked.

"Many people come through Iraq on religious pilgrimages. They all bring prayer rugs. They could not travel without one," Kashi said. "You see, a good Moslem must pray five times a day. When he's traveling, he needs the rug for these prayers. At night he needs it for a bed."

"Are many Persian rugs imported from Iran?" I asked.

"Not many," he replied.

"How do you get your inventory of Persian rugs?"

"Mostly from the pilgrims. In Iraqi customs they are entitled to the prayer-rug exception on religious grounds. But they must also pay their expenses on these pilgrimages. A good prayer rug brings several hundred dollars," Kashi explained.

Down, down, down the road drops from Khanaqin. This is land heavily eroded from overgrazing and fast runoffs. Now and then there is a village, but even these are scarce. Any shade is inviting in summertime; and when we saw from a distance the poplar trees of Shahraban, the invitation could not be declined. We pulled into the shade and had a sweet melon we had brought from Iran. We crossed and recrossed the first railroad we had seen since Meshed, the line that runs from Baghdad to Khanaqin. At Ba'Qubah we crossed a river, the Diyala, which joins the Tigris below Baghdad. Our crossing was on a one-way bridge used both by the railroad and by autos. The traffic was heavy and the line long. The station wagon coughed and wheezed on this stretch. Once or twice it died; and I had to grind the starter a long time to get the motor going again. It seemed we were headed for serious trouble and the only question was whether we would reach Baghdad before then. Yet once we finished with the starts and stops at Ba'Qubah, and settled down at forty miles an hour on the black-top road that now went almost as straight as an arrow toward Baghdad, the engine purred perfectly. The hills were left behind at Shahraban. From there on we were in the vast delta of the Tigris. The road was flat and smooth; and the thermometer was headed toward 130° F.

In Baghdad we had been invited to stay with Waldemar J. Gallman, the American Ambassador to Iraq. The first sign of Baghdad was a lone smokestack across the bleak, simmering plain. Then came the brick kilns. Then came the mud huts of the slums. Then we passed over the great dikes erected to save Baghdad from flood. Kashi, being sentimental about Baghdad, gave us a tour of the city en route to the Embassy. Though it was hot and we were anxious to get to our destination, he took us first downtown—by the Quein Aliya bridge where we turned to follow the banks of the Tigris. Here there are restaurants one after another along the mudbanks. Later we were to see this riverbank at night with twinkling lights, white linen tablecloths, and gay diners. Then the waters of the Tigris had a romantic sparkle. Now the tables were bare and unset; the bare mudbanks were ugly; and the muddy water of the Tigris ran slovenly to the sea.

But down by the water's edge men were preparing fires for the cooking of the famous *muscouf* fish that probably is a carp but is called a salmon in Baghdad. We stopped and I visited with these men. Some in the water up to their knees had a string of live fish on ropes in the river. They grinned as they held them up for me to see. Some were cleaning the fish and preparing them for cooking. Others were unloading piles of brushlike wood that is gathered on the islands of the Tigris and used for cooking the fish. The fish are opened up flat and fastened to stakes driven into the ground. They are cooked against a hot open fire. When the meat is cooked from the front, the fish is placed on its back in the embers. It is then sprinkled with salt and pepper and covered with sliced tomatoes and onions. This is the way it is served—one fish to each person. Some patrons pick out their own fish and have it killed and dressed before their eyes. Others require a chef of their choice to prepare the dish. *Muscouf,* we were to discover, is Baghdad's special dish. And there is none nicer, provided the fish is served right from the fire.

We stopped only briefly by the Tigris and then went directly to the American Embassy, which is a replica of our White House. I had not been there since 1950 and wondered if Esau, the efficient Arab head servant, was still there. We no sooner swung around the circle in the forest-green garden than I saw him standing on the steps with a broad grin on his face.

Thanks to the Ambassador and Esau, our arrival was like a homecoming. Even the thick dust on the baggage did not seem to matter. Servants with cloths and brushes were busy cleaning us up, and the baggage was sent to an air-conditioned suite. We were almost unpacked when I returned from the rear of the car with news for Mercedes.

"The right rear tire is down again."

Mercedes grinned and, thinking of the place of comfort we had reached, replied:

"If you wait awhile, I will fix it in a jiffy."

It's wonderful what the thought of a bath and an air-conditioned room in 130° temperature can do to a woman.

CHAPTER 2

FLOODS, DRAINAGE, AND IRRIGATION

The Tigris is about 1100 miles long, and the Euphrates nearly 1700 miles long. Both rise in Turkey. The Euphrates runs across Syria. The Tigris has tributaries that rise in Iran. Thus the river basins of these two historic streams involve four nations. But the most important segment lies in Iraq, the portion known through history as Mesopotamia. The two rivers unite below Basra to form the little-known Shatt al 'Arab, which flows to the Persian Gulf. There is great economic use of the waters of the streams below their point of unison (and in the region of Basra); but the main engineering and social problems of the rivers focus farther north.

Mesopotamia was the seat of ancient civilizations. Many call it the very cradle of civilization. Cave dwellings dating back fifty thousand years have been found in northern Iraq. And remnants of advanced civilizations have been found that date back eight thousand years. These two were located up north, for at that time the sea probably covered central and southern Iraq. By about 2100 B.C. settlers from the north and east had arrived and laid the foundations of organized society in Mesopotamia proper. The ancient cities of Ur, Babylon, Ctesiphon, and Nineveh marked its splendor.

Under Hammurabi, who ruled from Babylon about 1900 B.C., the waters of the two rivers were utilized to irrigate vast areas through a network of canals. Many invaders came—Hittites, Assyrians, Greeks, Persians, and Arabs. Under each the irrigation systems apparently grew or went on without much hindrance. They must have flourished, for Mesopotamia in those centuries had a population of 25,000,000. Today Iraq has close to 6,000,000.

When the Mongols sacked Baghdad in A.D. 1258 there was a different story to tell. They destroyed barrages (dams) and canals and created havoc. Moreover, they apparently killed the leaders and the elite, including the engineers. It is easy enough for unskilled labor to dig and clean canals. But it takes engineering skills to keep an irrigation system working efficiently.

The two main problems concern silt and salt. The pressure of grazing on the land and the cutting of timber result in erosion. More topsoil is carried into the rivers. Runoffs of storms are more frequent and more devastating. Streams become saturated with silt; canals become clogged with it. There is evidence, which American and Iraqi engineers have discovered, indicating that silting had been occurring even before the Mongols; and that it had picked up speed and power as a disintegrating force afterward, because that invasion robbed Mesopotamia of its engineering leaders. Some silting was so great that it caused the abandonment of canals. Sometimes it made reconstruction necessary. The over-all result was a contraction of available canals and the increasing disuse of irrigable land.

Salt probably caused even more damage than silt. The water of the Tigris and Euphrates has 400 parts of salt to 1,000,000 parts. That is sweet water by any definition. (Our own Colorado has 800 parts to 1,000,000.) Evaporation always leaves some salt; over a period of centuries it leaves a lot of salt. That is to say, constant irrigation without drainage accumulates salt in the soil, even though the water is sweet. Moreover, constant irrigation raises the water table. After centuries, the subsurface water becomes salt-saturated. The salt seeps up with the water. Pretty soon it appears on or near the surface. After a while the land becomes non-usable for agriculture.

The ancient irrigation systems of Mesopotamia were masterpieces, according to modern engineers. Those that survived Genghis Khan failed due to improper maintenance. But even if

Genghis Khan had left the irrigation systems intact, they would have shriveled and become largely useless. For the ancient engineers did not comprehend the salt problem and made no provision for drainage. Thus those old canals, though models of gravity flow, had within themselves the seeds of their own destruction.

This was part of the lecture on irrigation and agriculture which I received the day after we reached Baghdad. Ambassador Gallman arranged for a plane to take him and his staff of agricultural experts on a flight over the reaches of the Tigris and Euphrates. He invited Mercedes, Mary, and me to join him. We took off near seven o'clock and returned after twelve o'clock. Ray J. Lyman, Gordon Loveless, Barbara Brown, wife of Ben Brown, Director of USOM, and Reed Ligget were the experts who made the trip; and they took turns educating me. We flew northwest along the Diyala River. In this area remnants of old canals built by the Persians over a thousand years ago can be seen. They were mammoth affairs—about 400 feet wide and 30 feet deep, built for navigation as well as for irrigation. We saw two small dams or barrages on the Diyala that had recently been built and a large one, Derbend-i-Khan, that was under construction. Now we turned north, skirting the rough terrain of the lower slopes of the Zagros Mountains. Here we were over country where the wild licorice plant grows—of which the United States imports 6000 tons a year from Iraq alone. At the Lesser Zab River, another tributary of the Tigris, we passed over Dokan Dam, under construction. In the Baghdad area we had flown over land growing dates, cotton, and vegetables. Orange groves flourish there in the shade of palm trees. Now we were over vineyards, apricot orchards, tobacco fields, and great stands of walnuts. New lands to be irrigated by Dokan have rich black soil that will grow beets, cotton, and wheat. In this region were new industries, including a spick-and-span cement plant and several resettlement projects. One resettlement project that had opened up new farms had brought 7500 people to the Lesser Zab River basin.

We turned southwest from Dokan, circled the fiery furnaces at Kirkuk, and could see in the distance along the Tigris other dams under construction. We crossed the Tigris at the huge Samarra Barrage and went on to the Euphrates to the Ramadi Barrage. In between these rivers are remnants of ancient canal systems now taken over by salt. We followed one canal to the Wadi Thar Thar Depression. The Thar Thar Depression or storage lake for floodwaters is about a hundred and fifty miles long. A central problem has been to check the excessive runoffs of the rivers and store the water for future irrigation. The Thar Thar Depression is the largest of these storage lakes, designed to divert 265,000 cubic feet per second. The experts figure that in its 1956 operation it prevented more flood damage than the whole system cost. There are other storage reservoirs in the river basins. They will not only supply flood-control protection and irrigation, but also hydroelectric power. Water storage is as important to these river basins as irrigation itself. On the average 50 per cent of the total annual flow of the two rivers takes place in March, April, and May. And peak high flows have exceeded the average high flow by 170 per cent.

From Ramadi on the Euphrates we went south to the Hindiya Barrage, which is serving a vast resettlement area that we later visited by car. It is noticeably green and composed of small holdings. It has had the curse of salt on it; but new drainage canals that operate night and day reclaim some useless land in three years.

The two rivers have served navigation, as well as irrigation, through the centuries. Today the Tigris is navigable by barge to Samarra, the Euphrates to Syria. The development program serves commerce as well as agriculture.

The Ottoman Turks, who ruled Iraq for four hundred years, ending with World War I, and the British, who gave modern Iraq her independence in 1921, made some of these river basin improvements. But the great majority were made by the Iraqi government under the supervision of its Development Board and Ministry of Development. On the discovery of oil in Iraq and its exploitation, the government made an important decision. Oil, it decided, was not income like milk from a cow but capital that was not replaceable. This liquid capital should be put into capital improvements. So a law was passed requiring 70 per cent of all oil revenues to be treated as capital. That policy has been strictly adhered to with the result that, of all the countries in the Middle East, Iraq is making the greatest strides in improving her physical plant.

The day after our aerial tour of the Tigris and Euphrates, we went south of Baghdad on an inspection trip of drainage canals with Ray E. Goss, the American expert who conceived and executed the idea. We visited the Saklawiyah Abu Ghuriab Drainage Project. Here was land so salty that men swept the salt into piles, sacked it, and sold it in Baghdad. The table salt one gets in a Baghdad hotel comes from this supply. We saw the network of drainage canals built by bulldozers for lowering the water table and carrying the runoffs from rains. These canals run as feeders to a main canal. They are dug very deep, with the result that they cannot carry the water by gravity to the river. So at certain locations there are electric pumps which take the water from the deep drainage canals to higher brick-lined canals that return the water to the lower reaches of the river. The water that drains this salt land is not palatable, having 15,000 parts of salt to 1,000,000 parts. Constant irrigation and drainage—as in rice fields—will soon reclaim salt-ridden land. For land less frequently used, longer time will be needed. But there's practically no land in Iraq that cannot be reclaimed from salt.

If the land is not to be lost to cultivation by salinity, irrigation and drainage must go hand in hand. The modern plat calls for drainage ditches on three sides of a farm and an irrigation ditch on the fourth side. These lands rid themselves of salt in a short while and guarantee that the salt cycle will never get started. The experts have found that drainage ancillary to irrigation increases productivity two or three times.

The waste salt lands under drainage will be cut up into farms within a few years and people will resettle there.

On another day we visited some of these farms on the Rashayid Branch of the Greater Mussayeb Project south of Baghdad. Said Abdul Hamid, the project manager, met us at his headquarters and drove with us to the Rashayid Branch where farmers have just moved onto the reclaimed land. We visited one farmer and his wife who had been there only six months. The man, whose name I forget, was dressed in loose white trousers and a white shirt that came nearly to his knees. His wife was unveiled but dressed wholly in black. Their home, which was a grass hut, was neat and clean inside, though quite barren. One milk cow and a donkey were in a corral. By the side of the grass hut was an old-fashioned plow made of a forked stick. A young daughter of this couple was having trouble with her eyes; and before Hamid left he gave orders for her treatment at the headquarters of the project.

Five years ago nothing but salt grass would grow here. Now the land has been divided into thirty-acre tracts with irrigation and drainage canals in full operation. The irrigation ditches are cleverly designed so that, with a full ditch running, each farmer on the ditch gets twenty cubic feet of water per second. Experts are on hand to advise the farmers. Diversified farming is encouraged—ten acres in cereals, and five each in vegetables, fruit, cotton, and pasture; and the people own their own land. Though the farmers had only mud and grass huts to live in—houses no better than the average of the Middle East—that condition is temporary. Good houses will soon go up. Thirty acres is an economical unit in this part of the world. All farm work is manual; there is no machinery. But once these thirty-acre farms start producing, the standard of living will rise rapidly.

We had lunch at the headquarters of the Rashayid Branch of the Greater Mussayeb Project. We sat in a newly constructed brick building and ate the sandwiches Esau had made for us. It was very hot outside, the temperature marching to 130° F. But the cross ventilation made the room comfortable. One window looked across a field of sunflowers, several acres in extent. Beyond the field was a mound or tell.

"That is Cuthah," Hamid told me.

It was the ruins of Cuthah, referred to in 2 Kings 17. It now is only a desolate mound set in a lush green garden of hay and vegetables.

At Latifiyah, also south of Baghdad, we saw a new-lands project. This was good land that had recently come under a modern irrigation system and been resettled. The farmers get this land by lot. The ones at Latifiyah had been there long enough to be fairly well settled. They had neat houses. A village center had been built by the government. Here was a fine public school where we were served tea by Elizabeth Williams, who was introducing a course in home economics, and her assistant, Karima Shamis. There was a first-aid clinic run by a pleasant Arab, Farid Y.

Fadhli. There was also a trades school in full operation. Men were learning carpentry and furniture making from Khalil Jabbar; and women were learning spinning and weaving on hand looms from a Japanese girl, Masako Takikawa.

The supervisor of this project was Hasan Thamir, a young man about thirty. In the midst of our tour he was interrupted by a delegation of farmers, each with a black and white *kafeyah* for a headdress. It appeared that an important sheikh had a farm upstream on the irrigation canal from Latifiyah. The previous night he had opened the gates so that he got most of the water. When the farmers went to their fields in the morning they found the fields beginning to parch. So they marched to the project office. Not all of the 437 farmers were assembled there. But there must have been 100; and one, named Madthloom, was the spokesman. From their tempers and speech they were ready to march on the sheikh and take revenge; and Hasan whispered to me that it might be a good idea if they did.

Soon many new villages will spring up all over Mesopotamia. Each will have a village center like Latifiyah's. Iraqis think they have enough manpower, with the 2 per cent annual increase in population, to take care of the indefinite future. Their laws are so severe that immigration is practically nil. Only a few artisans can come in each year. Whether the nation that once had 25,000,000 can do the job ahead with less than 6,000,000 remains to be seen. Many experts think not. But a reluctance to open doors that might result in thousands of refugees from Palestine is a major factor in keeping all doors closed at least for the present.

The old as well as the new contributes to Iraq's growth. I stopped at Iraq College of Agriculture one afternoon to visit with the Dean, J. C. Russel of Nebraska. This college, started in 1953, graduated fifty-one students in 1957. The instruction is geared to Iraqi needs; and all graduates are pledged to work for the Iraq government a year after graduation.

Dean Russel told me that he worked five years in Nebraska trying to develop a plow that would break the soil and yet not turn it under. Middle East soil has little humus. It needs humus; and the worst thing is to plow it so that the humus turns under. Dean Russel found that the old wooden plow used in the days of Christ does the trick. It has a long swordlike snout, capped with iron. It breaks the soil but does not turn it under. The weed seeds are saved for another season; and in time humus is developed.

I had often heard lectures, telling how backward these people were in farming. But it took Dean Russel to teach me that their plow was better suited to their needs than anything we in the West could design.

CHAPTER 3

CTESIPHON

Ctesiphon was an ancient city and an ancient palace of the Persians, located on the east banks of the Tigris. It was in fact their winter capital when they held sway over the Middle East. The ruins which survive today are from a structure built about the fourth century A.D. They are about forty minutes by car from Baghdad and for us were the most rewarding of all the ruins we saw.

It is surprising that this should be true. For there is nothing at Ctesiphon but pieces of old brick walls nearly ten feet thick and one high vaulted ceiling. This great façade is the attraction. The ceiling is 121½ feet above the floor and the span of the arched ceiling is 82 feet wide. The floor was once carpeted by a rug 90 feet by 80 feet. The arch is unsupported except by the bricks that compose it. It is the widest single-span vault of unreinforced brickwork in the world. Mary compared it to the grandeur that was Rome.

This great vaulted room was probably the banquet room of the palace, one side of which was open. In the Middle East, when one visits a tribe, he finds a central tent, rectangular in shape and open on one side, where the entertainment and feasting take place. On each side are tents where the household lives and where the cooking is done. I had been in many such tents on my earlier journeys; and as I stood at Ctesiphon, I imagined that this was the design of this immense vaulted dining hall.

Ctesiphon fell to the Arabs in A.D. 637. The Arab who took Ctesiphon was the military leader Sa'd-ibn-Abi-Waqqas, who moved east conquering Persia as another Arab army swept west conquering Egypt and North Africa. A Persian, Salman Pak, who had been converted to Islam, showed the Arabs where to ford the Tigris. They put their mares and stallions into the stream simultaneously so that the horses would be more likely to stay together and swim the Tigris without casualties. Thus the Arabs captured Ctesiphon and plundered its riches. Gibbon's *The History of the Decline and Fall of the Roman Empire* tells us that the loot was worth many fortunes. Then the Arabs moved the capital to Baghdad and let Ctesiphon go to ruins.

Ctesiphon has character all its own. We saw it in lightness and in darkness. In the evening great flocks of pigeons whirled around the arch looking for nesting. Whenever we went there—night or day—a blind beggar appeared. He walked with a cane and with the help of a young boy. He sat on a rock and strummed melancholy tunes on a guitarlike instrument. He kept on strumming even after a tip of a thousand fils (twenty-eight cents); and his music followed us all the way to the car.

As we drove off, Kashi said that the old man paid us a compliment.

In talking to Kashi about us, the blind man said, *"Kareem, kareem." Kareem* means generous; and it is one of the highest compliments an Arab knows.

One sees the great arch of Ctesiphon for some miles before he reaches it, rising in great splendor above a rather depressing scene. There is a squalid village nearby named Salman Pak. Some say it was named for the Persian who showed the Arabs the crossing of the Tigris. Others say that Salman Pak is the name of the man who washed and prepared for burial the body of Ali, Mohammed's son-in-law. Still others say that the Salman Pak for whom the village is named was Mohammed's barber; and some Iraqi schools teach this version. The barbers of Iraq have adopted him as their patron saint, just as throughout history local butchers and artisans have adopted famous Arabs as their patron saints. Every spring the barbers of Baghdad go to visit

Salman Pak's tomb. This pilgrimage has developed into a picnic in which all the townsfolk join.

One evening we stopped briefly at Salman Pak on our return from Ctesiphon. I walked the street with Kashi and stopped to talk with a middle-aged Iraqi. I asked him about the Salman Pak who was Mohammed's barber. He scratched his head and appeared to be in meditation. Then he removed his white *kafe-yah,* exposing a head that was wholly bald. This amiable Arab was a comedian. He made a wry face and said: "What can a bald man owe to the barber's mother?"

CHAPTER 4

BABYLON

We know about Babylon from the Book of Daniel where it was related how Nebuchadnezzar captured Jerusalem and carried the Jews to Babylon in captivity. This city, located on the Euphrates, was known in the beginning as Babel. Its origins are lost in history. Under Hammurabi it became the capital of a vast empire; and over the centuries it changed hands many times. Also before Nebuchadnezzar it had been completely destroyed by the Assyrian, Sennacherib. Nebuchadnezzar, who came into power in 604 B.C., made Babylon famous for its "hanging gardens." These gardens were a consequence of Babylon's design. The city sat on a vast plain that runs practically flat to the horizon. It had no natural defense except the lazy Euphrates River, which ran through the middle of the city. The city was defended by walls, one within others; and some of them were so broad that Nebuchadnezzar had gardens laid out on top of them. Hence the "hanging gardens" that were among the seven wonders of the ancient world.

Cyrus conquered Babylon in 538 B.C. When he marched his armies around the city, it appeared to be unconquerable. He announced a siege; but, according to Xenophon, the Babylonians smiled, for they had a twenty-year supply of corn within the city and they would never want for water as the Euphrates ran through the town. Cyrus appeared to make preparations for a siege. He dug trenches and with the dirt erected towers. But unknown to the Babylonians the trenches were designed to divert the great river into a depression and make the river bed the conqueror's path into the city. In the darkness of one night Cyrus diverted the Euphrates. This was a night of great revelry in Babylon. Belshazzar, son of Nebuchadnezzar, was now King. This was the night when, according to the Book of Daniel, Chapter 5, Belshazzar saw the handwriting on the wall. One word, translated by Daniel, was *"Peres,"* which meant "Thy kingdom is divided, and given to the Medes and Persians" (Daniel 5:28). That night Belshazzar was slain and the Persians took Babylon. The Persian army walked up the river bed in water no more than knee deep and caught the garrison unawares.

The rule of Nebuchadnezzar had been so benign that, when Cyrus gave the Jews the right to return to Palestine, few availed themselves of the opportunity.

Alexander the Great, who took over an empire from the Persians, planned to make Babylon his winter capital. There he went to prepare a campaign against Arabia; and in Babylon he died of malaria, after which his successors moved the capital to Seleucia on the Tigris. In those days Babylon apparently was an attractive metropolis.

Herodotus wrote that Babylon "in magnificence . . . surpassed every city of which we have any knowledge."

Babylon in its heyday had broad streets terminating at great bronze gates. One known as Procession Street was comparable to our Constitution Avenue and the Champs Elysées of Paris with Ishtar Gate serving as an Arc de Triomphe. In the center of the town was the main temple, topped by a ziggurat or stage-tower. This was a tower made of brick with a path or trail winding around the tower all the way to the top. The ziggurat still survives in Iraq. The day when we flew over Mesopotamia we came low over Samarra and saw a ziggurat with a winding path around it broad enough for a jeep. This ziggurat at Samarra is the best preserved of any. It was a Babylonian temple tower. Then it became a Zoroastrian fire temple. Afterward it became the minaret of a mosque built at its feet. The temple and mosque disappeared; but the ziggurat remains as one of the great relics of the Middle East. We had also seen ziggurats on the plains south of Baghdad.

They are made of brick and mortised with cement and reed matting. Some of them are thought to be four thousand years old and still in fair condition. Their origin is not certain. It is thought they were first erected to worship the Moon God. Herodotus described the path around the ziggurat at Babylon: "The ascent is by a path which is formed on the outside of the towers; midway in the ascent is a resting place, furnished with easy chairs, in which those who ascend repose themselves."

According to Herodotus, there was great traffic on the Euphrates. The boats were made of willow frames covered with skins; and they were round as a shield. The produce was floated down great distances from the north and a burro went as cargo. When the load reached Babylon, the cargo and the frame of the boat were sold and the skins loaded on the burro for the return trip north.

Young marriageable women were auctioned off once a year for marriage. The ugliest were sold with a dowry made up of a part of the purchase price of the prettiest ones.

There were no physicians in Babylon. The sick were brought into public places, where any passer-by could give him advice. "To pass a sick person in silence without inquiring his complaint, is deemed a breach of duty," wrote Herodotus.

Today there is nothing in Babylon except desolation.

Babylon is fifty-four miles south of Baghdad on a good paved road. We visited it one day about noon after we had spent the morning at some of the new resettlement projects which I have already mentioned. We would have been wiser to go to Babylon in the cool of the morning; but we could not fit it into our crowded schedule, except on this visit to the resettlement project. So the sun was reaching its peak of intensity when we turned off the main highway a quarter mile to what remains of the great city. A small two-story brick museum and a small house, home of the caretaker, sit under the shade of tamarisk trees. An Arab guide—a young man in his twenties, dressed in a white *kafeyah,* red gown, and sandals—came flying to greet us. He spoke halting English and was filled with a passionate interest in these ruins. The guidebook had said:

"It is the Babylon, which rose during these final years of prosperity, the city of Nebuchadnezzar and capital of the New Empire, of which one must form a mental impression before visiting the ruins, and it can at once be said that a good deal of imagination is necessary in order to see in them as they have survived, more than a sad expanse of brickwork and rubble."

I must admit that my imagination was not equal to the task. Once we reached the top of the rubble heap behind the museum all sense of anticipation disappeared. I saw pieces of small straight streets; remnants of walls and here and there a cornice. The guide pointed excitedly to the Lion of Babylon, a stone statue of a huge animal standing over a man on his back. A high corner of some ancient building housed a nest for cranes—birds which had migrated north for the summer. Most interesting of all, according to the guide, was a large walled-in space perhaps 40 feet by 20 feet which he called the lions' den. The rubble was piled so high we were looking down twenty feet or more into this den. The walls were brick adorned with fine enameled reliefs of griffins and bulls. The enamel was badly weathered; but the figures in relief still stand out. The young Arab had raised his voice and was fairly shouting:

"The lions' den," he said.

"What lions' den?" I asked.

"Why, Daniel's, of course," he answered, surprised that anyone should be so ignorant.

On second thought it looked like an ideal den for lions. The victim could not possibly escape. A lion would have him completely at his mercy. The miracle of Daniel grew and grew as I looked down into this hot pit.

Mercedes, Mary, and I spent an hour walking the hot bricks of Babylon, dropping down into its torrid pits and climbing again to a height of debris. All the while the young Arab kept talking. He pointed out every point of eminence of the ancient city—the main avenues, the palaces, the quay, the temple, the bazaar, the series of walls, the place where Cyrus breached them. I looked and looked but my imagination was not equal to the task. All I could see was rubble—not rubble with pattern and design but rubble in disarray and desolation.

As I stood in the heat viewing the vast expanse of rubble that once was Babylon, I kept thinking of the words of Isaiah:

"For I will rise up against them, saith the Lord of hosts, and cut off from Babylon the name, and remnant, and son, and nephew, saith the Lord.

"I will also make it a possession for the bittern, and pools of water: and I will sweep it with the besom of destruction, saith the Lord of hosts" (Isaiah 14:22, 23).

Finally I felt faint. My feet seemed to burn. The heat of the bricks was so great they made a furnace of my shoes. I had to keep walking to be comfortable. When I stood still, it seemed my shoes would ignite. I ended in a half trot in the intense heat of Babylon. I thought I would collapse before I reached the shade of the tamarisks. A thermometer on the wall of the museum showed 135°F. It must have been 110°F. in the shade. The interior of the car, which had been parked in the sun, was a furnace. The plastic steering wheel was so hot we could not touch it. Mercedes took ice cubes from the Bahai chest and, wrapping a cloth around them, wiped the steering wheel until it cooled.

All the way back to Baghdad, I regretted the expenditure of effort on Babylon. Like Balkh in northern Afghanistan, Babylon has practically nothing left from which one's imagination can reconstruct a pulsing city. I mentioned this disappointment to Dr. Naji al-Asil, the Director of Antiquities of Iraq, at luncheon the next day.

"That's true," he said. "The place to see Babylon is not here."

"Where is it?" I asked.

"Berlin," he answered.

"Berlin?" I asked in a perplexed tone.

"Yes. You see, when Iraq was a province of the Ottoman Turks, the Germans got permission to excavate Babylon. That was at the beginning of this century. The Germans as usual did a thorough job. Now Babylon is in Berlin."

CHAPTER 5

BAGHDAD

One day in Kashi's rug shop, I asked about the population of Baghdad. Kashi's father—slight, short, and soft-spoken—replied:

"During the war years we had sugar rationing. Judged by the applications made for sugar, Baghdad had about 2,000,000 people. During the war years we also had a draft for the army. Judged by the householders responding to the draft, Baghdad had less than 100,000 people."

Baghdad was built in four years, beginning in A.D. 762. Its builder was Abu-Ja'far, who took the title al-Mansur, which means "Rendered victorious by God." He was an unscrupulous man who had much blood on his hands. But he built a handsome city whose name means "Given by God." He chose it first as a military site and second as a port reaching Asian as well as inland commerce. The nearby ruins of Ctesiphon served as a source of building material for the new city. This city was circular in form and heavily fortified. It lay on the west bank of the Tigris. Before long it was to spread to both sides of the river, where it lies sprawled today. This city—the scene of *The Arabian Nights*—grew to be a great emporium of trade and the political center of the Moslem world. The Arabian Empire was divided into over twenty provinces, all ruled from Baghdad. This political rule extended to Spain and Sicily on the west, to the Indus on the east, and to Bukhara, Samarkand, and Ferganah (all now in Russia) on the north. Of the many Caliphs who ruled from Baghdad before its fall, one was Harun al-Rashid, known to the West as the Caliph in *The Arabian Nights.*

It takes works such as Hitti, *History of the Arabs,* to give the story of the full flowering of civilization at Baghdad under the Arabs. Here was the earliest school of pharmacy. Physicians were subjected to medical examinations so as to weed out the quacks. Traveling medical clinics were organized to service outlying areas. Astronomy and mathematics flourished. The Arabic numerals, borrowed from the Hindus, were introduced in Arabia and spread to the West.

The worst, but not the last, disaster that struck Baghdad came in A.D. 1258 when the Mongol Hulagu captured it and massacred 800,000 civilians. The Caliph and his entire family were executed, leaving the Arab world without a person who was a symbol of the unity of church and state. But Hulagu, who had a Christian wife, did not molest the patriarch of the Nestorian church.

We were discussing those matters one night in Baghdad, Kassim As-Sa'adi and I. Kassim is a radio and TV commentator who works at the Baghdad station. Our discussion took place on a live TV show. It was the Baghdad version of *Meet the Press.* The studio had not yet been air-conditioned. A few small fans hummed in a corner. But they made no impression on the heat from the bright lights bearing down on us. He had a much more difficult job than I. For he had to put all of his questions first in Arabic, then into English, and my answers into Arabic. The program was unrehearsed; and I led the discussion for a half hour into the ancient glories of Ctesiphon, Babylon, and Baghdad, and then to the great contributions which the Arabs had made to civilization. We discussed particularly the contribution of Avicenna, whose tomb we had visited in Hamadan; and the great role in public health which the clinics, traveling out of Baghdad, had played in the eleventh century.

It was near the end of the program when I suggested to Kassim that but for the Arabs we might never have been able to work out the mathematical formula for the atomic bomb.

"Why do you say that?" he asked.

"Think how the use of the Roman numerals would have slowed up mathematical advances," I said.

In the eleventh century mathematicians who did not use the Roman numerals sometimes followed the Semitic practice of using letters of the alphabet and, worse still, of writing out all numerals into words.

We closed the TV program with a unanimous decision in favor of the decimal system.

Baghdad has been described by some travelers as a miserable place of filth, beggars, and prostitution.

Like any big city, it is partly that. When I first saw it a decade ago, I thought it was one of the sinkholes of creation. But my opinion radically changed with renewed visits.

Though the heat of Baghdad is severe, the nights are comfortable. On the hottest of days, when the temperature tops 130°F., one can sit in comfort in a garden at night; and before midnight a lady may need a scarf or shawl.

One night Esau cooked *muscouf* in one corner of Ambassador Gallman's garden while we visited with some Americans in the Foreign Service. One of them was a young doctor, George Mishtowt, who practiced medicine for a while in Washington, D.C., and then decided to turn his talents to the public service. Stationed in Baghdad, he ministers to the needs of the American community and carries on research in the problems of public health in the Middle East. What he told me changed the course of my thinking about Mesopotamia. The chief diseases there are tuberculosis, trachoma, and bilharziasis. The latter comes from a worm that affects those who work in rice and other crops flooded with river water. Its intermediate host is a water snail. The parasites that leave the snail burrow through man's skin. Once they reach the blood stream, they are distributed throughout the body. They cause blood in the urine. Eventually the pelvic organs become severely affected and the bladder fills with stones. Bilharziasis is a scourge in Iraq as it is in Egypt. But amoebic dysentery, which I feared the most in all my travels, is no more common in the Baghdad area than it is in the United States. The reason is the low humidity and the high temperatures. The 135°F. we experienced at Babylon helps desroy the amoebic cyst. That cyst, which flourishes in Karachi and Delhi, has a much lower incidence in Mesopotamia.

Moreover, Baghdad today has a fine water system. The supply is pure. One can drink water safely out of any tap in the city. That cannot be said of many cities in the Middle East.

One evening we stopped at some of the hovels on the outskirts of Baghdad, made of mud and occupied by bedraggled people. The children were bringing in camel dung, paper, twigs, and any flammable material. With these, at evening, open fires were started outside where the cooking is done. In the flickering fires of dusk even miserable hovels take on an aura of beauty.

There are vile-looking tenements in the city. Some lead off Rashid Street, the main business thoroughfare. On one of these the prostitutes live; and on what I judged to be a chance turn by a chauffeur, I went through the district in late afternoon. I had not gone far when a young Arab boy came up alongside the car and followed it for a block or more, shouting, "Pretty girls. Pretty girls." There they were in all their glory, sitting on a first-floor porch. One was Sudanese with a broad grin and gold earrings the size of silver dollars, her red dress low on the bosom and pulled up well above her knees. A fat Arab woman about thirty, her lips highly rouged and her face thick with powder, sat poutingly by the side of the Sudanese. A young olive-skinned girl perhaps eighteen years old waved as she wrapped a cotton print kimono around her and crossed and recrossed her legs. One older brunette sitting at the young one's feet showed her legs and white teeth as she grinned. Then they were gone; yet I could still hear the young boy shouting, "Pretty girls. Pretty girls."

Here came porters with great loads on their backs. They carry goods from railroad or bus depots or from caravanseries. Or they'll take a purchase from the bazaar to one's home. These porters of Baghdad, I learned, are mostly Kurds from up north, noted for their stamina and muscular power. The Kurds are numerous in Iraq, making up about one sixth of the population. These porters were bent low, balancing their loads with a head strap that crossed the forehead. Some were barefoot; others had "sorry old shoes" like the footwear of the porter in *The Arabian Nights*. One had an upright piano; another a cotton bale; one several hundredweight of rice; another a box big enough to hold a good-sized electric refrigerator. They flowed through the crowds like a boat through water—people, donkeys, burros, and even cars making way for them. "*Ballek, ballek* [Look out, look out]," they shouted as they walked a beeline down the crowded street. And an occasional nudge of a sharp corner of their baggage punctuated their cries.

There are shops in Baghdad as Western as those in Yakima, and filled with as wide a variety of goods. Iraq has plenty of dollar exchange. Most of the merchandise one needs can be found there—whether it is a set of golf clubs, a tennis racquet, an outboard motor, or a filter for a camera lens. Baghdad also has the covered bazaars or *suks*.

The bazaars of Baghdad, like those of Isfahan and the other Eastern cities, have high vaulted roofs and many avenues. The avenue of coppersmiths is filled with a din; the rug avenue and the avenue where cloth is on display are as quiet as church. The avenue we enjoyed the most was the one near the river and outside the covered *suks*. It is River Street, where the silversmiths are gathered.

These are the Mandeans. They have long been in the lower plains of Babylonia, living close to the river. They are included among the People of the Book—that is to say, religious minorities tolerated by the Moslems. They are ruled by a Bishop.

It takes a book like Drower, *The Mandeans of Iraq and Iran,* to give a full-blown account of their religion. To the Mandeans, the symbol of the Great Life is the flowing water, a concept in tune with the role of the Tigris and Euphrates in the alluvial plain of Mesopotamia. Light is a second important symbol to them as it was to the Zoroastrians—the symbol of cleanliness, health of body and mind, purity of conscience, obedience to moral law. The third fundamental in their religion is immortality of the soul.

John the Baptist is not their prophet but a great teacher of their faith. Jesus, on the other hand, was to them a heretic who flouted the rules of purification.

They consider celibacy a sin and procreation a religious duty. The pollution of moving water with urine or feces is banned. They eat all things grown from seed (which excludes mushrooms). Fish may be eaten except those without scales. Eggs, chicken, and mutton are lawful foods. Pork, rabbit, and beef are forbidden, as are all birds of prey and fish-eating birds.

The Mandeans advertise themselves as Baptists. They have a ritual of constantly recurring baptisms. Though they claim John the Baptist, they also claim St. John.

When they pray they face the north star. They go in for astrology and horoscopes. They not only submit to immersions every Sunday as routine; they also bathe when they have contacts that are not pure, e.g., butter that has not been prepared by a Mandean. They number not more than 10,000 and they are mostly in the valley of the Tigris and Euphrates. They are either boatbuilders or silversmiths. The ones we met were silversmiths.

River Street is lined with them, each with a shop about a dozen feet wide and maybe twice as deep. They melt the silver, pour it in molds, polish it, and engrave it, all before one's eyes. They sit on the floor doing this delicate work. They are good-looking people. The compliment "as handsome as a Mandean" is often heard in Baghdad. Their dress in summer is the white, loose pantaloon with the white cotton shirt that hangs below the knees. Each one is barefoot; and most are bearded. The first one we came to handed us a card reading "Daiel John Baptist." He claimed to be a direct descendant of John the Baptist. Mercedes bought a few items—ash trays, a small sugar and cream set, and thimbles delicately engraved. Some of these silversmiths up and down the street were short and fat, some tall and rangy, some thin and aesthetic-looking. The faces of a few closely resembled the face of Jesus which we are accustomed to see in classical paintings.

As we went along River Street, I noticed that each merchant had the name John Baptist. When we returned to the shop that Daiel John Baptist owned, I commented on that fact. He drew me close and whispered:

"They all claim John Baptist. But I am the direct descendant."

One afternoon Mercedes and I visited the Iraq Museum whose curator, Dr. Naji al-Asil, is an outstanding public servant. Baghdad is waiting for its new museum designed by Frank Lloyd Wright. Its present one is very crowded. But the collection is rich. We spent some hours looking at the works of art gathered from the length and breadth of Iraq and displaying its ancient splendor. The Greek, Persian, Arab, Mongol, Assyrian, and Turkish influences are all there. The glories of empires were on display—empires that had reached a zenith and then decayed either from internal decay or outside assault or both.

Mary picked out as her favorites some gold ornaments from a tomb at Ur, a harp with a golden bull's head, a white marble head from Warka, 3000 B.C., an ivory carving from Nimrod, 710 B.C.

In one room pottery pieces, fresh in from a drainage-canal digging near Babylon, were being fitted together and glued. These modern bulldozers that are used to dig ditches often come up with great finds; and when it is known that they are on archaeological sites, they proceed with caution while the experts supervise. One recent digging had produced a tomb containing a mummy with many jewels. This day in Baghdad experts were tenderly handling the pieces, trying to make a perfect restoration.

I was seeing with my own eyes the dust to which great empires had been reduced. Each seemed to travel a cycle of greatness and then collapse. The story was partly the rise of the tough and the strong and the decline of those who had become soft. I remembered the sentence, "History is the sound of heavy boots coming up the stairs and the rustle of satin slippers coming down." The "sound of heavy boots" in the Middle East had once been the Arabs and every other national or racial group that had overrun it. Now the "sound of heavy boots" was Russian.

There are those who think that these cycles are inevitable, that every nation must meet its destiny in aggression and conquest, that we are living in a cycle in which it is Russia's turn, so to speak. We talked of these matters at the museum, and I expressed my doubts. The empires that fell had within themselves the seeds of their own destruction. The primary causes of collapse come from within. Once there is an inner strength, people can withstand the external assault even beyond any predicted breaking point, as England illustrated during World War II.

The Arab Empire was built by force out of many races, none of which ever gave up struggling and striving for its own independence. Persians were subdued; but they never became part of an Arab commonwealth. There never was a plan which would make it possible for them to become such. Any preferments they obtained were the result of favors, not of right. What the Persians felt, the Turks felt. And there was the same cleavage between Arabs from the south and Arabs from the north.

A related reason was a central administration with no opportunity for local autonomy. Provincial interests were subordinated to the capricious desire of Baghdad. The people were governed but they had no opportunity to participate in government. The result was an exploitive central government interested in profits for itself, not service for the communities it governed. Discriminatory taxes were laid on the people. The rich got richer and the poor got poorer. Landlords made heavy exactions from their serfs. The poor felt the ravages of disease and suffered the ravages of the floods. Government seldom gave the helping hand. It was, indeed, the oppressor. The appearance of an invader on the horizon might even lift the hearts of the people as promising some relief.

An equally important reason, I think, for the internal decay of the Arab Empire was the union of church and state, with the consequent relegation of minorities to inferior positions. There was one state religion and it was Islam. Other religious groups were allowed to live. But they suffered rank discrimination and were denied what we would call the equal protection of the law.

The religious minorities in the Arab world were the People of the Book, who by the Koran were entitled to protection, but barred from service in the army, and subject to discriminatory tax action. The Caliph Uwar in A.D. 635 went further and adopted the policy that in the Arabian Peninsula only the Moslem religion was to be tolerated. He expelled the Jews and Christians from the territory; and in the other parts of the empire he placed discriminatory taxes on them. By A.D. 717 Christians and Jews had to wear distinctive dress; and they were disqualified from holding public office. In A.D. 807 many of their churches were destroyed. In A.D. 850 it was decreed they should affix images of the devil to their houses, wear yellow outer garments, ride only mules on wooden saddles especially marked, and level their graves even with the ground. Moreover, Moslem courts ruled that the testimony of a Christian or Jew could not be accepted against a Moslem.

These practices sowed seeds of discord in the Arab Empire. They produced divisive influences, tending to pull the nation apart in times of trouble. When the great stress and strain came there was not the mucilage to hold the country together. The people did not share enough together in peace to be willing to share together the ravages of war. Wherever possible they went over to the conqueror without a struggle.

Mercedes and I talked of these things at the Iraq Museum and on our way back to the American Embassy. That night at a garden party at the home of the Minister of Education, Abdul H. Kadhim, I brought some of my Arab friends around to the same subject. We discussed it over delicious *muscouf* fish which Mrs. Kadhim had prepared especially for us.

Iraq has done much to ferret out corruption in government. Corruption is the cancer in some Asian governments, as it is in some of our own municipalities. The wealth which Iraq has from oil tempts some public servants. The Iraqis adopted a unique way of dealing with it. A law was passed setting up an administrative board, known as the Purge Committee, to investigate cases of alleged corruption of public officials and with power to remove any official found guilty. An administrative edict against an official barred him from office for three years. The law had a short duration, expiring of its own terms in June, 1957. During its life, seventy-five public officials were "purged" and removed from office for corruption.

The Purge Committee was dissolved on June 10, 1957. It had been appointed by the Cabinet, serving under a temporary law, giving the committee power only to remove officials for dishonesty, etc. A new law, which established a Civil Service Council, to be appointed by the Cabinet, became effective November 2, 1957. There are five members of the council and each is appointed for five years. The council has full control over the appointment of all men in the public service below Cabinet rank, the determination of their fitness for the office, the scrutiny of their conduct during office, and the power to remove anyone except Cabinet officers. This is a permanent law.

In these and other respects, Iraq, prior to the military *coup d'état* in July 1958, was making great progress in building a civilized society. But she has not yet faced squarely the issue of freedom of speech and of the press. Article 12 of the Constitution provides: "Freedom of expression of opinion, liberty of publication, of meeting together, and of forming and joining associations is guaranteed to all Iraqis within such limits as may be prescribed by law." But the law prescribes exceedingly narrow limits. One who visits the newsstands in Baghdad gets the impression of great activity by the press. Baghdad has eight daily newspapers. They are, however, all on one side of public issues—the government side.

At the garden party at the home of the Minister of Education, already mentioned, I met some members of the Bar who were discussing this problem.

"Would an anti-government paper be tolerated?" I asked.

"No," said one lawyer.

"Why?" I asked.

The answer was one in which all the lawyers seemed to agree.

"We are young as a nation. It takes time to develop the tradition of criticism. If you write an editorial today criticizing a minister, he takes it personally. Our officials cannot stand public censure. Some call it the necessity to save face. But it's really immaturity in self-government."

We went on to discuss political parties.

"They were all abolished in 1954," this lawyer said.

"Why?" I asked.

"Well, there was a party called the National Democratic Party that was opposed to those in power. The head of that party criticized the government. He was tried by court-martial and sentenced to three years in prison. The officials of our government can't stand criticism."

I moved around the garden, talking to various people. I ended with the wife of a former minister. She asked me if I knew whom I had been talking with. I replied that he was a prominent member of the Bar.

"Yes," she replied. "But he's also one of our most dangerous people."

"Is he a Communist?"

"Not exactly. But he's about as dangerous."

"Why do you say that?"

"Because he's always stirring up trouble."

"What kind of trouble?"

"Oh, all this nonsense about freedom of the press. He'd really stir things up in Iraq if he had his way; and the Communists would take over."

Every newspaper in Iraq must have a license from the government to operate. The Minister of Justice is given broad powers to prosecute editors. The Minister of the Interior has broad powers to suspend the license, for a day, for a month, or for an indefinite period. His action is reviewable by the Council of State, a body made up of Cabinet officers. There is no court review. No independent agency sits in judgment on the suspension order. Political considerations alone control.

Shortly after our visit two papers were suspended. *Al Yagdha* was suspended for one year because it came out against the government's policy on Suez. *Al Bilad* was suspended for three months for several reasons: first, because it criticized certain projects of the government—the management of a T.B. hospital and the construction of a dam; second, because it gave more space to an article on Nasser than it did to an article on the birthday of the Crown Prince; third, because "you failed to praise the government."

The government uses financial pressures on the press as well as the threat of suspension. The Iraqi government has much advertising to dispense, such as the specifications of bids on public projects. I talked with newspaper editors who had been critical of the government and who had lost all government advertisements as a result.

"In the old days," one said to me, "we used to go to prison. But our officials have learned that a prison term only makes heroes and future opponents out of us. Now they try to reach us first through our stomachs. If they can dry up our revenues, they expect us to be humble."

The jail sentence is used. Kemal Chaderchi, leader of the opposition party which was banned by the government in 1954, was later sentenced to prison. Chaderchi's offense was that he petitioned the King for a return of the party system of government. He was tried for "attacking the government"; and the body that tried him was a military commission. As one editor put it to me, the central government declared martial law to protect it "against the wrath of the people" on the Suez issue.

When martial law is proclaimed in Iraq, the military take over and all criminal laws are suspended. Chaderchi was convicted by the military and sentenced to three years. And from his prison cell in Baghdad, he's becoming a symbol of the struggle of the editors for freedom. As one editor said to me, "It would be a pleasure—a real pleasure, I assure you—to go to jail for the great cause of freedom of the press in Iraq."

When martial law is declared in Iraq, the military not only take over the courts; they move into every newspaper plant as well, and censor all items. One editor told me what happened in his office during the martial-law regime at the time of the Suez crisis.

His paper has a section devoted to jokes, some of which are sent in by the readers. One person sent in a joke about leukemia, which in Arabic means "poverty of the blood." The joke went like this:

Doctor: "You have leukemia."

Patient: "Now my poverty has reached even to my blood."

The army censor came to my friend, the editor, and said, "You cannot publish this joke."

"Why not?" my friend asked.

"Because talk of poverty leads to Communism," the officer retorted.

The Communist influence in Iraq was practically nil. The abolition of political parties, prosecution of those who opposed the government, surveillance of the press, ruthless suppression of trade unionism—these were the conditions that made Iraq ripe for the *coup d'état* of July 1958.

These dissident elements, joining forces with the army, gave the July 1958 uprising a broad popular base. The slogans were Arab nationalism and independence from Western influence. But the seeds of discord over grievances against the government had been sown again and again.

CHAPTER 6

THE BURNING FIERY FURNACE

We said goodbye to Ambassador Gallman and to Esau one August morning at four-thirty o'clock. We were headed north to Mosul and we wanted the cool of the morning for the crossing of the cruel sands above Baghdad.

There is a railroad from Baghdad to Mosul via Kirkuk, a line that goes on to Istanbul in Turkey. Many people put their cars aboard the train and take them off at Kirkuk or Mosul, thus avoiding the hot, dreary wasteland that the road traverses. But we chose the road; and we packed the car with a view to our comfort on the crossing of these badlands.

The Bahai ice chest was filled with fresh ice, Pepsi-Cola, and soda water. We also had a huge gallon thermos that Mercedes had found in Meshed. In Iran we had not used it much. In Iraq it was as indispensable as the ice chest. Now it was filled with fresh water and ice cubes. Since the tap water in Baghdad is pure, we were sure of both the water and the ice. Esau also had some melons for us, and some sweet Baghdad peaches that turned quickly into sweet liquid at the touch of the lips.

The car was in excellent condition. At the garage it was discovered we had broken six leaves in the rear springs. These were replaced. The rack on top had become loose as a result of the tight cinches we had thrown over the baggage. The roof had indeed bulged downward from the great weight on top. These were fixed. The generator had caused trouble. I suggested we buy a new one; but the chauffeur at the American Embassy knew a place where generators were rewound. So we took it there, and it seemed to be in fine working order when we left. Brake adjustments, motor tune-up, and the replenishment of our supply of baling wire completed the car job.

The city was still asleep when we left. Lampposts cast lonely shadows on empty streets. We met only two vehicles as we turned east and put the sleepy city behind us—an auto with sputtering yellow headlights and a creaking bullock cart pulled by an ancient horse. It took us a half hour or more, traveling east, to find the road north to Kirkuk and Mosul. It too was vacant and by daybreak we could see the desolate plain we traveled. Part of it may be reclaimed and turned into a garden. But today it looks like sandy wasteland. Nothing grows there but camel's-thorn and it has difficulty catching hold. There are miles and miles of desert that run flat to the horizon. Most of it was a dull lifeless gray. After some miles the ground had a reddish tinge and soon we came to outcroppings of rocks and dark ledges. Now the land was more broken. Gullies washed it. Escarpments appeared as low hills. We gained perhaps five hundred feet in elevation and came to the small village of Tuz Khurmatli.

The sun was now up and the shops that line the highway on both sides for a block were open. A garageman had petrol in four-liter cans; and we bought some. A small fruit and confectionery shop across the street had a supply of soft drinks and we decided to protect our own supply and buy some; but they were not cold. So the proprietor obliged by sending his twelve-year-old son running down the street to a competitor to buy us bottles that were icy to the touch. This kindly shopkeeper had fresh grapes. Where they came from, I do not know. Grapes would not grow in the searing desert surrounding the village. Yet in spite of the distance they must have come, they were firm and sweet.

The sun was now showing its authority and the thermometer was mounting to 120°F. The road to Kirkuk beyond Tuz Khurmatli was as uninviting as that out of Baghdad. There was not a touch of green along the roadside. Usually, as one travels the byways of the Middle East, he sees lone trees standing on a hillside or in a distant ravine. The natives call these *jin* trees, no matter their genus or species. They are *jin* trees because, as I have said, some spirit is thought to guard them. How else could a tree survive in the fierce environment where rainfall is scarce, where every tree or shrub struggles to get a foothold, and where goats give each sapling the kiss of death by eating its bark? The view of the distant mountains to the northwest was the only relief from the monotony of this desolate rolling country. These were the Zagros bordering Iran and Iraq, which we crossed going to Baghdad, and which we were to recross in another week. There were no snow-capped peaks in the distance; but the mountains were purple in the thickening heat haze and inviting to those who traveled the hot plains.

The first sign of Kirkuk, which we saw about eleven o'clock, was the flaming jets of natural gas escaping from the oil fields. Behind them were oil rigs and still farther in the background were the outlines of many oil refineries and storage tanks. Kirkuk is the center of a vast petroleum industry operated by the Iraq Petroleum Company, known locally as IPC. It is from Kirkuk that the pipeline runs to the Mediterranean—the pipeline cut by the Syrians when the Suez Canal crisis set the Middle East afire. It is the revenue from IPC that finances the great capital developments in Iraq—particularly the irrigation, drainage, and flood-control projects that we saw the length and breadth of Mesopotamia.

We stopped to see Mr. and Mrs. Lee Dinsmore at the American Consulate in Kirkuk. Mr. Dinsmore put a guard by our car so that we could leave the windows open. It was a fierce sun overhead; but it was cool in the Dinsmore home, where we had lunch and a nap.

Mr. and Mrs. G. F. Stutz of USIS were there; and after lunch we went to see the enterprising reading-room project that this energetic couple established in Kirkuk.

We talked much about development work in Iraq—flood control and drainage; oil resources; new industries; and Point IV. And whatever we discussed or whoever we saw, the talk always came back to Henry K. Botch, who represented Point IV in Kirkuk for a few years. I never met the man. But he's a legendary figure in Iraq.

Botch at one time was a county agent in America. He had

Yankee inventive genius and a practical know-how. He could do anything needed to be done around a farm. He was well trained technically; and he was endowed with a personality that made it easy for him to reach through to people's hearts. He went around northern Iraq in a car, visiting farms. He knew the Arabic language. He carried new seeds and samples of fertilizers with him. He carried medicines for livestock. He also carried handy new gadgets for use around the farm, including currycombs. He was willing to take care of an ailing horse or cow, investigate a new blight, work out a remedy for worms that were destructive to crops, teach the farmers about plowing and seeding, or meet any emergency that arose. They tell about the day he broke a horse that some Iraqi farmers were afraid to ride. From that day on Botch could just about write his own ticket. Farmers sought him out. He did more for adult education in agriculture than anyone in the modern history of Iraq.

He also got some industries started. Raw milk is dangerous in Iraq as elsewhere. Pasteurized milk was non-existent. Botch campaigned about the virtues of pasteurized milk. He finally induced two Armenians to put up a pasteurization plant in Kirkuk. This enterprise turned out to be a great success. When we were there in August, 1957, the demand for pasteurized milk far exceeded the supply which the plant could turn out. The Armenians could not get enough raw milk to meet the needs. So they were beginning to develop their own dairy herds.

Botch introduced another industry. It has traditionally been a slow process for women to grind rice by hand and remove the husks. Botch knew about a Japanese machine that did the husking. He could get no one to buy it. So he bought one himself for about seventy-five dollars and brought it to Iraq. This machine turns out a ton of rice a day. It was so great a success that now there are three machines in operation in the Kirkuk region.

At Baghdad we had heard about the new flood-control reservoirs that would be miles long and hundreds of feet deep and where a new fishery industry could be started. No private capital could be interested. At Kirkuk we heard about the new hotel that was needed. IPC brings many businessmen to Kirkuk. There's no hotel adequate to meet their requirements. IPC guaranteed a fifteen-room occupancy year around to any entrepreneur who would put up a small hotel. No private capital was interested. When we were in Kirkuk, the municipality was starting construction of its hotel.

In Iraq, as in other Asian countries, there has been such an air of uncertainty about the country and its future that capital has been timid. As I said before, in this region capital likes to go into land, which is indestructible, or into jewels, which are easily removed or hidden, rather than into plants and factories, which can be seized or destroyed. This was the psychological factor that Botch fought. It is the great barrier to the development of private industry in the Middle East and a main reason why these countries are developing on the socialist pattern.

IPC has about 12,000 employees in Iraq; and 4000 of them work in and around Kirkuk. They have an eight-hour day and wages that are high by Iraqi standards. IPC also has schools for the workers' children and hospitals for the families. It also has a pension system for its workers.

The trend of population in Iraq is away from the farm. Sharecroppers here usually get 40 per cent of the crop. A cash income of sixty dollars a year per family is average. In the cities a worker can make twenty dollars a month or more. At the same time, farm machinery is on the decline. Of 1200 tractors in Iraq, only 800 are in use. First, the parts are expensive; and second, repairs are difficult due to the shortage of skilled mechanics. High-cost agriculture is having a hard time pushing low-cost agriculture out. Yet low-cost agriculture is driving peasants off the farm. Iraq in this and in other ways is midstream these days. Her most serious internal problems lie ahead.

Kirkuk is an ancient city renowned for the Burning Fiery Furnace. We went with the Dinsmores to visit it. It was Nebuchadnezzar who commanded that Shadrach, Meshach, and Abednego be cast into the Burning Fiery Furnace:

"Then these men were bound in their coats, their hosen, and their hats and their other garments, and were cast into the midst of the burning fiery furnace.

"Therefore because the king's commandment was urgent, and the furnace exceeding hot, the flame of the fire slew those men that took up Shadrach, Meshach, and Abednego.

"And these three men, Shadrach, Meshach, and Abednego, fell down bound into the midst of the burning fiery furnace.

"Then Nebuchadnezzar the king was astonished, and rose up in haste, and spake, and said unto his counsellors, Did not we cast three men bound into the midst of the fire? They answered and said unto the king, True, O king.

"He answered and said, Lo, I see four men loose, walking in the midst of the fire, and they have no hurt; and the form of the fourth is like the Son of God.

"Then Nebuchadnezzar came near to the mouth of the burning fiery furnace, and spake, and said, Shadrach, Meshach, and Abednego, ye servants of the most high God, come forth, and come hither. Then Shadrach, Meshach, and Abednego, came forth of the midst of the fire.

"And the princes, governors, and captains, and the king's counsellors, being gathered together, saw these men, upon whose bodies the fire had no power, nor was an hair of their head singed, neither were their coats changed, nor the smell of fire had passed on them" (Daniel 3: 21–27).

We went to a level spot in a low canyon where natural gas was escaping from the ground. There was a low, hot flame burning. It has been burning from time immemorial. Once in the 1920s the fire was extinguished. IPC brought in a great well that was rich in gas as well as in oil. There was so much gas in the air that it was dangerous even to strike a match. The fire of the Burning Fiery Furnace was covered with dirt and choked. All stoves and lamps in Kirkuk were extinguished for a whole month, while IPC supplied the town with dry rations.

There is so much pressure at Kirkuk that the oil wells are not pumped. Petroleum engineers say that in biblical days these gas fields would have had so great a pressure that they could blow people sky high. Perhaps the spot that we went to was not the precise spot of the Burning Fiery Furnace that Daniel describes. There are several depressions where escaping gas burns, as well as this flat spot. There is one pit about twenty-five feet deep that is ablaze at the bottom. The walls are tar; and the guide said that the pit was dug over the decades by people carrying the tar away on donkeys for fuel. Yet others say this pit was the Burning Fiery

Furnace. Whoever is to be believed, it seems certain that the Kirkuk oil field was the site of the Burning Fiery Furnace.

I took pictures of Mercedes walking through it. I was not sure I got the pictures I wanted. So I asked her to repeat the performance. She objected loudly and vigorously, claiming that her shoes had been burned the first time. I looked at the soles of her shoes. They were, indeed, scorched.

CHAPTER 7

THE DEVIL WORSHIPERS

We stayed at the Station Hotel in Mosul. The hotel is in the railroad station. But the rooms facing the street side are quiet; and the hotel is one of the best we visited on our journey. The rooms are air-conditioned, the food good, the service excellent. We had no sooner reached our rooms with our baggage than a bellboy arrived with a message that the Prince had arrived to pay his respects. My mind was a blank for a second. I could not think of any Prince. Then it dawned on me that this was Prince Tahsin Saeed of the Devil Worshipers.

In Baghdad I had met Michael Kaju, a young Iraqi attached to the American Embassy, who knew the Prince. Michael's father and the father of the Prince had been close friends. Michael had promised to send word to the Prince of our arrival in Mosul. I had beaten the Prince to the hotel by less than five minutes.

Dirty as I was, I went down to see Prince Saeed. He is a man in his twenties, over six feet tall and of big frame. His hair is coal black and he wears a heavy beard. His brown eyes are deep-set and slightly bulging; the flesh of his face is slightly puffy; his fingers are long and slender, almost delicate; his hands had a clammy feel. He wore typical Iraqi clothes: loose white trousers; a white shirt that was coat length; and a white *kafeyah* with a black cord or *argayl* to hold it on. Tonight he wore a dark Western coat over his white shirt; and once when he got up from his chair I noticed that he wore a holster and a revolver around his waist.

He greeted me through an interpreter and asked if we would have dinner with him. I excused myself because of our late arrival and unkempt condition but made a date to meet him at seven o'clock in the morning. So it was that we were introduced to the Devil Worshipers, known in Iraq as the Yazidis.

We took two cars the next day—the station wagon and another Chevrolet owned by the Prince—and made a tour of the shrines of this sect, visited some of the elders, and had lunch at a village of the Devil Worshipers. Michael Kaju, who had arrived from Baghdad, went with us. And Kashi, as usual, was our interpreter. I had not been long in the car with the Prince before he said:

"You are an American. So I want to congratulate you on the Baghdad Pact."

"Thank you," I replied. "Do you think it is a good compact against Communism?"

"I do not know about Communism," the Prince answered. "But the pact is good for the Yazidis."

"Why?" I asked.

"You see, there are many Yazidis in Turkey. Since World War II, I have not been able to visit our members there. But since the Baghdad Pact, the travel restrictions between member nations have been made easier. I can thank America for bringing the Yazidis of Turkey and of Iraq back together."

I asked him how many Yazidis there were in Iraq. He said there were 280,000—a figure which Iraqis say is much too high. In Turkey, he said, there are 15,000. And in Russia, according to the Prince, there are 3,000,000 Yazidis. He was visibly disturbed by border barriers that kept him from his flock.

"Turkish members are delinquent in dues," he said.

"How about Russians?" I asked.

Waving his hand hopelessly, he said, "The Communists won't let my people pay their dues."

I learned on this trip that the Prince always is armed. His father and his grandfather were both murdered. Few of his predecessors died in bed. In each case it was a relative who wanted the lucrative job. It is his relatives whom the Prince fears most.

His job as chief of the Yazidi community is inherited. The

heir must come from a marriage with a close kin, say a first cousin. The son of the chief whose mother is closest kin to the father is the heir. This is a problem, for polygamy is practiced among the Yazidis. Each man is entitled to as many wives as he wants. Prince Saeed is younger than a brother who also went with us. But this brother's mother was a more distant relative of her husband than the mother of the Prince.

The Prince plainly does not trust his brother. For he told me that he could not talk religion in front of him. I asked the reason and he said that since Kashi, my interpreter, spoke Arabic, which his brother understood, his brother would know that the Prince violated a principle of this sect by discussing its theology publicly. The brother then might take revenge.

There are 400 members of Saeed's royal family who must be supported. The levies on the Devil Worshipers amount to $750,000 a year. This is tax-free money. The Prince not only levies and collects taxes from his people but sits in judgment on them also. In Iraq each religious community has its own courts. These courts, recognized by law, deal with the personal affairs of members of that particular community such as the making of wills, inheritance of property, marriage, divorce, separation, alimony, the adoption of children, and the like. The Yazidis have this religious court; and the Prince either presides over it or designates a deputy.

Crimes, such as murder, and litigation, such as highway accidents, come before the Iraqi courts, not the religious courts. But the Yazidis told me that, if a murder involves only two Yazidis, the Prince will try the accused. He even imposes the death sentence.

"How is the death sentence executed?" I asked a Yazidi.

"The Prince merely hands down word that the man shall die. He turns the convicted person loose; and we hunt him down and kill him in private."

"Has that been done recently?" I asked.

"Last year," the Yazidi told me.

By this time we were at a crossroads about thirty miles northwest of Mosul. Here in the brilliant sun of early morning were twenty or more Yazidis lined up to greet us. They were all priests or elders and each kissed the hand of the Prince. I was introduced all around and Mercedes took pictures. Then we turned off the main road to the village of Ba'Shiqah. It has bleak stone houses and cobblestone streets. The Yazidis have a shrine there, half of the people who live there being Yazidis. The other half is made up of Syrian Catholics. We stopped only for a few moments to take pictures. The Prince and a few of his followers stood in the shade while Mercedes photographed women drawing water from the community well, filling their pitchers, and carrying them on their heads. These were all unveiled women, with heavy turbans wound round their heads. A few were quite pretty and all were shy of the camera.

While it is not beneath the dignity of a man to draw water, he will not do so if a woman is there to do it. And this day the women far outnumbered the men at the well in the village of Ba'Shiqah.

From Ba'Shiqah we went to another small village called Ba'-Zani. This is a Yazidi settlement. On its outskirts is a shrine called Sheikh Bakher, where we stopped to greet another group of priests and members of the Devil Worshipers. The shrine is set in a small grove surrounded by an iron fence. The building has a square marble base topped by a crown that is shaped like an inverted cone with ridges on its surface, making a fluted conical spire. This is the telltale mark of Yazidi architecture. What it symbolizes, I could not find out. Others have borrowed it. The Yazidis use it consistently.

This shrine marks the tomb of one of their holy men. The sill in the low doorway is never stepped upon. A Yazidi always takes off his shoes, kisses the sill, and enters the room. I followed suit except that I omitted the kissing. Inside was a bare room with pans and colored rags hanging on the wall. The pans, square shallow vessels with four lips, are for burning olive oil; the rags are twisted and used as wicks in the pan. The design, according to Drower, *Peacock Angel,* represents the four corners of the earth and the path of the sun. This is the light used in Yazidi ceremonies.

After Ba'Zani we headed cross country on a very poor dirt road to another Yazidi village, Ba'Athra, a small place on a barren slope dotted with mud huts. One square stone house that overlooks the scene is the home of the brother of the Prince. We parked our cars there and climbed steep steps to enter it. A dozen or more armed men were lounging there as we entered. These were bodyguards of the Prince. The interior was rather barren, with plain couches and low tables. The Prince, his brother, and several guards joined us in the front room. The Prince, speaking Arabic to Kashi, asked us if we would like drinks. We ordered soft drinks. To my surprise the Prince ordered whisky. It was served to him without ice and with but little water in a large glass. He drank it like lemonade. I expressed surprise that this religious order, which is an affiliate of Islam, should sanction alcoholic beverages. I was told in a whisper by a Yazidi:

"We drink what the Devil would want us to drink."

This is not the sole key to the Yazidi religion; but it explains features of their creed. They believe in God and maintain that God is good, forgiving, and all-wise. God, however, does not need to be propitiated, for He can be counted on to do the right thing. The force to reckon with is the Devil. While God will eventually rule the earth, the Devil, according to the Yazidis, rules at present and will rule for the foreseeable future. Therefore he must be constantly honored. The Devil is propitiated by revelry and feasting and drinking; and he is worshiped.

The Yazidis believe in reincarnation. An evil man is reincarnated into a lower form of life—into an insect if he is evil enough, or into a donkey or camel. Most people are reincarnated as men or women, the highest reward being reincarnation as a Yazidi.

The Koran is one of the books of the Yazidis; and it is considered holy. Christ and Mohammed are both considered to be prophets.

Yazidis, like Moslems, pray five times a day, washing their hands and faces before starting. Each time the worshiper faces the sun as he prays, not Mecca.

Most teachings of the Koran are followed. But every reference to the Devil in the Koran is blocked out. The Yazidis paste paper over that part of the script. The Arabic word for Devil is *Sheitan.* That word does not appear in a Yazidis' Koran or in any of his literature or conversation. In fact, a Yazidi never pronounces a word with the letters *sh* in it, for even that sound might displease the Devil. This has serious consequences. Luke, *Mosul and Its*

Minorities, relates how the British after World War I decided to open public schools in Yazidi territory in northern Iraq. The Arabic symbol which represented the sound *sh* had to be eliminated from the textbooks. The word *Sheitan,* of course, could not be used. Neither could any word that rhymed with *Sheitan.* That often meant a long search for synonyms. For example, the usual word for river was *shatt,* which had to be replaced by *nahr.* The barriers which the British encountered forty years ago are now encountered by the Iraqis in their educational programs.

The Yazidis have two religious books in addition to the Koran. One is the Black Book, which gives an account of the Creation. A more important book is the *Jaliveh* or *Jeliva,* which contains the teachings of Satan. Its opening lines are, "I was, I am, and I shall be unto the end of time, ruling over all creatures and ordering the affairs and deeds of those who are under my sway." The book ends with a command that all of the teachings of the Devil should be treated as *secrets* by the followers.

These were our whispered conversations as the Prince drank not one but three huge tumblers of whisky. Then we were invited to eat.

We were given chairs at the heavily laden table. But the Prince and his brother stood. It is a Yazidi custom to eat with the hands. Though there were knives and forks at our places, the Prince urged us to follow his example and use our fingers.

I had read or been told that the Yazidis had a list of forbidden foods which include beans. But there were beans on the table this noon—string beans, eggplant, roast chicken, fruit, *doogh* (water mixed with *leban* or yogurt), and a whole roasted sheep. The taboo foods include lettuce, pumpkin, fish, and gazelle. I could not learn the reasons for these taboos, nor did I discover why they outlaw the color blue.

The Yazidis have no taboo on gluttony. I never saw men eat as they did this noon. In Baghdad I heard the Arab proverb, "Eat like a camel and be the first to finish." This luncheon brought the proverb back to mind, for the Prince and his relatives went feverishly at work on the huge pile of food and uttered hardly a word until they finished. They tore great pieces of flesh from the sheep. Over and again they came back for helpings and chided us for our meager servings. The food was delicious; the *doogh* was excellent; the sheep was precisely and nicely baked. Even the eggplant—which is not my favorite—was a tasty dish.

There was no siesta after this lunch. We had a long way to go. So after much picture taking on the steep stone steps we again went cross-country—this time to Shayk'Adi, which lies northeast of Ba'Athra and close to the Turkish border.

We left our cars at the village of Shaykhan, parking them in the shade, and locking them, and transferred to two old 1938 or 1940 Fords belonging to the Prince. The road from this point goes up a narrow winding canyon where a clear cold stream runs. The walls are bleak and barren except for an occasional oak in a draw. Higher up there are flat stretches near the creek where small rice fields make bright green splotches on a dull gray background. The road has a high center and deep ruts. We climbed steeply, bearing to the left up a narrower canyon. In ten minutes or so we came to the head of this small canyon where walnut, olive, mulberry, oak, poplar, and fig trees grow in profusion. We could see stone buildings through the thick foliage. Here the drivers stopped; and as we got out of the cars we could hear the radiators boiling. The air was delightfully cool, as we were close to 6000 feet in elevation.

Cobblestone paths led upward to the buildings. We came to one on the left that had a stone-floored patio roofed over by a huge mulberry tree. At the edge of the patio was a concrete pool fed by a lively spring of fresh cold water. We washed at the outlet of the pool and then sat on the patio visiting with several Yazidi priests who came out to greet the Prince and kiss his hand. Servants brought bowls of figs, grapes, and plums. The figs were the sweetest I could remember eating. They were grown at Shayk'Adi. They and the other fruit are the exclusive property of the Prince. No fruit can be picked, no tree can be cut at Shayk'Adi without his permission.

There is a strain of nature worship in the Yazidi creed. They worship trees and water, the stars, the moon, and the sun. They kiss the spot where the sun first hits in the morning. They honor the moon by burying their dead facing the north star. They honor fire by never spitting in it. Some say these influences came in part from the Zoroastrians. I do not know. The Yazidi is reluctant to talk about his religion; and perhaps not even the Prince knows all the origins. One thing is certain and that is that Shayk'Adi did not start as a Yazidi shrine. In the sixth century it was a Christian (Nestorian) monastery. The Yazidis came in the eleventh century, massacred the Christians, and took over. They made it their Holy of Holies.

The Yazidis have two main holy days. One is the first Friday after April 1. That day they have a feast. They assemble at one of their shrines where they eat, drink, and dance. On the second Friday after April 1 they make a sacrifice at Shayk'Adi. About 5000 people make the pilgrimage to this shrine at that time. They bring a yearling bull and after various ceremonies turn him loose and kill him in pursuit. Then they cook the bull and have a feast. This too is a day of revelry.

These were our whispered conversations under the mulberry tree on the patio at Shayk'Adi as we sipped *doogh*. Then we visited the Holy of Holies. We climbed stone steps to a courtyard shaded by mulberry trees and enclosed by stone walls. Then we passed to the courtyard of the temple, laid with flagstones and almost completely covered by a mulberry tree. A cistern of running water is in this courtyard. Here we took off our shoes. Facing us was a door set in marble that marks the entrance to the Holy of Holies. An Arabic script is over the doorway. On the right-hand side of the door, cut in stone and colored with black lead, is a shiny black serpent—the symbol of the Devil. Its head is pointed skyward and it has a lifelike twist in its body. The threshold stone is worn smooth from kissing. The Prince took us into the dark interior. It was pitch-dark. An attendant had a lamp which he lighted. It was the same pan-with-olive-oil type as at Sheikh Bakher. With that as a guide we entered two pitch-dark naves that had vaulted ceilings. In a corner of one is a spring that is said to be connected with the underground stream that flows in Mecca at a spring called Zemzem. The other nave opens into a square rock-lined room over which rises a fluted spire shaped like an inverted cone. Here is a casket draped with cloth.

We stood with the Prince in silence around the casket. He knelt and prayed. The oil lamp flickered, casting weird shadows. I had an eerie feeling. It was a relief to get back to pure sunlight.

There are numerous buildings at Shayk'Adi, all of unmortared masonry. Priests, who are the custodians of the secrets of the religion, live there. So do several ladies in white. Few of the secrets are known to the flock. The people merely submit to the authority of the Prince, who has great sway over them.

"He can appropriate any farm, any oxen, any food supply from a member," a Yazidi told me.

"He can appropriate any woman and draft her for his harem," he added.

"Who is buried at the shrines?" I asked.

"Adie was a Nestorian. He was gardener here. But he turned to Islam for his faith and took the Nestorian priests and made them his gardeners."

"Where is the peacock kept?" I asked.

He would not answer. It was only later that I learned that here the peacock is guarded. The snake is the symbol of the Devil; the peacock is God. Some say the peacock represents the Devil; and perhaps he does, indirectly. The Greek word for God is *Theos*. In Arabic *Theos* means peacock. And so the Yazidis made a godlike symbol out of the peacock. Some say there are several images of the peacock, each cast in bronze. My information is that there is only one. It is not, of course, a live one. It is made of silver and is kept at Shayk'Adi. Only the Prince is allowed to handle it. He takes it out on holy days and holds it in his hands. Then the faithful gather and kiss it, making their contribution to the Prince.

After our return to Mosul, I talked with Michael Kaju about the Yazidis and asked him why the Prince had gone out of his way to be so nice to us. Michael, who is a devout Catholic, told me that in previous days the Yazidis had been horribly persecuted by the Moslems.

The Koran, as I have said, extends protection to the People of the Book—the Christians and Jews who follow a revelation. But that protection is not given to idolaters. Though the Yazidis had their books, they were treated by Moslems as idolaters, perhaps, as Wigram, *Cradle of Mankind,* suggests, because for years they concealed the existence of those books. Being a renegade Moslem sect, they were insufferable to the Moslem world. Yet since they were not an offshoot of a Christian sect, they were better received by the Christians.

"A Yazidi," explained Michael, "is always eager for a Christian ally. And who is a better Christian ally these days than an American?"

After it was all over, I had a melancholy feeling. I remembered that no Yazidi I met had smiled. They were always melancholy. They seemed eternally sad, and rather cowed. There was no simple lighthearted moment in our long day together. They worship the Devil out of fear. Their rites are based on expediency. Their attitudes seemed always negative, reflecting a scheme in which they only shield themselves from harm. An important element was missing from their religion. Love was not there. Tenderness, kindness, service to others, resignation of self, the outgoing attitude of a desire to serve one's neighbor—all these were absent. I could only remember the way in which the Prince gulped his whisky, the limpid handshake on departure, the slightly bulging eyes that were filled with fear and infinite sadness.

CHAPTER 8

JONAH, THE WHALE, AND HATRA

Mosul sits on the west bank of the Tigris River in northern Iraq not far from the borders of Syria and Turkey. The name means "Crossroads"; and such it was for centuries until the Suez Canal sent east-west traffic by ship. Mosul has other names to the local people. It is sometimes referred to as "The Hunchback" because of the silhouette of hills one sees as he approaches from the east. Others call it "Mother of Two Springs" because both its spring and autumn seasons are unusually mild. Marco Polo referred to Mosul as a busy trading and manufacturing region from which the word *muslin* is derived.

Mosul, like other Middle Eastern cities, suffered the ravages of invasions, particularly at the hands of Hulagu and Tamerlane. Its modern history dates from A.D. 1516 when the Ottoman Turks incorporated it in their empire. The Ottomans ruled through Governors who were always military men. One Governor resided in Damascus, one in Baghdad, one in Mosul. They did little to develop their colonial countries.

Though some maintain that the Ottoman colonial rule was not oppressive, all must agree it was not enlightened. They played a divisive role in countries like Iraq, pitting religious group against religious group, race against race. And Maxwell in *People of the Reeds* shows how they set tribe against tribe in southern Iraq. They were primarily concerned with collecting the taxes and keeping control. The Turks stayed until the British took over in 1918. About the only imprint the Turks left on this ancient city are the barracks where they kept their troops, some remains of their fortification, and a few mosques.

Mosul is filled with mosques, nearly a hundred of them. Most are merely museums; only a few are used for the Friday prayers. Nebi Shit is a Turkish mosque with a spearlike minaret typical of Turkish architecture. It was built in 1815 and is supposed to contain the tomb of Seth, the third son of Adam. The roof above his tomb is made up of a cluster of fluted conical spires like those found on all Yazidi shrines. Seth in historical perspective has moorings in Jewish, Christian, and Moslem tradition.

Of greater interest is the Great Mosque with its leaning minaret. This minaret is like many we saw in Persia—made of brick overlaid by hand-baked tile of various colors. The tower is rather massive; and it is about 190 feet tall. The man responsible for its construction—an architect whose name I forget, but well known in Arab circles—either planned unwisely or executed the project carelessly. For as the structure passed the halfway mark, it came out of alignment and began to tilt. Today it looks like a rather droopy candlestick. When we stopped in the bazaar—made up of narrow winding streets partially covered by low roofs streaked with holes that bring in the sunlight—and inquired of the merchants about the leaning minaret, we got various accounts. Generally the local people agree that the distinguished architect was filled with grief at this miscarriage, prostrated himself before the King, Nur-ed-Din Zengui, and promised never again to put his hand to construction work. As a pledge he had his right hand cut off.

Of still greater interest is Nebi Yunus, across the Tigris to the east of Mosul. Nebi Yunus is known as "The Hill of the Prophet Jonah." From a distance it looks as if it rests on a low line of earthworks. This site is a part of the site of ancient Nineveh. Nebi Yunus rests on the rubble from the residence of the ancient Assyrian King, Esarhaddon. A nearby mound, marking the palace of Sennacherib, has been excavated. But the *tell* or mound where Nebi Yunus stands has never been explored by the archaeologists. For it is a spot holy to Moslems and therefore barred to excavators.

The shrine is an imposing edifice, capped by a fluted conical spire on the pattern of the Yazidis. One climbs long stairways to reach the shrine; and when he gets there, he has a wonderful view of Mosul and the surrounding country. Inside, there is a Moslem mosque heavily carpeted with Persian rugs. After we removed our shoes, the guide took us through this chapel down winding corridors into a room very dimly lighted where a huge marble sarcophagus almost fills the space.

"Jonah's tomb," the guide said. Then, pointing to the wall on the left-hand side of the tomb, he said:

"There is the whale."

We saw pieces of bone hung against a dark satin cloth high above the floor.

"Is that a whale bone?" Mercedes asked.

"Looks more like the beak of a swordfish," I answered.

But the guide insisted the bones were from Jonah's whale.

I asked why Jonah, a Jewish prophet, would be so honored by a Moslem community. The answer was not clear. There is, indeed, no clear answer. Luke, *Mosul and Its Minorities,* maintains that Jonah is not buried here, that the tomb holds the remains of John the Lame, a Patriarch of the Nestorian Church. This edifice was once a Nestorian church, taken over by the Moslems. Then a transformation took place. Jonah became not only a Jewish prophet but a Moslem saint.

Jonah was told by the Lord, "Arise, go to Nineveh, that great city, and cry against it; for their wickedness is come up before me" (Jonah 1:2).

Jonah went to Nineveh and cried out, ". . . Yet forty days, and Nineveh shall be overthrown" (Jonah 3:4).

The response of the people of Nineveh was to proclaim a fast. The King declared:

". . . Let neither man nor beast, herd nor flock, taste any thing: let them not feed, nor drink water" (Jonah 3:7).

The fast that saved Nineveh continues to this day. It is called the Rogation of the Ninevites. It is a three-day fast in the month that precedes Lent. All of the social and religious groups join in this fasting—Moslems, Yazidis, Nestorians. They honor the Prophet Jonah by offering gifts to God for the salvation of their ancestors.

So it is that Jonah, who went to Nineveh to proclaim its destruction, is honored there. Jonah through the centuries has become identified with the salvation of Nineveh rather than with the prophecy of its destruction.

That is the legend. But in truth there was no Nineveh at the time Jonah lived. Nineveh was destroyed 612 B.C. The Book of Jonah was written about 350 B.C. By that time the people had even forgotten what Nineveh was like. Hence the late Dr. A. Powell Davies concluded that the story of Jonah and the whale was not based on history but was a satire inspired by a new and robust Jewish humanism. The moral, according to Dr. Davies, was that one could expect nothing from God merely because he was a Jew, or indeed because he belonged to any other type of Chosen People. As the Book of Matthew put it, God "made the sun to rise upon the evil and the good and sent his rain upon the just and unjust."

Most that is left of ancient Nineveh lies along the Tigris about a half mile north of Nebi Yunus. We are told from the Book of Jonah that in Jonah's day it had a population of 120,000 people. Now one sees only a long stretch of low mounds. Once there was a wall about the city, twelve miles in circumference. Here were three fortified palaces built by ancient Assyrian Kings—Sennacherib, Esarhaddon, and Ashur-Banipal. Nineveh was indeed the capital of the Assyrians—the fourth and last capital of an empire that once included Mesopotamia, Syria, Palestine, and Egypt. Sennacherib destroyed Babylon in 689 B.C., leveling it to the ground. Nineveh was destroyed by the Medes and Babylonians in 612 B.C. The destruction was so great, the leveling so complete that when Xenophon marched by two centuries later he was unaware that Nineveh once occupied the spot. Many excavations have since been made, especially by the French and the British; and the Louvre and the British Museum are filled with the relics. But these days there is nothing at all to see at Nineveh except one gate. This is the Nergal Gate on what was the north end of Nineveh. It has been reconstructed, showing one colossal winged bull and part of another. This is all one sees of Nineveh except, of course, the nondescript mounds where the city once stood.

I vaguely remembered from Sunday school the desolation of

Nineveh. When I returned to the Station Hotel I got out the Bible:

"And he will stretch out his hand against the north, and destroy Assyria; and will make Nineveh a desolation, and dry like a wilderness" (Zephaniah 2:13).

When Assyria was at its prime, there was a village southwest of Mosul by the name of Hatra or Al Hadhr. After the Assyrians fell and the Parthians came to power in Persia, Hatra was made into a fortress. Its walls were twenty feet thick. It had a moat and high towers to guard it. It had deep wells within its walls that guaranteed enough water for any siege. It was located on a flat fertile plain that produced many cereals. It withstood many sieges, the most notable being the one by the Roman Emperor Trajan in A.D. 116. The heat of the sun and the lack of water defeated Trajan, as they did others. Severus was also turned back in A.D. 198. Finally, the Persian King Sapor I captured and sacked the town in A.D. 250. After that Hatra turned to dust and rubble.

We went down to Hatra on a blistering hot day. It's about a three-hour drive. The first hour and a half is on the paved highway that runs south of Mosul along the Tigris. After about an hour's drive we turned right and west onto remnants of a paved road that apparently had been laid by IPC to serve some exploratory mission. But after ten miles or so this broken paved road ends and we traveled on dirt. The turnoff from the main road was unmarked. There was no signpost all the way down to Hatra. The dirt road was hardly more than a trail. It seemed to have innumerable branches and side roads. We could not possibly have found it by ourselves. Even Kashi, our interpreter, would have been of little help, as we met few people on this long drive and passed close to no village. Our guide was a member of the gendarmes in Mosul. There is a garrison at Hatra where this man had worked. So he knew the trail as I know my back yard.

Some accounts say this stretch of land around Hatra is a desert. Viewed from a distance, it has that appearance. But this is actually fairly good winter wheat land, some of it worked by machinery, and most of it owned by those who work the fields, not by landlords. There are a few villages of a dozen or so families on this desert, located beside deep wells. They are far off the road and looked from the car like dark splotches against the horizon.

The wheat had been harvested; only the stubble was left. There had been no rain for weeks on end, so the ground was powder-dry. The wind made countless whirlwinds that we could trace for dozens of miles across the plain. Some of them encompassed us and passed on; and judged by our speed, they were moving perhaps forty miles an hour.

Just before reaching the ancient city we crossed a gully in which a small stream flowed. It apparently has a fast runoff in the spring and is known as the northern end of the Wadi Thar Thar. The day of our visit a few cattle were grazing on a thin strip of grass that grew in the bottom of the gully.

The village of Hatra has a few dozen souls and a garrison of gendarmes. When we arrived we drove the car through what once was a hole in the thick wall. There at a deep well men, boys, and girls were drawing water for their sheep and goats. Camels, including a baby albino, lay chewing their cuds. Most of the sheep of Hatra were in the mountains to the west along the Syrian border. The wolves—big gray ones—had followed them there and the hyenas had followed the wolves. Gazelle were still on the plains. Here too were bustards with a white meat delicious to eat. We saw some of the three kinds of partridge that flourish on this plain.

Hatra is hot, dusty, barren, and wind-blown. There are no trees or grass there. There is no fuel except camel dung. One who sees it easily jumps to the conclusion that this place is cursed by poverty and oppression. That, however, is not true. There is pure well water at Hatra; and the wheat, the sheep, goats, and camels provide the people with a fair living by Asian standards.

The ruins of the old city of Hatra are quite substantial. There are remnants of numerous buildings, all substantially built from blocks of limestone and marble which plainly have been hauled a long way, as no quarry is near at hand. The Parthians built seven main palaces here and a Temple of the Sun. The temple and the royal residence were in the center of the city. The buildings had a basement or underground room that could be entered through a small door at ground level from the outside. We went underground and discovered that, while it was blistering hot in the sun, it was quite cool in the basement.

The halls of the palaces reminded me somewhat of Ctesiphon:

they were open on the east side just like a tent of an Arab sheikh. The main arches and lintels are ornamented with carvings. There are many sculptured heads there. And on one wall are groups of carved masks. These heads and masks are badly mutilated. I asked the guide why they were mutilated.

"The tribesmen who have guns like to shoot at the old statues," he replied.

"Why?" I asked.

"The statues are symbols of evil," he replied.

"Why?" I inquired.

"There is only one God and that is Allah."

That is to say, the sculptured heads were taken by the unknowing Moslems to be the images of gods. And perhaps they were. But they are also matters of great archaeological interest.

The sun was high and burning with intensity when we returned to the present village of Hatra to meet Commandant Said of the gendarmes. He's short, plump, and swarthy. His headquarters are in a group of one-story adobe buildings. Outside were two large tents with double roofs which are set up in summertime to accommodate tourists. It was here that Said met us. He had gendarmes bring us cold soft drinks. They were dressed in khaki and wore Sam Browne belts heavy with cartridges. Over their heads was the black and white *kafeyah.*

Said brought a guestbook for our signatures. Many travelers come here, as the guestbook makes clear. Most of them are Iraqis, Britishers, or Germans. A few are Americans. Signing a few lines above us were the British historian, Arnold Toynbee, and the American newsman, Joseph Alsop.

Luncheon was in one of the adobe buildings. The windows were open and covered on the outside by a wooden frame filled with camel's-thorn. We had seen these devices before in villages south of Baghdad. They are air coolers that work very efficiently. The ones we install at home are more expensive and more durable. But the principle is the same as the one employed at Hatra.

It was cool in the darkened dining room. After washing our hands and faces in water poured by an Arab attendant from an earthen jar, we sat down to one of the best luncheons we had had on our trip. There was *koski* on the table—whole lamb stuffed with rice and baked. *Leban,* rice cooked with almonds, fried cucumbers, and eggplant were passed. For dessert we had melon and watermelon, both grown at Hatra in fields that get their moisture from the spring rains. The cantaloupe and the watermelon were exceptionally sweet.

At luncheon we talked of Said's command. This is headquarters for the patrol of the Syrian border to the west. Said is more than a gendarme. He is judge as well. He sits in all civil cases that arise among the people of Hatra and renders judgment. Appeals from his decisions go to the Sessions Court in Baghdad, which reviews both the law and the facts. Said impressed us as being not only hospitable and warmhearted, but able as well—a credit to the civil service of Iraq.

After Turkish coffee was passed, Said invited us to a siesta. He put cots in several of the rooms used as offices, turned on overhead electric fans, and left us for an hour's sleep.

Wind-blown and desolate Hatra had treated us well, so well that I was tempted to accept Said's invitation, stay all night, and see this barren land under the stars.

We had not gone far across the hard-packed plain on our return trip to Mosul before we met villagers—some on foot, some on donkeys—returning home from a visit to some market. They were carrying brightly burnished metal pans and buckets that carried milk and *leban* to the market. There were others on camels—one man riding and several walking at a brisk rate. These camels all had packs on their backs, with ropes and straps hanging down as if they too had just completed a trip to some market, carrying freight.

Iraq has an ambitious program in education. The Ministry of Education plans to have enough *primary* schools for compulsory education throughout Iraq by 1965. To date there are primary schools for only 40 per cent of the boys and less than 30 per cent of the girls. The new schools are all co-educational, thus making a break with Moslem tradition. Only 10 per cent of the students are presently taken care of in *secondary* schools. It will take fifteen years or more to fill the country with high schools enough for all the children. The blueprint is an excellent one. It provides for two years of English as a second language in the primary schools, and four years of English in the high schools.

In Baghdad and Mosul we met many urchins who were beneficiaries of this educational program. But none of the children on the road out of Hatra had a school to attend. They were destined to grow up illiterate just like their mothers, who tended the milk buckets, and their fathers, who minded the camels.

These women were unveiled. The old order requires the women to wear the *aba* whenever they appear in public, or whenever they are in their own homes or in other homes where men, not members of the immediate family, are present. This *aba* is a robe —usually black—which comes over the head and completely covers the body. It is used with a veil drawn over the face. The *aba* is disappearing in the larger cities—not as a result of legal decrees but as a matter of choice. As a practical matter, Iraqi women are not yet on the same equal footing with men as American women are. But they are in law, medicine, teaching, nursing, and social work. Moreover, in the civil service they get for equal jobs equal pay with men. Those are changes that have taken placc largely since the beginning of World War II.

Only in their work, however, do these Iraqi women have the freedom that women of the West enjoy. Marriages are still arranged in most communities. A woman, after the office has closed, steps back several centuries when she returns home. She may not go to a movie with a man unless she is chaperoned by a male relative. Nor may she entertain a male friend at home unless her family is present. And it would be hazardous for her to sit in a café having tea with a man or even to drink orange crush with him alone in public. Moreover, women in Iraq do not vote, though they have been promised the franchise by 1962.

We could not make out whether or not these women who met us on our return from Hatra were Moslems. But these taboos on women, though Moslem in origin, apply as much today to the Christians, the Jews, and the Yazidis in Iraq as to those who embrace Islam.

CHAPTER 9

CHRISTIAN MINORITIES

Iraq has made progress in guaranteeing religious freedom. Article 13 of the Constitution provides: "Islam is the official religion of the State. Freedom to practice the rites of the different sects of that religion, as observed in Iraq, is guaranteed. Complete freedom of conscience and freedom to practice the various forms of worship, in conformity with accepted customs, are guaranteed to all inhabitants of the country, provided that such forms of worship do not conflict with the maintenance of order and discipline or public morality."

Article 6 of the Iraq Constitution guarantees equality to all nationals, "whatever differences may exist in language, race, or creed." Article 16 gives various communities "the right of establishing and maintaining schools for the instruction of their members in their own tongues." Article 18 provides that no distinction shall be made between Iraqi nationals "on account of origin, language, or religion." And Article 37 states that the law regulating the election of members of the National Chamber of Deputies shall prescribe "the necessary representation of the Christian and Jewish minorities."

The 1946 Electoral Law provides in general for one Deputy for every 20,000 registered male voters. In addition, the law provides that Jews and Christians shall have in addition a prescribed number of Deputies from Baghdad, Basra, and Mosul. In effect, this latter system is the electorate register system of the kind the British introduced into India, since in each of those designated districts only a Jew or a Christian, as the case may be, is returned to the Chamber of Deputies. But in all the other districts a deputy can be returned irrespective of his race or religion. Likewise, the voters enjoy the same rights, irrespective of their race or religion.

The minorities of Iraq are no longer treated as the People of the Book—that is to say, as protected but subordinate groups. In theory they have equality. Indeed, a Jew and a Christian have been members of the Cabinet.

Prior to the exodus of Jews to Palestine, they had six members in Parliament. Now there are less than 10,000 Jews left in Iraq, too few to give any representation under the Electoral Law. But there are eight Christian deputies in Parliament. Yet religious prejudice lies close to the surface in Middle East affairs, as evidenced by the massacre of the Assyrians in Iraq in 1933 and the pogrom against the Jews in Baghdad in 1941. The process of building a society that gives equality to all religious groups is a new experiment in the Moslem world. It takes time to perfect. Iraq has made greater progress than any other Arab nation and, apart from Turkey, greater progress than any Moslem country.

We found religious minorities flourishing there. I have already mentioned the Mandeans and Yazidis. In and around Mosul we saw and visited with the Armenians, Jacobites, Nestorians, and Catholics.

There are not as many Armenians in Iraq as there are in Iran. But they have a Patriarch in Baghdad and settlements in that city, in Mosul, and Kirkuk. An increasing number have gone to Kirkuk in recent years to work in the oil fields. One bright August morning we visited the Church of the Virgin Mary in Mosul, an Armenian church that serves not more than 150 families. The priest—the Reverend Father Khoram Khasabian—was away. An eighty-five-year-old lady, Kharima Zakrain, showed us the church. She was spry for her age and fairly galloped over the huge flagstones that lined the courtyard leading to the chapel. This is an ancient church; and the chapel is heavily hung with lights, brightly painted drapes and furniture, and decorated with an ornate altar covered with a white cloth. It was the most ornate chapel I had seen—so filled with relics as to leave the impression of disorderliness.

The most threadbare Christian church we saw was also in Mosul. It was St. George's Church, whose pastor is the Reverend Father Zaia Bobo Debato. He is dark, thin, and pleasant. He was dressed in a black robe and a round brimless black hat that had four tiers to it. His face was calm; and it had the philosopher's look. He is perhaps forty years old; and he had five bright-eyed boys ranging from about three years to twelve. He called them and they all came running. He lined them up according to age, facing me. He then tapped each one on the head, calling off his name. Each had a famous Assyrian name, the oldest boy being named after the famous King Sennacherib. The other names I forget. We crossed the barren courtyard to the chapel. The room had an altar and benches. There was a cross over the altar. But with that the decorations ended.

There was no picture of Christ in this chapel, as the Nestorians abjure holy pictures, perhaps due to the Moslem influence, as Fortescue suggests in *The Lesser Eastern Churches*. This was the most barren chapel I ever saw. It was not only barren; it had the mark of poverty on it. It was hard to realize that we were standing in a church whose prelates once ruled as far east as China. This is the only Nestorian church in Mosul; and it was not even listed in the guidebook.

Others have told of the rise and decline of the Nestorians. As good an account as any is Luke, *Mosul and Its Minorities*, already mentioned. When the Arabs conquered Persia, in A.D. 641, they took the Nestorians under their wing. These Christians had a higher order of learning than their masters. The Arabs used them at court as physicians, scribes, and secretaries. Their influence at court grew so that they were allowed their Patriarchs. They were freed from military service, their clergy was exempt from taxes, and a Christian woman who worked for a Moslem need not change her religion or her religious practices. They sent missionaries to India and to China. The Chinese Emperor Tai-tsung introduced Christianity into his country. Soon there were Bishops the length and breadth of China. This Chinese Church sent a delegate to Pope Nicholas IV in Rome, to Philip IV of France, and to Edward I of England.

It was Tamerlane who toppled the Nestorians in Asia. Hulagu, who preceded him, tolerated Christianity and Buddhism, as well as Islam. His son Abaqa married a Christian. Some of his relatives were baptized. But Tamerlane was the scourge of religion. He engaged in wholesale slaughter, leaving only a few remnants of the Nestorian Church. These remnants were mostly in northwest Persia and northern Iraq. The great Church of the East was no more. "So great was the terror inspired by this brutal conqueror," wrote Lamsa in *The Oldest Christian People,* "that millions of Nestorians in China, India, and Tartary became Mohammedans."

Then began a new disintegration. In the nineteenth century the Kurds began bloody massacres of the Nestorians. They were so devastating that the Nestorians in Mosul date their years not from their early beginnings but from 1845 when these awful Kurdish massacres ended. The Nestorians closed ranks and tightened control and made their Patriarch hereditary. They were massacred again in World War I by the Kurds. These massacres caused many Nestorians to go over to the Catholic Church. Through the French Consul they had the protection and influence of a European power. So their ranks dwindled.

These Nestorians follow Hebrew customs. Jewish holidays are observed; the eating of pork is banned. The practice of animal sacrifices is followed. An ox or sheep is sacrificed at the door of the church. The meat is eaten by the church officials and the poor of the parish. The hide is given to the church; and the fat is used to make candles. These present-day Nestorians are Assyrians; and many think they are members of Jilu, one of the lost tribes of Israel. The religious books of the Nestorians are written in the language which Christ spoke.

There are now about 500 Nestorian families in and around Mosul. They live at last in peace and quiet. Father Debato spoke to me of the ancient glory of the Nestorians, of the extent of their great influence from Rome to China. His eyes light up as he talks of the ancient sphere of influence of the Nestorians. His hopes are in the five young bright-eyed youngsters who do not yet know the cruelty of the world. But his eyes are full of infinite grief because he knows the bloody history of his little band.

We also visited three Jacobite churches—one in Bartalle and

one in Ba'Shiqah, two small towns to the northeast of Mosul, and one in Mosul.

In Mosul we visited the St. Thomas Church of the Jacobites of which the Reverend Father Bashara Numan is the head. This is an active church serving 800 families. It has two church schools —one for boys and one for girls—that go through six years. There is in addition a kindergarten attached to the church.

We visited briefly at the Jacobite church at Ba'Shiqah, which has 420 members. The pastor was absent. We only saw the caretaker, Joseph Georgis, who told us with pride that this church was three hundred years old.

Our best visit with the Jacobites was at Bartallc (sometimes spelled Bartley) where we talked with Father Elias Eshaya. This church is named after an early woman martyr, Mart Ishmooni. It is four hundred and eighty years old and serves today 400 families. It is a big congregation as Jacobites go. For in all Iraq there are only 6000 Jacobite families, or 30,000 people.

The Jacobites, like the Nestorians, are not in communion with either the Orthodox Church or the Church of Rome. They have a Patriarch residing in Antioch. Historically they were confined to Mesopotamia and northern Syria. But, like the Nestorians, they grew in power under the early Arab rule, extending their power into Persia and to Malabar in India.

The priests are bearded and dressed in black raiment and a unique black hat that is round and much narrower at the rim than at the top.

Father Eshaya, after posing for pictures in the quiet courtyard of his church, showed us the chapel. Here is an altar curtain that portrays a horrible picture. It shows the saint, Mart Ishmooni, and her husband viewing the slaughter of their seven children.

The account is related in 2 Maccabees 7:

"And it came to pass that seven brethren also with their mother were at the king's command taken and shamefully handled with scourges and cords, to compel them to taste of the abominable swine's flesh. But one of them made himself the spokesman and said, What wouldest thou ask and learn of us? for we are ready to die rather than transgress the laws of our fathers. And the king fell into a rage, and commanded to heat pans and caldrons: and when these forthwith were heated, he commanded to cut out the tongue of him that had been their spokesman, and to scalp him, and to cut off his extremities, the rest of his brethren and his mother looking on. And when he was utterly maimed, the king commanded to bring him to the fire, being yet alive, and to fry him in the pan. And as the vapour of the pan spread far, they and their mother also exhorted one another to die nobly."

Father Eshaya told me another version; he said the reason for the persecution was that Ishmooni was the first lady publicly to proclaim for Jesus. Whatever the cause, the executions took place in the first century A.D. when King Antiochus IV ruled Palestine on behalf of Rome. The saint was first made to witness the execution of her family before she herself was executed.

Apart from that inflammatory altar curtain, the chapel was rather bare and drab.

We went across the street with Father Eshaya, entered another courtyard, and climbed to a second-story balcony where he served us cold orange squash. He talked to us through Kashi about the history of the Jacobites and their present activities. Unlike the Nestorians, they have a theological school, located in Mosul. The services of the Bartalle church are conducted in Assyrian. The Jacobites have no sister orders. Their priests marry. They have no hospitals or orphanages. They maintain no separate schools for children in Bartalle. Their children go to public schools; and the Iraqi government allows any public school in a village that has a Christian majority, as Bartalle does, to have a teacher of the Christian religion. The Jacobites hire the teacher but his salary is paid by the government; and he sees to it that Jacobite children in the school are inculcated with Jacobite principles. This is the kind of practice held unconstitutional by *McCollum v. Board of Education,* 333 U.S. 203, because it violates our principle of separation of church and state. But it is a flourishing practice in northern Iraq and is used by every religious group in every village having a Christian majority. It is justified there on the grounds that, since Arab village schools teach the Koran, Christian village schools should teach the Bible.

We visited several Chaldean Catholic churches, and a Chaldean Catholic monastery. These are all Uniat organizations who have communion with the Church of Rome. In Mosul we visited with the Reverend Father Emanuel Dady of the Church of Our Mother of Help and learned from him that in all Iraq there are about 200,000 Chaldeans. In Ba'Shiqah we met the Reverend Father Bahnam Al-Sanian, who showed us his hunded-year-old church, which has 300 members. We made two visits to Bartalle to see the Reverend Father Basil Agoulla. On our second trip we had a long visit with him and with Sister Mary Behnam of the Dominican Order. It was hot in the barren, rocky, wind-blown courtyard where we talked for a few moments and took pictures. Then we sat in a room in the parish house where open windows brought a cooling wind and sipped Turkish coffee with Father Agoulla and Sister Behnam. Father Agoulla is about forty, slight and dark, with an earnest, aesthetic face. He is most learned; and without a touch of prejudice he talked about each of the Christian minorities in Iraq. He gave me new light on the Mandeans, Jacobites, and Nestorians. He also talked at length about the Yazidis and their religious rites. He knew each of these groups, the Yazidis in particular. He told me about the Chaldean Catholics and their union with Rome. They have everything in common with the Roman Catholics except the liturgy. The Chaldean Catholics conduct their mass in Aramaic.

"It's the language Jesus used," Father Agoulla said.

"Has it not changed over the centuries?" I asked.

"In some places, yes. But we Chaldeans think we speak the pure Aramaic," he answered.

I asked if he would please give me a sample of the liturgy. The good man stood up and went into deep meditation for perhaps three minutes. Then, standing with bowed head, he gave a prayer in Aramaic from the Chaldean liturgy.

One day we made a long trip on dusty roads to Alqosh, which takes several hours to reach from Mosul. It's almost due north from that city and quite close to the Turkish border. Alqosh is noted for several reasons. Here is the tomb of Nahum, who cried out against Nineveh:

"And it shall come to pass, that all they that look upon thee shall flee from thee, and say, Nineveh is laid waste: who will bemoan her? whence shall I seek comforters for thee?" (Nahum 3:7.)

Here too is the monastery of Rabban Hormizd. Alqosh lies up against a high hill on the northernmost edge of the plain of Mosul. The face of this hill is steep. Here Hormizd came in the sixth century. He was a Persian who went into seclusion in a cave in this cliff and renounced life just like an Indian *saddhu.* Other men followed his example; and soon there were many caves of hermits in this cliff. In time churches were built here. There's still a hermitage on the cliff that looks like an eagle's nest from below. It belongs to the Chaldean Catholics; and one priest and four brothers live there. This monastery, known as Rabban Hormizd, offers little but a view these days. It has two interesting relics. One is an iron collar attached to a stone wall that is said to cure insanity (sometimes), if the victim wears the collar one night through. There is another room carved in the rock where two iron rings are fastened to the ceiling. These are rings through which ropes were passed to keep Hormizd in a kneeling position, year after year.

Of greater interest is Sayada or the Virgin Mary Monastery at the foot of the cliff. It is part and parcel of Rabban Hormizd; and it was built about a hundred years ago to house the priests and the brothers and to be headquarters for supervision of the vast agricultural interests of the Chaldeans in the valley. Here at Sayada we met five priests and some of the thirty-five brothers. It's a pleasant place, built around a large courtyard that is shaded with trees. In the middle is an old well from which the monks still get water with a windlass. Our host was the senior priest, Father P. Samuel Chauvitz. He showed us a pleasant chapel that contains the burial place of the Patriarchs of Babylon; and after that he took us to an interesting library off the chapel. The books in this library are written in various scripts, one of which is Syriac but none of which was familiar to me. Father Chauvitz, who studied at Notre Dame in France, assured me they were very old and very valuable. We had tea under a grape arbor in the courtyard while a vicious dog growled from the far side. These brothers make a red wine famous in northern Iraq. We were served tea, and as we had our tea and biscuits, Father Chauvitz talked of the work of the monastery. It feeds the poor and it takes care of the spiritual needs of the villagers of Alqosh. But even more important to this good man was the orphanage which the order has established in Alqosh. That institution takes care of forty-four young ones; and it was their welfare that was his greatest pride.

I mentioned earlier that all Christian villages are made of rock, while Moslem villages are usually of mud. All the houses in the Christian villages I have mentioned had rock buildings. Alqosh is no exception. Neither was Tall Usquf where we stopped on returning from Alqosh. Tall Usquf means Bishop's Hill. It too has a Chaldean church, though we did not visit it. We had stopped on the outskirts to take pictures of villagers coming in from work in the fields. Then we went to a community well where girls and women in gay dresses were drawing water with buckets and filling earthen jars. After traveling another block or so, we were attracted by the sound of music. As soon as we parked the station wagon by the curb, friendly villagers came up and invited us to the party. It was a wedding. The celebration had been going on for three days; and this was the end of the third day. The ceremony was over; and the bride and groom had, unfortunately for our visit, left. But the dance continued. The dance was in a courtyard of the bride's home. The music was a wooden horn and a drum. Young men and women formed a line, their arms around each other's shoulders; and they moved forward and backward—and sometimes sidewise—to the music. The sun was low and it was too dark and too crowded in the courtyard for good pictures. An eager villager escorted us up stone steps to a roof overlooking the courtyard. For some minutes we were absorbed with the movements of the dance and our picture taking.

Hearing a noise, I happened to turn around; and when I did, I saw one of the most interesting village scenes of our entire journey. Being on a roof, we had a good view of the neighboring houses. Each was built of stone, and was two-storied. Each also had a courtyard that shut the community out and turned the members of the family to each other. This was late afternoon, close to evening; and the livestock were home. On the ground floor in the courtyard were the cattle, each house having at least one animal. On the porch of the second floor, reached by stone steps, were the sheep, each house having a few. On the roofs were the housewives bringing out blankets and making up beds for the night. This is hot, dry country; and the people invariably sleep under the stars during summertime.

Our most interesting visit was in Tall Kayf, northwest of Mosul. This is a town of over 10,000 people. The Chaldean church has 10,000 members. It's a neat, tidy village, though almost barren of trees. This is wheat country; and when we were there the wheat was on the thrashing floors being separated in the ancient way. We stopped briefly at a convent owned by the Dominican sisters. These sisters have a school in Tall Kayf but no orphanage. The church is an attractive one. In church services the women squat behind a rail to the rear of the church, the men in front. The priests wear beards and round black hats with red tops. We met the priest outside, the Reverend Father Peter Kattoula, who speaks some English. As we were visiting with him, an older man came along. He must have been seventy years old, dressed in a red *kafeyah* and a Western coat over a flowing Arab gown. He introduced himself as Yussif Hakim. He was a former Mayor of Tall Kayf. Learning that we were Americans, he asked us at once to his home for tea. We followed him through winding cobblestone lanes to his house. It was late afternoon and the cattle and sheep were being driven home by boys. We came to his stone house near the center of town and climbed steep stone steps to a second-floor porch. This porch, like all others in Tall Kayf, had no guardrail. We entered a small room off the porch and sat on comfortable chairs. The walls had biblical pictures on them. In the center was a small table. Yussif excused himself, returning in about five minutes with a gallon glass bottle of wine. It was wine made of Tall Kayf grapes and bottled by Yussif ten years ago. It was sealed with enough wax to weigh a quarter pound. After the wax was removed, he brought out huge tumblers and poured drinks around. Then we drank to his health and the health of Tall Kayf.

It was good wine, though quite heady. Since sipping was in order, we sat for an hour. The conversation took a wide range—from the gypsum pit near Tall Kayf to the wheat crop to politics. Women are not veiled in the Christian cities. But the Moslem influence is so strong socially as to keep women in the background. Yussif's wife did not appear during our tea. As I said, women are segregated in church services in these Christian villages. But they are treated equally in all other respects. Christian villages always have Christian Mayors; Moslem villages, Moslem Mayors. Religious tolerance has not yet developed to the point that a Christian gets the Moslem vote, or vice versa. Tall Kayfis have vast interests in Iraq. Practically all the hotels in Baghdad are owned by Tall Kayfis. They own many, if not most, of the taxicabs and a lot of the brothels and movie houses. They also are the waiters in hotels and clubs in Baghdad. We talked with Yussif about the business interests of Tall Kayfis. Then he brought the conversation around to America.

"Tall Kayf in Iraq is proud of Tall Kayf in America," he said.

"Tall Kayf in America?" I asked.

"Yes, Tall Kayf, Detroit, Michigan," he said.

He went on to explain that about 250 families from Tall Kayf have migrated to Detroit. There they keep a Tall Kayf community alive.

"Do they keep up contacts with the Iraqi Tall Kayf?" I asked.

"Yes, certainly," Yussif replied.

He went out of the room to get a letter just arrived from a nephew in Detroit—John H. Hakim. He was proud of his nephew's progress.

"Do these people from Detroit ever return here?" I asked.

"Certainly," he said. "Most of the Tall Kayf boys in Detroit come back here to get married."

"Not girls from Detroit?" I said.

"No, no. Tall Kayf boys, wherever they are, come back here to marry Tall Kayf girls. They like the Tall Kayf girls best."

CHAPTER 10

SALAHADDIN AND HAJI OMRAN

One night on our return to Mosul from one of the Christian villages we had carburetor trouble. The engine coughed, wheezed, and stopped. Each time it stopped, I had difficulty starting it. Finally in the midst of Mosul evening traffic, and right beside a policeman's wooden stand at a street intersection, the engine died and the starter would not work. Mercedes was under the hood in an instant; and it took the ingenuity of the traffic policeman to keep a great crowd from gathering. In a few minutes Mercedes diagnosed the difficulty as generator trouble. There was no tow available. We could only recruit the good people of Mosul abroad this evening to push us. They would push a block; and then I, by using the gears, would get the car started. In a hundred yards or so the engine would die again. We would recruit a new street crowd for pushing and repeat the performance. Finally the gendarmes sent out a jeep to our rescue and pushed us to their headquarters and compound. The commandant, a tall, thin, pleasant man in his thirties, then took charge. Our job of generator repair in Baghdad had not lasted long. The commandant would have a new generator put in the car by morning; and with that assurance he returned us to the Station Hotel in one of his cars.

The station wagon was ready at seven o'clock the next morning. The commandant had found a new generator; the carburetor had been adjusted; and the car once more ran as good as new. We loaded up for our return trip to Iran; and as we left Mosul we stopped by the gendarme heaquarters to settle our account with the commandant and to say goodbye to him and the others who had been so kind to us.

We crossed the Tigris on the bridge leading to Nineveh and headed east. This morning farmers had brought to Mosul hundreds of watermelons; and they were all piled in stacks under this bridge. Some of these stacks were six feet or more high; and the watermelons were the largest I have seen, nearing three feet or more in length.

Soon we quit Nineveh and bore east by south on the black-surfaced road to Erbil (Arbela). This is rolling wheat land that lies between the Greater Zab River on the north and the Lesser Zab on the south. It was in this neighborhood (about fifty miles to the north) that Alexander the Great defeated Darius in the battle of Gaugamela. Darius, in all probability, had 500,000 men. It was a miscellaneous collection of men of various races from Central Asia. Alexander was outnumbered ten to one, having 40,000 infantry and 7000 cavalry. The Persians had scythes, chariots, and elephants. But Alexander, riding his prize horse Bucephalus, led the oblique attack from the right wing while the Macedonian phalanx held the center against the scythed chariots and elephants. The Persian host was shattered and Darius fled. This battle, on October 1, 331 B.C., marked the end of the Persian Empire. Every battle after this one was for Alexander an anticlimax.

Erbil now is a city of perhaps 25,000 people. It's a typical nondescript town of the Middle East with ordinary bazaars and no touch of civic charm and beauty. It has two claims to distinction: first, its proximity to the battle of Gaugamela; and second, its claim to be the oldest city in the world that has been continuously inhabited.

We first saw it from the airplane the day we flew north from Baghdad with Ambassador Gallman. The center of the town seemed to rest on a high mound. From the air it looked like an old fortified place. When we arrived by car it was apparent that the mound was not a fort but debris from ancient times. When old mud houses fell, the ground was leveled and new houses erected on the same site. In this way the height of the mound grew by about three feet a century. It is now at least two hundred feet above the plain. This mound, known as a *tell,* undoubtedly holds archaeological treasures. I heard it discussed by antiquarians the length of Iraq. But no shovel has touched the *tell* to this day.

We took pictures at its base; and then moved on to the busy bazaar for more photographs and cold drinks. After studying the maps we decided to have an early lunch at Erbil and then drive to Salahaddin, our destination that day. Kashi and I found a nice teahouse where we had four lamb *kababs* cooked on skewers. We wrapped these in the big round pieces of unleavened bread for sale in every market. Then we bought a watermelon and took our food to a place called the Railway Rest House. The gendarmes at Mosul had told us of the place; but we thought it was a rest house only. We learned that it had a nice kitchen and dining room as well. But with the permission of the good-natured manager we ate our lunch in the lobby. The *kabab* was perfect. The manager supplied hot raw onions and tea. The melon was cool and sweet.

The Mosul gendarmes had sent a jeep escort with us to Erbil. Now the Erbil gendarmes sent a jeep with us to Salahaddin. This town is less than twenty-five miles from Erbil in a northeasterly direction. But it took us well over an hour to get there. The road is black-surfaced and good. But the curves are sharp and the grade is steep. The car did not have the power it once had. And to make matters worse we lost the muffler. There was no excuse for it. I was driving and the road was clear except for a couple of rocks that had rolled down a bank. They looked like thin rocks to me. But they were solid and just high enough to rip the muffler. Once more we had a hot piece of metal inside, rather than under, the car. But this time the gendarmes obliged by driving the station wagon back to Erbil later that day, welding the muffler back on, and returning the car to Salahaddin by evening.

Salahaddin, named for Saladin, the great Kurdish military genius who was born near here and who took Jerusalem from the Crusaders, lies on the east side of the Zagros Mountains. These mountains have been a refuge throughout history. Marco Polo mentioned that in these mountains "there is a race of people called Kurds, some of whom are Christians of the Nestorian and Jacobite sects, and others Mohometans. They are all an unprincipled people, whose occupation it is to rob the merchants." When the Assyrian Empire fell in 612 B.C., the Assyrians (Nestorians) took to the hills. The plundering armies then, as later, kept to the valleys and the passes. This part of the Zagros, often referred to as Kurdistan, became an asylum for the Assyrians. After Tamerlane's scourge, the remnants of the Nestorians took refuge here. But as a result of the great disturbances in the Middle East during and after World War I, and the vast movements of population, the Nestorians who once occupied these hills are now in the plains; and the people of the hills are now almost wholly Kurdish.

These hills abound in bear and wolves and in some places wild boar. There are many magpies in these canyons; and bluejay, kingfisher, and the hoopoe, called "the bird of Solomon" by the Nestorians, are common.

Salahaddin, being about 4000 feet in elevation, is a delightfully cool place and an ideal summer resort. It has several nice hotels. We stayed at the Salahaddin Hotel, which is modern and clean, and has an excellent cook. A strong wind came up at night; and it seemed strange after the heat of Baghdad, Kirkuk, and Mosul to need blankets for sleeping. The coolness of Salahaddin was an omen of cool weather that was to accompany us the rest of our journey.

The road from Salahaddin to Iraq's border town of Haji Omran is black-surfaced and excellent all the way. It is one of the most scenic drives of any in the world. The road follows canyons most of the way, breaking out of one to cross an intervening ridge and then to drop down to another. It does this twice before entering the Rawanduz Canyon. There is water in each of these canyons; each carries a tributary of the Greater Zab River, which runs into the Tigris below Mosul. The first of these canyons that we reached out of Salahaddin is where the Mawaran River runs. It's a narrow valley dominated by crags and filled with chestnut and oak trees. An attractive village, Shaqlawa, lies deep in the shade under an overhanging cliff. Iraqi Boy Scouts had a camp on the edge of town and were going through signal practice when we passed. Here we stopped for tea.

We were alighting from the car when I saw a young man, either American or British, talking with a group of Arabs. I introduced us to him. He was Robert A. Fernia, of the University of Chicago, who was working in southern Iraq on his Ph.D. He and his wife were passing through Shaqlawa on a vacation trip. They too were headed for Haji Omran; and we had dinner with them this same night.

Fernia was interested in tribal organizations now in transition in the Middle East. The settlements on the new lands that Iraq has reclaimed draw heavily on tribal areas. Fernia is interested in the dislocations in tribal and family relations which result from this program. Moreover, he is concerned with the problem of educating the youngsters in tribal areas. When the Iraqi government sends an Iraqi to college, it has a claim on his services. In the field of education, the state gets two years of service for every year of college education. But in general it is one year for one year. But the boys and girls coming from tribal areas are not sent back to the tribes. The result is a disintegrating effect; and the tribes, mostly backward, get no benefits from their eager graduates who make good in Baghdad.

The breakup of old, established institutions in Asia has profound ramifications. Tribes, like castes, give people the feeling of security, of belonging. When the institution breaks up, the people are at loose ends. This is when power vacuums are created, which Communists in particular exploit. We touched on these matters as we sat on a crowded porch of a teahouse at Shaqlawa.

After this village the road follows the Barazan River canyon downstream for several miles, then crosses over an intervening ridge to the Rawanduz. At this point the most beautiful scenery starts. The rocks are highly colored; the cliffs and peaks take fascinating shapes, sometimes almost human. At Gali Ali Beg there are waterfalls. The river falls steeply; the canyon is filled with roaring white water. There are calm, deep blue pools and small cascades from tributaries. The road crosses and recrosses the river over narrow bridges. There is no sign of any fortification. But this is the main invasion route from the north. Should Russia's troops ever move south to begin World War III, they would undoubtedly pour through this canyon. In World War I, Russian troops moved down this gorge, as far as the town of Rawanduz, building a road on the opposite side of the canyon. They undoubtedly would head this way again. And if they did, Iraq would undoubtedly be prepared. I have no idea what the defenses are. But every time the canyon narrowed to fifty or a hundred feet, I imagined that here were mines that would effectively close the canyon to any invader. This is mere surmise. But this beautiful canyon provides such an easy and swift access to the plains that it has high military value.

The town of Rawanduz that the Russians destroyed at the end of World War I lies on the opposite side of the river and off this main highway about five miles. We made the detour to visit it. The city is pitched on a very steep hillside, so steep that our radiator was boiling when we finished the climb. It must have been a spectacular approach by camel train. Then one would see this city-set-on-a-cliff for hours. One loses much of the approach view when he comes by car; for he travels so quickly that the dramatic effect of the location is lost. Actually there is nothing to the city of interest except that approach. We went beyond the city to a high point that overlooks it. It's rather plain and dreary, made up of flat-roofed houses with small yards. The women were dressed in gay colors. But they ran like gazelles with the result that no photographs of consequence could be obtained.

We stopped at a small teahouse below Rawanduz for lunch. It was entirely under one huge oak tree. A cold-water creek ran into a stone-enclosed pool and out below. Here we washed up and rested, while the proprietor and his small son prepared our lunch. He cooked alternate pieces of lamb and tomatoes on a skewer over charcoal. He served this *kabab* with thin unleavened bread, excellent onions, and tea. For dessert he gave us sweet yellow figs. It seemed that every teahouse lunch was better than the last one. Certainly this one was outstanding. And the roar of the small creek and the cool of the shade added to its pleasure.

Above Rawanduz the river forks, one coming in from the south, the other from the east. The road follows the east fork through an oak-studded canyon to Haji Omran, which we reached in about two hours.

This is a village of a few dozen souls just below the top of the pass over the Zagros. It lies nearly 6000 feet high. And it is famous as a ski resort in winter and as a place of rest in summer.

The evening temperatures average about 50° F.; it is seldom over 70° in the daytime. Most of the houses are made of mud and stones. A few are thatched with oak boughs and rice mats. These are the summer houses. There is a year-round rest house with five bedrooms, a dining room, and a kitchen. It was there we stayed. Harold Josif, American Consul at Tabriz, had driven all the way from there to meet us. Lee Dinsmore had come all the way from Kirkuk to say goodbye.

The peaks around Haji Omran rise a couple of thousand feet above the village. Some were touched with snow; but their slopes were barren. We were now above the oaks. This is a big country with turf that has stood up well under the centuries. It is still heavily pounded by sheep and goats. Every June whole families bring their flocks up this canyon for grazing. Their destination is Iran, where they graze high up all summer, making their return trip in October. They pay the Iranian government for this grazing privilege—so many rials a sheep.

I went for a hike out of Haji Omran. Below it I came to a cold mineral spring that has been cemented into a pool. Here several tents were pitched under ancient willow trees. The King's photographer, A. Abbosh, was camped here. He is a stout, rotund man who likes to hunt. He told me about the gazelle and wild boar of Iraq and more particularly about the spring beside his camp. That water is noted throughout Iraq for its medicinal qualities.

"It discharges any kidney stone," he told me. "Doctors send patients all the way from Baghdad merely to drink this water."

We were joined by Fowzi Saib Qaimaqani, the administrator for this district. He, like most of the people in northern Iraq, is a Kurd. These days most of the Kurds are sedentary. But some still tend flocks and migrate in the spring and fall. These Kurds are mostly Sunni or orthodox Moslems. The Iraqi Kurds are organized by tribes, five in number. The leading one in northern Iraq is the Herki tribe. Tribal organization is still strong in the mountains. Loyalty to tribe has long been superior to any other loyalty. They agitated during World War I for a separate Kurdish state. They ended up in large part in Iraq, though some still live in Iran and Syria. This led to revolts in the thirties and early forties.

Kurds and Arabs hated each other for centuries. The Arab had this to say of the Kurd: "There are three pests in the world —locusts, rats, and Kurds." And the Kurd would reply: "Just as the camel is not much of an animal, so the Arab is not much of a man."

There was a day, not many years back, when the Baghdad government did not trust the Kurds. But times are changing. The Kurds are more and more contented. I asked Qaimaqani for the secret.

"There is no secret," he answered. "Once we were foreigners in our own country. Now we are equal with the Arabs. More and more Kurds are coming into positions of importance."

"Is the campaign for an independent Kurdistan ended?" I inquired.

"There's not much sentiment for it these days," he said. "All of us Kurds in Iraq are coming to think of Iraq as our nation."

"Why not?" he added after a pause. "Now we have schools. We are no longer treated like subject people."

We talked about the matter at dinner and decided Qaimaqani had understated the position of the Kurds. The Prime Minister who served until 1956, Nuri Al Said, was part Kurdish. His successor, Ali Jowdat, whom I had met in Baghdad, was a Kurd. The Kurds were no longer making revolution in Iraq; they were running the government.

As I have said, the Kurds are Moslems; and most of them are Sunnis, that is, members of the orthodox branch of the faith. While the issue of Kurds versus Arabs has greatly lessened in recent years, there is another serious fracture within the Moslem community in Iraq. It is the cleavage between Sunnis and Shiites or Shi'as. The Shiite faith, which took root in Iran, has spread throughout the Moslem world; and today the Shi'as are reported to outnumber the Sunnis in Iraq. The Shi'as have important roots in Iraq. For Hossein, the martyred Imam, already mentioned, is buried at Kerbela; and Ali, whom the Shi'as think was the rightful successor of Mohammed, is buried at Najaf. Though the Shi'as use the same mosques as the Sunnis, there is great political rivalry between the two in Iraq. During the Ottoman rule the Sunnis were greatly preferred. The Ottomans were Sunnis; and they saw to it that the Shi'as played second fiddle. Political patronage followed the Sunni line; Shi'as had difficulty getting government jobs. The discrimination was so deep as to reserve the few seats in the public schools to Sunnis. On this trip an Arab friend in Baghdad told me that when he was a boy his father, with tears in his eyes, had told him that under the Ottomans he had been denied entrance to the public schools because he was a Shi'a.

There have been in recent years no overt acts in Iraq to bring religious differences into an ugly clash. But though there is harmony on the surface, old prejudices lie in wait to flare up on any provocation.

Those who managed the July 1958 *coup d'état* recognized the religious-ethnic complex in Iraq. The Council of State or Sovereignty Council which they established has three members—a Sunni, a Shi'a, and a Kurd. The Constitution submitted by the new government goes so far as to proclaim that Kurds and Arabs are now partners in Iraq.

PART 5

PERSIAN KURDISTAN AND AZERBAIJAN

CHAPTER 1

A KURDISH SHRINE

We hated to say goodbye at Haji Omran. We had become specially attached to Kashi. He rode the few miles to the border with Lee Dinsmore. They then turned back to Kirkuk. Hal Josif and his jeep took the lead in escorting us into Iran.

Haji Omran lies only a little west of and below the pass that marks the line between Iraq and Iran. There is no guard at the line—no building, no gate, no barrier until one drops off the mountains on the eastern slopes and reaches the village of Khaneh.

The Shah sent Lieutenant Colonel Mansour Ghadar to be with us on this the last leg of our Iranian journey. The Colonel had his own jeep; and it was he who expedited our clearance through customs and immigration at Khaneh.

This is handsome country. From Khaneh, looking east, there is a great huge bowl many miles long and wide. There are no trees except in draws and along creeks in the bottom lands. The slopes were barren; a few peaks in the background had patches of snow; dark green streaks showed canyons where there was water; as far as one could see, the hills seemed to be covered with a soft brown nap. They looked as soft as velveteen. High cumulus clouds cast moving shadows across them. This day the basin at our feet was a thing of rare beauty. I wondered as I stood there how Alexander the Great felt when he came this way. He had already defeated the Persians near Erbil. Now he was headed up the Rawanduz Gorge to Khaneh, Persepolis, and the Indus River. If the day when he stood at Khaneh was like this day, Asia must have been a powerful magnet. Here is land to embrace. Here one can ride with the wind to almost limitless horizons. It does something to the possessive instincts to see rich land rolling to the horizon.

This was my first view of Persian Kurdistan since 1950; and I felt at home. I had found the Kurds to be friendly people and came to admire their fierce sense of independence. They had much blood on their hands throughout history. But these days they were becoming more civilized. I was eager to be with them again.

We dropped off the slopes below Khaneh to the broad valley and visited briefly an American construction project at Ushniyeh. Our host was Lieutenant Colonel J. J. Hawkins of the Army Engineers. An American firm was erecting barracks for the First Division of the Iranian Army at Ushniyeh. This is a $30,000,000 gift from America. The Iranian Army customarily stays in tents during the winter. This project insures comfortable barracks for the soldiers, administrative headquarters for officers, garages for motor vehicles, and a hospital for the sick. Colonel Hawkins, a most competent engineer, showed us the plans as we sipped good American coffee at his Khaneh headquarters—our first good coffee since New York City. Then we went to see the construction going on at Ushniyeh.

Ali Amir Ashayeri, head of the Mamash tribe of Kurds, sent word, inviting us to visit his place at Pasveh, about twenty miles from Khaneh. There are some fifteen tribes of Kurds in Kurdistan these days. Most of them are sedentary. The Mamash, 10,000 strong, are entirely so.

We left our station wagon at the construction camp and went with Colonel Hawkins by jeep to Ashayeri's home. We had gone only a few miles when we met him and a group of other Kurds, all in jeeps. We stopped and visited for a few moments; then Ashayeri, a huge, broad-shouldered man with immense hands, led the parade of jeeps to his home.

We passed several small mud villages. Each one had many

storks on its rooftops and high stacks of thistles collected for winter forage. Storks are sacred birds in Persian Kurdistan. The natives call them *hadji lac lac*. A *hadji* is one who has made the pilgrimage to Mecca. *Lac* means "to Thee"; and *lac lac* is taken to mean "To Thee praise, to Thee thanks." The storks migrate south every fall. That is the direction of Mecca. Hence their nickname in this valley.

Ashayeri's home is on a knoll perhaps a hundred feet above the valley. Once it was a fortified place. It commands the valley in all directions. The valley immediately below it is dotted with flat-roofed mud villages where this day women were making patties out of cow dung and putting them out to dry for winter fuel. The manor house is a huge, roomy affair built on a courtyard. Mercedes and Mary had a great dividend from this visit. While I stayed with Ashayeri, they visited with his sixteen-year-old wife, his mother, and other ladies of the house. That visit was arranged by Ashayeri's physician—an Indian doctor by the name of P. A. Satralker. This man, a Presbyterian, came from India to the Caspian Sea area to join the staff of the American Hospital at Resht. He had been in Iran for over twenty-eight years and speaks Persian fluently. After he was transferred to the Khaneh construction property he won his way to the hearts of all the Ashayeris by his medical skill. Mercedes and Mary went with him to visit the ladies. They reported drinking tea while sitting cross-legged on a heavily carpeted floor. Their conversation covered the full range that women's tea-party talk touches anywhere in the world. I gathered that Ashayeri's mother and aunt did most of the talking and, if anything, outdid the American ladies. Dr. Satralker was a busy interpreter. Ashayeri took the rest of us upstairs to have tea. The sitting room where we gathered was thickly covered with Persian rugs, one laid on the other. Apart from the rugs, the room had a barren look. There were no curtains, no tables, no flowers of any kind. Tea was served by a barefooted, obsequious servant who had shaved his head.

Ashayeri, like most Kurds, is not retiring. First he told of his gift of land for a part of the Khaneh project. Then he told of his efforts to get the Kurds to put up brick kilns and to find rock quarries for the building materials necessary for the Khaneh projects. He apparently had been successful. For he spoke in glowing terms of the value to local industry of this $30,000,000 American project. As I listened to him talk, I got new light on our foreign aid policy. The amount of American aid a country receives has come to be regarded as a gauge of its political importance. The great aid poured into the project at Khaneh had raised Khaneh and all Iran notches in importance.

I interrupted to ask, "Why should America present Iran with a $30,000,000 army barracks when Iran *per capita* is one of the richest countries in the world, judged by its oil reserves?"

He brushed that question off as his horse in August brushes off the horsefly and went at once to a matter that was very much on his mind. That question was Communism, on which this forty-year-old Kurd had many views.

During World War II the Russians had occupied northern Iran. Ashayeri had been imprisoned by them for thirty-five days. He told me how he had escaped by strangling his guard. The Soviets retaliated by killing seven of his nearest relatives.

Later, when Mossadegh came to power, Kurdistan, according to Ashayeri, was filled with Iranian Communists.

"I killed three myself," he said.

"How do you know they were Communists?"

"I knew. Moreover they supported Mossadegh."

"Did you get into trouble for killing these three men?"

"No," he answered. "I went to the General of the Army here in Kurdistan and told him what I had done."

"What did the General say?"

"He told me to kill as many Communists as I wanted."

He brought out an attractive young boy, not more than twelve years old, whose father the Russians had killed. He was the boy's uncle and was raising the lad to hate Communism with all his heart.

Turning to me, he said, "You are a judge. You can help us fight Communism in Kurdistan."

"How?" I asked.

"You must educate our *mullahs* to be aggressive opponents of Communism. The *mullahs* have real control over the people. You can make them active agents against Communism."

I was saved from this assignment by Dr. Satralker, who came

to tell me to come join the ladies. I went with him across an inner courtyard and up high stone steps into another wing of the house. There I was introduced to Ashayeri's mother, an extremely plump and heavy-set woman, and his very shy and reticent sixteen-year-old wife. Both of them had dressed up specially for the occasion. They wore long full cotton print dresses—the wife white, the mother blue. Each wore an overskirt and bustle of crushed print in contrasting color low around the waist and tied in the back. They had sheer white scarves on their heads; and these headdresses were adorned with gold jewelry, much of it in coins. This jewelry is what is known as their "bank"—the liquid wealth of the family, which in Kurdistan is usually invested in gold. After some cold drinks, we went outside for Mercedes to photograph the ladies. While she photographed them, I photographed her. Then I wandered around the huge estate. In a corner of a courtyard, I found firewood piled to the eaves. I examined it carefully; it was the trunks of young conifers. The wood must have been brought for miles. Any conifers in Kurdistan are high up and few and far between. These conifers were perhaps a dozen years old. Moreover, they had been pulled up by the roots. A land already practically denuded of trees was being scoured. The episode affected me deeply.

As the crow flies from Khaneh to Mahabad, it cannot be even fifty miles. But it takes at least five hours by car, since the road follows two sides of a triangle to avoid high hills. Our first stop was at Naqadeh, a small town not far from Lake Urmia, Iran's great salt lake. We had lunch with the Khosrovis, members of the Qarapajah tribe of Kurds.

Our host was Dr. Bahman Khosrovi, who practices medicine at Mahabad. The luncheon was at the home of his father, Qolamreza Khosrovi. The doctor's mother was present. The home is a typical country home of a middle-class Persian. It is on the outskirts of Naqadeh and headquarters of a large farm. The house is made of stone and is two stories high with an open second-floor porch guarded by a railing. This porch had been recently whitewashed; and it was covered with Persian rugs.

This is country where olives, figs, plums, apricots, and sugar beets are grown. At Naqadeh there's a sugar beet factory owned by the government. Government capital was necessary to build it, as well as the new cement and tobacco factories that have been constructed. For private capital has been too timid to venture into industry.

We sat on the porch of this Kurdish home, cracking pistachio nuts and talking of sugar, as we waited for lunch. Sugar, next to bread and *chai,* is the most important item in the diet of the Persian people. Sugar is always taken with tea. It is served in huge coarse lumps. Four or six lumps may be put in an average-sized cup. Sometimes a countryman may put several lumps in his mouth and sip the tea through them.

Sugar in Iran is a government monopoly. Governments fall if sugar is unavailable. The government monopoly is designed to insure a firm supply. The planting of sugar beets is encouraged. Sugar beet factories are spotted all over Iran. The one at Naqadeh had recently gone up. In 1953 there was a serious shortage of sugar. Iran had not become self-sufficient. Some sugar came down from Russia. Other nations imported it. But Iran was very short. It uses 200,000 tons a year and it had only half that amount. Some villages were indeed completely out. One hundred thousand tons of sugar from the United States saved the day; and some think it may have prevented the emotionalists of Iran from sweeping the nation to the Communists.

The luncheon was one of the most elaborate ones we experienced on the trip. I counted twelve distinct dishes of food on the table. It was served all at once as is customary in informal Persian meals. The table was so heavy with food that even if one sampled each of the main dishes he would have more than he could eat. I took the *kabab* and some *doogh* and finished with delicious stewed cherries and a watery sweet melon.

Then Mercedes assembled the family group in the back yard—women as well as men, and during the course of much giggling and banter took pictures. A baby awoke somewhere in the house. The mother raced to pick it up. But soon she was back to join the group for more picture taking.

The men wore the Kurdish turban—tightly wound with tassels and dark blue. Kurdish men also usually wear a brightly embroidered vest, coarse wool pants, and a brightly colored *kamarband.* One of the Kurds on the porch had been dressed that way; and he had such an attractive face that Mercedes took his picture. But these Khosrovi men wore Western suits—only the blue turbans marking them as Kurds. Their women—who are never veiled—wore pantaloons, gaily colored dresses, sleeveless embroidered jackets over long-sleeved blouses, and sheer white scarves. One who had a magenta skirt over black pantaloons wore a dark cape of velvet over one shoulder—the garment in which the Khosrovis wrapped a Kurdish woman's outfit that they presented to Mercedes.

This turned out to be a two-and-a-half-hour stop for lunch. So we hurried out of Naqadeh, heading north for Lake Urmia. Before reaching there, however, we went off the road a few miles to a place called Hassanloo. Here the University of Pennsylvania Museum has an expedition digging into an ancient *tell*. The man in charge was Robert H. Dyson, Jr. His assistant was Brewster Grace, also an American. The expedition had two jeeps, one called Cyrus, the other Darius I, after two of Persia's great.

These young men are extremely able and personable. They took us on a quick tour of the diggings. In this one *tell* they found artifacts of the Iron Age (1250 B.C.), the Brass Age (1500 B.C.) and the Copper Age (2500 B.C.). They even have traces of the Neolithic Age (3000 B.C.). Their diggings are far from completed. But what they have found is as fascinating as a detective story. One civilization was built on top of the ruins of another. So the *tell* grew in height over the centuries. To put the pieces of pottery together to form a utensil is fairly easy. To identify it by age is not too difficult. But to tell how the household of which it was a part met its end—whether by fire, earthquake, or invasion—is the exciting problem. Listening to young Dyson talk made me see for the first time how exciting those rare moments in an archaeologist's life can be.

When we reached Lake Urmia we were in the midst of a strip of wasteland. Nothing seemed fertile; everything seemed desolate. Yet I remembered a knoll where I had stopped in 1950 to take pictures. When I climbed this knoll, I learned there was life even around a sterile salt lake. For here I found a lovely flower of the mallow family that is now in the National Herbarium, Washington, D.C. It was the flower-of-an-hour (*Hibiscus trionum*), which has sulphur-yellow flowers with purple centers, loved by some but classified as a weed by the experts. We were so late this trip that we did not stop. We roared on in thick dust to Mahabad, arriving at dusk.

Mahabad did not seem to have changed since I saw it in 1950—no growth, no new houses except for one. A new house had been erected for the General of the army in charge of this district. It's a two-story modern brick house set at the back of a small green garden. Its occupant in 1957 was General Karim Varahram; and he met us at the bottom of the steps when our station wagon drew up.

There was a minimum of social amenities this night. For we were all dead tired. We arose early for the long day's journey to Tabriz. There were several stops we wanted to make in Mahabad. First was the Bulagh Chai River, which runs through town. This is a great meeting place in early morning. Here the townsfolk come to get water for drinking and cooking.

One woman had two burros with jugs tied on the side of one and metal tanks or cans on the side of the other. She filled them from the river with a big dipper. Other women brought buckets for filling. Two men brought down a red Persian rug for washing. Men drove their horses and wagons down for watering. Many wagons also forded the river at this point instead of using the bridge. Mercedes and I took pictures for a half hour or so, when I returned to the car to get some new film. As I opened the car door, a lady stepped up and introduced herself. She had come to Mahabad as a young lady from America. She came as a nurse in the Lutheran mission that once was located in Mahabad. That was thirty-two years ago. She married a Kurd and settled down in Mahabad. Her name is Martha Dahl Habibi. She has a son who teaches school there. I asked her how she liked the city.

"The people here are wonderful," she said. "The Kurd is a very superior person."

"Is this a healthy place?" I asked.

Pointing to the river, she said, "See that dirty water? The poor have to drink it. Some of us have deep wells. But most people cannot afford anything but river water."

"What disease is most common?"

"T.B.," she said. "T.B. as a result of the river water and the crowded living conditions."

"Is it very common?"

"A third of the people in this town have T.B.," she said.

Our second stop in Mahabad was at the bazaar. One reaches it by a lane that leads off the main street. There is a covered section or *suk* such as one finds in the large Eastern cities. Here we found the embroidered skullcaps for which Mahabad is famous. Here too we found the turned-up slipper with the pointed toe—typically Kurdish in style. Off the covered bazaar is a compound perhaps a half block square. It is paved with cobblestones. The sides are filled with small shops, each with an awning. In the center are stands of vegetables and even piles of grain. Here the farmers have their markets. Here too are the quilt merchants, who walk up and down, as proud as peacocks, displaying their brightly colored merchandise.

This morning the covered bazaar and the compound too were packed with people. Most of them were men and all of them were Kurds. A dagger was in many of the *kamarbands*. Each man had fierce brown eyes; most of them had a mustache but none a beard; all of them had gleaming white teeth. These are typical of the million Kurds in northern Iran today. The Kurds of Mahabad are of the Mokry tribe. Once they lived on the range, moving with their flocks. Today they are largely sedentary. Many are in professions and in business. Most of them are farmers. They are great individualists with whom Americans would find kindred interests. There still stirs in Persian Kurdistan a desire for an independent nation or at least an autonomous Kurdish state. It was around that political problem that our third mission in Mahabad revolved.

That stop was at the grave of Qazi Mohammed. He was the head of the Kurdish People's Government, with headquarters in Mahabad, from December 15, 1945, to December 15, 1946. Russia had occupied northern Persia during World War II and, before she withdrew her troops in the spring of 1946, established two separate states in northern Persia—one at Mahabad and one at Tabriz. Qazi Mohammed, a deeply religious Kurd, became a tool of Soviet interests, though he himself was not a Communist. His political program during the year he was in power had a Kurdish nationalist slant and served Communist ends. When the Persian Army retook Mahabad on December 15, 1946, Qazi

Mohammed was arrested. And on January 3, 1947, he was hanged.

He is buried at Mahabad and his grave is a Kurdish shrine. Pilgrims come there from hundreds of miles away to pray.

The graveyard is on the immediate edge of town; and like all Moslem cemeteries, it has no grass and few trees or shrubs. There are two small trees that mark the grave. It is the middle of three graves. Each has a head and a footstone; and each is sealed with a concrete slab that rises a few inches above the ground. The grave on the left as one approaches it from the town is that of a nephew. It is marked. But the grave of Qazi Mohammed in the middle and his brother on the right are unmarked. His brother was a Deputy in the Parliament of the Kurdish People's Government. Both he and Qazi were implicated in Soviet schemes. So, like all dishonored men in Persia, they lie in unmarked graves.

Yet, as I have said, Qazi Mohammed, though dishonored by the central government, is honored and adored by the Kurds. Many lined the street leading to the cemetery when we left. They had assembled there during our visit. And each bowed courteously out of appreciation for our visit as we departed.

I stopped to chat with some of the Kurds about Qazi Mohammed and Kurdistan before we left Mahabad for Tabriz. The spirit of independence still burns in Mahabad. I mentioned that in Iraq the movement was no longer strong, that there the Kurds were being absorbed into an Arab state. The answer I got was illuminating.

"Yes, but in Iraq the Prime Minister is a Kurd. In Persia no Tehrani would think of putting a Kurd in the Cabinet."

What my Kurdish friend said is partly true. The tribes of Persia have never been given the rating of political equality which the Kurds of Iraq enjoy. They have seldom been represented in the Cabinet. Ardalan, the Foreign Minister, is a Kurd. A few Kurds have served in the Majlis. But they are the exceptions. A Tehrani often looks with respect on the tribes. Yet he considers them somewhat inferior. I was reminded in Mahabad that Iran had not yet learned the lesson in equality which Iraq is exploiting so successfully.

CHAPTER 2

THE MONGOLS AND A SALT MONOPOLY

The road from Mahabad to Maragheh is a second-class dirt road. It is also a historic route. Some of the Moguls who came down from the north passed this way. And in December, 1946, it was the route traveled by two adventuresome Americans—Clifton Daniels of the New York *Times* and Joseph Goodman of the Associated Press.

Before the Russians evacuated their army from Azerbaijan in the spring of 1946, they helped create two autonomous states in northern Iran. I have already mentioned the Kurdish People's Government in Mahabad headed by Qazi Mohammed. The other was headed by Jafar Pishevari, a Communist who established a "democratic" government at Tabriz. Like the one at Mahabad, it also lasted from December, 1945, to December, 1946.

The Persian Army moved against these two governments, entering Azerbaijan on November 24, 1946. It took one town and waited for orders. No orders came, for Tehran was not sure what organized opposition existed in northern Iran. Clifton Daniels and Joe Goodman were covering "the war." They had a jeep; and for identification purposes they painted an American flag on the side of the jeep. The Persian General in charge of the operation had no orders to allow them to go ahead of the army and no orders to stop them. So they went ahead in their jeep decorated with the American flag. As they moved from town to town word spread that the United States Army was on its way to liberate Azerbaijan. That news went ahead of Daniels and Goodman. Riots took place among civilians. The Pishevari groups attacked the anti-Pishevari groups. Over 500 civilian casualties resulted. By the time Daniels and Goodman reached Tabriz, Pishevari had fled to Russia, taking ten trucks full of loot, including carpets and silverware, with him.

The two newspapermen found Tabriz in a state of war with much street fighting going on. This was nighttime; and to save the jeep from being fired upon they turned out the headlights, one walking ahead with a shielded flashlight to spot the curb. They finally found the Tabriz radio station. No one was there but two Persian engineers. They located the American Consul, Lester Sutton, who suggested to the Persian engineers that the station be opened. They complied and Daniels and Goodman contacted Tehran, arranging for a time when they could relay their stories. Then they sat down and wrote the stories, reopened communication with Tehran, and gave their reports. The story of the fall of Tabriz was in the New York *Times* before it was in the Tehran papers. That was not the only *coup*. Daniels and Goodman reached Tabriz about forty-eight hours before the Persian Army.

Prior to Sutton, Gerald Dooher and Robert Rossow, Jr., had been our Consuls in Tabriz. Both had done heroic work. Late in 1945 and early in 1946, pressure was mounting in the United Nations to make the Russians quit Azerbaijan. The Russians kept telling the United Nations that they were withdrawing their forces. Rossow saw from the window of the Consulate the new Russian tanks that were filling Tabriz. It was Rossow's and Dooher's dispatches from Tabriz that saved the day.

The dirt road north from Mahabad keeps on the 4800-foot plateau where Mahabad is located. The first main town is Miandoab where we stopped to visit a Community Development Project being assisted by our Point IV program. The young Persian in charge, Parviz Sadeqi, invited us into his cool office; and after cold soft drinks were served he addressed us. He had had notice through Hal Josif of our coming, and so he had his remarks prepared. His speech was one of welcome to the three of us and a word of appreciation to me for telling Americans about the Iranians. What he was trying to say was that people-to-people relations were the best way to build understanding and international good will.

Sadeqi has twenty villages in this one Community Development Project. These villages contain 300 people each. He and a small group of Persian workers are endeavoring to modernize them. The first task is to get a pure water supply. For this he resorts to artesian wells that supply a community with water uncontaminated by surface drainage. The second task is to provide a school. The next is to build better houses.

We went with him and two of his workers to one of the twenty villages, a small community called Taghiabad. They had on display a model house, built of brick made in the village. It was a three-room house with a fireplace in one room. A small storage room was off the kitchen. This is a house that any villager could build with his own hands out of bricks baked in the sun of Taghiabad. It was cool in the heat of this August day; and it would be warm in winter when the cold winds blow off Lake Urmia a few miles distant.

Next to the model home was a schoolhouse under construction. In the fields nearby bricks were being molded and placed by hand in the sun to dry. They were collected by wheelbarrows and brought to the base of the wall being built. Bricklayers were on the wall and men were tossing them bricks from below. This schoolhouse was being made ready for the 1957 fall term. It was a primary school; and it would make a break with Moslem tradition and be co-educational. This block of twenty villages had no secondary school; but some were planned by Sadeqi.

This quiet young man talked excitedly about the beginnings of democracy in his twenty villages. Each at last had a council of three to govern it. One member was elected by the people, one was the "graybeard" or leading old man of the village, and the third was appointed by the government. This was a crude beginning in self-government. But it was a start at the grass-roots level. Traditionally the only real voice of authority in the village was the voice of the landlords, who were interested in financial return, not in schools, hospitals, and self-government. The landlords would probably have the loudest voice in these councils of three. But at last other voices would also begin to be heard.

Maragheh lies at 5500 feet about twenty miles east of Lake Urmia. To the north and west are mountains between 8000 and 9000 feet high. The town is set deep in shade and surrounding it are many peach and apple orchards. Here we saw grapes planted in a curious way. The plants were in trenches nearly six feet deep; and the vines grew along the walls of the trenches. Delicious grapes grow here; but there is no winery. The grapes are used mostly for raisins.

The railroad north from Tehran had long stopped at Maragheh. When I visited with the Shah, he told me of his plans to extend the road from Maragheh to Tabriz and from there west to Turkey. Another project would carry the line eastward to West Pakistan. In a few years, the Shah said, a person could get on an air-conditioned train in Istanbul and step off at Karachi, avoiding all the heat, the dust, and the adventure of our seven-thousand-mile automobile journey. When we reached Maragheh we saw the construction to Tabriz under way. And by now it is completed; and that line is today connected with Russia.

Hossein Diraya, Director of Education in Maragheh, was our guide in that city. He took us on an interesting tour. Here Hulagu had his capital. He chose Maragheh for its rich grass, its forests, and its wonderful water—each important for good grazing. Good grazing was high on the Mongol's preference list, for their horses were superb; and they depended heavily on sheep and goats. Hulagu built many edifices in Maragheh, including a library and museum. These buildings are now gone; only a few tombs from the Mongol period remain. One is the Gonbadeh Gafarieh—square-shaped and made of bricks. Another is the Blue Tomb or Gonbadeh Kabud, which is said to be the burial place of Hulagu's mother. But these places, like other ancient buildings in Maragheh, are in great disrepair. Only occasional patches of tile show the ancient beauty of these buildings.

The Safi Rud runs beside Maragheh. Two stone bridges built by Hulagu still stand; they are in daily use and in a fine state of repair.

There are few points of distinction in the city. No one knows for sure where Hulagu was buried. He died in A.D. 1265 and the story is that beautiful maidens were buried with him. Mongol Khans were secretive about their burial places. They wanted to protect their tombs against vandals. One story is that Hulagu was buried in Maragheh; the other is that his tomb is on an island in Lake Urmia. Shahi Island is near the eastern edge of the lake in its northern waters. Here Hulagu built a vault to protect his treasury; and some say the faithful buried him there also.

The Governor of Maragheh, Malik Matani, tendered us a luncheon. Many officials were present, including the exceptionally able Mayor of Mahabad, Mohammed Taqi Alp. We had missed seeing him in Mahabad and he came all the way to meet us here. It was an elaborate lunch topped by sweet Maragheh grapes and Turkish coffee.

The luncheon conversation turned to monopoly versus competition. Historically there have been many monopolies in Iran, some exploited by the government, some by private parties. One monopoly was opium; but that ceased in 1955 with the prohibition of the cultivation of poppies. By a law passed in 1931, the government, to protect the country against control of trade by the Russians, issued licenses for all imports and exports. Quotas were assigned to individuals over various commodities, who thereby acquired a monopoly in the export-import field. But that law has fallen into disuse. There are, however, other monopolies existing today.

The government owns and operates a red oxide mine.

Caviar is a government monopoly. Caspian Fisheries is a government agency that operates on the Caspian. It sells caviar to the highest bidder; but most of the fish goes to Russia under trade agreements.

The match trade is by law a monopoly. In practice, however, the government allows anyone to manufacture matches, imposing only an excise tax on all matches sold and prohibiting all imports.

Tea is another government monopoly. Import licenses are granted only to growers of tea.

Tobacco is also a government monopoly, though here too the government imposes only an excise tax.

Sugar is a monopoly. All the domestic plants are owned by the government. The right to import is held by the Sugar Administration, which sells at a uniform retail price, paying certain taxes to the central government and to the municipality where the sugar is consumed.

The government also has a salt monopoly that is farmed out to individuals on the basis of the highest bid. Mohammed and Ahmed Valanejad are brothers who have the salt monopoly. It's not complete; but it covers from 80 to 90 per cent of all salt consumed in Iran. The monopoly precludes anyone but them from making salt at Lake Urmia, or mining salt in the known quarries. Governor Matani talked at length about the curse of this monopoly. The Valanejad brothers raised the price of salt three times in 1956–1957, causing a great outcry among the householders. The Governor moved into action. He could not get the salt monopoly broken, for it is a grant by the government. But he got the owners of the monopoly to sign a contract reducing the price of salt in Maragheh and agreeing to keep it below a certain level.

I told the Governor about our Sherman Anti-Trust Law and he exclaimed:

"That's what we need in Iran."

CHAPTER 3

THE RED MOUNTAIN

Tabriz is close to the Russian border in northwest Iran. It lies at about 5500 feet. It is surrounded on the north and south and east by orange- and red-colored hills. Its setting is one of the loveliest of Persian towns. It's the second largest (300,000 people) and for a long time was (and probably still is) the largest commercial emporium in Iran.

It has a large colorful bazaar, covered like the one in Isfahan and known as Ghaza. This bazaar has the reputation of being one of the very best in Asia. Marco Polo visited Tabriz and praised its markets. In those days merchants from Europe, Russia, and India met there. Marco Polo observed that, while these merchants were wealthy, "the inhabitants in general are poor." And so it is to this day.

Ibn Battuta, the Moroccan tourist who passed through there in A.D. 1325, wrote that Ghaza was "one of the finest bazaars I have seen this world over." It was so famous for its artisans that when Sultan Salim, the Ottoman Turk, captured Tabriz in 1514 he moved some 3000 artisans and their families to Istanbul. Many think that it was these Persian artisans who gave the Istanbul bazaar the prestige it enjoys today.

Mercedes, Mary, and I roamed the Tabriz bazaar in 1957 but found it disappointing after Isfahan.

We picked up a *droshky* after we left the covered bazaar.

Droshkys fill the streets of Tabriz. The driver sits up front in a higher seat than the passenger. It is pulled by two horses; and old-fashioned lanterns are on each side of the buckboard. These seats are lined with leather, usually red and green. The streets are cobblestone; so the ride is bumpy. But this is the way to sight-see. The business streets of Tabriz are lined with small shops. Most of them are filled with the products of Tabriz factories—leather goods, cotton products, perfumes, silverware, and rugs. Here too are wines of high quality. Many of the shops have American and European products. The Germans fill the camera shops with their film. We fill household appliance shops with electric refrigerators, toasters, and electric mixers.

We visited one factory at Tabriz—the Javan Rug Factory. This factory is thirty-two years old and is typical of the classical capitalism that Karl Marz inveighed against. It employs 2000 people, 400 of whom are women. There is a law that prohibits the employment of anyone under sixteen years of age. Yet I saw many rug weavers who were not more than six or eight years old. I took pictures of them weaving and the proprietor became so nervous that he barred my camera.

This man has the workers organized into a party "to fight Communism." It's a company union of the worst type. They have a band and they often march the streets. There is a restaurant where the children and oldsters may buy lunch. The proprietor has classes for the workers. It is a primary school that starts when the children quit work at five o'clock; and it continues for three hours. Since they work twelve hours a day, Mercedes asked, "Aren't these children too tired to study when they go to school?"

She got no reply.

The beginners get five rials (six cents) a day; the older children, say from twelve years up, get fifteen rials (eighteen cents); the men and women (they are in the minority) get thirty to forty rials a day (thirty-six cents to forty-eight cents). (Note: unskilled labor in Iran gets from twenty to fifty rials [twenty-six to sixty-six cents] a day).

I asked the proprietor why he employed these children.

"There is unemployment in Tabriz. I find work for these people."

"But why employ these little tots?"

"I keep them out of trouble by keeping them off the streets."

"Don't their parents object?"

"Certainly not. They ask me to employ them."

What he said has some truth to it. There is family pressure to put the children to work; and this sweatshop provides an opportunity. A match factory in Tabriz competes with the rug factory for the available child labor. It pays children ten rials (thirteen cents) a day. Their quick little fingers fill more boxes in a minute than I could in an hour.

On another day we saw some of the ruins of Tabriz—quite ancient compared with the sweatshop in the rug factory. Our guide was a learned instructor in the Tabriz High School, A. Bahrelelumi. We saw the Ark which marks the ruins of a mosque built in A.D. 1300 and called Masjed-e Ali Shah. There is very little left these days except one high wall which we reached by a ladder. The Ark was once a fortress and shows marks of its military use. From the top it gives a grand view of Tabriz with the barren mountains in the north running to the Russian border. It was from this high wall, the guide said, that unfaithful wives used to be thrown to their death.

The other ruin we saw was the Blue Mosque or Masjed-e Jahen Shah, built in the thirteenth century. Its main part is largely in ruins, only some of the deep blue tile remaining. On a side that faces a miserable street one room has been repaired for use. Here the faithful come to pray five times daily.

Marco Polo wrote that the Moslems of Tabriz were "treacherous and unprincipled." There is an old Persian saying, "From a Tabrizi thou wilt see naught but rascality." He is different from a Tehrani or Shirazi—more rough and ready, less polished. His life along a troublesome border has made him more severe perhaps, more suspicious of foreigners. But he is a stout individual, one whose pledge of friendship is worth gold. There is a strong Turkish influence in his culture.

The Seljuk Turks took over Iran in A.D. 1055. Persia flourished under their rule; for while the Seljuks conquered by arms, the Persians conquered by culture. Seljuk art, literature, and learning were primarily Persian. Yet the Turks made a big dent on Persia. There are Turki-speaking people in various parts of Iran today. Most of the merchants in the bazaars of Tabriz speak

Turkish. My Tehrani friend, who spoke only Persian, could no longer function as my interpreter.

Tabriz was once called Ta-e-Vrezh, which meant "This is revenge." Some say it was given that name by King Chrosroes I of the Armenians, who sacked the town near the middle of the third century. Others say the Armenian victory was under Arshak II about a century later. One authority thinks these two Armenian events may have become fused in time, both of them happening. The Persians do not accept these stories. They say that Tabriz was founded as a result of a visit of a wife of the famous Harun al-Rashid to gain relief from a fever. Since Queen Zulaikha recovered, the place received the name Tab-Riz, i.e., "the fever has poured out or gone." The difficulty with this version is that Zulaikha lived about A.D. 800, which was long after Tabriz had become known by that name. Perhaps the best version of all is one passed on to me by one of our foremost experts in this area. In 714 B.C., Sargon II, a famous Assyrian King, conquered a fortified region around Tabriz. The name of the fort, transliterated from the cuneiform, reads Tawra, a word from a lost language that became corrupted into Tabriz. That means that Tabriz is at least 2700 years old.

The Mongol ruler Arghun (1284–1291) made Tabriz his capital. Hulagu, his grandfather, had inaugurated a rule of tolerance for all religious minorities. Bar-Hebraeus, Christian historian of the thirteenth century, wrote: "With the Mongols there is neither slave nor free man, neither believer nor pagan neither Christian nor Jew; but they regard all men as belonging to one and the same stock." Arghun sent emissaries to Europe to enlist the help of Christendom in liberating Syria and Palestine from the Mamaluks. He even declared that he himself would become a Christian if Jerusalem were taken. Nicholas IV, Pope of Rome, was in friendly alliance with him. Islam trembled for fear the Temple of Mecca would be converted into a cathedral.

Under the early Persian dynasties (539–331 B.C.) the Jews had flourished and enjoyed considerable autonomy. Alexander the Great favored them, in line with his policy of letting minority cultures develop without hindrance. But it was not until the Mongol Arghun that the Jews were beneficiaries of a rank discrimination.

Arghun went so far as to issue a decree that only Christians and Jews were to be given administrative posts. As a result Sa'd ad-Daula and other Jews rose to top ranks in government; and Moslems were banned from court. Sa'd ad-Daula was a physician whom Arghun found to be indispensable. From doctor he became adviser to the King. Then he moved up to Investigator of the Revenues and from there to Controller. At last he became First Minister or Vizier. But the cry against "Jewish domination" soon meant his ruin. Shortly before Arghun's death Sa'd ad-Daula was murdered.

Arghun's successor, Gaykhatu (1291–1295), also summoned a Jew, Rashid ad-Daula, to his staff. But the next, Il Khan Ghazan (1295–1304), put an end to this tolerance. He became a Moslem and dashed the hopes of Christianity. Once more, Christians and Jews became People of the Book. Now the Jew Rashid ad-Daula turned Moslem and became Rashid ad-Din. He, in turn, became Vizier. But his enemies did not let him hold power long. He was murdered and his head dragged through the streets of Tabriz. A century after his death the ruler of Tabriz had the bones of Rashid ad-Din removed from the Moslem cemetery in Tabriz and put in the Jewish cemetery. This intolerant Il Khan could not allow the body of a Jew to lie next to bodies of true Moslems.

Tabriz was the scene of the execution of the Bab, founder of the Bahai religion. On July 9, 1850, he was hung from a scaffold by a rope under his arms. His companion, also executed, was Agha Mohammed Ali, a young merchant of Tabriz. Their execution was by a firing squad. At the signal the shots rang out. Ali was killed but the Bab was not touched. The bullets merely cut the ropes by which he was hung and he fell to the ground unharmed. The firing squad refused to fire again, and in that instant it seemed that the miracle of the Bab might sweep Iran from its Moslem foundations. But a quick-witted officer summoned another firing squad which quickly killed the Bab, putting an end to any mysticism about his powers. His corpse was then dragged through the streets and cast out of the city to be devoured by jackals. After much movement and concealment of the body, it was brought years later to Mount Carmel in Israel, where it now rests.

One day in Tabriz as Mercedes, Mary, and I were window-shopping, a tall heavy-set man about forty years of age came out of a shop and called me by name. How he knew me, I do not know. He was a Bahai who runs a shop in Tabriz. He invited us in, produced cold soft drinks and huge pistachio nuts, and brought us up to date on the Bahais. They are 1200 strong in Tabriz. They meet in each other's homes and are very active proselytizing their faith.

I asked if there was a shrine of the Bab here in Tabriz. He said there was not; and he took me down the street to show me why. There on the spot where the Bab was executed stands a new public school with all the appearance of a permanent institution.

"The site was chosen so that this spot could never become a Bahai shrine," my friend added.

We stayed with the Josifs in Tabriz in the commodious home that sits in the center of the American compound. Tabriz is short of water; so none of the gardens or compounds is as green as those in Isfahan. But the American compound is nonetheless attractive, adorned by small peach trees and shrubs. It's a peaceful, relaxing place in the summer. But come winter when the north wind whistles, the wolves often enter the compound and howl.

One evening we went with the Josifs and some other American and Iranian friends to Shah Gali for dinner. This is a restaurant on the side of an artificial lake built on the outskirts of Tabriz. There are boatmen with inboard motors to take one across. On the way out we came to a height of land where I could see the northern mountains that lie between Tabriz and Russia. Here was the Red Mountain for which Tabriz is famous. The last glow of sunset was on it. In Arizona the Red Mountain would have reminded me of symphonies or of poetry. In Tabriz it reminded me of all the blood this border town had spilled.

It seemed in that instant that the fanatics of all religions were the same the world over. Persia in a sense was the victim of that fanaticism; and the story of how she recovered from it and survived is one of the most interesting chapters of modern history.

Before the Arabs conquered Persia, the Persians were accustomed to call Semites "lizard eaters." They held the Arabs in low esteem. The Persians were Aryans. Iran, indeed, means The Home of Aryans. After the Arab conquest, the Persians accepted Islam because it was forced on them. But they took it only skin-deep and modified it. They became Shiites or Shi'as rather than Sunnis. And Sufism modified their philosophy.

The Sufists drew from the Koran the philosophy that only God—not the Islamic creed—is supreme. "All else is but a vision that disturbs the sight." To them God is not only the pure and holy but the eternally beautiful Being.

The aim of life is the renunciation of self by the release through love. The love of men leads up to God. Jami wrote:

> Though in this world a hundred tasks thou tryest,
> 'Tis love alone which from thyself will save thee.
> Even from earthly love thy face avert not,
> Since to the Real it may serve to raise thee.
> Ere A, B, C are rightly apprehended,
> How canst thou con the pages of thy Kur'an?
> A sage (so heard I), unto whom a student
> Came craving counsel on the course before him,
> Said, "If thy steps be strangers to love's pathways,
> Depart, learn love, and then return before me!
> For, shouldst thou fear to drink wine from Form's flagon,
> Thou canst not drain the draught of the Ideal.
> But yet beware! Be not by Form belated;
> Strive rather with all speed the bridge to traverse.
> If to the bourn thou fain wouldst bear thy baggage
> Upon the bridge let not thy footsteps linger."

Each nation seems to have a dark, ugly streak somewhere deep in the subconscious. Persia has one. But her spiritual side, part of which is expressed in Sufism, finds expression in compassion.

Compassion is reflected in many Persian attitudes. One of the most conspicuous is the provision of Persian law that no one over sixty years old shall be executed for any crime, no matter how heinous. Another is that no woman shall ever be executed for any crime.

CHAPTER 4

LANDLORDS AND TENANTS

One day in Tabriz the Josifs arranged a picnic for us. Hal Josif could not go. His wife Sylvia and daughter Elaine went; and so did Mr. and Mrs. Clifford A. Rajala, Jared Jones, and Hossein Zadeh Fard. We traveled by jeep up the canyon of the Talkeh Rud, which runs by Tabriz, taking one of the spurs to the northwest. It was a good hour-and-a-half drive, the cars climbing all the way. Our destination was Lighvan, a village perched on the side of the canyon wall about 7500 feet high.

This village of almost 100 families overlooks a fertile valley well watered by a small tributary of the Talkeh Rud. In the valley they grow apples, wheat, vegetables, and hay. The land is all owned by the Lighvani family, three of whom were there to greet us—Abdullah Ghasem, about seventy years of age, and Davoud and Mousa, both middle-aged.

Why the village is located high on the canyon wall is a mystery. Most Persian villages lie snug in a valley, getting some protection from winter blasts in thick stands of poplar or willow. The villagers of Lighvan are much more exposed, especially since their houses are on the northern slope of the canyon wall. Perhaps they are there to avoid heavy runoffs in the spring. For the snow lies deep in this valley in wintertime. But they are more likely on the canyon wall because a wonderful spring of clear cold water is located there. It is a community well where women come frequently with jugs and buckets for water.

The Lighvanis have a summer house on a wide ledge below the village. It's a five-room comfortable house which they turned over to us for the day. It commands a fine view of the valley where the fields are located and to which the villagers must descend every morning for work.

By the time of our visit most of the work in the fields had ended. The harvest was in or coming in. The wheat, cut by hand sickles, had been tied in sheaves, placed on the backs of donkeys, and brought up to the village. Now the wheat lay on the thrashing floor while animals walked in a circle to pound out the heads. The thrashing floor was the flat roof of the house. As we climbed about four hundred feet to the top of the canyon and looked down upon all the houses we saw that every rooftop was a thrashing floor. Some were in the process of thrashing. Other villagers were pitching the straw in the air so the wind would separate it. Still others were putting the golden wheat in sacks for the winter.

Each house had a cow; a few had sheep. Boys were busy bringing bundles of hay, thistles, and weeds up the canyon for winter fodder. Beneath this great activity was a plan for each family. No household has a drone. The tiniest child picks up sticks, straw, and dung for fuel. Everyone has a job to do.

Lighvan represents a typical landlord operation that is not particularly enlightened. Nor is it unduly oppressive. It results, however, in a cycle of unenlightenment and stagnation.

There is no school, hospital, movie house, or drugstore at Lighvan. For amusement the people have only themselves. There are dances at weddings. But the big day of the year is *No Ruz,* the Persian New Year. While the Arabs foisted the lunar calendar on the Persians, the Persians do not count their New Year on that basis. *No Ruz* is truly a New Year, for it comes at the vernal equinox, on the first day of spring. This is the real holiday of all Persians. They dress up, exchange gifts, and dance. The humble villagers of Lighvan try to taste sugar early that morning to ward off misfortune for the rest of the year. And they eat *pilau* with greens in it to assure that they will not be penniless or hungry during the New Year.

There is no village council in Lighvan. The only voice of

authority is the landlord. This landlord is not malevolent. The Lighvans take care of their villagers. But to one born there no opportunity for escape exists. He is doomed to the dreary treadmill his ancestors walked. The brains from this bottom stratum will have no chance to enlighten the nation.

Azerbaijan has been notorious for its landlords. Here there has been greater exploitation of sharecroppers than anywhere in the Middle East. The worst offenders are not those, like the Lighvanis, who live in the village. The oppressive practices have come from the absentee landlords. I had seen much of these evils on my earlier visits. Though in general on irrigated land the tenant gets two thirds of the crop and on unirrigated land four fifths, his annual return is greatly cut down by the interest the landlord charges on loans. There is no agricultural credit system for the farmers of Iran. The landlord (and the grocer) are the two main credit institutions. The interest rate depends on what the market will stand—100 per cent is common; 400 per cent is not uncommon. Many a tenant never gets out of debt. He often is paying on what his father or grandfather borrowed.

As a result of my previous experiences in Azerbaijan, I expected to find that it had made the least progress in land reform. But I was mistaken. Azerbaijan is way out front in village development work.

No small credit is due to the Governor, Ibrahim Zand, whom I had first met in Isfahan in 1949. I called on him in Tabriz to pay my respects; and he told me over a cup of tea of his pride in the village development work. He said that this program was in 4000 of the 7000 villages in Azerbaijan. I found that this was a conservative estimate; for by late summer 1957 projects were under way in 5000 Azerbaijan villages.

In these villages councils have been selected. In some there are three members of the council; in most there are five. One is always elected by the people; one is always the graybeard; and the balance are named by the Governor. In practical operation this means that the landlords control the councils.

There is a school on the Veramin Plain, near Tehran, for village-level workers. They take a nine months' course there and then are assigned to the villages. Where a program has succeeded, it has been due entirely to the village-level worker.

The 5 per cent law, already mentioned, works pretty well in Azerbaijan. The 5 per cent of the crops set aside is administered by the village councils. Since this 5 per cent comes from the landlord's share of the crop, he wants to get credit for improvements. Often he now does things on his own, such as building a schoolhouse or installing a sanitary water supply, without waiting for the 5 per cent to be collected. These improvements are often in addition to those made from the 5 per cent fund. The 5 per cent law has, in other words, made the landlords more village conscious. No great revolution is sweeping the villages of Azerbaijan. But progress is being made, bit by bit, to bring the decencies of civilization to communities that have known nothing but desolation throughout time. The greatest stride forward is in the introduction of primary schools. These are cropping up everywhere these days. For the first time in history a child born in a mud hut of Azerbaijan may not be destined to illiteracy.

Of all the primary schools started only one so far is co-educational. Old habits and *mores* are hard to change. The pressure both from the family side and from the *mullahs* is for segregation of the sexes. So in modern Azerbaijan segregation is the order of the new day.

We talked of these village programs the day we had the picnic at Lighvan. The Lighvanis—the landlords—have not yet moved to place Lighvan under this new program. But they have had cruel warning of the arrival of a new age. When Pishevari's government ruled Azerbaijan, terrorists were sent against the landlords.

The master of this terror was not Pishevari but Mohammed Beria, Minister of Labor, Education, and Propaganda. He was a little man with a dark mustache. He was very tough and cocky. He had risen to power through the Street Cleaners' Union of Tabriz. He had a goon squad known as the Society of Friends of Soviet Azerbaijan. One night the goon squad came to Lighvan and killed seven members of the Lighvani family.

On December 12, 1946, after the Russian troops had withdrawn from Tabriz and before the Iranian troops had reached the city, a mob seized Beria and killed him, dragging his body up and down the streets of Tabriz behind a jeep.

CHAPTER 5

WHERE IS THE MOON?

We had the good fortune to meet in Tabriz Captain Victor H. Wood, head of our military mission there. Learning of our car troubles, he assigned Sergeant Anthony S. Bifora to look it over. As a result of this fine mechanic's diagnosis we had extensive repair work done. We had the brakes relined. He found several leaves in the rear springs broken. We replaced them. We installed new spark plugs and new points; and we bought new American tires in the bazaar. The Sergeant's careful inventory showed that somewhere between Baghdad and Tabriz we had broken the casings in three tires and that we were now headed for some resounding blowouts.

Hal Josif had government business in Maku so he accompanied us in his car, when we left Tabriz in the early morning of August 27 for Turkey. It is less than three hundred miles; but the roads are all dirt; and there are stretches where travel is very slow. For this reason we started bright and early, planning also to take a side trip to Lake Urmia while we were en route east. It was this side trip that was costly in time and that put us into Maku quite late at night.

We left the main road from Tabriz to Maku at a village called Sufian. It's not much over fifty miles from there to Lake Urmia. But it took us over two hours to make it. This road was crossed by innumerable irrigation ditches and creeks.

After traveling this road, I came to understand why it was a pious act for a Zoroastrian to build a bridge—in which definition I would include a culvert. Our car was so low that we had to creep across these ditches and creeks and usually angle them so as not to scrape bottom. We had deep ruts to avoid and high centers to ride. It was midmorning when we reached the end of the road at Sharifkhaneh on the northeastern shore of Lake Urmia.

It is across the lake at Resaiyeh that Zoroaster is supposed to have lived. In that vicinity are found ash hills or mounds that marked the fire shrines of the Zoroastrians. Sharifkhaneh is a hot, bleak, and barren spot where the Russians in World War II built a spur track to connect with the railroad line that they extended from Julfa in Russia to Tabriz. The spur track from Lake Urmia was constructed to pick up traffic coming across Lake Urmia from Resaiyeh on the west shore by ferry. To facilitate the handling of this traffic, the Russians built a quay about one mile in length into the lake. Railroad tracks run the length of it.

Our reason for visiting Lake Urmia was not the traffic; for precious little of it moves across the water these days. We went there to see the mud bathers. Lake Urmia is noted for its mud. This black malodorous mud is said to have medicinal qualities. People with arthritis, rheumatism, tendonitis, bursitis, or just ordinary aches and pains come here for mud baths. There is no sanitarium here. Men use one section of the beach about a mile from the place where the women enter. One goes to the beach with as little clothes on as possible and rolls in this thick oozy mud that is several feet deep. He becomes caked with it. After lying for hours encrusted in it, he takes to the water and bathes. There is a grove of poplars back from the beach where some people come for weeks and take their daily baths.

"How they stand the stench of the mud, I do not know," Mercedes said.

Many were in the mud when we arrived. But even so it was an hour before we got our pictures, which meant we got back to the main road in five hours after we left it, or about two o'clock. This was most embarrassing because Governor Dehgan had invited us to luncheon at Khoi. We were still seventy-five miles from that town; and hurry as fast as we could, we did not reach it until nearly five o'clock. On this journey we were so much in a hurry we did not even stop at shady Marand where Noah's wife is supposed to be buried. This is pleasant rolling country with the bottom lands well irrigated not far from Khoi. While we stopped to look at a tire, Colonel Ghadar pointed out a small shrine on a height of land.

"People who have hydrophobia or snakebite go there to be cured," he said.

"Are you teasing?" I asked.

"By thy precious life, I am not," he said.

A gray-haired Persian named Hairik A. Mayva, who works in the American Consulate at Tabriz, was with Hal Josif on this trip. So I turned to Mayva and asked: "Why did the Colonel swear by my life rather than by his own?"

"In Persia," Mayva answered, "to swear by one's own life is to swear by something not as precious as the other man's life."

The Governor was waiting at the steps of his administration building when we drove up—four hours late for lunch. We all apologized. But this hospitable man brushed away our concern with friendly handclasps and ushered us into his office where we took turns washing up. Then we went upstairs to a large room where lunch was served.

There were many toasts at this luncheon—all in Pepsi-Cola—and a few speeches. The lunch was closer to an American meal than any we had had on our trip—vegetable soup, meat patties, broiled chicken, and fried potatoes.

We ate and ran, for Governor Mohammed Ghaffari had invited us to dinner in Maku and it looked as if we would be late to it too.

Colonel Ghadar told me not to worry, that he would telephone ahead.

"Moreover," he added, "you must remember that in Iran no dinner is served until 10 P.M. or even later."

That is true. One invited for an eight o'clock dinner sits down at the table a couple of hours later. The Persians use the few hours before a meal for conversation. Dinner is served very late. And when it is over, etiquette requires that the guests leave at once.

This custom saved us at Maku. It was dark within an hour after we had quit Khoi. The wind came up. It fairly howled down from the north, sweeping ahead of it great clouds of dust. Fortunately it blew crosswise of the road. Yet even so there were times when we were momentarily completely lost in dust, making it necessary to come to a stop. There was no shelter from this howling wind, for we traveled most of the way on high ground, either on an exposed plain or on an escarpment, never on the lee side. About an hour out of Maku the road makes an elbow to the northeast. At this point we were only sixteen miles from the Russian border. Hal Josif in the lead stopped his car not far from the Iranian village of Poldasht on the Aras River. Beyond the Aras were a group of blinking lights. They marked the town of Shakhtakhty in Azerbaijan SSR.

Maku is an ancient town, noted largely for the fact that here the Bab was imprisoned for some months before his execution in 1850. A huge rock cliff with a vast overhang is to the right of the road as one enters from the east. Most of the town is built on the slopes leading up to this overhang or immediately under it. The site was chosen originally for the protection it afforded against invaders. The overhang gave some protection and simplified the problem of defense.

In A.D. 1403, Clavijo, Spanish Ambassador to Tamerlane, came through Maku and found the place ruled by a Roman Catholic. There was a Dominican monastery there. The castle of the King stood at the foot of this cliff; and a great wall surrounded the place, running up the slopes to join the cliffs.

Not even the cliff could be seen this dark dusty night. The lights in the houses under the cliff were all extinguished. Maku lay in pitch-darkness except for a lantern on the edge of the main street. This marked the entrance to Governor Ghaffari's home. When we stopped, he soon joined us; and with his jeep escort leading the way, we went ten miles east of Maku to a famous old palace called Bagh-cheh Jough where we stayed the night.

I had been in this palace before in 1950. It's a gaudy and pretentious place built early last century. It's set in the midst of apple trees, nicely terraced. There are neat gardens and a lovely pool. The rooms are high-ceilinged. The walls are covered with decorations, some grotesque. There are paintings of voluptuous women on some walls. In the main reception room on the second floor is a ceiling painted to show a Persian meal being served. Another panel shows a Western meal being served. Wherever one looks a painted wall greets him. Overhead are large cut-glass chandeliers. On the floor are many Persian rugs.

The man who built Bagh-cheh Jough had a principality of his own. He had an army and he administered the affairs of this northwest corner of Persia. His son took his place and Reza Shah, father of the present Shah, deposed the son, seized the palace, and made it an Iranian government show place.

I figured that each bed was so large it would hold at least four people. The bedrooms were on a balcony of the second floor. One looked down from his bedroom onto a dance floor at ground level. In the candlelight the shadows created an eerie feeling.

"Not even a guard rail," screamed Mercedes.

So we lined up chairs and moved furniture to protect a sleep-walker from a dreadful drop of one story.

A sumptuous dinner was served by Governor Ghaffari at eleven o'clock. Some of his staff, including the Judge Advocate General Hassan Farjadi, were there. Many toasts were offered, including toasts to President Eisenhower and His Majesty the Shah.

We talked of Mount Ararat, which looks down on Maku from the northwest. The legend is that Noah landed his Ark there. In recent years expeditions have climbed Ararat, looking for pieces of the Ark. The persistence of the legend is indicated by the fact that the people in Maku often refer to Ararat as the Mountain of Noah.

The origins of Maku are lost in history. Those present at the dinner would not venture a guess as to its date. Some said that Alexander the Great marched through here. But that, I thought, was borrowing prestige, for Alexander entered Iran farther south. Finally I turned to the Governor and asked:

"What does Maku mean?"

He gave me a long account of an ancient King of Maku who moved in the moonlight one night against his enemy. The aim was to catch the opponent off guard. The troops with the King in the lead marched quietly through one of the canyons that empty out on the plain around Maku. At one point the canyon walls rose so steeply that they shut out the moonlight. In the pitch-dark of the canyon the King cried out:

"Ma ku? Ma ku?"

"What did he mean?" I asked.

"He meant," the Governor answered, " 'Where is the moon?' "

PART 6

TURKEY

CHAPTER 1

MERHABA

The morning of August 28 was cool, bright, and glorious. The air was fresh. There was no cloud in the sky. We could hardly wait for our tea and soft-boiled eggs, served in the garden of the palace, to get on the road to Turkey. Two weeks earlier I had sent word to the Turkish government that we would be at Bazargan, the point of entry on the Iranian-Turkish border, at 8 A.M. on August 28. We had had to push to make that schedule. Now that we were so close, I wanted to keep it. We also wanted to see Maku in daylight and to photograph Mount Ararat early. In the summer, clouds form around its top before the day is far gone. Early morning pictures of it are the best.

On our way back to Maku we got excellent shots of Ararat across stands of corn and tobacco fields. By the time we had photographed Maku, filled our tank with gasoline, and said our farewell to the Governor and his staff, it was seven o'clock. Then we headed the fifteen miles or so to Bazargan and the Turkish border. The road out of Maku is an excellent dirt highway. We were making good time, when we saw a great number of nomads on the move. We parked our car and ran across fields of thistles to get a picture of several families with a dozen or more camels, each heavily loaded, headed north toward the Russian border. We no sooner got this picture, with Mount Ararat as background, than another group appeared. They too had camels. Once more we started back to the car when we saw still another group following. They were on horses and donkeys. We waited to get pictures of them. It was apparent that this was a tribal migration. Inquiry developed that these were Jalali Kurds headed for some new camp along the Aras River, which marks the Soviet border. This was the advance contingent. The rich Jalalis had the camels; the poorer ones, the donkeys. Here came the sheep by the thousands, herded by big gray dogs. Beautiful horses came into view, while dogs trotted behind. Women rode some of these horses. They had large woven bags on each side of the saddle to hold their small children. Each bag was designed to fasten under the child's armpits so that his arms were out and the body was held up. One lady had a child on each side of her saddle, both asleep. She obliged me and stopped so that I could get some pictures.

Once we ran out of film and had to race back to the car to refill the cameras. We returned on the run to get pictures of new family groups. They kept coming over a hill to the south. How many hundreds of familes there were in this migration, I do not know. It looked as if it would take hours for them to pass. This was a photographer's heyday, for the light, the setting, and the people were fascinating.

But when I looked at my watch to discover it was already eight-thirty o'clock, I called the picture taking off and we resumed our journey. I was needlessly in haste. For although we reached the border at 9 A.M., the Turks did not expect me so soon. For there is a time zone along the Turkish-Iranian border that puts Turkish time an hour and a half behind Iranian time.

Outside the main building at Bazargan twelve Iranian gendarmes presented arms as we passed. At customs and immigration, Hasham Sattani gave us quick service. The buildings at Bazargan are arranged in the form of a courtyard, the border running down the middle. A young man in his twenties, Vedat Uras, crossed the courtyard to greet us. He was sent by the Turkish government to be our interpreter.

We hated to say goodbye to Hal Josif. He had been with us almost continuously for a week and we had developed a deep affection for him. But time pressed on us. Our stop this night would be in far-off Erzurum, Uras said. So we drove the station wagon across the courtyard and arrived in Turkey at the far side. As we waited for customs and immigration clearance, Uras said: "There is a guard of honor to meet you."

I walked with him through an archway of the customs building to find on the side of the road, leading to Erzurum, a group of nine Turkish soldiers. They came to attention and presented arms.

Uras whispered, "You are supposed to say '*Merhaba*' to them."

"*Merhaba,*" I shouted. And they shouted back:

"*Sagol, sagol.*" Then they marched away.

"What did we say?" I asked Uras.

"*Merhaba* is a salutation like the English hello; and *sagol* means long life."

It warmed our hearts to get this hearty welcome. And in retrospect it seems that *merhaba* and *sagol* were symbolic of the Turkish hospitality we received along fifteen hundred miles of roads.

Never have we been taken so quickly and so completely into the hearts of a people.

CHAPTER 2

A GRACIOUS GOVERNOR

Eastern Turkey is handsome country. The dirt road ahead of us stretched over rolling hills as far as the eye could see. As I stood at Turkish customs facing into Turkey, Mount Ararat was straight ahead. Shortly the road bore south, putting snow-capped Ararat on the right. Now it seemed close enough to touch. Beyond it was Little Ararat, free of snow; and in between was a swayback saddle. This is big country. From the border looking west there's no sign of habitation. It looked to me much like our Wyoming and Colorado. It's country for horses and cattle, for riding with the wind, for unfenced pastures, for unlimited horizons.

This is part of the country known to Marco Polo as Armenia Major. He mentioned the legend connecting Noah with Ararat; he called it "the mountain of the ark." The early Greeks called this "good horse-pasturing" country. Marco Polo commented on how abundant the vegetation in this valley was, how good the pasture for cattle, how cold the weather and deep the snow in winter. Xenophon and his Ten Thousand came through here on their great retreat from Persia. It was here that Xenophon experienced cold, drifted snow, and a howling north wind. He wrote in the *Anabasis:* "One of the augurs, in consequence, ordered that they should sacrifice to the wind; and a sacrifice was accordingly offered; when the vehemence of the wind appeared to every one manifestly to abate."

The day we crossed this region, white cumulus clouds dotted a deep blue sky. The air was freshly washed by a storm that had preceded us. The good dirt roads—for which modern Turkey has become famous—had been so thoroughly sprinkled that there was no dust. There were no washboard ruts crosswise of the road, no high centers to ride. This was true the entire fifteen hundred miles across Turkey, east to west. A nation, once notorious for poor communications, has now superb dirt highways everywhere.

For thirty miles or more beyond the border we were in a big handsome bowl running northwest by southeast. There was no farming in sight. Not an acre of ground seemed to have been tilled. This is grazing land—and de luxe land at that. Mount Ararat gives it beauty and water gives it fertility. This huge bowl runs northeast to Russia. Once it was part of ancient Armenia. There are many blood-and-thunder stories written of massacres and persecutions in this broad pleasant land of eastern Turkey. But they are all a part of history. Hardly any Armenians live here any more. They are not banned; they just chose to leave. Most of them left Turkey for Armenian SSR twenty years or more ago. Some went northeast up this broad valley across the Russian border thirty miles distant. Others caught Russian boats going from the Persian Gulf and Mediterranean ports through the Black Sea to Batum. They traded much of their freedom for a homeland in Russia. Today, Armenia Major is filled only with memories of bloody conflicts. Of the 24,000,000 people in Turkey now, only about 55,000 are Armenians. One finds a family here and there in eastern Turkey. But practically all of them now live in Istanbul.

After thirty miles we came to the first Turkish town, Dogybayazid. It's a small place of a few hundred families. It has on it the mark of the poverty of the East. The houses are rather ugly stone affairs. A few spindly trees adorn the place. But there is no grass or shrubbery. No touch of husbandry. The men who gathered round, when we stopped the car for pictures, were dressed differently than most villagers from the Indus on west. There were no more flowing pantaloons and long oversize shirts that hung below the waistline. No more turbans. No more *kafeyahs.* The Turkish villager is Westernized in dress—trousers, belt, shirt, and coat. He has one distinctive mark—the coarse cap. This we were to see all the way across Turkey. The women of Turkey have made less of a break with Middle Eastern attire than the men. They have the right to vote and the right to hold office guaranteed by Articles 10 and 11 of the Constitution. In these and in other ways Turkish women have equal political rights with men. There is no such thing as *purdah* in Turkey. Ataturk abolished it in the 1920s. But women's styles and habits are not easy to change and customs have their deepest roots in rural areas. We were to see few veiled women on the streets of any Turkish cities. In Dogybayazid, however, every woman wore a scarf over her head; and it was wound loosely around her face so as to show only her nose and eyes. Some of these scarves were white, some blue or black. But every peasant woman wore one. It was mostly for protection against wind and weather. It was in part the residue of the veil which long relegated woman to the background and that still keeps the bulk of the women of the Middle East in second-class citizenship. In Turkey it is a stylistic tie to an ancient past.

It is a bit over fifty miles from Dogybayazid to Agri; and we took not much over an hour to cover the distance. The car purred beautifully. It was a pleasure to drive. The road was smooth, hard-packed, and almost as straight as an arrow. It went up and down over low hills such as one finds in South Dakota, passing cornfields where the harvest had been pretty well finished. Mount Ararat was always on the right, hiding Little Ararat from view as we moved west. White fleece clouds were low around the snow-capped peak, giving it a halo. The sight of corn harvested and the tang of cool air made fall seem close at hand.

Agri—pronounced Ah-ree—might well be a cow or sheep town in the fringe areas of our own West. Agri was known in the beginning as Bayazid and once as Karakose. It was an Armenian town where many massacres took place. It now has 20,000 people. The streets are not paved; a couple blocks have cobblestones. There are few trees for shade. Several buildings are two-storied; every structure is of stone. They are built for warmth, since Agri in the winter lies deep in snow under freezing temperatures.

Agri is the capital of a province that has 200,000 people. We stopped on the main street at a building which by its imposing nature showed that it must be the administrative headquarters for the province. While the ladies waited, Uras and I went inside so that I could pay my respects to the Governor. We walked up a flight and were soon escorted into a spacious office of the Governor, Ali Akseven. He is a bachelor—short, dark, slightly corpulent, and about forty years old. He is pleasant to meet, quick-witted, and a fine conversationalist. He speaks a bit of English as shown by a letter we received shortly after our return to the States:

"The heat of your friendness is deep enough to reach us though we are far away. We are very sorey that we couldn't do what we want during the very short time you have been in Agri. We are being friends with all Americans and your very much valuable personals. We send our best wishes to the Douglas family."

On my arrival in his office this August day he invited us to lunch at once. He apologized for the restaurant in Agri, though we were to learn that Turkish restaurants, even in the small country towns, were good. The luncheon to which we were invited was to be in his home; and before we left his office to meet the ladies downstairs, he had telephoned his sister, with whom he lives, that we were on the way to the house.

The house might well have been one from our own Midwest. The low mud wall around it was indigenous to this part of the world. But the stucco finish of the house, its high ceilings, its coal-burning stove in a corner of the living room, the lace curtains, the rather decrepit chandelier with its electric bulbs, family pictures on the wall, an old-fashioned rocker and couch, the indoor plumbing fixtures—all these suggested to me a middle-class family home in America built about 1910. They are probably the reason why I immediately felt at ease. His sister, large-framed, pleasant and courteous, and also an excellent cook, greeted us. And while she went to work in the kitchen, Akseven entertained us in the parlor.

Akseven, like all provincial Governors, represents the central government at Ankara. He is appointed by the President on recommendation of the Ministry of Interior. Each province is divided into townships and each township into boroughs. The head of the township is the *Kaymakam;* the head of the borough, the Director. These are subordinates of the Governor and, like him, are appointed by the central government. Each province has an assembly elected by the people every four years. The Governor and his subordinates are civil service men—career men specially trained and serving their country irrespective of what political party may be in power. There is no fixed period of service in a particular place. Akseven has been in Agri four years and may stay another two. But usually a Governor is slated for a move after that length of service.

Municipal affairs are not in the hands of the Governor and his subordinates. Each town or village has its council and Mayor elected by the people every four years. There is universal suffrage in Turkey, everyone eighteen years of age or over being entitled to the franchise. Felons, of course, cannot vote. But there is no poll tax nor any property qualification.

Akseven boasted of Agri's hydroelectric power plant located on the Murat River, a tributary of the Euphrates. It's a municipal plant on which the city makes a good profit. I asked Akseven about private enterprise in eastern Turkey. There is little, apart from the shops and the farms. Turkey has gone further than any other Middle East country in industrial development. But socialism has done it. Private capital in Turkey seeks a quick return, such as in apartment houses in the larger centers. Little private capital is available for power plants and factories. I first learned in Agri a story, to be repeated over and again on our journey, that in Turkey the central government owns all the hospitals in the nation. There is the private practice of medicine; and medicines are not free. But all hospital care is free; and the free hospitalization includes operations performed by hospital doctors. In these and in many other ways Turkey, the nation that has done so much to promote the democratic ideal and to defend freedom, has marched mainly under the socialist banner.

The Turkish Constitution says, "The Turkish State is republican, nationalist, populist, statist, secular, and revolutionary." Statism is socialism, and that is the constitutional flavor of modern Turkey.

Agri, the Governor explained, is an agricultural center specializing in sheep and goats. There are over 1,000,000 of them in the province. The wool, though not first class, provides a cash crop. Wheat and corn are secondary.

About this point in our conversation, Miss Akseven announced lunch. We sat at an old-fashioned table that pulled out for extra leaves, and all the food was put on the table at once, all except dessert. It was a wonderful meal. There were green beans cooked in olive oil and served cold. Tasty lamb stew with many vegetables was served piping hot. Miss Akseven had baked leavened bread the night before, one of the first batches we had had since leaving Karachi two months earlier. Dark yellow butter was on the table. Dunking was in order, the Governor said. So we soaked up the juice of the stew with large hunks of this delicious dark bread.

When the table was cleared for dessert, the Governor turned to Mercedes and asked if we would like coffee. This offer was the ultimate in Turkish hospitality. For Turkey, the nation known for its good coffee, has no coffee these days. Turkey has no foreign exchange with which to buy it. A few have a precious reserve of coffee left from earlier years. Akseven is in this group. But there's no coffee for sale; there's not even a black market. Coffee is practically non-existent in Turkey.

Mercedes, knowing these things, quickly answered:

"No, we prefer tea."

So black tea made in a big earthen pot and served in heavy porcelain cups was served. And with the tea was served a unique and sweet dessert—yellow watermelon. This melon, grown in Agri, is one of the sweetest watermelons I have tasted. So I carefully collected all the seeds for shipment to Beltsville, Maryland, to see if this Turkish variety would grow here.

There was one more treat coming to us. After we had returned to the parlor, Miss Akseven passed a confection well known here—Turkish delight. Then came offers of a siesta and an invitation to stay all night.

But having scheduled Erzurum for tonight's stop, we said farewell to the Aksevens. This lively Governor, however, hung onto us for some time. First, he took me to the yard where apple trees and lilacs grow. Stepping beyond the trees and shrubs, we came to a clear point where Mount Ararat could be seen. Pointing to it, he said proudly:

"We're named after the mountain."

"The town?" I asked.

"Yes," he replied. "In Turkish, Ararat is Agri."

Then the Governor announced he would escort us out of the city. But first we needed gasoline. We followed his Chevrolet to first one filling station, then another. There was no gasoline to be found. Turkey often runs short, especially in her eastern cities. Her sterling and dollar balances reduce these imports also; and her domestic production is not enough to satisfy her needs.

The Governor then announced that he would take us to the next town—Eleskirt—about twenty-five miles distant and see that we got gasoline there. I tried to dissuade him but there was no use. He was off in a flash, headed west. We followed in a few minutes. But we were not far out of town when we saw that the Governor was in trouble.

Eastern Turkey has little mechanization on the farms. The work is done mostly by oxen. They pull the plows in the fields and the carts on the road. These carts, with squeaky wooden wheels, fill every highway. They usually take and keep the center of the highway. Auto and truck traffic has to make its way around the oxen as best it can. The Governor, faced with this problem, turned out to the left. At this point the road was on an embankment about a dozen feet high. The sides were soft and steep and they ended in a watery slough. The Governor in his eagerness to squeeze by this ox team got his two left wheels onto the soft steep bank. The rear wheel slipped downhill a few feet, and when he stepped on the gasoline, it spun.

We stopped to be of help. Uras and I pushed while the Governor sat behind the wheel. But with each spin of the wheel, the rear of the car slipped farther down the bank. It was now at a precarious angle—dangerous to the Governor. I told him as much. Yet the danger was easier to describe than to avoid. How could he get out of the car without causing it to roll? He first thought of trying to escape out of the right-hand door. But he could not negotiate the pitch of the seat. So he jumped from the left front door. As he jumped, his head hit the top of the door and the car started to hurtle after him. Miraculously the front door swung open just far enough to catch on the slope and hold the car up.

The Governor and I had a consultation. We were to go for help. Down the road five miles or so was a gendarme station. We were to alert them and then go on to Eleskirt and wait for the Governor. We followed instructions; and within the hour we were in the small town of Eleskirt where tiny shops, offering very few consumer goods, lined the cobblestone streets. The only gasoline station in town was out of gas. We had no alternative but to wait.

In a half hour here came the Governor in his Chevrolet, bouncing merrily down the cobblestone street.

"How did you get out?" I asked. "Did they send a truck?"

"A truck?" he said in a surprised voice. "If I had waited for a truck, I'd be there until morning maybe. Out here in eastern Turkey we use the oxen. Two oxen got me into the ditch. Two other oxen pulled me out."

Then the Governor went to work giving orders right and left to gendarmes who went running. In five minutes they returned with two four-gallon tins of gasoline and filled our tank.

"I'd rather not give you the gasoline," the Governor said.

"Why not?" I asked, a bit puzzled.

"Because then you'd have to stay all night and maybe tomorrow too. For the next tank truck won't come through until then," he replied.

CHAPTER 3

A FLAT TIRE AND A MELON

The balance of the journey to Erzurum was highlighted by some highway episodes. We had not gone far from Eleskirt when we saw several groups of farmers thrashing wheat. The method was as ancient as the one used across the Middle East. On some thrashing floors girls rode sleds drawn by cattle that walked round and round the thrashing floor. On others men drove cattle around the circle. Though there are many thousands of tractors and combines in Turkey, about 50,000, I believe, we saw none in eastern Turkey. The farmers in that part of the nation own the land they till. Indeed 80 per cent of all Turkish farmers own their farms. The Ottomans developed landlordism in their empire. But they did not foster it in Anatolia. The Turkish peasant under the Ottomans was a free man so far as land tenure was concerned. But the holdings are small, making mechanization difficult. Moreover, there are in Turkey about 177 different varieties of tractors. This makes the problem of parts difficult since foreign exchange is hard to get. Turkey does not yet manufacture her own farm machinery. The result is that if the rulers of the old Ottoman Empire returned they would see few physical changes on the farms in eastern and northern Turkey.

We stopped for pictures of this primitive thrashing operation. We soon were joined by a number of male bystanders. One of them came up to me and shook hands, introducing himself. He had on a Western suit of clothes; his beard was rather heavy; and he wore a white turban. Uras explained to me that this man was a *mullah* or *hodja* who was welcoming us to Turkey.

I had traveled far and wide in the Middle East and met many *hodjas*. Some who were judges had been friendly. But most of those who were clergy had been aloof and even hostile. So many of them were filled with prejudice against Westerners (the infidels) that they were unapproachable. It was therefore a surprise to find a friendly gregarious clergyman.

We had a good visit, he and I. Mustafa Kemal or Ataturk, who led Turkey's revolution against the *status quo* in the 1920s, had stood firmly against merger of church and state. Islam had become so much a part of the lives of the people that it even dictated the form of their headdress and the trimming of the beard. It subjugated women. It conditioned all scholarship, turning it inward toward the Koran and its mysteries, not outward to science and to the conditions of modern living.

The Arabo-Islamic world beginning about A.D. 800 had a golden era in science and literature. By that time the conquest of other lands had been made and the administrative controls of the new empire were established. Then a period of ease and relaxation began in which the intelligentsia flourished and religious and racial minorities were allowed to make their unique contributions. But due to historical circumstances, particularly from the East, this creative spirit did not continue its development under the Ottoman Empire.

Under the Ottomans, Islam conditioned the whole mentality of the people to inertia, resistance against change, prejudice to new ideas. The Ottoman Empire, which crossed the Dardanelles in 1357, had fostered the union of church and state. Ataturk abolished the Caliphate—the office that blended temporal and spiritual authority. He did away with Islamic law as the code governing private affairs and introduced the Swiss civil code. He designed a public school system to give his people a secular, not a sectarian, education. Ataturk attacked Islam at all points. He abolished all religious courts. He did away with the Islamic calendar and substituted the Gregorian. He gave women the right to vote and the right to obtain a divorce. He abolished the fez and made men wear hats. He abolished polygamy. He tore the veils from women's faces. He banned the wearing of clerical dress in public. He made Sunday an official day of rest. He replaced Arabic with the Latin script; and he decreed that all prayers be said in Turkish, not Arabic. He designed a phonetic Turkish alphabet. In these ways he tried to cut off the oncoming generations from their reactionary religious heritage. Finally he made the intrusion of the church into politics high treason.

We talked of these reforms by the roadside near Eleskirt. Even the *hodja* thought they were good reforms. He went on to say, however, that the religious pressures had been so great that the government had to make some concessions. He referred to the alliance in 1950 of many *hodjas* with the Democratic Party, which promised that the church would regain many of its lost prerogatives. The first result was a regulation promulgated by the Minister of Education, providing for religious instruction in the public schools. The instruction is optional with the pupils, not mandatory. The Council of State of Turkey, in a suit brought by a parent, held, contrary to our own ruling in *McCollum* v. *Board of Education,* 333 U.S. 203, that this practice did not violate the Turkish concept of separation of church and state.

The second result was restoring Arabic as the language for prayers at the mosques. Ataturk, knowing the power of the priests over the people and their manipulation of formalism to perpetuate their authority, required all religious ceremonies to be rendered in Turkish. Then the people knew what was being said and came to a better understanding of the utterances and attitudes of the clergy. The priests did not like that dilution in their power. And over the great objections of young Turks, they recently got Arabic restored as the church language. Some of my Turkish friends think this is the greatest retrogression of all.

Uras and I were in the midst of a discussion of these problems as we drove along. Soon our car was flagged down by an American Mercury. We stopped to discover that the Governor of Erzurum, Nurettin Aynuksa, had come to meet us and to escort us to his home. He is a tall, pleasant-faced Turk about fifty-five years of age and serving in the Turkish civil service. The Ottoman Empire ran its affairs mostly through army officers; the military were the first to get the benefits of Western education; the military, not the intelligentsia, led the revolution of Ataturk. The Governors we were now meeting in eastern Turkey were products of the civil service system that Ataturk installed in Turkey. They are career men who survive any political upheaval in Ankara—unless they engage in partisan activities.

When Aynuksa met us there were lowering clouds in the west. Lightning played on the horizon. Shortly we were on the edge of the storm and felt rain for the first time since the shower in Kabul. The road, having been soaked, was now packed firmly; and we roared along at fifty miles an hour. Once the Governor, who kept the lead, stopped to show us a bridge. It was a stone structure with graceful arches built by the Seljuk Turks who took Baghdad in A.D. 1055 and ruled Persia, Mesopotamia, and Anatolia for a couple centuries. Miller, *The Loom of History,* develops the theme that Seljuk art, learning, and literature were primarily Persian. Certainly the Seljuk bridge which the Governor proudly showed us as being a thousand years old had the mark of Persian design; and to add to its charm a rainbow suddenly formed with one end apparently resting on the ancient bridge.

We had resumed the journey, with Mary driving, when suddenly the car, which had caused us no trouble since Tabriz, started weaving. We stopped to find we had a flat tire on the right rear wheel. The Governor's chauffeur returned to join us; and we watched as he changed tires. He no sooner started than a truck stopped. Three men got out and helped the chauffeur. This pattern was to be repeated over and again on our Turkish trip. Those who travel the highways of Turkey, like those who travel Afghan roads, take care of their fellow travelers.

This is rich farming land as far as the eye can see. Wheat is grown here; and this afternoon the checkerboard of fallow land and cultivated land was beautiful under the rainbows that kept forming. Along the banks of streams, where the bottom land looked especially rich, there were great stretches of cabbage, headed out and nearly ready to harvest.

We changed the tire at the crest of a hill, where we could see the highway for several miles to the west. A motorcycle carrying two men stopped at the bottom to let a passenger off. Then the driver came charging up the hill on a sputtering machine and stopped near us. He was a German in his thirties and missing one leg. The machine was not powerful enough to carry two of them up and over Turkish hills. They were headed for Delhi via northern Afghanistan. That was the road we had traveled—the road with the rough washboards, deep ruts and steep hills, and angry dogs. I told the one-legged German about the roads and especially about the dogs. I could visualize one of these dogs pulling a man from a motorcycle. The one that had leaped at our car certainly would have killed a motorcyclist. But this blue-eyed, pleasant German only grinned. He had all the road information he needed and none of it was bad. The Governor asked him if he should not reconsider his routing. But he only shook his head. And his young companion who now joined him was as resolute. With a roar they were off for high adventure in the East, waving their arms and grinning from ear to ear as they turned to say goodbye.

We were still twenty miles short of Erzurum, when the Governor's car stopped. By the time we pulled up, his chauffeur had the hood up. Something was wrong with the motor and the trouble was not easy to diagnose. A truck pulled up and several Turks climbed down to help the Governor. Time passed quickly in this interval of dusk. New storm clouds blew up and then in an instant it was dark. I got out the large flashlight with the red blinker and placed it by the side of the car. The light attracted every truck driver who came by. Soon we had a dozen or more men helping the Governor's chauffeur. Finally he followed the advice of one of the volunteers, took the hand pump, hooked it up with the gas line, and pumped furiously. When he reconnected the line, the motor started at once.

This is a highly militarized area. Traffic through Erzurum must register at check points on either side of the town. Passports are picked up to insure that the owner will not flee; and every foreign car is given an escort through the town. Indeed, a Turkish soldier takes over as chauffeur until one leaves the military zone. But we were not burdened with these regulations. The Governor spoke to the sentries and we were waved on to Erzurum.

The Governor's home at Erzurum is a one-story commodious structure made of stone. It is set in a large garden surrounded by a wall. The house is completely modern and most comfortable. The Governor, a devout Moslem, lives with his wife, Saadet, and his sister, Refia. They had a delicious informal dinner for us, built around beef goulash as the main course.

The next morning with the sun streaming in the windows we had our first Turkish breakfast—small ripe olives, marmalade made from wild oranges, goat cheese, bread, pears, peaches, grapes, and tea.

We learned at these meals much about Turkish history and Turkish heroism. Erzurum, a town of 60,000 people, is less than a hundred miles from Russia. In the last three hundred years Erzurum has had 127 battles with Russian troops, though there have been only twelve official Russo-Turkish wars since 1672. There is no family in all Erzurum that does not feel some loss as a result of those conflicts.

Erzurum, a city of ancient Armenia, is now entirely Turkish. It is sprawling and not well laid out. Its distinguishing mark is the architecture of the homes—stucco finish and four gabled roofs covered with tiles. The city lies 6000 feet high; it is the community center of vast barren rolling country and head of the province where 560,000 people live. The summers are dry and cool. The winters are severe. The Governor has hopes of developing Erzurum as a ski resort. It already boasts a ski jump east of town that one can see from the city.

The economy of Erzurum is based on sheep, goats, sugar beets, and wheat. The city has a sugar beet factory and a meat-packing plant, jointly owned by the government and by private capital. At Erzurum we talked again about Turkish socialism. What Ataturk demanded was a complete social and political revolution. The stodgy influence of Islam had to be dissipated, and the faces of the people turned to the West where the Industrial Revolution had long been achieved. Turkey had a great distance to go to catch up. Mechanics as well as artisans and architects had to be trained. Plants had to be built and managers found. A nation in as great a hurry as Turkey to catch up could not wait until private capital got the necessary confidence in the revolutionary government to come out of hiding. The revolutionary government had to create the confidence by building the industrial plant or at least getting it well on its way. Socialism was thrust on Turkey.

One of Turkey's greatest needs was and is education. A new

university is being built at Erzurum; and it will be called Ataturk University. The school that serves as the model is the University of Nebraska, which is giving technical advice on the building of this new institution. This new university will fill a great void in eastern Turkey by providing an agricultural extension service. Even more important, however, is the Village Training College located in Erzurum. This is the college that trains teachers for the village schools. Education is compulsory for girls and boys from seven to fourteen; and the schools are co-educational. The problem is not only the building of schools but the training of enough teachers. Turkey, like other nations in Asia, is finding difficulty getting college graduates to return to their villages to work and live. Most of them want to escape to positions of greater luxury and comfort. It was that trend that helped undermine China and open it to subversion by the Communists. The intellectuals returned to their ivory towers; the political and ideological vacuum in the village was filled by the Communists. Turkey is working hard to avoid this disaster. Teacher-training centers are in every province. Teachers are trained, not in far-off Ankara, but in the provinces for the tasks at hand there.

The Aynuksa women brought the conversation around to Turkish women and their rights. There is no doubt that in Turkey they have a degree of equality not generally achieved in the West. Turkish women receive the same pay as men in commercial and industrial work. The professions are filled with women—medicine, law, engineering. Several doctors and several lawyers in Erzurum are women; and one woman in that city is a judge. There have been as many as three women on Turkey's highest court—the Court of Cassation—at one time.

These were the matters we discussed with the Aynuksas at dinner and at breakfast. And we dallied so long over breakfast that we ruined our day's schedule. For when I went out to the Governor's garage to get the station wagon, I learned that we were in trouble again. Some sand or gravel had apparently got into one of the brake drums. The back wheel made a terrible noise as I backed out of the garage. Mercedes made an inspection and discovered the drum was badly scored. That meant we had to remove the wheel and send the drum for turning to the garage of the Turkish Army—the only one in town.

We sat three more hours with this affable Governor under his locust, poplar, and maple trees discussing affairs of state before the drum had been turned and the wheel assembled. It was eleven o'clock by the time we were loaded and on our way.

To save time we decided to pick up our lunch in the bazaar. While Mercedes, Mary, and Uras went for gasoline, I went alone to do the shopping. First I bought a loaf of bread—the round leavened black loaf that is in every Turkish food store. I found peanuts which, though unroasted, were sweet and tender. Erzurum has sweet white grapes and small juicy peaches. I bought some of each. My last purchase was to be a watermelon. There was a large pile of them on the walk in front of this ramshackle wooden shop. I went through the pile, picked my choice, and took it inside to the young Turk with a black mustache, white teeth, and brown cap. He smelled it first; then he put it to his ear and squeezed it. With that he shook his head and returned it to the pile outside. He went through the pile making his own selection and using his nose and ear in the process. Finally he beamed and handed me a melon.

We followed the railroad track out of Erzurum, headed west. This is the broad-gauge line that connects Ankara with Moscow. The section from Erzurum to Russia was built by the Russians in World War II. A heavily loaded freight train headed for Russia passed by just before we crossed the tracks and turned north for Kopdagi and Zigana passes. At 8000 feet we stopped to cool the radiator. There we had our lunch. I cut the melon on the running board of the car. It was wonderfully sweet. I told Uras that a merchant who had a good chance to do a foreigner in had done a fine favor instead. I was to find this trait in all the Turkish tradesmen and merchants we met along fifteen hundred miles of roads.

CHAPTER 4

TRABZON ON THE BLACK SEA

It is a long hard drive from Erzurum to Trabzon, the Black Sea port. The country east of Erzurum is vast wheat, cattle, and sheep country, with rich valleys and rolling hills, mostly barren. In a little over fifty miles the road turns northeast and starts up a long grade that follows many canyon walls, coming out on top occasionally and then heading for another ridge to climb. This is the Pontic Border Range, which is split up into two parallel chains running east and west. The southernmost is called the Cimen Kop Fortum Range. To the north of it and overlooking the Black Sea is the Rize Range with Mount Kackar (12,915 feet) as its highest peak. We had to cross both ranges to reach Trabzon. It's a good dirt road with plenty of room for the big trucks full of gasoline that roar over the mountains from the Black Sea. As I said, we stopped once on an elbow of this steep grade of Kopdagi Pass to have our lunch. And we stopped several more times to cool the engine. One of these was at Gomosane where clear cold water comes up from a spring. The sun set while we were still climbing to Zigana Pass, promising a fine day on the morrow as it turned to a golden disc and sank below a barren peak in the distance.

It was dusk when we crossed Zigana Pass (9700 feet) and felt the motor relax as the wheels rolled downhill. Not far over Zigana Pass on the north side is the small village of Hamsikoy. It's little more than a truck stop, though there are a few shops and a couple of restaurants in the one block that marks the turn. Here we stopped for a dinner. The restaurant we chose was called Yayla. It was lighted by gasoline lanterns hung from the ceiling. The tables seated four people and were covered with soiled linen. The place was pretty well packed with truck drivers whose vehicles filled the street. The waiters wore shirts, trousers, and soiled aprons; and there was not one who did not need a shave. There was a service counter between the kitchen and the dining room where the waiters picked up the orders. They shouted them across the room to the cooks; and when the cooks had placed the orders on the counter they shouted back. Their shouts filled the place. Dark-skinned men, most of them with caps, sat at the tables dipping black bread in the gravy of their stews and sucking black tea out of thick white cups. The clank of dishes, the scraping of chairs, the guttural sounds of the customers, the shouts of the waiters made the place seem like bedlam. And the soiled linen, the dim lantern light, the unshaven men set up in all of us, I think, doubts as to the wisdom of our choice of a restaurant. But that feeling quickly passed. One of the waiters came up to the table where we had sat down and invited us to the kitchen. The kitchen was a joy to behold. It was clean and neat as a pin. A large iron stove about 6 feet by 12 feet held all the dishes that the cook had ready. And he was ready to cook any other dish to order.

This was as appetizing a display of food as we had seen. Mercedes and I ended with boiled beef, potatoes cooked separately, tomato *dolmeh,* rice, and bread. Since there was no wine available in this restaurant or in the village, we drank *chai* in thick white cups. On leaving I expressed our gratitude to the owner of the Yayla Restaurant and congratulated him on his fine food. And I told Uras, as we walked out, that this place, though grimy, was a restaurant where I would be happy to eat every day of my life. Mercedes, who shared my feeling, had only this to say: "In Turkey, as in America, truck drivers always know the best restaurants along the highway. Where you see the big trucks parked, that is the place to eat."

It was a dark night; and the traffic out of Hamsikoy was heavy. Trailer trucks going downhill were swinging crazily; the diesel-powered ones coming up from the Black Sea were growling in low. Soon we were in the conifers. Since the night was balmy, we opened all the car windows and slowed down so that we could smell the pine. They were the Mediterranean type, the first we had seen all summer in thick stands. Somehow those pines lining the lovely dark road gave us as hearty a welcome to Turkey as the Governors at Agri and Erzurum and the restaurant owner at Hamsikoy. Somewhere along the road one gets the first glimpse of the Black Sea. Xenophon relates the joy of the Greeks, retreating from Persia, when they saw the blue sea that marked an easy highway to their homes. We saw nothing in the night except the headlights of oncoming cars and the limbs of pine that our own lights picked up. In about an hour and a half the lights of Trabzon came into view and the road straightened out. A jeep was waiting for us at a gendarme station on the outskirts of town. We followed it into the city and then back in the direction we had come. Trabzon lies on low hills that come gently down to the sea. Our destination this night was "Ataturk Kosku"—Ataturk's massive stone mansion, which he left to his nation. The road was cobblestone and climbed steeply past many darkened homes. Soon we were high above the city. We continued to climb for some minutes until we came to a flat shoulder of the hill where we turned into a gate. Ataturk's home—big and spacious with high ceilings, Persian rugs, magnificent cupboards, and modern plumbing—was ablaze with lights, awaiting us.

When the bags were up and the car locked, I stepped onto a balcony off our bedroom. This was wide and spacious, guarded by an iron grill of delicate design. It seemed from this dark vantage point that we were on a cliff looking down on the city. In the morning from the same balcony the town was some miles distant and beyond it the Black Sea, blue and calm to the horizon. A slight fog had apparently settled during the night; and it had not quite risen. So there was a misty effect which seemed to heighten the deep dark green of the thick vegetation between us and the water. In a few minutes I felt suddenly relaxed. I sensed the reason for it. The bright burning sky of the Middle East produces intensities of heat, of color, and of other sensations. The blue sky of Persia has an infinity that other skies do not know. The mountains of West Pakistan and Afghanistan are barren and seared. They show a monotony of grays and browns. The searing heat of Mesopotamia is enervating. The desert wastelands, though bright with color at sunset, produce a tension in man from which he ultimately needs to flee.

The thick lush vegetation of the Black Sea was suddenly and noticeably relaxing. The green countryside did something soothing to the eyes and through them to the nerve ends. This was my first sensation on seeing Trabzon by daylight. The welcome of the Black Sea was so friendly, it at once became a favored spot the world over.

We hurried through a breakfast of black olives, goat cheese, marmalade, bread, and tea to pack the car and go down to Trabzon. On the way we came to several small tobacco farms with drying barns quite like those we have in our own South. This morning boys were putting some of the tobacco out in the sun to dry. The leaves were hung on cords across large open trays that ran on wheels following wooden rails laid upon the ground. These trays were about 15 feet wide and 25 feet long. The track ran for perhaps 150 feet so that about ten of the trays could be placed in the yard at once. Tobacco is a main crop in Turkey. The government has a floor under the price to the farmer. The Ottomans were interested only in squeezing taxes from the farmers and in drafting their sons for military duty. Only since Ataturk has the farmer been treated considerately and with dignity and raised to full first-class citizenship in Turkey. Though his farm and his farming methods would look familiar to the Ottomans if they returned, his new political stature would be startling to them.

After the tobacco barns were behind us and we were on the fringe of Trabzon, we met a new kind of merchant. He looked like a mendicant, so poor was his attire. His merchandise was all aboard a burro. Around the animal's neck hung a freshly caught fish weighing ten pounds. On its back were loaves of bread, fresh eggs, grapes, and various vegetables. We were to see his type in rural Turkey, peddling his wares from house to house.

We stopped in the city to pay our respects to the Governor, Muhlis Babaoglu. He, the Mayor, one of the local judges, and some of their staffs were present. They were filled with curiosity as to the workings of our judicial system and the interplay between our state and federal courts. I conducted a seminar on American law and government for nearly an hour as a lemon drink called *gazoz,* which is very popular in Turkey, was served.

We visited the harbor of Trabzon where a new breakwater has been built. A Victory ship called SS *Linfield,* from Portland, Oregon, that we had seen in American waters was being unloaded. Wheat poured through canvas funnels onto trucks that lined up to take the precious cargo. A Turkish coastwise vessel was loading tobacco and fruits for Istanbul and other Black Sea ports. A policeman in civilian attire by the name of Selahattin Gediz took us on a tour of the harbor in a large dory with an inboard motor. There were fishing boats off Trabzon. Many handlines were out and small fish about eight inches in length were being hauled aboard.

When we docked we bought lemonade from a peddler dressed in a long white coat and wearing a chef's white hat. He carried lemon concentrate in a jar and thc fizz water in a big jug on his back. These soft-drink peddlers seemed to be everywhere; and once in a while a man with an ice cream cart went by. Everyone was headed for the city square. We followed suit, to find a large crowd already assembled. This was a celebration of Zafer Bayrami, which falls on August 30 each year. On this day in 1922 the Turkish Army won a decisive battle over the Greeks. It is now celebrated in every town in Turkey. In Trabzon the people and the city and provincial officials were gathered for the event. Soon several companies of infantry came by. They lined up and came to attention while the national anthem was played. Then the poet of Trabzon, Aziz Aktulga by name, stepped before a loudspeaker and recited poetry. It was his own composition and it concerned the power and the virtues of the Turks. It was such an emotional account that the poet himself was in tears at the end. Then came the parade, headed by the infantry. Tanks, trucks, and anti-aircraft equipment followed.

We ate lunch in the Imren Restaurant on the main street of Trabzon. A roll of lamb was laced on a skewer, placed on end, and rotated before a charcoal grill. This is called *doner kabab* in Turkey and is a favorite dish in rural sections. Thin slices of the lamb are cut off and served with grilled tomatoes and long green peppers about the size of a man's finger. For dessert we had delicious green figs grown at Trabzon.

Trabzon, where Xenophon and his Ten Thousand reached the Black Sea, is filled with Greek relics, and the mark of Christendom. Alexius I, known as Grand Comnenus, established a Greek colony here in A.D. 1204. The ruins of his castle are still here. A few Byzantine churches are in evidence, and one Armenian. Some are missions; most are converted to other uses, such as mosques or caravanseries. The best-preserved is Santa Sofia, some of whose thirteenth-century frescoes are still intact. It has two massive columns made of porphyry. Our guide said that one of these columns drips water. He called it weeping; and none of the townsfolk knows why the column weeps. Beyond Santa Sofia and above it are cave shrines in poor condition; and overlooking the town are the ruins of a Greek monastery, the center of a Greek religious movement in the thirteenth or fourteenth century that the Turks claimed was subversive.

There had been a light wind from the north when we were cruising the harbor. By early afternoon when we left for Giresun it had died down. The Black Sea was like a mirror. Now the sun was hot. As we headed west by the coast road we kept looking for bathhouses where we could change clothes and go for a swim. But we found none. Someone suggested, perhaps Mary, that we each find a clump of bushes for a dressing room. But once more, time pressed us to get to Giresun before dark, as Governor Ali Cahit Betil and his wife expected us for dinner.

The coast road is very reminiscent of the Pacific highway along the Washington and Oregon coasts. The mountains, heavy with vegetation, come right down to the sea. Sometimes there is a narrow, flat valley washed by a creek that the road crosses. For the most part the road follows the contours of the hills, taking the serpentine course which the ravines and shoulders of the mountains design. The engineering of the road was herculean. Landslides were one problem; straightening the road was another. They say that in the old days the road was the slowest, the worst road imaginable. Today it is a fine dirt road, but still quite slow. The Menderes government, representing the Democratic Party, has made road building one of its prime activities. As we traveled between Trabzon and Giresun, great earth-moving machines were at work. In a few years this winding road will cut much straighter along the coast line and have many turnouts where travelers can stop to drink in the magnificent view which every promontory gives.

But in 1957 the curves were still sharp; and it was impossible to average more than twenty miles an hour. When we got up courage to go faster, we were almost invariably met by a huge bus or truck crowding us to the brink.

The result of our slow travel was that we covered the sixty-odd miles to Giresun in a little over three hours. We saw it in the distance at sunset, marked by a new jetty running into the sea. As Mary was commenting on how Mediterranean it looked, we heard a clatter underneath the car, which meant only one thing —that the muffler was off again. Fortunately we were in a straight stretch of road about two hundred yards long.

Mercedes got out the rice mats which we bought in Peshawar and, using them as a carpet, got under the car. As the muffler was hot to handle, she had to wait for it to cool. Then she tried to wire it up tightly enough to last until we reached Giresun. That would not work. So she tried to take it off. But one end was stubbornly attached to the tail pipe. At this point Uras went under the car to help Mercedes. Then two trucks stopped and four men piled out. They too went under the car. When they got the muffler off, the exhaust pipe was dragging. They worked hard to take it off too. But it was so designed as not to come off unless the chassis were off the axle. By the time that lesson was learned it was dark. I put out the red blinker light on the highway to warn traffic. The crew of six under the car kept hollering for more and more baling wire. Mary and I took the red blinker light and used its flashlight beam to search the roadside where recent construction had been completed. There in the dark we found the strands of baling wire needed to complete the job. The four volunteer helpers drove off with grins, one of them shouting:

"We Turks are proud of your wife. She's a fine mechanic."

CHAPTER 5

HAZELNUTS AND BUTTERMILK

Giresun was an old Roman city. The modern town of 18,000 people has remnants of structures built by the Venetians, who came by boat about A.D. 1200. They built a fort to guard it; and we went up the cliff in the morning to see the ruins. The design of the fort can be made out; but there is little left of it. An old, old cannon is on the bluff in front of the fort. How old it is, Governor Betil did not know. It is used these days to announce the beginning and end of Ramadan, the month when no devout Moslem takes food or drink or any puff of a cigarette or pipe between sunrise and sunset.

I felt more at home in Giresun than in Trabzon, though both are beautiful. Giresun seems more Mediterranean than any Black Sea port we saw. The mountains rise steeply behind the town. The houses are made of stone. They are square and each has a four-gabled tile roof.

On the cliff I found delicate saxifrage and the brazen dandelion. The Giresun gardens have chrysanthemums, asters, and hydrangeas. I saw in one garden a saucy stand of snapdragons, a flower the Turks call "the lion's mouth." There are orchards of figs in Giresun. No lemons are grown along the Black Sea. But Giresun boasts of oranges, tangerines, and olives. It has tea plantations too, but only on an experimental basis. Like Trabzon, it grows tobacco, eggplant, okra, and melons. But it is most famous for its hazelnuts. We saw them on the hillsides both above and below the road from Trabzon. The trees are bushlike and not over ten feet high. They thrive in this belt along the Black Sea. Corn used to be Giresun's chief product. Now the city needs imports of cereals to feed its people, for everyone grows hazelnuts. The Governor told me that in 1956 this province alone produced 70,000 tons of hazelnuts. A late frost cut the 1957 crop down to 12,000 tons.

Governor Betil reminded me in looks and mannerisms very much of Justice William J. Brennan of our Court. But he is given to overweight; and his wife, Iclal, was teasing him about it at breakfast, served in their garden. He laughed at her and, patting his stomach, turned to me and said:

"There is a saying these days that the fattest men in Turkey come from Giresun."

"Why Giresun?" I asked.

"It's the hazelnuts," he replied.

There are several hazelnut factories in Giresun. The farmers first husk the nuts, using the outside shell for fuel. Then they lay the nuts out in the sun to dry. Any sunny place will do. Some lay sheets of burlap on the beach and dry their nuts there. Others use the open fields or their own lawns. Some use the sidewalks in the village. This was the last of August, and the hazelnuts were being harvested. We saw the nuts drying in all sunny spots available. After drying, the nuts are taken to factories built by the government. There are several in Giresun. Here the shells are cracked and the nuts removed for packing. The smaller hazelnut, the one that is full of oil, is selected for export as it stands shipment well and does not dry out.

We saw hazelnuts drying by the roadside all the way west to Ordu. We stopped several times to take pictures and each time some man or woman filled our pockets. In a few hours we had gallons of hazelnuts in the car. We used the two pairs of pliers for nutcrackers, one for the front seat, one for the rear. But Uras did remarkably well by using one nut to crack another by hand.

At Giresun we had asked Governor Betil for advice on beaches for swimming. He had telephoned ahead to the police at Ordu, a city that hangs on a mountainside. The police met us east of town and escorted us through Ordu to the western outskirts where there is a lovely beach. It is the custom in Turkey for people in June to erect small huts on the beaches as dressing rooms and to remove the huts by September. All the dressing rooms at this Ordu beach had been removed except one. It too was to be dismantled this day. But the owner kindly let us use it. It was a three-walled affair with a wooden floor, but no roof or fourth side. That side, facing the sea, had a blue curtain.

The north wind was up and there was a grand surf. The sand was soft. This is volcanic rock country; and the black rock, pulverized into soft sand, has given the sea its name. This is one of the nicest beaches we know. There are no weeds, no grass as far out as one can wade. The water is clear and only slightly saline. The water temperature is about 68° F. or 70° F., cool enough to be invigorating and yet not cold enough to be forbidding. Here in the soft sand, we found fields of white lilies. There were hundreds of them in bloom. They were miniatures of our Easter lily and most fragrant. We dug up some of the bulbs and shipped them to Dr. S. M. Emsweller at Beltsville, Maryland, for his experimental work with lilies.

The police offered us a luncheon in Ordu. But wanting to make Samsun this night, we declined. We had not gone far out of Ordu, when we came to the largest hazelnut operation we had seen. Several dozen men and women were at work on various stages of the process—some husking, others laying the nuts on burlap in the sun, others turning the nuts so they would dry uniformly. We stopped to take pictures. All were co-operative, even the women. In the midst of our picture taking the owner came out of the house to greet me. He was a tall, thin, red-haired Turk by the name of Ali Karaarslan. He was about fifty-five years old. He was happy to welcome us. He wanted me especially to meet his seven sons. When he called, they came running. One must have been thirty; one was a babe in arms carried by a daughter. Each one had his father's red hair. After meeting the sons and finishing our pictures, we turned to go. But Karaarslan would have none of that. He insisted we come into his house.

It was a stone affair in two stories. The downstairs was more or less a storehouse for household goods and farm supplies. The family lived upstairs. The kitchen, bedroom, and sitting room were on the second floor. There were no beds in the Western sense. Each member of the family had a bedroll that was laid on the floor at night. Now they were neatly rolled up and piled one on the other in the corner.

Our host gave orders that sent a couple of daughters flying. They came back in a few moments with trays of buttermilk, called *ayran* in Turkish. There is electricity along the Black Sea; and this farmer friend of ours had an electric icebox. The result was cold buttermilk, which I had craved many times on the journey. One glass followed another, and with them came much conversation.

This farmer was old enough to remember the Ottoman Empire. The ruling institution of the Ottomans was the army and the Sultan. Most officials of government were soldiers—army officers holding civilian posts. The host of employees under them were slaves who had to become Moslems to receive promotions. These slaves, mostly Christians who were bought while young, were well trained for government service in peace and in war. Many sons of goatherds rose to positions of great power and prestige in service of the Ottomans. Religious minorities were allowed their own courts and a degree of freedom. But Moslem and non-Moslem alike who were not in the hierarchy received few benefits from the Ottoman regime. There were many perquisites for the ruling classes but few for the masses.

The taxes on the land ranged from 10 per cent to 50 per cent, depending on the fertility of the land as registered with a *cadaster*. But the custom grew of selling the taxes to high officials who resold them section by section, town by town. This process might be repeated several times until the amount wrung from the peasant might be twice what the Ottoman government received. The farmer got nothing in return—no roads, no schools, no hospitals. He lost his sons to the army and received no benefits from the government.

Karaarslan praised Ataturk, who abolished the tax on farm produce. Ataturk established instead the income tax and excise taxes. Farmers, like all consumers, pay the excise taxes. The income tax is graduated, stopping at 35 per cent; and the capital gains tax in Turkey is 15 per cent. But the unique thing about the income tax is that all farmers are exempt. Moreover, they pay only a nominal tax on their lands.

Our host walked to the car with us to say goodbye. His parting comment was praise for the Menderes government.

We stopped for lunch at a small village called Persembe. We found a restaurant by the highway, overlooking the beach and called the Senkardeslar. We had a delicious mutton stew, bread, and red wine. We talked of the farmers of Turkey and their new political status under the Menderes government. As I said, the farming countryside has not changed much since the time of the Ottomans. A few like Karaarslan have electric refrigerators. But the revolution that electricity brings has not reached many of the farms of Turkey. Not many farmers have automobiles. Oxen still plow most fields and haul most produce. But the Turkish farmer is at long last awakened to the political power which universal suffrage grants him. He makes up 85 per cent of the population. His voice is more and more heard in the councils of government. He enjoys his income tax exemption; and it will be difficult for any party to take it from him.

CHAPTER 6

GOOD CIRCUMCISION WEATHER

The Turkish government is making great strides in agriculture. Opium is a state monopoly and the poppy can be planted only where the government permits. The government protects the farmer in major products by putting a floor under prices. This price support is the key to the Turkish agricultural economy. The government has a monopoly not only on opium but also on all products that are exported, which include wheat, rice, hazelnuts, and cotton. It is doing much to introduce the scientific attitude into farming. And to further that cause it has experimental farms scattered across Turkey. We visited one east of Samsun that is known as the Geleman State Farm.

The man who welcomed us was Cenani Akcer, a forty-year-old associate director, who is steeped in modern agriculture. He insisted that we sample some of his experimental melons and fruits. We did so and found them very tasty. He beamed as he brought new dishes to our table in the garden.

"These are melons from Texas," he said.

We said nothing in reply as we sampled this variety. We never knew how this variety had reached the Black Sea. It was undoubtedly superior in Texas; but here it had become hard and bitter. Akcer kept grinning all the time we ate. So I could not tell whether or not he was enjoying a joke.

My special interest at Geleman State Farm was cherry seed.

My friend, Elon Gilbert, had written from Yakima, Washington, asking if Turkish mahaleb cherry seeds were available. He wanted some in the Yakima Valley to raise seedlings with which to bud the Bing and Lambert types of cherry. The botanical name is *Prunus mahaleb linn.* Akcer not only knew about the species but had some on the farm. The advantage of this Turkish species is that it produces a tree that is shorter and smaller and easier to pick. It also has a much stronger leaf area than ours. And Elon felt that it probably had greater winter hardiness too, an important factor in the Yakima economy. For in November, 1955, a freeze destroyed a third of Yakima's cherry trees.

We ran this errand for Elon, saw the trees, got the promise of the seeds, and started at dusk for Samsun.

As we left, Akcer gave me the interesting information that the first cherries Rome ever knew came from Samsun. Lucullus, the Emperor, brought them back to Italy.

Samsun, a city of 80,000 people, has sometimes been referred to as an ugly Black Sea port. It seemed attractive to us, though not as much so as Trabzon and Giresun. The reason is that here the hills are more barren than they are farther east; and the mountains come down to the sea gently, leaving wide sloping lowlands. These slopes are the habitat of partridge and quail. In the fall ducks and geese come down from Russia by the thousands. With them comes a species of quail that makes a non-stop flight to Samsun. It is so weak and exhausted on its arrival that the local people hunt it with nets as they would butterflies.

On one of the barren headlands above Samsun, Turkey has an elaborate radar system. Stationed in Samsun is an American military mission headed by Captain Leo D. Talbot of Grand Island, Nebraska. We stayed at the new modern Vidinli Hotel in Samsun and met in the lobby a couple of lonesome American privates who sent word of our arrival to Captain Talbot. The Captain called on us and invited us to visit his headquarters, which we did one bright clear morning. Samsun is too full of military secrets to talk about. So Captain Talbot showed us one of the hobbies of his staff. It was the exploration of the ruins of an ancient city at Samsun. This city was known as Amisus. It was established by the Greeks. The colonizer was not Greece proper, but the Greek colony, Miletus, in Asia Minor. The Black Sea export trade in those days was cattle, fish, corn, and timber. From here caviar and smoked sturgeon reached Greece and, later, Rome. The imports were clothing, wine, and many other articles from the shops of Athens.

Mithridates founded Amisus; and Lucullus, the Roman, conquered it and razed it to the ground. It never was rebuilt; and sand many feet deep has drifted over it. Captain Talbot took us in jeeps to see some of the old foundations and cisterns. Occasionally a whole room of a house has been discovered. But the barren headland where Amisus once stood is a lonesome place whose melancholy is heightened by the occasional outcropping of a piece of an ancient wall.

Samsun was rebuilt by the Seljuks. The Greeks built on the headland, the Seljuks on the alluvial plain. There is no tide in the Black Sea. So the houses are built to the water's edge. Samsun today is prospering. Perhaps the military personnel contribute materially. But more important is the wonderful port that is being constructed. Like Giresun, Samsun is being equipped with a causeway and dock system that will enable ten freighters and ten passenger ships to be unloaded at the same time. This project was not completed when we were there. So a passenger ship from Istanbul was at anchor offshore, being unloaded by lighters. But one berth for freighters was being used and a huge electric crane, like those at Trabzon, was unloading a vessel.

Samsun is now connected with Ankara and Istanbul by railroad. So it's on its way to development as a great Black Sea port. But the communication system that intrigued Mercedes the most was the narrow-gauge railroad that runs from Carsamba (pronounced Charshamba) to Samsun. It's mainly a commuter train; but it hauls some freight. The evening we came into Samsun we passed it. It was loaded with passengers—inside as well as out. Workers coming home completely covered the top of each car. We went down early one morning to see it come in. It's so small and tiny that it's almost a toy. But it's the pride and joy of Samsun.

We had dinner at the Vidinli Hotel with Governor Nihat Danisman and his wife Zuleyha and son Tarhan. Mrs. Danisman was one of the first women to graduate in political science at Ankara University. Tarhan speaks perfect English. In Turkey a student, after finishing primary school, takes English. Counting the college years, that gives him ten years of English. Tarhan, who had finished college in Ankara, was thus well grounded in English. So was Nezahat Ulusoy, a high school teacher in Samsun. The Mayor, Nuzhet Ulusoy, his wife Binnoz, and the District Attorney, Kani Verona, were also present at the dinner. But they did not speak English. Counting Uras, we had four good interpreters at the table. So we covered much ground that night.

Most of the talk centered on Ataturk. We had seen that morning the statue of him on a rearing horse in Samsun's park. Samsun especially honors Ataturk because this was his sanctuary. He made revolution not only against the Allies in occupation of Turkey at the end of World War I, but against the Sultan as well. The Sultan had a price on his head. He escaped Istanbul by ship and on May 19, 1919, reached Samsun where the Sultan had an army unit. Ataturk had an all-night conference with the Commanding General. As a result of Ataturk's persuasion, the General threw in his lot with Ataturk—a story whose sequel is told by Price, *A History of Turkey.* So it was that Samsun became the real staging ground for the great revolution that followed.

Turkey has no trade agreement with the Soviets. But these neighbors trade on a barter basis. Turkey takes no autos, which Russia has in abundance for export. She takes mostly consumer goods, such as pencils, paper, and rulers, and various kinds of machinery, including tractors. With any upsurge in trade with the north, Samsun will come into its own.

There was an aura of an American Chamber of Commerce about the dinner table this night. Moreover, Governor Danisman, like all other civil servants I met in Turkey, is intensely proud of its municipal achievements. All intercity busses, all railroads, and all airplanes are owned by the central government. The cities own the local bus lines and the power plants. The strides taken at the municipal level have been enormous in recent years. The high quality of the Governors and Mayors has been the determining factor.

In the morning we went four miles west of Samsun to a beach white with a pounding surf. Tarhan, the Governor's son, arranged with friends to keep a four-stall dressing-room shack intact so that we could have a swim. The black sand was hot this morning, so hot I could not walk in it barefooted above the beach proper. A brisk north wind was blowing; and the water was wonderfully refreshing. We were finishing our swim when a man came down to the water with cattle and started to bathe them. They had the crippling and highly infectious hoof and mouth disease that sheep had brought into Turkey from Syria. The Governor of Samsun had talked about it. The government was anxiously trying to collect the diseased stock for quarantine and extermination. We talked with the farmer who bathed his sick cattle in the Black Sea. He had tried all other remedies and they had failed. He had been told by the government that his cattle must be destroyed. But he hoped the salt water would help them.

"But how can I live without my cattle?" he asked.

Tarhan explained that the government would compensate him somehow or other. But the old man, like farmers the world over, had a close tie to these milk cows that he would maintain to the bitter end.

On our return to Samsun we packed for departure to Corum (pronounced Chorum) in the interior. We hated to leave the Black Sea that had treated us so well. Our problem of lunch was solved in one of the winding cobblestone streets leading to the hotel. Here was a vendor with a cartload of peaches as big and as bright as our own Hales. We bought a dozen or more from him; and they gave us one of our tastiest meals.

We were about to leave the hotel when the sound of music filled one of the side streets. Here came a procession of phaetons, known as the circumcision parade. In the front phaeton rode the victim dressed in a fancy skullcap. The next carriage had a band, playing full blast. Three or more carriages filled with young children followed. This was the gayest public gathering we had seen in Turkey. All participants were in a happy mood. They had come from the host's home where a party held forth and were headed for the home of a man authorized to perform circumcisions and to give vaccinations. He's not a *hodja* but a technician who passes a government examination to qualify for his profession. He performs a circumcision for a fee. The boy is circumcised before he is ten years old; and all his friends join to make it a happy event. Maxwell, *People of the Reeds,* relates that, among the Arabs in south Iraq, circumcision is a hot-weather rite, the feeling being that cool weather brings on infection. Not so in Turkey.

This was September 1; and I asked Uras if there was any significance to the date.

"No," he said, "except that this is good circumcision weather."

"How can you measure that?"

"It's good circumcision weather," he replied, "whenever it's cool."

CHAPTER 7

THE REGIME OF THE OXCART

The road to Corum and Ankara turns inland in a southwesterly direction right at Samsun. In a mile or two one gets his last glimpse of the Black Sea. The road enters a rather dry canyon and climbs a low ridge that marks the divide between the green northern country and the dry rolling interior of Turkey. This far west there is not as much vegetation on the north slopes as there is at Trabzon. On the lower reaches are terraces of hazelnuts. Beyond them are a few conifers. But most of the trees are oak and *sanjid* with much scrub in between. There is no real pass over this ridge into the interior. Rather the road climbs gradually through long canyons and drops gently over barren, rounded ridges into the interior.

We were not long on our way before we saw band after band of sheep and goats with dozens of limping animals. The hoof and mouth disease was galloping through Turkey. After we had reached the plateau of the interior we came to a dozen or more black tents stretched across a field of stubble where wheat had recently been harvested. These were not tents with side walls such as one sees in Iran but pieces of black wool stretched between poles to form a roof and one side. These were the first black tents we had seen in Turkey, which indicated that so far we had traveled areas where sedentary farmers lived.

These tent dwellers are not truly migratory. They are villagers who move with their flocks in the summer and who return to villages in the winter. There were several familes of them; and their leader was Ahmet Firinci, who was about fifty years old and whose distinguishing mark was his red beard.

Women, men, and children gathered round when we stopped for pictures. One young man in his twenties lectured Ahmet and protested vigorously against allowing us the privilege. But Ahmet waved him aside. The women, with scarves over their heads and across their chins, brought out a huge wooden churn that stood about four feet tall and looked like an inverted cone and went to work avidly on it. The men talked of politics and the fine quality of the Menderes government. They feared the crippling hoof and mouth disease. They were fringe people in Turkish agriculture who had not yet received many benefits from the revolution of Ataturk except stabilized agricultural prices and protection against vicious tax collectors.

I suspect the caramels we offered the children were the first candy they had known. The older ones went running to corral all of the youngsters; and when one in his mother's arms did not get there, one of the older boys took the caramel to the infant. Ahmet and all his people were illiterate. So we did not offer them the usual gift of a ballpoint pen. Instead we thanked him in American cigarettes, which contain some of the tobacco grown along the Black Sea at Trabzon, Giresun, and Samsun.

Corum is a rather bleak, barren place. This is cattle, wheat, and sugar beet country. The town itself, the home of perhaps 10,000 people, is neatly laid out and well maintained though it has few lawns or gardens to adorn it. One who viewed it from the air would be apt to identify it with a cow town in western Texas, but for the mosque. Turkish mosques are quite different from those we saw all the way from Karachi. They are small, modest buildings. Not many have brilliant and ornate exteriors. Rather, they are on the run-down side. Some look like old houses; some like one-story office buildings; some look like old warehouses. They have no architectural dignity or distinction except for one thing and that is the minaret. The Turkish minaret is less ornate than the Persian. It has no majestic cupola at the top. It rises spirelike and very narrow, ending with a thin, sharp-pointed shaft.

We stayed with Governor Cevat Copanoglu in Corum. His

wife was visiting in Istanbul where he had long been stationed. He had a house guest, Sungur Mavi, Director of Finance for their province. This spacious modern house might well be Des Moines, Iowa, vintage 1910. It was clean and tidy, thanks to a man and wife who work as servants for the Governor. This was a most unusual couple. The wife was an excellent cook; the husband was a butler *par excellence*. For the first time in weeks our baggage was thoroughly dusted and cleaned, our shoes were shined, our clothes were pressed. We had not experienced such excellent service since we left Baghdad. Mercedes and I became interested in the couple and had some talks with them. The man is not primarily a butler; he's the gardener; and he has a "green thumb."

"He makes everything grow," the Governor said.

The beautiful garden in barren Corum showed his handiwork.

"We'll take them both to Washington, D.C.," Mercedes said.

"Okay," laughed the Governor. "Ask them."

So Mercedes asked them. The man said eagerly:

"America? Yes, I've always wanted to go."

The wife dissented.

"No. This is our home."

That night I had a long talk with Mavi about the finances of Turkey. He rounded out the picture for me.

The government has an agricultural credit bank that loans money to the farmers at 2½ to 5 per cent interest. Turkey is one of the few places in the Middle East where the usurer—whether landlord or other moneylender—has been taken off the back of the farmer.

The federal government finances its operation largely through the income tax, from which the farmers are exempt. This income tax is collected through the agency of the sixty-seven provinces which make up Turkey. Each Governor has as one of his main jobs the supervision of that collection. The federal government also has many excise taxes on consumer goods, including, among others, benzine. This tax is called the "purchase" tax but is the equivalent of our own "sales" taxes. The local governments finance their operation through a tax on property, real and personal.

I heard again at Corum the reasons for the broad base of popular support which the Menderes government has. It's partly the price supports already mentioned—the floor under wheat, rice, cotton, sugar beets, hazelnuts, etc., which assured, as far as may be, a fair income to the farmer. The road-building program of Menderes has met much opposition in the cities but not in rural areas. This vast program is knitting all of rural Turkey into a cosmopolitan whole and is declaring great political dividends in the country districts. The third mainstay of the Menderes program is the industrial one. Factories, sugar beet plants, cement plants are going up like mushrooms. The opposition protests against it, saying the nation cannot afford it. But Menderes believes that Turkey must hurry to catch up and that new industries will make her independent of foreign sources of supply.

"All rural Turkey will applaud when we get our own farm implement factory," the Governor added.

Many poeple in Turkey complain that Menderes is going too fast. I heard him criticized for putting up thirteen cement plants all at once. But, having seen rural Turkey, I was not impressed with the criticism. As Uras said at one point of our journey:

"Look at all these farmhouses. Every single one is made of mud, dung, and stone. Think of the cement needed to give rural Turkey decent houses!"

Turkey is overwhelmingly agricultural. Eighty-five per cent of her population is engaged in agriculture. About 45 per cent of her national income is derived from agriculture. Her agricultural production has a high cost per unit, since little of it is mechanized. Turkey's problem is to move machinery onto the farms and move people off the land into factories. That means getting foreign exchange to buy machinery abroad and the capital to build her factories. Russia and Red China built their industrial plants out of the hides of the people. Turkey, like India and Israel, has chosen the democratic method. Turkey now has a minimum wage law; a law governing maximum hours; a child labor law; the beginning of a trade union movement; and a broadening scheme of social insurance. These gains for labor will not be sacrificed. Neither will the gains for the farmers, already mentioned.

Much of the capital must come from the outside. Yet the Turks would rebel at subservience either to a foreign government or to foreign capitalists. Ataturk once said:

"Economics means everything. To live, to be happy, whatever is necessary for civilized man; it means all of these. It means agriculture; it means industry; it means everything."

There is an urge in Turkey to get on with the job. The political pressures for an increased standard of living are enormous. The economics are complicated. The experts figure that an annual investment in capital goods equal to about 20 per cent of the national income must be made. Turkey has just about done this in recent years; but she has accumulated nearly a $1,000,000,000 external debt in the process and at the same time has maintained an enormous military establishment. Richard D. Robinson of Harvard, an American well and favorably known in Turkey, is convinced that governmental loans are not the sole solution; that private investment is essential. Incentives other than a friendly government must be offered; and these must include the creation of tax incentives by lowering income tax rates on income derived from investment by United States companies or citizens in underdeveloped countries.

Yet how can Turkey do all these things and still maintain her vast military establishment? During the last five years Turkey has allocated to defense about 40 per cent of her annual budget. Where can she get the capital to maintain her armies and air corps and still build the industrial plant necessary to raise the standard of living of her people? Can she do it without turning totalitarian?

These were the ideas we discussed far into the night and beyond the bedtime of the good people of Corum.

During the night a hard wind, carrying rain, came up; and the shutters of the Governor's home rattled. It seemed I had been asleep only a few minutes when I heard a weird ghostly sound. This was the moment between sleep and consciousness when the noise seemed more a part of a dream than reality. If it had been fleeting, I probably would have credited it to a dream, had I remembered. But this noise was so persistent that I awoke. When I raised the window blinds, the street was barely visible in the dusk that comes before dawn. The street lamps had not yet gone off. Coming into town was a long train of carts pulled by oxen. Some had two wheels, some had four. Most of the frames on the wagon beds were woven of reeds of willows. The wagons creaked and groaned at each turn of the wheels. Each wheel was a solid piece of wood with a rim of iron. The wheels were fastened to a wooden axle. The creaks and groans of the turnings could be heard a mile. That noise is the one distinguishing feature of rural Turkey. This morning that noise was an echo of the challenge of last night's conversation: the need to turn Turkey's oxcarts into tractors and to build an industrial economy.

We left Corum shortly after sunrise, as we had many stops to make and were due in Ankara for dinner. The smell of freshly wetted dust filled the streets of Corum. The feel of fall was very much in the air. We had not gone far before we came to fields where sugar beets were being harvested. All of the work was manual, huge heavy wooden forks being used—forks crudely but stoutly made with fingers fashioned from sturdy roots. These sugar beets were being dug by hand and loaded in the creaky oxcarts I had seen earlier.

"How's the crop this year?" I asked.

"Crop's fine," was the answer. "But the price is not too good." By which he meant what the American farmer would mean when he thought he was not getting a high enough percentage of parity.

These farmers were hauling their sugar beets by oxen twelve miles to the factory. Twelve miles by oxen takes a full eight hours non-stop, for these animals average a mile and a half an hour. By the time a man makes up a load, goes to the factory, and returns, the day is gone. When we reached the factory, we saw many groaning oxcarts unloading. Along came a large red dump truck which also unloaded. The old and the new—Western and Eastern agriculture—had met at this sugar factory. The Eastern method was still predominant. Men expended innumerable man-hours to do what a machine could do in seconds. As I photographed the scene, I thought of the farmers of Iran who spend all day taking a dozen melons to market on their burros. In the Middle East the machine has not yet taken the burdens off the backs of men. But Turkey has gone furthest in that direction—further than any nation except Israel. Turkey's aim is to shift the population from farm to factory with a program of industrialization that will make her more self-sufficient and that will raise her standard of living.

CHAPTER 8

THE HITTITES

The Book of Genesis speaks of the Hittites as one of the peoples of the Euphrates River basin (15:20). Esau married Hittite women (26:34). David had a Hittite among his guards (2 Samuel 23:39). Solomon exacted tribute of all the Hittites left in his realm (2 Chronicles 8:7). And 2 Kings 7:6 put the Hittites in the class of dread warriors and powerful kings:

"For the Lord had made the host of the Syrians to hear a noise of chariots, and a noise of horses, even the noise of a great host: and they said one to another, Lo, the king of Israel hath hired against us the kings of the Hittites, and the kings of the Egyptians, to come upon us."

These things I remembered vaguely from Sunday school days. But the Hittites were for me wholly legendary people without flesh and blood. I had not heard of the legions they had marched, the gods they had worshiped, or the architecture they had espoused.

I learned on this Turkish journey much about the Hittites. They were a great imperial power who ruled from the central part of Anatolia. Their capital was Boghazkhoy, midway between Corum and Ankara on the high rolling plateau of north central Anatolia. The Hittites, who ruled for at least six centuries, ending about 1200 B.C., moved south from Anatolia, conquering Aleppo in Syria and Babylon in Iraq. They were destroyed by some upheaval in Asia Minor that has not been definitely identified, although it probably came from the Mediterranean. Ceram in his recent book, *The Secret of the Hittites,* gives a fascinating account of the contest for power between the Egyptians and the Hittites. The Hittites introduced the two-wheeled war chariot drawn by horses and manned by a driver and two warriors. It was the charge of these chariots that broke the army of Ramses in the famous battle of Kadesh in 1296 B.C. Ceram shows with painstaking care the details of the detective work leading to the discovery that the Hittites were Indo-Europeans. Their language had long been undecipherable. But the root of the language, when discovered, was so familiar that Ceram says that "a Frisian living on the North Sea coast of Germany and a Pennsylvania Dutchman of Eastern North America would understand a Hittite's cry of thirst!"

Our first stop at the Hittite ruins was at Alacahuyuk or Alayahuyuk. This is the name of both a museum and a village. We visited the museum first and got a view of many of the relics from Hittite diggings. There are large stone vases there and pieces of several friezes. They show the eagle with two heads—the Hittite symbol which the Seljuk Turks adopted centuries later. The sphinx is prominent in the friezes. So is the lion. The smaller items show knives and daggers in bronze; dishes in stone, small, neat, personal seals in bronze; jewelry in gold that the curator said had been removed from tombs, a gold chalice, female figurines in copper. There are three-legged dishes of bronze; and vases and pictures fashioned in that metal. For weaving the Hittites had shuttles made of bone; and these are also on display at Alacahuyuk.

The village of Alacahuyuk is still inhabited. The day we were there women were preparing wheat for use as a cereal. One woman was driving a horse around a stone mill. The horse was hitched to a long wooden shaft that turned a round stone wheel over wheat and cracked it. The cracked wheat was then washed by irrigation water in a wooden trough. A few rods beyond this mill were the ruins of Alacahuyuk. The gate to this ancient palace is guarded by two huge stone sphinxes. I agreed with Mary when she said they were "weird monsters, quite terrifying." On each side of them is an eagle with two heads.

Alacahuyuk today is mostly rubble. There are foundations and walls to see; and here and there a design can be discerned. It takes works like Lloyd, *Early Anatolia,* to reconstruct the details.

Boghazkhoy lies in rolling country twenty-one miles south; and it rests on a hill that commands a valley. On this hill was a citadel heavily fortified. The fortress wall which was part of that defense was nearly five miles long. It apparently had four temples arranged around a court.

Two miles east of Boghazkhoy is the sanctuary known as Yazilikaya. It is the site of a Hittite temple built in the jaws of two limestone cliffs that open into a flat field. The field and the cliffs make up perhaps forty acres that lie six hundred feet above the small village by the same name. This is a quiet, dignified shrine. When one steps into the jaws of these limestone cliffs he seems shut off completely from the world. All is deeply still. Even the creaking and groaning of the oxcarts on the road below the cliffs are shut out.

Once a building lay across this entrance. Now only traces of its foundation can be seen. Today the two cliffs are open and unprotected. The left flank shows about sixty marching figures in bas-relief. At the narrow mouth of the opening is the profile of a goddess. Below her figure a trench has been cut in the rock. This trench slopes to a rock basin. Here water once ran; and the water pouring into the basin was holy water. That, at least, is the theory of the curator who accompanied us from Alacahuyuk.

The inner sanctuary bears off to the right through a narrow recess. Here one stands in a small roofless room. A fearsome figure in bas-relief guards the entrance. Rock carvings show the King being embraced by a young man. Facing him is the Dagger God—one whose body tapers into a huge poignard. The sanctuary is a place in which one can sit for hours. We, indeed, spent several there, watching the change in mood of the place as the clouds put the cavern in shade, as shafts of bright sunlight made the limestone glisten.

The experts seem to agree that the Hittites made little cultural contribution in architecture, art, military genius, or literature. But the further one probes the more impressive do they seem to have been in politics. Ceram asserts that "The Hittite Empire of the second millennium B.C. was the most splendid and amazing political phenomenon of ancient history." The Hittites had a federal system that included various groups of people. At least eight different languages were spoken in the Hittite federation. The Hittite government treated all equally. The federation had a legal system based not on the principle of retaliation—an eye for an eye—but on reparation. The Hittite regime sponsored no single religion. Many religions flourished. Tolerance rather than suppression was the Hittite theme.

The Middle East has seldom known any regime of tolerance, except for the golden rule of the Achaemenids in Persia (559 B.C.–330 B.C.). Down through the centuries its minorities have experienced mostly persecution and discrimination. The Hittites—hardly known seventy-five years ago—are coming into historical perspective as a result of recent diggings. If what the scholars have turned up to date survives professional analysis, we will owe the Hittites a great debt for their espousal of civil rights in the dark ages of the second millennium B.C.

The patient curator from Alacahuyuk had filled me with these noble thoughts of the Hittites. His talk ended with a strange coincidence. We returned to the main highway from Yazilikaya and stopped at Sungurlu for luncheon. We ate in a pleasant restaurant named the Erol Palas. We had beef stew, stuffed tomatoes, green peppers, and white wine. The *Kaymakam,* Yilmaz Ergun, joined us. He was hardly thirty years old but, like Uras, my interpreter, seemed like an energetic, idealistic, first-rate public servant. We talked of many matters, then I changed the subject to the Hittites and their high standard of civil rights. At this point Mercedes spoke up and asked me to look behind me.

I had not noticed a picture on the wall when I sat down. It was the Jefferson Memorial in Washington, D.C.

CHAPTER 9

ANKARA

In the time of Ataturk, Ankara was a small, dusty, country town. Today it is a bustling modern city of 500,000 and growing so fast that water has to be rationed. At the Ankara Palace Hotel where we stayed, the water was turned on for only four hours a day.

Ankara lies in a big broad bowl only slightly studded with trees. Those that dominate are the cypress. At least their lines were so majestic as to catch my eye. The old city of Ankara, known as Onculer, lies on the hill to the east where the roads are so narrow and steep that a jeep can hardly ascend. The shops here have the deep mark of time on them. They are as quaint as the sight of flocks of turkeys which we saw being herded to market on cobblestone streets by young barefoot boys. The new town has taken over the basin itself and the slopes of the other hills. It is on the whole well planned. The new government office buildings are light and airy. There is a fine university at Ankara; and one of its departments is busy training men for the public service, both in domestic and in foreign affairs. All of the Governors and *Kaymakam* we had met across Turkey were graduates of this school; and it is proud of them and the high standard of service which they have given the nation.

I met the Minister of Justice, Avni Gokturk, and the Chief Justice of the Court of Cassation, Munir Akyurek. Our conversation centered mostly on law. The Turkish system resembles more the German and the Swiss than the British or American. Turkey has the parliamentary form of government. The people elect the Parliament. Four parties compete for their votes. The National Assembly chooses the President, who has many of the powers of our President. The parliamentary head of government is the Prime Minister.

The courts can interpret and enforce the law; but they have no power to declare an act of the Parliament unconstitutional. The power has been withheld for fear of judicial supremacy. There is, however, a special court that deals with constitutional problems in the field of administrative law. It is the only constitutional check on the exercise of powers by the Executive. It can hold a *regulation* of an executive department unconstitutional but not a *law* of the Parliament. It is called the Council of State and is created by the Constitution. It examines and decides "administrative suits and conflicts." It is concerned only with contests between the citizen and the state over civil rights, including, of course, property interests. It is composed of five judges chosen by the National Assembly; and there are five divisions of it. The decision of one division can be appealed to a court composed of the Chief Justice of each division.

Judges of the regular courts have a large degree of independence, guaranteed by the Constitution. Their term is specified by law, not by the Constitution. They cannot be removed except for misbehavior; but after twenty-five years of service they can be pensioned by the government. There were stories circulating in Ankara that the government was combing the list of older judges for retirement with a view to removing those whose decisions had been unfriendly to the Administration. This the Minister of Justice denied. Certain it is that Turkish judges have on the whole been stoutly independent. They are by no means tools of the executive or legislative branch as in some Middle Eastern countries. They have taken a solid stand against arbitrary action and are developing a tradition of independence in the pattern of the West. They have one unique feature I have not found elsewhere. An appeal court is made up of five judges. If the judge, from whom the appeal is taken, is not satisfied with the decision by the appellate court, he can ask that it be reconsidered. His request puts in motion a procedure which calls the General Assembly of the judges to hear the case. The General Assembly is made up of thirty-five judges in criminal cases and forty-five in civil cases. Two thirds are required for a quorum; and two thirds of a quorum are necessary for a decision. The Chief Justice assured me that this is a procedure often invoked by a trial judge who is overruled on appeal. But I was unable to get the precise statistics.

Ankara is filled with stories of Ataturk—the great hero who took the country by the neck and shook it, established a dictatorship to get his program going, but wisely planned for a democratic regime when the people had developed a capacity for self-government. This took time, for the masses were mostly illiterate and had long been vassals of the Ottoman regime. But the evolution in a generation of a responsible democratic Turkish government is one of the reasons for optimism in the Middle East these days.

The old Parliament building is across the street from the Ankara Palace. The story is that Ataturk viewed the site, then empty, and said:

"In six months there will be a handsome hotel there where our foreign visitors can stay."

In six months, due to the pressure of the man, the Ankara Palace was built.

When we asked at the desk where a good restaurant was located, the old man in a faded blue jacket and round brass buttons would say:

"Would you like to eat where Ataturk used to eat?"

Or he would say:

"Would you like to eat where Ataturk's old chef works?"

Even the choice of restaurants seemed to this old man to turn on the strength of an association with Ataturk.

One night we chose the Bekir Restaurant where Ataturk's chef still works. We dined with Glenn and Gloria Smith of the American Embassy and found the service and food excellent.

The main boulevard in Ankara is named after Ataturk. It's a broad pleasant street with a center strip of trees and grass.

The most interesting spectacle in Ankara is the Ataturk Mausoleum. It is on Memorial Hill to the south of the city and commands it. Its shape from the air is a long broad T with Ataturk's tomb at the left corner of the cross piece. The stem of the T is a broad brick walk lined with grass, shrubs, and trees. This walk, about six hundred feet long, has the figures of three men in stone on the left as one enters and three women on the right—figures symbolic of the unity of the Turkish people. The mausoleum is made of reddish sandstone on the outside and marble and limestone on the inside. It shows eight columns as one faces it. The top of the T is a great patio paved with stone and lined with low buildings that house the guards and administrative offices. Low steps lead up to the mausoleum, so low one has to walk slowly. The interior has the open effect of our Jefferson Memorial but it is a high, square room. The tomb lies at the far end and in front of an iron grille faced with glass that lets the sun touch the casket and gives a beautiful vista of the city below.

It's a quiet, impressive place with soldiers on guard around the clock. The tomb has an inscription that reads:

"Independence Belongs Unconditionally to the Nation."

That was a favorite statement of Ataturk. The independence that he meant was twofold: (a) independence from the Allies who occupied Turkey at the end of World War I; and (b) independence from the Sultan's government in Istanbul.

The struggle against the Sultan was a struggle against merger of church and state, and a fight against a religious conservatism that trained the mind to the mysteries of the Koran, not to the mysteries of science. The Sultan kept the Western scientific attitude from the people; he made Moslem dogma the main influence in public affairs.

The Ottomans had no legislative body. The central idea of Islam was that new laws should not be made. The Prophet had revealed the final word. The problem was to divine the law. That was the work of judges. Turkey under the Ottomans was ruled by a judiciary, not by a legislature. It was practically the same as it would be in the United States if our Supreme Court governed the country, the Justices being selected from among bishops, priests, and other religious leaders, who looked to the Scriptures for their lawmaking.

The struggle against the Western powers was more than a

struggle against an occupation army. It was also a struggle against the capitulations that had long been a curse on Turkey. These were treaties, granted by the Sultans, which conferred to outside powers extraterritorial jurisdiction over their citizens within Turkey. Genoa, Pisa, and Venice all had capitulations from Turkey as early as the twelfth century. France obtained one in 1536 which granted French courts the right to try Frenchmen and other Europeans for offenses committed in Turkey. England obtained her capitulation in 1583. In 1740 France obtained a capitulation in perpetuity which could not be modified without France's consent. In the eighteenth century, practically all European countries obtained capitulations from Turkey. In the nineteenth century the United States obtained one. Under these capitulations foreign governments actually levied duties on goods sold in Turkish ports. Foreign powers set up banks, post offices, and commercial establishments in Turkey and made them exempt from Turkish taxes even though they competed with Turkish firms. Refugees from Turkish justice sought refuge with foreign powers.

France went a step further and got a capitulation giving her the right of protecting under her flag the subjects of nations which had no capitulations. This gave rise to much abuse. For example, the French Consul in Istanbul would sell Greeks and Armenians the privilege of protection, represented by a document which exempted them from paying duties on goods imported. The French and British went so far as to issue "patents of protection" to entire groups of Greeks and Armenians who were subjects of the Ottomans. These devices, used to protect Christendom, sowed the seeds of bitter conflict between Christians and Moslems, Turks and Greeks, Moslems and Armenians. Foreign powers became divisive influences inside Turkey. As protectors of Christians against Moslems, they became a political force in the country. Turkish minorities came to look to outside powers to help them. Price, *A History of Turkey,* shows how the Russian championship of the Christian subject races of Turkey aroused intense emotions and gave Russo-Turkish conflicts an abiding bitterness in the nineteenth century. The minorities in Turkey came to be an apparent fifth column within the country, working for an outside power. This led to acrimonious disputes ending sometimes in massacres. And it was those massacres that gave the Turk such a poor reputation in Christendom. Yet Christendom was a co-architect of the system that produced them.

Ataturk inveighed against these capitulations. They were finally abrogated by the Lausanne Treaty signed in 1923 by the Allies and Turkey. The United States did not ratify that treaty. But in 1931 it made a treaty with Turkey that recognized their termination.

CHAPTER 10

TURKS VERSUS GREEKS

It's a nice day's drive from Ankara to Istanbul. The road has a black surface; and it is well engineered. For the first sixty miles or so the country is open and rolling, as is all central Anatolia. Then the road cuts through the range of hills protecting the interior from the Black Sea air. Here at the pass are conifers; and then as the road drops one is back in the Black Sea environment. The hills are heavily wooded, mostly with hardwood trees. The valleys are planted to corn, peppers, tobacco, beans, sugar beets. Wild sweet blackberries run riot. Here the women weave bright-colored carpets out of a fiber made from some plant and brightly dyed. We stopped while Mercedes took pictures of the housewives busy at the looms on the front porches and in their yards. Here we came to markets dominated by big burlap bags filled with long peppers—some red, some yellow. Here we saw string beans over a foot long loaded in burlap bags many times the size of our gunny sacks. A group of farmers had brought them to the roadside to await a truck going to Ankara. They had pooled their crop, in the manner of a marketing co-operative, and hired a truck to take all of their beans to the market where they had arranged for a commission agent to dispose of the beans for a 7 per cent fee. Each farmer's share of the total load was being computed on old-fashioned scales that looked like teeter-totters and that had big flat stones on one end.

We had our last village luncheon of our seven-thousand-mile trip at Duzce, a small rambling town about eighteen miles from the Black Sea. We saw the distant spires of Istanbul about four o'clock as we reached the Sea of Marmara. By five o'clock we were on the Bosporus in the Asiatic part of Istanbul, squeezing by inches onto a heavily loaded ferry across to the European part of Istanbul. As the ferry pulled out, leaving Asia behind, I felt sad. As I stood on the stern watching the Asian shore line recede, I realized that after my many journeys I had finally left much of my heart in Asia. Asia with its mysticism, subtlety, indirection, and of course poverty, was somehow a home to which I would always have to return. I was so deep in these nostalgic thoughts that I had hardly noticed the sky line of modern Istanbul.

As I drove off the ferry and onto the narrow cobblestone streets of Istanbul and shifted into low for the steep hills, I was reminded of San Francisco. But after sixty days of travel on lonesome highways where only an occasional truck whizzed by, I was suddenly confronted with thick threatening traffic and its earsplitting noise. For a second it seemed I would have to learn to drive all over again. Then a tension took hold and I found myself fighting valiantly to maintain our position in this roaring tide of automobiles and trucks.

That night at dinner I sat with some young Turks talking of the new Turkey and the modern Istanbul. Istanbul had for centuries been the citadel that protected Christendom against Islam. It was long the head of the Byzantine Empire, which, though titularly Roman, was Greek in language, customs, and culture. When Mohammed the Conqueror took Istanbul from the Byzantines in 1453, the greatest losers were the Greeks. And it has been between the Greeks and the Turks that some of the deepest animosities in the Middle East have been aroused. They are long-standing; and just as they have no single specific beginning, so it is difficult to see a definite end to the feelings.

Some Greeks in Istanbul help keep the feeling of antagonism alive. The main doors of their churches are shut, only the side ones being open. The Patriarchs spread the word that the main doors will not be opened until Istanbul is returned to Greece. This makes the Turks boil inside and curse the Greeks. This feeling of antagonism is heightened by the Cyprus issue, both Turkey and Greece feeling keenly that the other is wrong. The Turks own 80 per cent of the land and yet are only 20 per cent of the people. They are the farmers; the Greeks are the merchants. It is unthinkable to a Turk that he could live happily in Cyprus under Greek rule. The racial, mercantile, and religious influences that are responsible for this feeling have produced prejudices that we have not quite known on this continent.

Some Turks in Istanbul also help keep this antagonism alive. When we were there a storm generated by the Turkish press was blowing up. It was the beginning of a new campaign to expel the Patriarch from Istanbul and to exchange the 80,000 Greeks in Istanbul for Turkish minorities in Greek Thrace who number about 100,000.

On September 6, 1955, these prejudices had erupted in a violent way. The evening papers of Istanbul carried a story that the birthplace of Ataturk in the Greek city of Salonika had been bombed. That night pandemonium broke loose in Istanbul. Greek churches were raided, their windows broken, their clergy assaulted. The bazaars were ransacked by the rioters. One section which is largely owned by Greeks was practically demolished. The streets were filled with refrigerators, tables, stoves, rugs, beds, and clothing. Some rioters had as many as six wrist watches on their arms. Great damage, since compensated, was done.

I talked with young Turks about this story, which was prominently carried in the American press. They agreed that the rioting was wrong. They were proud that the *Kaymakam* who closed their eyes and let the rioters have their way were penalized and that the *Kaymakam* who kept order were all promoted. They knew that one wrong in Greece did not justify another one in Turkey. Yet these young Turks, fair-minded as they were, roared at one episode.

"It was all quite wrong," a chap with a mustache said. "But we got one laugh out of the whole business."

"What was that?" I asked.

"In the midst of all the rioting we circumcised one Greek priest."

CHAPTER 11

ALEXANDER THE GREAT

I said that the streets of Istanbul reminded me of San Francisco. But the taxi drivers reminded me of New York City. Most of them have a smattering of English and without much effort one can get into an argument about anything from the weather to the Baghdad Pact, from the bombing of Ataturk's birthplace to the Menderes government. The drivers seemed mostly in favor of Menderes, stopping to show me what his government had done to tear down slums, to widen streets, to clean the exteriors of buildings.

Istanbul has a bazaar of shops as modern as any in Europe. It also has a covered bazaar, not as extensive as Isfahan's and not quite as Eastern, but nonetheless interesting. It is owned by the government, which leases stalls to the merchants and artisans. The floor is dirt; the ceilings are high and vaulted; small windows high up are barred. Kurds work here as porters. Here all sorts of articles are made, from wedding rings to samovars. Like all covered bazaars of Asia, the place is filled with cries of hawkers, the din of hammers on brass, and the odors of spices, candy, and leather.

We cruised the Bosporus on a clear September day and learned something of its history. In the Pliocene Era the Black Sea was an inland sea with no outlet to the Mediterranean. By the end of the Glacial Period the Bosporus had pierced the land barrier.

Since then the Black Sea has been running into the Mediterranean at surface levels, while at greater depths the Mediterranean pours into the Black Sea. We went up the Golden Horn, an estuary on the European side of the Bosporus, and saw ships of many different nations unloading. I talked to a Turkish sailor about this estuary; and he said it got its name, the Golden Horn, from the brilliant sunsets that shower it with gold. The Bosporus was heavy with traffic this day. Black, dirty ships low in the water with coal were looking for berths. Others were unloading corn and wheat by lighters. Dories shuttled back and forth with provisions. Passenger ships by the dozen were loading and unloading. Our skipper sounded the alarm to call our attention to two Russian warships entering the Bosporus from the Marmara Sea. They were returning from a visit to Albanian ports. One was a cruiser, the other a destroyer. All the officers and crew lined the deck, standing at attention. They were steaming full speed. As we turned to photograph them, we tried to keep up. But their pace was too much for us.

The captain told interesting tales of these Russians who have long coveted the Bosporus. When the Soviets set up Armenian SSR, they sent ships through the Bosporus to various ports picking up Armenians to take to their new homeland. When the ships loaded with Armenians came through the Bosporus, the immigrants lined the decks, just as the Russian officers and crew were doing, and played Armenian music and sang Armenian songs. The Turks and Armenians had been at each other's throats for centuries. These songs and the music were designed to make the Armenians who remained in Istanbul lonesome and unhappy.

Roberts College, the American institution that has done pioneer educational work in the Middle East, sits high on the bluff to the north of Istanbul. Below it is the castle known as Rumelihisari, which was built by Mohammed the Conqueror in A.D. 1452. It is composed of three main fortresses and eighteen minor ones that occupy the entire slope from top to water's edge. Hotels and restaurants line the Bosporus for miles, especially the European side where Roberts College and this castle are located. Many of them are at water's edge. Attractive summer houses line the Bosporus; and the guide pointed out the red-roofed house rented by my friend George C. McGhee when he was Ambassador to Turkey. It was from that cottage that he swam the Bosporus one summer day.

We spent some hours at the museum located on the point where the Bosporus and Sea of Marmara come together. The buildings of the museum were once called the Seraglio. Here was the head of the Ottoman Empire. It was here the Sultan lived and had his offices. Today the museum has a choice collection of items covering many centuries and many civilizations. One section is devoted exclusively to chinaware; another to jewels; another to royalty, including thrones and clothes; another to armor, etc.

Not far from the museum stands St. Sofia, which was built by Constantine in A.D. 347 and destroyed by fire in A.D. 404. It was then rebuilt by Justinian in the sixth century. When the Turks conquered Istanbul in 1453, they converted it into a mosque. It has the highest dome I have seen. Great mosaics depict Christ, the Virgin Mary, and Justinian. Candelabra dropped by long chains from the ceiling hang seven feet from the floor. Huge round discs, showing writings from the Koran, have been affixed high up on the walls. These discs, plus the addition to the exterior of four minarets, mark the conversion of St. Sophia to a mosque. Ataturk generously made it a museum; and such it is today.

Across the way from St. Sophia stands the lovely Blue Mosque, unique for its six minarets. It is Turkish in origin, having been started in 1609. Its blue reflects tilework almost as exquisite as that of Isfahan. The high dome pierced by 260 windows gives to the interior the effect of the outdoors, so spacious is it.

There are so many mosques and monuments in Istanbul, one could spend days seeing them. We were so weary from our journey that we visited only a few more than those already mentioned. But we returned one day to Seraglio to see the Archaeological Museum, which is filled with Roman, Greek, Arabic, Turkish, Persian influences.

A visit to this museum is a great experience. Mary pointed out the transition from Roman art, to early Christian, to Byzantine. "The forms seem to slide," she said, "into strangely stylized, elongated Byzantine figures, some of whom have an other-world quality symbolic of Christ or the Madonna."

My chief interest was the sarcophagus of Alexander the Great. As a result of this seven-thousand-mile journey and three earlier ones, I had now covered almost every mile of Alexander's long track.

I liked the man because he too liked horses. His horse Bucephalus was close to his heart. The horse when young was wild and savage. No one dared ride it. Alexander observed that the horse was frightened of its shadow. Turning the horse into the sun, he first caressed and calmed it, then mounted it, and rode off in complete command of the animal. From that day he and the horse were inseparable. It was named Bucephalus because its head resembled the head of an ox. Alexander lost Bucephalus at the battle of the Hydaspes near the Indus River and founded the town Bucephala in his honor. I honored Alexander the Great for more than that. I honored him for his tolerance and moderation, for the fact that he destroyed armies, not civilizations. Some maintain that by the time of his death Alexander had turned into a cruel tyrant. But the ideal with which he started was revolutionary even in Greece. For it related to the equality of man. He had learned from his teacher, Aristotle, the value of the spirit of free and critical inquiry. He found good in the "barbarians" he conquered, as well as bad. He tolerated their religions; studied their cultures; made agricultural, botanical and metallurgical reports on the new countries he conquered. He was interested in art, ethics, politics, and religion, as well as in natural science. Alexander, unlike Aristotle, did not believe that a slave population was necessary. He had the broader vision. To use his words, "God is the Father of all men, but the best He made peculiarly His own."

These were my thoughts as I stood at the great man's tomb in Istanbul. My mind also went back to a little-remembered British geographer, Sir Halford J. MacKinder. He wrote in 1919:

"North America is no longer even a continent; in this twentieth century it is shrinking to be an island." He added, "The joint continent of Europe, Asia, and Africa, is now effectively, and not merely theoretically, an island." Americans, he said, "must no longer think of Europe apart from Asia and Africa. The Old World has become insular, or in other words a unit, incomparably the largest geographical unit on our Globe."

The realization that Europe, Asia, and Africa were one and

that America had shrunk to an island was another dividend from this long journey. I had seen the many forces that are pulling Europe, Asia, and Africa together and pushing America away from them. As I turned from Alexander the Great's tomb to return to the hotel to pack for a flight to Athens and New York, I suddenly felt very lonely—the loneliness all Americans may feel someday soon. In this instant the odds and ends of innumerable Asian experiences suddenly jelled. The tragedy to America seemed stark and naked.

CHAPTER 12

A PRESS CONFERENCE AND A FLAT TIRE

We had not been long in Istanbul when two newspaper reporters—a man and a lady—asked for interviews. I put them off until the next day; and by the time the hour had arrived, forty correspondents had gathered. So we took over one corner of the spacious lobby of the Hilton for nearly an hour of intensive questioning. I had expected questions concerning the Middle East—the countries we had crossed, the development program under way there, the Baghdad Pact, the Eisenhower Doctrine, Turkey's progress compared with the others', and so on. To my surprise there were no questions of importance concerning these topics. Practically every inquiry touched on freedom of the press. The reason why the correspondents seemed completely absorbed with that subject can be understood only in light of developments in Turkey.

Turkey has a rather severe press law.

The publication or circulation of any Communist literature is a penal offense.

No comment whatsoever may be made on the conduct of a criminal trial until final sentence is pronounced.

Where the law makes meetings of agencies secret, no publication of the debates or decisions taken during the secret sessions may be published.

Punishment for unlawful comment on a criminal case and for disclosure of the proceedings at secret meetings carries fine and imprisonment and in addition suspension of the right to publish this particular paper or any other.

Letters of denial or contradiction must be published on the same page, in the same column, and in the same type as the offending article. An article offends if it affects or has been detrimental to "the signatory's honour, self respect or interests," and which has "in untrue manner reproduced the said person's behaviour, ideas or words either overtly or by implication." Failure to comply with the duty to publish a contradiction or denial is an offense carrying penalties of fine and imprisonment.

The broadest provision in the press law states:

"Anyone relating, describing or drawing events or happenings, actual or imaginary, with details capable of arousing emotion or in any manner inciting or provoking the individual to crime, or of a nature that will debase national morality or disrupt the familial order, any person or persons publishing pictures and details of cases of suicide in a manner that exceeds the limits of news information and in form capable of effecting influence on the reader are liable to sentence for penalties from 1000 to 10,000 liras."

These laws have recently been supplemented by the Parliamentary Law. Turkey, like the Western nations, gave immunity to a newspaper which reported what went on in Parliament. Under the new Parliamentary Law matters of "an offensive nature" may, when Parliament so provides, be barred from publication by the press, even though happening in Parliament.

The men and women in the circle facing me at the press conference were burning with zeal about the issues raised by these laws. Some were obviously defenders of the laws; others—and the greater number—were obviously opposed to them. The first, I learned later, represented papers that supported the Menderes government. The latter were reporters from the opposition press.

One asked me if I knew that one paper, called *Millet,* had had as many as four of its reporters and editors in jail for press law violations at one time. One mentioned Yalcin, an elderly editor opposed to the government, who went to jail for over two years for slandering the Prime Minister and the President. Other opposition spokesmen have been convicted of defaming officials of the government. As many as twenty-five editors and reporters have been in prison or under indictment at one time for what they published about Menderes and his Cabinet. The charges were that the paper made "insults to the honor of the Turkish nation," and impugned "the moral personality of the Grand National Assembly," or injured "the reputation" of an official.

In Turkey an editor or reporter risks prosecution if he writes anything that can be construed as reflecting on "the personal honor or integrity" of an official. The trial may be secret. The punishment may include exile to some town.

"Should we not have the right to publish anything that is true?" they kept asking.

They cited instances of prosecutions in Turkey where truth was disallowed as a defense. It is, indeed, the fact that an editor can go to jail for calling a minister a "thief," even if he has conclusive proof that the charge is true.

Another law mentioned by the reporters antedates the press law and concerns treason. Treason is defined as any utterance or act that is anti-republic. Thus, a man who denounces separation of church and state and asks for a return of the Caliphate is guilty of treason.

It was not for me, a guest, to hold a press conference on the equities or inequities of Turkey's press law or treason law. I tried, however, to put the Western law of libel and treason in perspective for them. I talked mostly about the law of seditious and criminal libel. I told them that at one time any statement scandalous to the government constituted a common-law crime; and truth was no defense. It took long years to get the rule changed and to control criminal libel in the interests of freedom of the press. I told them about the evolution in America of the doctrine of "fair comment." We have felt that the right to criticize official acts should be freely given, even though at times the charge may be false. Otherwise the advantage would always rest with government, which has vast resources of propaganda and prosecution to express its policies. The concept of "fair comment" has grown in America to give our press greater leeway in discussing public matters and public officials. Not all states adopt the "fair comment" rule, regardless of truth or falsity, but many of them do; and the tendency of the law is toward its expansion.

A reporter spoke up to say that any derogatory comment about Ataturk is a criminal libel; and he cited instances of arrests of people who had done no more than make an unkind remark about that Turkish hero. I told them that not many years ago the courts of the State of Washington had sustained the conviction of a man who exposed the memory of George Washington to hatred, obloquy, and contempt. I added, however, that that was an exceptional case and not representative of the trend of cases in America.

It was clear from this discussion that Turkey was now about where we were in 1798 when the obnoxious Alien and Sedition Laws were enacted.

Some of these Turkish trials reminded me of the trial of David Brown under the Alien and Sedition Laws and his conviction and sentence to eighteen months and a $450 fine. All he had done was to erect a "liberty pole" at Dedham, Massachusetts, with a sign: "No stamp act, no sedition and no alien acts, no land tax. Downfall to the tyrants of America: peace and retirement to the President: long live the Vice President and the minority."

It was also clear that while many of the offending articles in the Turkish press were highly personal, emotional outbursts against officials, the line between that kind of criticism and a criticism of government policy is not always an easy one to draw. Yet I could not find then or subsequently any instance where mere criticism of government policy as such had been prosecuted. Moreover, many of the charges brought against editors and reporters are dropped. Many are acquitted; and some convictions are reversed by the appellate courts.

It is, therefore, unfair to condemn Turkey as undemocratic. She has greater freedom of speech and of the press than any country in Asia, except Burma, India, Israel, and Pakistan. She has not yet developed the tolerance among political opponents that we of the West know. Both government officials and the opposition seem to attack each other quite freely, going so far as to call one another "professional criminals."

"It takes time to develop a tradition," I said to one reporter as the session was breaking up. "Particularly a tradition of tolerance for those who stand in your way."

I went on to add: "Don't forget that it took six hundred years to evolve the House of Commons as the model of the parliamentary system."

Turkey is young by any standard. She did not get a multi-party system until 1950. Prior to that time she had a dictatorship. Under the dictatorship the press was licensed and regimented. Editors were told what to print and what not; how much space to give to this item and how much to another. Violations of an order of the censor that aroused his ire resulted in suspension of the paper. I have a Turkish friend whose paper was suspended for five months for printing "Hitler is a donkey," at a time when Turkey and Nazi Germany were allied. Turkey has gone far since that time, even though by Western standards the Turkish press law is a retrogressive measure.

After most of the reporters left, a few gathered in small groups and continued the discussion. One young man said that infringement of freedom of the press was having serious repercussions on the courts. I asked him what he meant. He repeated rumors I had heard in Ankara that the government was retiring judges, who had served more than twenty-five years, for their rulings adverse to the government under the press law and other laws. This threat of retirement, he said, is influential in making judges arrive at decisions acceptable to the government. He showed me an editorial written by Nehat Erim of the opposition press, saying that this new law giving the government the power to retire judges has weakened public "confidence in justice." What the facts are, I do not know. But the deep feeling among the press indicates that some dark influence is working against the full independence of the judiciary in this new Republic.

The discussion turned to another law which gives the Minister of the Interior power, with the approval of the Cabinet, to ban any imported book. The authority extends not only to obscene books but also to those that reflect ideas against the national policy or are injurious to relations with allies. The Minister of the Interior is prone to ban books, while the Cabinet has a more libertarian attitude. One of the first publications banned was published in the United States. It is the *Watch Tower*, an organ of Jehovah's Witnesses, whose religious fervor and philosophy are antagonistic to Islam as well as to other organized religions. Occasional issues of American magazines are also banned; and the reasons are often hard to divine. In two instances I know, the reason was that a Turkish official felt that a picture of the Red Star over the Kremlin and a print of the Hammer and Sickle would offend the Turkish people.

After the reporters had left, Uras and I sat for a while talking about these laws. He said he thought reporters from the opposition press had overstated the case against the press law of Turkey. He repeated that the courts had dismissed several cases brought against journalists and that other defendants had been acquitted.

"Why should the press be used for character assassination," he asked, "rather than for discussion of public issues? Is it real freedom to be able to say publicly that an official is a man without personal honor?"

I left Uras and the reporters feeling that Turkey was handling her problems with maturity—by public debate, by legislative and judicial proceedings. The forces of Jefferson were allied against those of Adams in ancient Anatolia. What will be the outcome, no one can tell. But I was confident the Turks would find the answer within the framework of democratic traditions, provided the economics of their problem did not pull them into the whirlpool of the totalitarian state.

Ataturk's old paper, *Ulus,* was suspended in 1958 for a month and fined 10,000 lira for a cartoon which shows a policeman arresting a burglar near a safe which could be construed as being the national treasury. The policeman is telling the burglar, "Of course you would come out empty-handed. Don't you know there are bigger thieves than you?" Later in the spring of 1958 the judge who imposed this and other severe press sentences died. The newspapermen united and sent flowers to his funeral. In Turkey the contestants in public life tend to forgive and forget.

That reveals one of my reasons for thinking the Turks will find their salvation by democratic means. Another is their keen sense of humor. The Turk is proud and sensitive and quick to react to criticism. But he also has the ability to laugh at himself.

The Turks, like the Persians, have a legendary humorist. He may be the same as the Persians', for his name is Nasr-ed-Din

Hodja. His stories are legion. One concerns his two wives who came to him one day and asked which one he liked better. He tried to avoid the decision; but they kept pressing him. Finally one said:

"Suppose we were both in a boat on Lake Van and it turned over. Which one of us would you save?"

Hodja scratched his chin and, turning to the older of the two, said, "You can swim, can't you, my dear?"

This Turkish sense of humor is illustrated by a story that was current in Istanbul during our visit. A man, who heard that his wife had been arrested, rushed down to the police station and asked what was wrong. The police told him that she had been arrested because she had criticized the government for shortages of food in the market.

The husband pretended to swoon. Sinking into a chair, he said feebly:

"Please get me a cup of coffee."

"Coffee?" shouted the policeman. "You know there is not enough foreign exchange in Turkey to buy coffee."

The husband leaped to his feet and, pointing to the policeman, screamed at his senior officer:

"Arrest that man. He's criticizing the government."

We had many details to attend to before our departure. The car had to be delivered to a steamship company for return to America. We had to repack for air travel, sending many packages by ship. There was some shopping to do, correspondence to get off, calls to make on friends in Istanbul. The morning of the day of our departure by air arrived. It was a cool, clear September day. I arose early and went downstairs to run a few errands and to take a last look at Ali, the station wagon.

It was a sad farewell to Ali. The car, which at times had achieved the impossible, had become almost personal in its relations to us. I walked around it, touching it now and then. When I reached the rear, I had to smile. For the right rear tire was down. "Another job for Mercedes," I said to myself.

On my return to the hotel lobby I met a group of Americans, just arriving. Some of them I knew. Most were strangers. They were well dressed—indeed overdressed for the Middle East. They were a bit on edge for the adventure ahead of them. I stayed with them for some minutes, listening to them talk, answering their questions, watching their reactions. They were intrigued with Asia but full of misgivings. They had been conditioned to think that the only way to fight Communism was with guns and that the revolutions of Asia might somehow be stopped. Having no conception of the nature of these revolutions, they had never comprehended how they might become great democratic influences.

One lady had got a whiff of Turkish socialism and wondered if they were not a half step from Communism. A man demanded, "How can you afford to do business with socialists? You can't ever trust them." These American tourists were so far behind world trends as to be tragic figures. Moreover, they feared dysentery. They were fascinated by the colors and mysticism of Asia but nervous about its stench and its dirt. They wanted to enjoy in Asia the American standard of living. That meant that they would see Asia from luxurious hotels, not from the highways and byways. They would go to teas in Embassies and see something of the social whirl of the capitals. But they would never get close enough to the villages to feel the heartbeat of the people. They would meet their own kind in Asia and not come to know the men and women who are making their revolutions come true.

This should not have come as a shock, for I had once been one of them. But I had just left Asia where I had been lost in its villages and on its back roads for over two months. I now knew as never before the warmth of her people, their longing for equality, their great pride in race and culture.

The Asian wants a handclasp for friendship. He needs people who will stay with him in his hut, not in an air-conditioned house on the hill. He needs visitors who come without condescension. He likes the foreigner who will eat his bread and rice and not be dependent on frozen steaks flown in by air. He welcomes the stranger who will fill the role of neighbor, who will sleep on his rice mats, who will drink his tea and share his worries, who will feel the measure of his life by living with him, who will not lord it over him.

The Americans in the hotel lobby at Istanbul came to Asia

with different ideas. They were symbolic of the growing gulf between America and the East, the gulf that threatens to leave us in lonely isolation.

This worry was on my mind when I returned to our hotel room. Mercedes and Mary were completing the separation of their baggage, preparatory to our departure by air. Mercedes, noticing the worried look on my face, asked what was wrong.

"The right rear tire is down again," I announced.

"I know just the right bellboy to fix it," Mercedes said, as both she and Mary roared with laughter.

INDEX

Black Sea
Bosporus
Istanbul
Sea of Marmara
Duzce
Bolu
Samsun
Corum
Sungurlu
Alacahuyuk
Ankara
Boghazkhoy
Ismir
Turkey
Antalya
Cyprus
Syria
Lebanon
Mediterranean Sea
Beirut
Damascus
Israel
Jordan
Red Sea
Alqosh
Ba'Athra
Shayk'Adi
Shaykhan
Tall Usquf
Tall Kayf
Ba'Zani
Ba'Shiqah
Bartalle
Mosul
Erbil
Tigris R.
Miles
0 10
Mosul Area